NATIONAL STUDIES ON INTERNATIONAL ORGANIZATION

AUSTRALIA
AND THE
UNITED NATIONS

by

NORMAN HARPER and DAVID SISSONS

Prepared for

THE AUSTRALIAN INSTITUTE OF INTERNATIONAL AFFAIRS

and the

CARNEGIE ENDOWMENT FOR INTERNATIONAL PEACE

Manhattan Publishing Company
New York
1959

VOLUMES PREVIOUSLY PUBLISHED IN THIS SERIES

PRINTED BY BRÜDER ROSENBAUM, VIENNA (AUSTRIA)

Preface

This volume forms part of a series of studies on international organization initiated by the Carnegie Endowment for International Peace and carried out by private institutions and individuals in more than twenty countries around the world. This particular study has been prepared under the auspices of The Australian Institute of International Affairs by Norman Harper and David Sissons.

The decision, taken in 1952, to initiate this program reflected both the Endowment's long-standing conviction that international organizations, such as the United Nations, are central to the quest for peace and the assumption that their significance and functioning depend first and foremost upon the attitudes and policies of nations. The fact that the question of Charter review would be on the agenda of the General Assembly in 1955 seemed to afford a unique opportunity for assessing the strengths and weaknesses of the United Nations in terms of national expectations and their fulfilment during the brief but rich testing period of the first ten years. In sponsoring this series of studies the Endowment has sought to encourage an exchange of unofficial national views, with the object of stimulating a closer examination of the past record and future potentialities of the United Nations and of increasing understanding of differences and similarities in national attitudes toward the Organization.

In pursuit of these objectives, the participants in each country were asked to appraise their national experience in international organization, especially in the United Nations. In doing so they have considered such questions as: What impact has the United Nations had on both the content and the conduct of national policy? To what extent have the purposes and principles set out in the

Charter served as adequate guides to the organs of the United Nations in their operations? Have developments in the practices and the procedures of the United Nations made the Organization more or less effective as an agency to achieve the purposes for which it was established? What is, and should be, the relationship of the United Nations to other forms of international organizations, including regional systems? Does experience suggest the need for formal revision of the Charter?

These studies have been undertaken on the initiative of the Carnegie Endowment for International Peace. However, they have been carried out independently of that organization and the responsibility for the contents of the individual volumes, therefore, lies with the authors.

In exercising its responsibility for the decision to publish the volumes in this series, the Endowment has been assisted by an advisory review committee, comprising Dr. Alberto Lleras Camargo, former Secretary-General of the Organization of American States; Sir Ramaswami Mudaliar, Vice-Chancellor of Travancore University, India; and Dr. Bernard H. M. Vlekke, Secretary-General of the Netherlands Institute of International Affairs. Their faithful and wise counsel is most gratefully acknowledged.

The conclusions of the individual studies have been summarized and their significance analyzed in two final volumes prepared independently by Robert M. MacIver, Lieber Professor Emeritus of Political Philosophy and Sociology at Columbia University; and Maurice Bourquin, Professor in the Institut Universitaire de Hautes Etudes Internationales in Geneva.

No prefatory note which did not exceed its proper dimensions could possibly acknowledge all the debts which the Endowment owes to scholars and officials in many parts of the world for the help which they have graciously given. To the Australian Institute of International Affairs, and to the two authors, particular thanks are due for their co-operation in making the present volume possible. The Endowment wishes to record its deep appreciation not only for the scholarship and thought which are reflected in the following pages but also for the patience and unfailing courtesy they have shown in this venture in co-operation over several years.

The Endowment wishes to express its gratitude to the Ford Foundation for providing a grant which, by supplementing funds supplied by the Endowment and the co-operating institutions themselves, made it possible to carry out the project on a broad and comprehensive basis.

October 1958   JOSEPH E. JOHNSON
President
Carnegie Endowment for International Peace

Foreword

Assessing national attitudes is in itself a difficult task. It poses complicated problems of technique in a field that is as yet largely unscientific. There are no adequate devices for weighing and measuring opinions that are amorphous, ephemeral, or only partly considered. The analysis of attitudes towards the United Nations presents special problems in the handling of the daily and periodical press, in evaluating public opinion polls, in assessing the views of propaganda bodies or of organizations either marginally interested in the United Nations in general or interested in one or another specialized aspect of its work. Examination of parliamentary debates also presents difficulties; generally the major contributions are quickly made in the opening speeches by the parties and the backbenchers are allowed considerable freedom in rounding out the debate.

The occasion for this study was the impending approach of a Charter review conference provided for under Article 109 of the United Nations Charter. It was considered that a stock-taking of policies and of attitudes, revealing trends of policy and changes of opinion about the functioning of the United Nations, would be of value in clearing the ground for any such conference.

The field of study is immense, and accordingly it has been necessary to be rigidly selective. Problems that have bulked large in Australian thinking, or towards the solution of which Australia may be said to have made some contribution, have been singled out for analysis. Those upon which there has been no distinctive attitude (e.g., disarmament) have been ignored; others have been treated briefly where it has been felt that the main Australian contribution has viii

been made outside the framework of the United Nations (e.g., technical assistance which for Australia has been implemented primarily through the Colombo Plan).

This study has been carried out with the assistance of study groups convened under the auspices of The Australian Institute of International Affairs in five of the main capital cities. The membership of these groups was as follows:

Melbourne:
Sir Ian Clunies Ross, C.M.G.
 (Convener)
Mr. R. W. T. Cowan
 D eputy Convener)
(Mr.K. A. Aickin
Professor W. Macmahon Ball
Mr. T. N. M. Buesst
Mrs. C. Couchman, O.B.E.
Mr. Frank Crean, M.H.R.
Miss Constance Duncan
Mr. Paul Freadman
Mr. N. F. Goss
Mr. N. D. Harper
Dr. J. Leyser
Mr. Gerald Packer
Mr. J. Finley Patrick
Professor W. Prest
Mr. D. C. S. Sissons
Mr. R. L. Stock
Mr. Douglas Wilkie

Brisbane:
Professor G. Greenwood
 (Convener)
Dr. S. R. Davis
Mr. C. Grimshaw
Mr. R. Joyce
Mr. R. G. Neale

Canberra:
Mr. T. Pyman
 (Convener)
Professor C. M. H. Clark
Professor J. M. Davidson
Lord Lindsay of Birker
Professor G. Sawer
Mr. K. W. Thompson
Mr. H. F. Whitlam

Adelaide:
Mr. A. M. Ramsay
 (Convener)
Mr. J. Adams
Mr. C. Crase
Mr. J. Forres
Mr. B. Hunter
Mr. C. Walker

Perth:
Dr. J. D. Legge
 (Convener)
Mr. L. J. Downer
Mr. E. K. Greville
Mr. J. Huelin
Sir Ross McDonald
Mr. A. G. Staples

Each of the groups considered a series of discussion papers prepared by the Research Worker, Mr. David Sissons. The final draft, evaluating the group discussions, was the joint work of the Research Worker and the Director. The two thousand miles separating the groups prevented complete agreement on a number of contentious issues that could have been obtained round a table. Accordingly, the Director must accept responsibility for the final manuscript, particularly the concluding chapter on which no preliminary draft was submitted to the study groups. Opinions described in this report as "official" represent the views expressed by the government in Australia or at the United Nations.

The thanks of the Institute must be expressed to the conveners and members of the study groups for their contribution to the study. It should be pointed out that those who accepted invitations to participate in the groups do not necessarily subscribe individually to all the conclusions.

The preliminary papers for a number of chapters were also discussed with or by a number of people with a special competence in particular fields. Among those who gave material assistance in this way were: Mr. H. D. Black, Mr. J. Chinnery, Mr. J. Hodgetts, Miss Eileen Powell, and the late Miss Camilla Wedgwood, to whom the authors are also indebted for the special study appended to this report on the attitudes of the native peoples of Papua and New Guinea.

The drafts of particular chapters were discussed with a number of people—trade union leaders and representatives of employers, churchmen, and journalists—who cannot be mentioned by name. The Australian Association of United Nations, especially the Queensland and Victoria divisions, also freely expressed opinions and gave considerable assistance.

The Research Worker and the Director would like to express their appreciation of the deep interest of the late Sir Frederic W. Eggleston in the project, and of Mr. T. Pyman of the Canberra Branch for his invaluable help with documents.

The carrying out of the study has been largely possible because of the enthusiasm and careful work of the Research Worker, Mr. David Sissons. Valuable assistance in the final stages of revision (1957-58) was given by Mr. John New. Both the Institute and the Director are heavily indebted to them.

University of Melbourne
December 1954; June 1958

NORMAN HARPER
Director

Contents

PART ONE

chapter one

Background to Australian Security

"No nation can escape its geography. . . . there is nothing we can do to alter our geographical position."[1] Australia is a large semi-continental area on the rim of Asia, linked to Asia by a bridge of islands. "Geographically, Australia is next door to Asia and our destiny as a nation is irretrievably conditioned by what takes place in Asia. This means that our future depends to an ever increasing degree upon the economic stability of our Asian neighbours, upon the economic well being of Asian peoples, and upon the development of understanding and friendly relations between Australia and Asia." Australia's geographical position has not changed since the first settlement in 1788 but the shrinking of the world through the

---

[1] See the statement by Mr. Percy Spender (Minister for External Affairs) on Australian foreign policy, 9 March 1950, in *Current Notes on International Affairs* (Dept. of External Affairs, Canberra), Vol. 21 (1950), pp. 153-72, especially p. 160.

transport revolution, particularly of the air age, has altered the kind of conclusions that political leaders drew from the geographical facts.

Australia has always been relatively remote from the main centres of power and potential conflict: its proximity to them has varied according to the means of communication. Traditionally, it has been the terminal of a 10,000-12,000 mile sea route from Great Britain, a sea-lane of crucial importance; today Australia lies at the end of global air lines linking it with North America, Asia, and Europe.

Australia's population of some nine millions, although widely dispersed, is concentrated primarily on the southeastern fringes of the continent. It occupies the fertile crescent from Rockhampton through Melbourne to Perth. The extensive migration program of the post-war period has added more than three-quarters of a million people to the more settled areas of this southeastern crescent.[2] But a limited rainfall in many parts of the country means that many areas of submarginal rainfall will continue to be sparsely populated. The southwest is separated from the settlements on the eastern seaboard by desert country so that it assumes many of the characteristics of an island. Large parts of the northwest of Australia would be military liabilities both for an invading and a defending power, even supported by air strength. The striking thing, however, is the great population disparity between Australia and the other countries of the Pacific area: Mainland China, 621 millions; Indonesia, 84; Japan, 90; Korea, 31; Laos, Cambodia, and Vietnam, 32; Malaya and Singapore, 7; Philippines, 22; and Thailand, 21 millions—a total of 910 millions in east and southeast Asia. In south Asia, Burma has 20 millions, Ceylon 9, India 392, and Pakistan 84 millions, a total over 500 millions.[3]

---

[2] W. D. Borrie, "Immigration to Australia, 1945-53," *The Commonwealth: Special Problems of the Member Nations* in G. Greenwood, ed., *Australian Papers*, Commonwealth Relations Conference, Lahore, 1954 (Melbourne: Australian Institute of International Affairs), p. 3.

[3] *United Nations Demographic Yearbook, 1957* (New York: United Nations, 1957), pp. 128-31.

Although its export income is dangerously dependent upon wool prices, Australia has become increasingly industrialized in the last two decades. Capital investment, private and public, rose from £475m. in 1948-49 to a new peak of £1,180m. in 1951-52. Large-scale development programs are aimed primarily at increasing the capacity of the country to absorb a larger population: the marked expansion in expenditure on fuel, power, and communications has military as well as economic significance. The expansion of secondary industry—the creation of aircraft, automobile, and tractor plants— has been significant. But Australia is still far short of industrial self-sufficiency and is deficient in strategic raw materials such as oil and rubber. Despite promising bores, no major oil strike of importance has yet been made. Hard coal output is 19.6 million tons (as compared with 46.5 million in Japan). Iron ore production has risen by 1957 to 2.58 million tons, pig iron to 1.9 million tons, and steel to 2.3 million tons. Uranium deposits and production are considerable. Although relatively small, Australian output of strategic materials is important for the west Pacific region. Australia is a secondary centre of industrial power; it is not comparable to European, North American, or Russian concentrations, but rather to those of India, China, and Japan. The concentration of industrial development in the southeast, remote from Asia, makes these industrial centres vulnerable only to air and atomic attack. "From a military point of view, Australia would be more efficient if the continent were a quarter of its actual size, premising that the quarter left should be the southeast quadrant. Her population and her industrial power are comparable to those of the smaller states of north-west Europe, say the Netherlands or Belgium. But they must defend an enormous and virtually empty glacis fronting on the Indian Ocean and towards Indonesia."[4]

The approaches to the Australian continent lie in part through the island archipelagoes which could furnish bases for attack by

---

[4] O. H. K. Spate, "The Pacific: Some Strategic Considerations," *The Commonwealth: Special Problems of the Member Nations, op. cit.,* p. 9.

an enemy strong in sea and air power. Although the major centres of population and economic development lie in the southeast and east of the country (facing, or close to the Pacific) Australia is a two-ocean country, with the whole of Western Australia and part of the Northern Territory bordering on the Indian Ocean. While Britain ruled India, the Indian Ocean was to all intents and purposes a British ocean. The main line of communication between Britain, Australia, and the Far East has always run through the Indian Ocean and this area has constituted the traditional axis of Australian defence plans.

As Australia's physical isolation began to disappear during the late Victorian period, a fear of external attack developed. The potential enemy varied from time to time: the vague fear of French settlement during the Napoleonic wars was replaced by a concern over German policy as Bismarck moved into New Guinea in 1884. Russia's spectacular advances into central Asia in the 'seventies and 'eighties created a fear that India might be bypassed and northern Australia attacked. The Sino-Japanese war (1894-95) intensified the fear of Japan when it was felt that Australia's vacant north might possess an irresistible attraction for the peoples of Asia. The ocean at one time had been regarded as a perfect defence. With the development of the steamship and the emergence of modern Asian states, the ocean ceased to be a barrier and came to be regarded as a broad highway for the approach of invaders. The crumbling of Australian geographical isolation brought a demand for a greater voice in foreign policy and a greater willingness to assume responsibilities for defence.

With British control of the Australian colonies, an independent Australian foreign policy was at once superfluous and constitutionally impossible. Only when the implications of self-government were worked out in the last half of the nineteenth century could Australia begin to contemplate a separate foreign policy. As late as the Imperial Conference of 1911, Whitehall made it clear that Britain was unprepared to relinquish control over foreign policy to the self-governing colonies. The British Prime Minister, Mr. H. H. Asquith, declared that the responsibility of the Imperial government for the conclusion of treaties, the maintenance of peace, and the declaration of war "cannot be shared." He flatly rejected a proposal for the creation of an Imperial Council of State on which all the Dominions would be represented because it would be "fatal to the very fundamental conditions on which our Empire has been built up and carried on."[5] Not only was the British government solely responsible for Empire foreign policy: it was also responsible for imperial defence. This took the form of naval defence, each of the Dominions being responsible for its own local defences. The Foreign Office, however, was not impervious to suggestions from the Dominions. In fact, on occasion it modified its policies to suit Australian demands, though usually to a degree considered inadequate.

Before 1914 Australia had been groping towards an independent policy: of primary concern were the problems of security, trade, and immigration. Rising Australian nationalism from the early 'nineties onward led to pressure for independent policies. Underlying this was a firm determination to retain at all costs the essentially British character of the Australian nation. "With us it is not a mere question of sentiment or racial prejudice, but the grave question of whether we shall preserve our existence as an Anglo-Saxon people, and prevent the Australian continent from being swarmed over by races that do not assimilate, but might in their multitudes alter or sweep away the institutions we are so carefully building up for ourselves and our children."[6] The achievement of security and the preservation of ethnic homogeneity meant not only close collaboration with Great Britain within a broad imperial framework but also the assumption of the responsibilities of collaboration and of increasing independence. Here Australia parted

---

[5] A. B. Keith, ed., *Selected Speeches and Documents on British Colonial Policy* (London: Oxford University Press, 1918), Vol. 1, pp. 302-03.
[6] *Sydney Morning Herald*, cited in Jack Shepherd, *Australia's Interests and Policies in the Far East* (New York: Institute of Pacific Relations, 1939), p. 9.

company with Laurier, the Canadian Premier, who exclaimed: "Do not call us to your councils lest we be made responsible for your policy." Because of its geographical isolation, Australia was particularly concerned with Pacific problems, and sought spasmodically, with varying success, to influence British policies in this area. Australia wanted responsibilities, but not unlimited responsibilities: a navy of its own to take over regional naval defence subject to British Admiralty control only during war; compulsory military training but with service limited to Australia. There was an almost complete reliance upon the Pax Britannica and the British fleet for security.

Australian participation with other Dominions in the First World War brought a wider self-consciousness, a new self-confidence, and a greater maturity of outlook. Britain recognized the importance of the material aid of the Dominions by inviting them to share in the direction of the war from 1916 onward through participation in the Imperial War Cabinet. Throughout the war, Dominion prime ministers received high level information on matters of foreign policy; this practice was continued after the armistice. Finally, the Dominions were given by international consent independent representation at the Paris Peace Conference and in the League of Nations. As separate signatories of the peace treaties there was little to distinguish them from sovereign states. In addition, as a member of the British Empire, Australia like the other Dominions attended meetings of the British Empire delegation at Paris to hammer out a common policy on major problems. Here, W. M. Hughes, the Australian Prime Minister, because of his vigour, his intransigence, and his popularity with the English press usually succeeded in having his views adopted. His claims were then set forth as those of Great Britain at great power meetings, while at plenary sessions the Empire as a bloc supported them. This method of diplomacy was in marked contrast with that followed by Australia at San Francisco in 1945.

The quest for security was the central problem of Australian and British Commonwealth foreign policy between 1919 and 1939. The

relative security of the pre-1914 period had disappeared: how could
it be regained? If Australia were to assume new international responsibilities, within what type of organization should it be? In
the new League of Nations or in the rapidly developing British
Commonwealth of Nations? The problem was complicated by the
relative decline in British naval strength. As a small power, Australia
tried to make the best of both possible worlds. Australian leaders
supported Sir Robert Borden of Canada and General Smuts of
South Africa in demanding an increasing share in the formulation
of foreign policy. Separate representation in the League of Nations
was clear proof of the new adult status. The Balfour Report on
Inter-Imperial Relations in 1926 and the Statute of Westminster in
1931 reflected the new concern with equality of status and gave
legal recognition to it. In an attempt to assert not merely equality
of status but also of stature, Australia and the other Dominions
insisted upon continuous consultation on Commonwealth foreign
policy. As a symbol of the new status, Australia began to develop
a small Department of External Affairs.

Yet there was a clear appreciation of the fact that stature was
unequal within the Commonwealth and also a reluctance to assume
the burdens which logically would follow the translation of constitutional and legal principles into hard pragmatic reality. As
W. M. Hughes had put it at the Paris Peace Conference, "Australia
outside the Empire would, although the nation were armed to the
teeth and prepared to fight to the last ditch for what it believed
to be essential to its national existence, have failed to turn the
Conference from what was only too obviously its settled purpose."[7]
This was equally true throughout the 'twenties. A comfortable feeling
of geographical isolation, reinforced by the Washington treaties,
lulled Australia into a false sense of security for over a decade. It
was easier to accept in theory constitutional rights (Australia did
not ratify the Statute of Westminster until 1942) than to formulate

---

[7] William M. Hughes, *The Splendid Adventure* (London: Ernest Benn, 1929),
pp. 108-09.

an effective foreign policy; Australia accepted through choice rather than through constitutional necessity British direction of foreign policy.

The alternative source of security lay conceivably in the League of Nations. In 1919, Australia's pertinacious Prime Minister, W. M. Hughes, who personally conducted Australian foreign policy, was antagonistic to the idea of a League of Nations and sceptical of the chances of success of any international organization. He was openly hostile to President Wilson's Fourteen Points and his scheme for international co-operation: these would interfere with Australia's tariff policies, the exercise of British sea power, and Australia's claim to possessions in the Pacific. The principle of racial equality which the President supported would, if acknowledged by the League, weaken Australia's right to continue its policy of excluding Asian migrants. To Hughes, since equality depended upon power, British sea power and to a lesser extent American goodwill provided the only reliable protection for Australia. There was however no point in continuing opposition to the League: the British Cabinet and Clemenceau accepted it.[8]

His comments on the draft Covenant indicate that he desired to restrict both the scope of the League and the obligations of its members to an absolute minimum. To him, the draft savoured too much of international government; it tended to obscure the proper functions of the League as "a standing international Conference or an organ of consultation." "It cannot be too strongly emphasized that the large body [i.e., the Assembly] is not a Legislature, and the small body [the Council] is not an Executive. . . . Both are organs of international consultation." He eschewed the notion that either a part or the whole of the League had the right to pass "binding resolutions." The suggestion that the Council was authorized to dictate to a member its scale of armaments was "a position which

---

[8] See in general, Ernest Scott, *Australia During the War*, Vol. XI of *The Official History of Australia in the War of 1914-1918* (Sydney: Angus and Robertson, 1936), pp. 739-824.

can hardly be contemplated." His criticism of the clause in which members bound themselves to sever relations and intercourse with a Covenant-breaking state is, in the light of subsequent events, most interesting. "A pledge of this sort, to enter into a state of war automatically in a certain event, is a mistake. The weight of the League behind the bare Covenant is itself a sanction which would be as effective as a pledge. The League ought to be left to take counsel when the case arises, without a cast-iron pledge."[9] He proposed that this article be limited solely to an affirmation of the right to make war against a Covenant-breaking state. He concurred completely with the reservation that matters solely within the domestic jurisdiction of a state were outside the power of the Council. Other matters, too, were outside the scope of the League's activities. Just as the United States, citing the Monroe Doctrine, insisted that there should be no outside interference in the affairs of the Western Hemisphere, so Hughes asserted that "the Pacific . . . at least within the area and sphere of our influence . . . is covered by a doctrine that is for us [Australia] to settle, and for nobody else."[10]

At the Conference, Hughes fought the mandates system tooth and nail within the British Empire delegation and before Wilson himself. He demanded outright annexation of New Guinea as merited by Australia's contribution to victory and as absolutely necessary "in the interests of Australian security and not in the interests of the British Empire." He attacked the arguments upon which the system was based. The more direct the government, the better that government would be. He contended, "The Australians were on the spot; Australia knew what New Guinea wanted far better than any League of Nations. Australia actually at the present moment repre-

---

[9] Quoted in David H. Miller, *The Drafting of the Covenant* (New York: G. P. Putnam's Sons, 1928), Vol. 1, pp. 363-68.
[10] Commonwealth of Australia, *Parliamentary Debates* (Canberra: Commonwealth Govt. Printer), Vol. 90, 10 Sept. 1919, p. 12172. (Hereinafter cited as *C.P.D.*)

sented the Nations and if the claims of Australia were not now
accepted, what more attention would it in future receive from the
League of Nations?"[11] Any appeal to the League against Australian
administration would in fact merely be an appeal "from those who
knew to those who didn't know."

He accepted the application of the system to New Guinea only
when his own staff had devised a special type of mandate which,
he was satisfied, gave Australia virtual sovereignty over the territory.
This type of mandate (class C) differed from the others in that it
did not impose free trade and equal treatment for the citizens of
every member of the League: it would save the principle of trusteeship and concede Australian demands for effective possession.
"There could be no open door in regard to those islands near
Australia. There should be a barred and closed door—with Australia
as the guardian of the door."[12] The first ordinance passed in New
Guinea after the mandate was established applied the Commonwealth Immigration Act to the mandated territory. Hughes accepted
the prohibition on fortification of mandated territories because it
prohibited Japan's fortification of the Carolines, the Marshalls, and
the Marianas. After a most determined struggle which won reluctant
British support, he obtained the rejection of the Japanese proposal
to insert the principle of racial equality in the Covenant of the
League. Wilson ruled that, despite majority support for the Japanese
proposal, unanimity was essential on such a vital proposition.

Australia's attitude at the Peace Conference was influenced very
considerably by its assessment of the effect of the growth of Japanese
naval power upon Australian security. The Anglo-Japanese alliance
of 1902 had represented a British attempt to solve a problem at
once imperial and regional: it ended British isolation and imposed
a check upon Japanese Pacific expansion. As a result, Japanese

---

[11] U.S. Dept. of State, *Foreign Relations of the United States: The Paris Peace
Conference 1919*, Vol. III, Publication 1958 (Washington: Govt. Printing Office,
1943), p. 746.
[12] Scott, *op. cit.*, p. 787.

warships had helped convoy Australian troops to the Middle East in 1915. Japan's seizure of German Pacific islands and the sub-sequent granting to Japan of League of Nations mandates over them did not allay Australian concern at the extension of Japanese influence southward towards the equator. During the war, W. M. Hughes had argued that Australia must send troops to France to strengthen its claim to British protection should the "White Australia" policy be attacked.

By 1921, the balance of power had changed in the Pacific, and Hughes pressed for the conversion of the Anglo-Japanese alliance into a tripartite treaty by the inclusion of the United States. This was not feasible politically. The Washington treaties were designed to terminate the arms race which threatened to develop between the United States and Japan and to preserve the status quo in the Pacific by regional arrangements. Yet neither imperial diplomacy nor Australian membership of the League appeared to enhance Australian security. The Washington treaties were, after all, nego-tiated by the great powers outside the League. In 1923, Mr. S. M. Bruce (Prime Minister 1923-29) pointed out to Parliament that Australia's defence was inadequate and that Australian armaments were below "the lowest level consistent with national safety."

Australian defence policy increasingly came to be based on the assumption that British naval power alone could provide adequate security, and this involved close co-ordination of Commonwealth defence and foreign policy. The 1923 Imperial Conference noted the "deep interest" of Australia, New Zealand, and India in the provision of a base at Singapore "as essential for ensuring the mobility necessary to provide for the security of the territories and trade of the Empire in Eastern waters." It recognized, too, the need for protecting the Mediterranean-Suez route to the Pacific. Accepting the strategic principles underlying these decisions, Australia intro-duced in 1924 a five-year defence program giving priority to naval construction. Australian offers of substantial contributions to the cost of a Singapore base were rejected by a British Labour government convinced of the importance of air as opposed to naval defence. The Australian Labour government which came into office in 1929 reduced defence expenditure and abolished compulsory military training although it retained voluntary training. The world depression postponed any increased expenditure until 1933-34 when a pre-dominantly naval scheme was introduced by a conservative govern-ment. The Defence Minister, Sir George Pearce, declared that Aus-tralia's defence policy must "dovetail with the Imperial defence policy" and justified naval orientation of the scheme on the grounds that "if Australia's markets were closed and her imports and exports stopped by enemy action, she could be forced to sue for peace without a single enemy soldier coming within sight of her shores."[13] By this time, however, the "blue water school" of strategy came under serious criticism. W. M. Hughes, John Curtin (later the Labour war-time Prime Minister), and a number of military men argued that an attack on Australia would come when British naval forces were preoccupied elsewhere and that air and land forces were more important. Despite criticism the government continued to rely primarily upon naval defence.

Australia, then, gave primacy to the British Commonwealth rather than to the League of Nations as the effective source of security. The government complacently accepted the Balfour Report of 1926 with its accompanying explanation that "in the sphere of defence, the major share of responsibility rests now, and must for some time continue to rest, with His Majesty's Government in Great Britain." There was a general feeling that, in the absence of the United States, enforcement action by the League would depend in the last resort upon British power.

Although the Australian delegate to the League of Nations, Mr. S. M. Bruce, achieved an international reputation as an expert in the social and economic field and as Council chairman during the Abyssinian dispute, Australia never attempted to enunciate an

[13] Paul Hasluck, *The Government and the People, 1939-1941* in the series *Australia in the War of 1939-45* (Canberra: Australian War Memorial, 1952), p. 42.

independent policy in the League: it was content in the main to establish the principle of equality of status within the Commonwealth and to entrust the actual formulation of policy to Great Britain. An important reason for Australia's opposition to the proposed Treaty of Mutual Assistance (1923-24) was that it was considered undesirable for Great Britain to undertake commitments in Europe which might have priority over its world-wide commitments under the League Covenant. The latter included the obligation to prevent or resist aggression in the Far East, a matter of great importance for Australia. While agreeing with Great Britain that the acceptance of the Geneva Protocol (1925) "would have accentuated existing obligations without achieving the objects aimed at," Australia felt that compulsory arbitration might endanger its position if an attack were made on the "White Australia" policy. Additional objections to the principle of arbitration were based on Australia's almost unique experience with compulsory arbitration in industrial disputes. Such a system tended to encourage disputes since the claimant had nothing to lose and possibly something to gain from litigation. Moreover, an arbitrator was in fact a legislator, since he frequently created a new law rather than applied an existing one. There was a real danger that international law could develop in an unpredictable fashion.[14] Australia was perfectly satisfied with international law as it stood, grounded firmly on the principle of state sovereignty as the basis of the international community.

Australia took a firm stand on the question whether tariffs and economic policy were, and should continue to be, matters of domestic jurisdiction. In the debate in the League Assembly in 1926 on the proposal to hold a World Economic Conference, the Australian delegate, John Latham, expressed concern at the possibility "that the Conference might feel itself entitled to make recommendations upon which the League might be asked to take action . . . Matters

---

[14] See statement by Sir John Latham, cited in C. A. W. Manning, *The Policies of the British Dominions in the League of Nations* (London: Oxford University Press, 1932), pp. 52-53.

might be allowed to drift in such a way that it would be assumed that all problems were to become subjects of enquiry by the League. . . . It was in the true interests alike of the League and of the world that it should . . . confine itself to the legitimate functions which it has under the Covenant. The League would serve its best interests . . . by avoiding domestic questions which were not truly international in character."[15] Similarly in 1929 when the British Labour government proposed a tariff truce, the Australian delegate, Mr. McDougall, regretted "the tendency . . . to suggest that the League of Nations stood for a definite economic policy of free trade and further to suggest that tariffs imposed for protective purposes were against international ideals."[16] However, as a country exporting agricultural products and suffering from the depression, Australia became one of the countries advocating co-operation to increase consumption. In 1935 Australia strongly urged the League to study means to improve world nutrition. Australia was also closely associated with the proposals (1938-39) to co-ordinate and expand the facilities for economic and social co-operation through the League.

Australian views on the question of greater representation for the small powers on the League Council differed sharply from those it was to adopt at San Francisco in 1945. When the question of admitting Germany arose in 1926, some of the small powers took the opportunity to press successfully for an increase in the number of non-permanent members on the Council. Mr. Bruce stated his government's very firm view that permanent seats should be given only to the great powers with world-wide interests and great responsibilities— powers that would be able to view all questions with a full sense of their own responsibilities and obligations. "However much one may desire to see the nations of the world on absolute equality, it would be destroying the League if the Council were so constituted that it could dictate to the Great Powers. If that were the position

---

[15] *Ibid.*, p. 75.
[16] *Ibid.*, p. 81.

of the Council it would inevitably break up. To-day it has the cordial co-operation and assistance of the Great Powers."[17]

Although Australia administered a League mandate, no Australian was ever a member of the Permanent Mandates Commission. Australia never went to the lengths of New Zealand either in denying the Commission's power to give advice on administration or in expressing regret at the publication of the Commission's reports. Australia did, however, join Great Britain and the other Dominions in denying the right of the Commission to hear petitioners in person and in opposing the enlargement of the scope of the Commission's questionnaire.

After the League's failure over Abyssinia, the question of amendments to the Covenant was raised in the Assembly in 1936. A special sub-committee of the Australian Cabinet was established to report on the question. It agreed with the British proposals for the abolition of the unanimity rule, the formation of regional pacts including countries outside the League to strengthen general security, and resort to the provisions of the Covenant for revising treaties. It supported British suggestions for a League enquiry on raw materials and the separation of the Covenant from the Versailles Treaty. The sub-committee, while accepting economic and financial sanctions, also supported the acceptance of the interpretative resolution of 1921 which gave to the individual members of the League acting separately the right to determine whether for the purpose of Article XVI a breach of the Covenant had been committed. Briefly, the Australian proposals can be explained as attempts to make the security system more universal and more orientated to the Pacific; at the same time they would ensure to members full freedom of decision on the vital question whether to go to war.

A further but subordinate reason for the government's adherence to the League was that the League was a useful instrument in preventing the pursuit of conflicting policies by members of the

---

[17] Melbourne *Argus*, 19 March 1926.

British Commonwealth. Thoughtful Empire statesmen feared that with Dominion autonomy, which all supported, it would be difficult to maintain a common foreign policy without which, it was felt, the Commonwealth might disintegrate. The League could deal with *all* international disputes and determine them in accordance with its stated principles, which all Dominions supported. Thus, it was argued, it would be impossible for the Dominions to be in disagreement on international questions. This thesis was apparent in an official memorandum prepared by Australia for the delegates to the 1937 Imperial Conference. Noting that a course of action emanating from the Imperial Government need not necessarily be acceptable to individual Dominions, it paraphrased an argument of the Australian Attorney-General, Mr. R. G. Menzies, as follows:

> If that policy were based purely on European considerations, then the Dominions might well be unwilling to cooperate. Fortunately, the League of Nations and the principles enshrined in the Covenant provided a focal point for a common Empire policy, and of recent years the declared policy of Great Britain and the Dominions had been based on League principles centred round the ideas of collective action, arbitration, conciliation and peace. These principles, world-wide in their scope, lessened the chance of any disruption and facilitated a consistent and unified Empire foreign policy.[18]

On a general level this argument was that the existence of the League and the acceptance of its principles by the members of the Commonwealth prevented their following conflicting policies. On a more specific level the argument was that the League was useful to Australia in committing Great Britain to resist aggression in the Pacific since in the absence of the League Great Britain might be inclined to withdraw to Europe. This was the same approach Australia had adopted almost a decade earlier during the debate on the proposed Treaty of Mutual Assistance. At that time Mr. Menzies' predecessor as Attorney-General, John Latham, had also argued in

---

[18] Hasluck, *op. cit.*, Ch. 13.

the abstract that the League of Nations ensured unanimity of the Empire in foreign policy which otherwise could be a serious problem.

> The existence of the League contributes in a very real sense towards the solution of some of the problems of the British Commonwealth which would, in the absence of the League, create very acute difficulties. It has already been argued that it is not necessary that all parts of the Empire should have identical policies in their relations with other nations. It is upon the issues of peace and war that the Empire must act as a unit if it is to continue to exist. It is exactly in this sphere that the League comes to help to solve the problem. The Covenant of the League . . . binds Great Britain and each of the Dominions to abstain from going to war against members of the League, except in pursuance of or subject to the provisions of the Covenant. All parts of the Empire have therefore already abandoned the right of making separate declarations of war on their own account against other members of the League. . . . They would all be equally concerned in a declaration of war made under the auspices of the League against a covenant-breaking State though each would be the judge of the degree in which it would actively participate in belligerent operations. . . . However, if the Covenant is obeyed by the nations which have solemnly accepted it, all parts of the Empire will necessarily be in a state of legal belligerency if any one part of the Empire is at war. . . . The establishment of the League has gone far to remove one of the fundamental obstacles to the idea of the British Empire by greatly diminishing the probability of the Empire breaking up by reason of divergent action of its parts upon the issues of war and peace.[19]

The attractions of this possible role of the League as the catalyst of a Commonwealth foreign policy should not of course be over-emphasized: practice rarely coincides with theory. These examples are interesting not as illustrating fundamental reasons why Australia was content to belong to the League but rather as indicating un-

---

[19] Sir John Latham, *Australia and the British Commonwealth* (London: Macmillan, 1929), pp. 41-43. Sir John, unlike Mr. Menzies, was writing an academic treatise, not an official memorandum.

expected ways in which the existence of the League was felt to accord with Australia's interests.

The two great tests of the League were Manchuria and Abyssinia. The Japanese invasion of Manchuria evoked little comment in the Australian Parliament despite a general concern at the growth of Japanese power. There was no appreciation of its significance from the point of view of collective security, and from no quarter in Australia came any suggestion that a strong line should be taken against Japan. Mr. J. Scullin, the Labour leader, pointed out that "we shall be wise if we do not anticipate trouble, and refrain from making statements that might aggravate the present strained relations between China and Japan."[20] Similar views were expressed by the non-Labour Minister for External Affairs, Sir John Latham. "It is inadvisable to make a statement in this Parliament concerning the possibility of aggression by a nation which is now friendly to us . . . The Government is doing everything within its power—a very limited power in such matters—to bring about a peaceful settlement of the present unfortunate trouble in the Far East."[21] At the special session of the League Assembly in March 1932, when the majority of the smaller powers emphatically condemned Japanese aggression, Australia and New Zealand were silent, although Canada and South Africa supported the majority.

On the Abyssinian question, Australia substantially accepted British policy without criticism. W. M. Hughes, however, had to resign from the Cabinet for publishing his views that sanctions extensive enough to be effective would result in war, that the League was useless, and that extensive and immediate rearmament by Great Britain and Australia was essential to save them from threats by Germany and Japan.[22] Mr. Eden's resignation from the British Cabinet was accepted by the Australian Parliament merely as a

---

[20] *C.P.D.*, Vol. 132, 14 Oct. 1931, p. 709.

[21] *Ibid.*, Vol. 133, 19 Feb. 1932, p. 142.

[22] This is the thesis of his book, *Australia and the War To-Day* (Sydney: Angus and Robertson, 1935). See especially pp. 95-96 on sanctions against Italy.

domestic political incident of no concern to Australia. In concert with Great Britain, Australia had imposed incomplete sanctions against Italy and had withdrawn them when they proved ineffective. Shortly after Munich, however, Australia encouraged Great Britain to conclude an agreement with Italy which would ensure peace and security in the Mediterranean and at the same time give *de jure* recognition of the incorporation of Abyssinia into the Italian Empire. On Czechoslovakia and the Munich Agreement the Australian government was fully in accord with the Chamberlain policy.

Similarly, the Japanese attack on China in 1937 evoked little comment. A section of the Labour party deplored association with the League lest the China question should embroil Australia in another capitalist war. The government contented itself with declaring that "peace can best be assured by a respect on the part of all nations for the terms of international agreements and by a universal acceptance of the view that international differences should be settled by methods of conciliation and consultation." It deplored the private boycotts of Japanese goods, chiefly by sections of the trade union movement, deprecating "single-handed action by any country, or a section of a community, which would prejudice any attempt at conciliation by agreement, and would not assist either side in the dispute."[23] By 1937 the breakdown of the Washington naval treaty had produced an unrestricted naval race; Germany had rearmed and a new political orientation had taken place in Europe with the Rome-Berlin Axis; the Spanish war had increased the complications for imperial defence created by the Abyssinian war. At the Imperial Conference of 1937, Australia, concerned at the possibility that international commitments would leave Great Britain unprepared in the Pacific, urged rapprochement between Great Britain and Japan. Reiterating the principle that Australian defence was inseparable from Empire defence, Australia pressed for a detailed statement of British political aims and military plans in the Far East

---

[23] *C.P.D.*, Vol. 155, 30 Nov. 1937, p. 6, and 3 Dec. 1937, p. 202.

and took the initiative in arguing the case for a detailed examination and closer co-ordination of imperial defence policy.

The Australian government eagerly supported the British government's efforts to appease Italy and Germany and later gave equally strong support for the final stand on Poland. When Great Britain declared war, the Australian cabinet's concept of the nature of the British Commonwealth led it to decide without delay that Australia was automatically at war. It was also felt that, independently of feelings of loyalty, Australia's existence was at stake. As Mr. Menzies put it, "We in Australia are involved, because in plain English, the destruction or defeat of Great Britain would be the destruction or defeat of the British Empire and would leave us with a precarious tenure of our own independence."[24]

In the inter-war period, then, a succession of non-Labour governments in Australia gave general support to the League of Nations. Accepting it as a "league of peace and not of war," they hoped it would provide general security but demand of them only limited and occasional aid. While assuming the obligations of members to collaborate in the preservation of peace, Australia was reluctant to be drawn into European affairs. A Canadian delegate to the League, M. Dandurand, expressed very clearly a point of view shared by Australia and Canada. "In this Association of Mutual Insurance against fire, the risks assumed by the different States are not equal. We live in a fire proof house, far from inflammable materials. A vast ocean separates us from Europe."[25] Great power pre-eminence in the constitution of the Council was therefore regarded as necessary and proper. The League would assist in the smooth functioning of British Commonwealth relations and in preventing Great Britain from becoming exclusively preoccupied with Europe. There was no thought of departing from a common Empire policy in the League.

---

[24] Cited in Hasluck, *op. cit.*, pp. 149-50.

[25] See Gwendolen M. Carter, *The British Commonwealth and International Security: The Role of the Dominions, 1919-1939* (Toronto: Ryerson Press, 1947), p. 117.

Within the ambit of League membership, Australia and the other Dominions would be free to work out their own social and economic policies. This necessitated complete freedom of action for all members of the League on vital questions that might be regarded as within the domestic jurisdiction of a state, particularly questions of economic policy and race relationships. There was a clear unwillingness to restrict sovereignty in matters of disarmament and the declaration of war. Each member must decide for itself how far it could participate in the solution of international problems as they arose. Australia, unlike New Zealand, Eire, and South Africa, was opposed to any system of regional or general guarantees and insisted upon the right to decide each case on its own merits, insisted in fact upon the ultimate exercise of a veto in all matters of action. The realization that "a vast ocean separates us from Europe" and an appreciation of a lack of power made Australia reluctant to give solid support to League policies and led to a tendency to support appeasement instead of collective security. The impact of the world depression was so strong that in economic matters Australia was prepared to consider the expansion of League activities to encourage world consumption of primary products. It was here that Australia's Mr. Bruce played a very active part at Geneva in drawing attention to the urgency of the world's nutritional problems.

With the outbreak of the European war in 1939 and the collapse of the League of Nations, the Australian government was faced with the alternatives of concentrating its military strength in the Middle East or of conserving that strength for a possible Pacific war. Partly aware of the weakness of the Singapore base, it deliberately chose the strategic alternative of sending its main forces to serve with the imperial armies in the Middle East. It felt that the defence of the Middle East was vital to Australian interests and that the despatch of Australian troops to this theatre would facilitate an Allied victory. At the same time, it strongly urged Great Britain to strengthen the defences of Singapore by stationing adequate imperial air and naval forces there.

Feeling that British diplomacy was lethargic and ineffectual, the Australian government frequently tendered advice to London on the conduct of relations with Japan. Its view was that it was necessary in the last resort to make concessions to Japan on non-vital questions, and that precise assurances of American support were so desirable as to warrant a considerable modification of Commonwealth policy to secure them. Thus when the United States froze Japanese assets, Australia urged the necessity for the Empire to follow with similar extreme measures. Australia stressed the importance of pointing out to the United States the possibility that an attack on Australia would follow the adoption of such measures and of obtaining a declaration of United States intervention in that event. Australia was, however, prepared to urge that, independently of the United States, Great Britain should inform Japan that any encroachment on Thailand would mean war. However, it was Japanese action and not Australian diplomacy that brought the United States into the war. As had been feared, the inadequate British naval forces in the Far East were destroyed, and the Australian Prime Minister (now Mr. Curtin) dramatically declared that Great Britain was unable to defend Australia and successfully called for assistance from the United States.

During the inter-war period, Australian foreign policy, Australian attitudes to the British Commonwealth and to the League of Nations, were formulated by a series of conservative governments except for the brief interlude of the Scullin Labour government from 1929-32. Yet during this period, the Labour party, like the conservative governments, was slowly formulating attitudes to foreign policy rather than a foreign policy.[26]

The Australian Labour party in origin was alike strongly nationalist and socialist. It emerged in part as a protest against imperial control of Australian policies during the period of early ebullient

---

[26] The only published analysis of Labour foreign policy has been made by Hasluck in *The Government and the People, op. cit.*, and he has been heavily drawn upon for this section.

Australian nationalism. A political observer described its leaders in 1918: "They began by being anti-conscription, they went on to be anti-British and ended by being anti-war."[27] Like the Australian community, the party split over W. M. Hughes's attempts in 1916 and 1917 to introduce conscription for overseas service; it was over this issue that Hughes and his supporters were expelled from the party. In June 1918, before the defeat of Germany, the Labour party passed a series of resolutions which attributed the outbreak of the war "to commercial rivalry, territorial greed and dynastic ambitions" and demanded the immediate initiation of peace negotiations. It refused to assist recruiting. With its socialist and anti-imperialist heritage, the party found it easy to add to its main objectives "the prevention of war through the settlement of international disputes by a tribunal clothed with powers sufficient to enforce its awards." There was at the same time an equally strong distrust of the motives of the "capitalist" governments comprising the League and a traditional isolationism which deplored any dependence upon or connection with Europe as likely to drain Australian resources and weaken its independence.

During the 'twenties, however, Labour spoke enthusiastically about the League but conveniently chose to ignore the fact that it was a collective security organization. Accordingly the Labour party opposed Mr. Bruce's defence policy and did not criticize the British decision to cease work on the Singapore base. When Labour came to office in 1929 compulsory military training was abolished on principle. Thus the Australian delegate to the League of Nations in 1930 could say with satisfaction: "Australia tells the world, as a gesture of peace, that she is not prepared for war. . . . We have drawn our pen through the schedule of military expenditure with unprecedented firmness. We have reversed a policy which has subsisted in Australia for twenty-five years of compelling the youth to learn the art of war."[28] Yet in office Labour was considerably less

[27] Quoted in Scott, *op. cit.*, p. 395.
[28] Attorney-General F. Brennan, cited in Hasluck, *op. cit.*, p. 39.

pacifist than the delegate suggested. Until the depression voluntary military training was continued and the navy and air force were maintained at their previous level.

When Japan invaded Manchuria (1931), Labour's greatest anxiety was lest Australian lives should be sacrificed in a war for Chinese markets. Labour's former Minister for Defence, while deploring aggression, expressed satisfaction that "the only nation from which Australia has anything to fear is engaged to-day in an almost impossible task, which will keep it fully occupied for the next 40 or 50 years."[29]

With the rise of the dictators there came a gradual but definite realization within the Labour party that it was useless merely to denounce war. A war which Australia was powerless to prevent could end in the conquest of Australia. The beginning of the change was evident when some members of the party supported the government defence estimates for 1933-34. There still remained a fear of unlimited liabilities arising from membership in the League of Nations. When the question of the application of sanctions against Italy arose as a result of the Abyssinian crisis, Mr. F. Forde (subsequently a Deputy Prime Minister during the Second World War) declared that Labour wanted "no war on foreign fields for economic treasure." It wanted Australia "to be kept free of entanglements leading to a repetition of the horrors of 1914-18." It was strongly opposed to "war camouflaged as sanctions."[30] The inability of the League to provide an alternative insurance of security led Labour to oscillate between isolation and a revision of defence policies.

Criticism of Britain's appeasement policies was most vocal from the pacifist section of the party. The defence group was equally opposed to the principle of collective security. The Opposition was united in attacking the government's bill for sanctions against Italy on the grounds that a "vote for sanctions means a vote for war."

---

[29] *C.P.D.*, Vol. 139, 26 May 1933, p. 1860 (Mr. A. E. Green); see also Vol. 132, 29 Oct. 1931, p. 1371 (Mr. E. J. Ward).

[30] *Ibid.*, Vol. 147, 23 Sept. 1935, p. 36.

The views of Mr. Curtin (leader of the defence group) on collective security had a traditional anti-capitalist content as well as a security basis (greater fear of Japan than of Germany).

> So long as the world is organised on its present [i.e., capitalist] basis, I say that it is essential that the workers should understand that a great deal of change must precede the organisation of collective security. . . . The workers do not control the governments of the world. Until they do, it would be suicidal for the workers of Australia to join in supporting pacts, treaties, understandings or obligations of any sort which would involve them in war against the workers of another nation . . . at the dictate of capitalist governments. . . . The Australian Labour Party stands to its policy of non-participation in European wars while ensuring that we shall attain to the maximum of self-reliance in order to repel aggression.[31]

On defence policy, the party remained divided, but the group favouring a defence effort was in the ascendant. The 1937 election campaign is an interesting example of the division. On that occasion, the federal executive of the Labour party attacked the government's defence program, but itself demanded extensive military preparations. At the same time, a large section of the industrial, as distinct from the political, wing was intent on organizing the masses against war and was opposed to the executive's policy of defence preparedness. Yet there was no division in the party on the question of isolationism: if there were to be a defence program, it should be for the defence of Australia in Australia, an independent defence by an Australian air force, not a contribution to imperial defence by sea.

On the outbreak of war in Europe, the Labour party, although it supported Australia's declaration of war, opposed the despatch of Australian troops to the Middle East. Labour was consistently more reluctant than the government to take risks in the Pacific in the interests of victory in Europe over Germany. When the situation

---

[31] Quoted in Hasluck, *op. cit.*, p. 88.

in the Middle East deteriorated, Labour advocated complete British withdrawal from the area as well as from the Mediterranean in order that a defeat should not leave Britain with no forces for the eventual defence of Singapore. At the same time, Labour's traditional beliefs in the efficacy of local defence alone to protect Australia had been quickly jettisoned. There was complete agreement among all parties that the despatch of British capital ships to Singapore was the greatest need in Australian defence.

Until Japan entered the war the Labour party continued to oppose conscription even for home service. After Pearl Harbor, the Labour government introduced conscription for service anywhere in the Pacific. The return of the Australian Imperial Force from the Middle East and the arrival of large United States forces in the Australian theatre meant that, for the rest of the war, Australian policy was to be concerted more closely with the United States than with Britain. This inevitable shift in emphasis was accompanied by some coolness in imperial relations, not because of the change but rather because of the mode of its announcement: It was heralded by a newspaper article signed by the Australian Prime Minister, Mr. Curtin, in which he attacked the "beat Hitler first" policy and called for United States military assistance "without any inhibitions of any kind" and "free of any pangs as to our traditional links with the United Kingdom."[32] However this coolness was only temporary. The older machinery of the full Imperial Conference had become largely outmoded and was being replaced increasingly by "a continuing conference of cabinets." Mr. Curtin in 1943 was sufficiently impressed with the usefulness of the imperial connection to propose the establishment of a permanent secretariat to facilitate continuous and intimate consultation among Commonwealth governments. The proposal was brushed aside by other Commonwealth Prime Ministers as likely to create binding commitments.

A significant move in the direction of an autonomous foreign

---

[32] Melbourne *Herald*, 27 Dec. 1941.

policy was made in January 1944 with the signature of the Australia-New Zealand agreement (the ANZAC Pact). Its principal feature was the declaration of a regional defence zone in the Pacific, including the arc of islands to the north of Australia, and the assertion that the peace settlement must contain no redistribution of territory in the Pacific in which both Australia and New Zealand did not concur. The agreement asserted the predominance of Australia and New Zealand rather than imperial interests in the area. Great Britain was informed rather than consulted in the matter. The assertion of the right to participate on an equal footing with the great powers in the peace settlement indicated another trend in the new foreign policy of the Labour government which was to be strongly in evidence in the following years: the assertion of the rights of the "middle powers." The agreement was in fact partly aimed at the Cairo Declaration in which the three great powers (China, Great Britain, and the United States), without consulting the other belligerents, had declared that certain Japanese possessions would be returned to China.

In the inter-war period, then, Australian external policies were worked out broadly within the framework of the British Commonwealth of Nations, all the members of which were also members of the League of Nations. There was a preoccupation at first with the great debate on constitutional forms within the Commonwealth. Australia was furthermore reluctant to burn its own fingers or to allow them to be burnt by Great Britain. The implications of equality of status but not of stature or function were largely burked by Dominions who were "free but not equal." With only an infant Department of External Affairs, Australia was rarely capable of formulating the independent policies which should have been a logical consequence of the Balfour Report. It was felt preferable to rely on informal and indirect influence on British policy than to attempt the onerous obligations of independence within the Commonwealth and as a member of the League of Nations. As Mr. Menzies pointed out in 1938:

> We may, as indeed some of our predecessors did, claim that
> we are equal in all things in point of foreign policy, but the
> fact will remain that the great issues of peace and war will be
> much more determined by the gentleman who sits in a room
> looking across the Horse Guards Parade than it will be by
> my colleagues in Canberra or one of our colleagues in Ottawa
> or Pretoria.[33]

It was largely this attitude, together with a feeling of geographical
isolation and remoteness, that produced a general support for policies
of appeasement by the League, policies supported by Great Britain.

Australia's preoccupation with the problems of the Pacific, and
the gradual realization of the changing balance of power, led to
oscillation between a hesitant support for collective security and a
groping attempt to develop a cautious Pacific policy of its own.
Japanese aggression in Manchuria and in China in 1937 and a
growing apprehension at the weakening of effective British power
in the Far East produced an independent attempt to build Pacific
security through a regional pact of mutual aid to repel aggression.
The United States was not a member of the League of Nations
and Japan had left the League. With the breakdown of the Washington treaties, Australia appeared to be exceedingly vulnerable to
attack. Mr. Lyons, the Australian Prime Minister, had in 1937 proposed a broad Pacific pact, but a pact that had not been worked
out in any detail. It had met with a cool reception from all the
Pacific powers. With the collapse of this proposal for a regional
pact, Australia expanded its own defence program, increased military
collaboration with Great Britain, and even contemplated closer
military relations with the Netherlands East Indies.

In 1939, then, there were Australian attitudes towards or opinions
about foreign policy, but no foreign policy as such. The old sense
of absolute security throughout the Commonwealth was dispelled

---

[33] Cited in H. V. Hodson ed., *The British Commonwealth and the Future:
Proceedings of the Second Unofficial Conference on British Commonwealth
Relations, Sydney, 3-17 September, 1938* (London: Oxford University Press,
1939), p. 219.

in 1941; the implications of autonomy were unresolved and there was no clear machinery for adequate Commonwealth co-operation or consultation. The Second World War acted as a catalyst for an independent foreign policy. Dunkirk, the battle on the Kokoda trail, the bombs at Darwin—these irretrievably shattered Australia's isolationism as well as its sense of remote security. They produced in the Labour government a new and firm determination to reassess Australian interests and to assume a prime responsibility for the Pacific policies of the British Commonwealth. As Dr. Evatt declared,

> Australia is setting out to make her own assessments of the problems of the Pacific. By so doing we may speak with a fresh, direct and independent voice in the councils of Pacific nations. It is our wish and intention to play a dynamic part in achieving, as a member of the British Commonwealth, a world comity. It is our destiny and duty to play that part in the Pacific.[34]

In so far as there were to be parallel or common policies in the Pacific, these should be determined primarily by the Pacific Dominions.

The war brought a rapid maturing of the Australian outlook; it also brought a greater maturity in foreign policy to the Australian Labour party. In the pre-war years there had been a steady narrowing of the gap between the parties on foreign policy. Labour, traditionally anti-imperialist, suspicious of British policy, and inclined to regard the League of Nations as a "capitalist club," no longer regarded war as a nefarious contest between rival profiteers, a contest which Australian action or indifference could help to prevent. War could not be averted by ignoring it, and Australia could not achieve security by isolation or unilateral defence. To a relatively small country, vulnerable to attack, collective security through international organization assumed a new importance.

With this increasing awareness of problems of post-war security went a greater sensitiveness on the part of the Labour government

---

[34] *C.P.D.*, Vol. 186, 13 March 1946, p. 200.

to questions of status, stature, and perhaps function. This was evident on the one hand in the Australian initiation of the Pacific War Council at Washington, proposals for the establishment of the Far Eastern Commission, participation in the British War Cabinet, and the formulation of the ANZAC Pact. On the other hand, there was an increasing sense of frustration at being snubbed by the great powers. The Australian government received its first information about the Cairo Declaration from the press communique. It was ignored in the discussions of European armistice arrangements. The European Advisory Commission, set up in October 1943, was limited to Great Britain, the United States and the USSR; the British Dominions as well as the smaller European powers were omitted. As Dr. Evatt pointed out, "the major powers excluded everyone else from the scene," even though all these powers had been co-belligerents.

chapter two

Prelude to San Francisco

The question of a post-war international security organization was not discussed in the Australian Parliament until July 1944. Although some clear indications of the principles and functions of the proposed organization had already been given, the Big Three did not consider the details until the fall of 1944. The Atlantic Charter (August 1941) had mentioned the eventual establishment of a "wider and permanent system of general security" and declared, *inter alia*, the intention of bringing about the "fullest collaboration between all nations in the economic field with the object of securing for all improved labor standards, economic advancement and social security." The Declaration on General Security, signed by the United States, the United Kingdom, the USSR, and China at Moscow on 30 October 1943, had recognized that such an organization must be based "on the principle of the sovereign equality of all peace-loving states" and be "open to membership by all such states, large and small." A meeting of Commonwealth Prime Ministers in April-May 1944 had discussed in London the British proposals for an international organization and issued a statement emphasizing the need for such a body to possess "the necessary power and authority to prevent aggression and violence."[1]

In Australia, the Department of External Affairs had been working on the concrete problems of post-war co-operation since 1942. On 14 October 1943 Dr. Herbert V. Evatt, the Minister for External Affairs, had stressed the importance of the effective participation of smaller nations, of regional defence in the Pacific, and of the improvement of the welfare of the native peoples of the Pacific and South East Asia.[2] (The latter two points became the subject of the ANZAC Pact in January 1944.)

In the absence of a draft charter or of detailed proposals, Parliament could discuss only broad principles. The debate in July 1944 showed the Labour government and the Opposition to be in substantial agreement on both the desirability of a security organization and on its structure and scope. Nevertheless, there were differences of emphasis between the parties, differences springing from something more fundamental than the Opposition's duty to oppose.[3]

To the Prime Minister, Mr. John Curtin, and to Dr. Evatt, who put the Labour government's views,[4] the cardinal weakness of the League of Nations lay in its lack of military power and its emphasis upon disarmament, a negative rather than a positive approach to peace. The new organization must, therefore, have force at its dis-

---

[1] Commonwealth of Australia, *Parliamentary Debates* (*C.P.D.*), Vol. 179, 8 Sept. 1944, p. 615.

[2] H. V. Evatt, *Foreign Policy of Australia* (Sydney: Angus and Robertson, 1945), pp. 135-53.

[3] For information on Australian political parties, see Appendix A, pp. 372 ff.

[4] Unless otherwise noted, all statements in this chapter attributed to Mr. Curtin are from his two speeches in Parliament on 17 and 21 July 1944. See *C.P.D.*, Vol. 179, pp. 36-38 and 377. Statements attributed to Dr. Evatt are from his speech in Parliament on 19 July 1944. *Ibid.*, pp. 229-34.

posal and a combined military, naval, and air staff to apply it.[5] The greater part of that force would have to be supplied by the great powers. The Prime Minister said:

> I have always maintained that as the great powers had the greatest responsibilities and resources they had the right to make the major decisions regarding the conduct of war. It follows equally that we must look to the great powers with their resources to ensure the preservation of peace, until a permanent and effective system of security can be established.

A further fundamental weakness of the League had been that it had never been universal; some of the great powers had refused to join out of a fear of being embroiled in war by the actions and decisions of the smaller powers. Responsibility for the maintenance of peace was not limited to the great powers; self-defence and the preparedness for it must be the positive duty of all members. "The weak must recognize their responsibility for doing what they can towards the defence of their territories and by co-operation in the wider system of regional security in the areas in which they and their territories are situated." Australia must therefore supplement the power of the world organization by retaining its own and the Empire's military resources. There must be a greater flexibility in the definition of preventive action and a more realistic allocation of responsibility for the maintenance of peace in the new organization.

While admitting the need for great power leadership, Mr. Curtin was emphatic that "the pendulum must not . . . swing too far in the other direction of might being right. A corrective against such a tendency must be provided in the shape of an assembly of nations, where policy can be moulded by ascertaining the highest common

---

[5] An Australian public opinion poll suggests that the general public shared this view: 67 per cent of the sample were in favour of the League of Nations having an armed force after the war; only 15 per cent were opposed. See *Australian Gallup Polls*, Nos. 205-12, July 1944 (Melbourne: Australian Public Opinion Polls).

denominator among the opinions expressed." Both he and Dr. Evatt applauded the assertion in the Moscow Declaration of the "sovereign equality of all peace-loving States" as the basis of the new organization. This "excluded any fear of a super State comprising the Big Three or the Big Four" (Evatt).

Prevention of war necessitated the removal of root causes. Peace could not be maintained without a general improvement in social and economic conditions. "Conditions of social betterment are not attainable without a lasting peace, and a durable peace is not possible until those causes of war, which have their origin in wrong social and economic conditions, are corrected" (Curtin). Force alone was inadequate. "You can only be sure of peace if you remove the temptation of national leaders to embark on acts of aggression against other countries because of internal social discontent" (Evatt). Maintaining and improving standards of living in accordance with the Atlantic Charter ranked among the organization's objectives as of equal importance with the preservation of peace.

Mr. Curtin did not entirely rely on the efficacy of conciliatory measures such as the removal of just grievances and the improvement of living conditions.

> Whilst a world organization can do a great deal to remove the causes which lead to war, we have had the experience that nations have gone to war without what those governed by goodwill and reasonable intelligence would regard as adequate justification; that is to say, the causes which lead to war were not present. When the known causes which led to war have been removed, it can be said that a contribution has been made to the peace of the world; but that in itself would not constitute a guarantee of peace. Therefore, a concert of nations of like minds must be maintained.

The effectiveness of the organization in maintaining peace depended on accord between the Big Three. "A prolonged period of peace is essential for recuperation and reconstruction after the war, and unanimity of the Great Powers on the need for it is, I think, sufficient assurance that it will be realized." Dr. Evatt was perhaps a little

more cautious: his attitude to continued close co-operation between the Allies was one of "guarded optimism."

Neither Mr. Curtin nor Dr. Evatt placed complete reliance upon the world organization for collective security. Mr. Curtin declared:

> The experience of the British Commonwealth has shown that the growth of cooperation has been slow, notwithstanding that we have so much in common. It remains to be seen how quickly and effectively we can develop and maintain a system of world security, but we dare not fail our own people in providing the security for which they so greatly yearn.

He pointed out that the security of Australia or any other part of the British Commonwealth in the future would rest on three safeguards, each wider in scope than the next: national defence, the degree of empire co-operation that could be established, and a system of collective security which could be organized on a world and regional basis. "These safeguards are complementary to each other, and none is exclusive of the others." The extent to which the Australian government would rely on self-defence and on imperial defence would depend on the extent to which confidence in collective security appeared to be justified.

How could membership of the new organization affect Australian collaboration with the British Commonwealth, traditionally its first line of defence? Particularly important in the light of their previous attitudes was Labour's emphasis upon defence—the obligation to maintain local defence and the intention to participate in imperial defence. At the London meeting of Commonwealth Prime Ministers in April 1944, Mr. Curtin, who had become particularly interested in the problem, had strongly argued for a system of closer representation and co-operation within the Commonwealth. He made it clear to Parliament that there was no conflict of interest or policy here: Australia would act in the organization in concert with other members of the Commonwealth.

> The strength of Britain has been described as her "alliance potential," when she speaks with the united voice and author-

ity of the whole British Commonwealth. This is also true of
the Dominions, for individually we are weak, but united we
are strong. Co-operation in regard to our policies should,
therefore, be such as to ensure that, mutually, each commands
the support of the others . . . It is as an integral part of the
British Commonwealth that Australia can most influentially
express itself in the world organization, and I have no doubt
whatever that the unity of the British Commonwealth will, in
the problems of the future, give to His Majesty's subjects
everywhere an authority in the consultations with other countries, that will enable our concept of life to influence greatly
the decisions which have to be made so that all we have
fought for can be achieved.

This did not mean the subordination of Australian interests to the
United Kingdom's: it meant rather consultation among equals. As
Dr. Evatt pointed out:

The British Commonwealth must present towards that world
organization the spectacle of a unified entity in matters of the
highest import. That does not mean that we have to integrate
our governments, nor does it mean that we have to present
the spectacle of an absolute Empire bloc against the rest of
the world. The Dominions, rather than the Motherland, have
the largest interest in authoritative declarations whereby a
British Prime Minister may speak for the Empire as a whole.

There was no point on which the Leader of the Liberal party
Opposition, Mr. R. G. Menzies, substantially disagreed with the
Labour leaders; the differences were differences of emphasis. He
welcomed the Moscow Declaration which recognized that the world
organization was to be based on the sovereign equality of states,
thereby rejecting any suggestion that it was a superstate. He agreed
that the chief weakness of the League lay in its lack of military
power and that the new body must possess force.

We shall not ignore the conception of and the necessity for
power . . . We shall endeavour to get out of the comradeship
of mighty races in this war a permanent association in peace
and the maintenance, for their common purposes, of such

power that there will be no room left for war by revengeful and defeated enemies.[6]

It was in their greater emphasis on the problem of power that the Opposition differed from the government. Realizing that success depended on great power agreement, Mr. Menzies was even more cautious than Dr. Evatt who, as Minister for External Affairs, could hardly have been pessimistic in public. Mr. Menzies could see that serious divisions were already developing among the war-time allies, that cracks in the facade were becoming visible.

The principal difference between the two main parties is evident in the omission by Mr. Menzies of any reference to the need for economic and social improvement. To Labour, influenced by traditional socialist conceptions of the causes of war, this was fundamental. The other differences were slight. Mr. Menzies agreed completely on the importance of national and imperial defence. Labour had stressed the need for regional defence along the lines of the ANZAC Pact between Australia and New Zealand (1944) as a component of the wider system of collective security. Mr. Menzies' chief reservation was that undue attention to Pacific defence might blind Australia to European dangers.

Finally, Mr. Menzies cautioned against expecting too much from the proposed organization in its early stages: it must not be overstrained. As an imperial statesman he placed greater reliance upon the Empire than upon the world organization.

> Many a good policy . . . has failed in the past because of the attempt to go too far, too fast. I am not sure that the League of Nations did not try to run before it had learned to crawl. We, I believe, while maintaining our great ideals on these matters of world control and world organization, must never lose sight of the fact that, for us, the immediate world organization, the one that we now have, is the British Empire itself.

---

[6] See Mr. Menzies' statement, *C.P.D.*, 18 July 1944, pp. 102-05.

Country party leaders,[7] while in general agreement with the Labour government, had a slightly different approach from both the Liberals and the government. To Sir Earle Page, an experienced former cabinet minister, the chief hope of a peaceful world lay in the naval power of Britain and the United States, and in cultural exchange among English-speaking peoples. His interest in an international security organization was secondary, although he did believe in the importance of international economic planning, co-operation, and consultation to ensure that output did not exceed demand. "The democratic countries, to prevent war, must solve fairly the economic problems that lead to war."[8] Here, his enthusiasms approximated more closely to those of Mr. Curtin and Dr. Evatt than of Mr. Menzies, although socialist explanations of the causes of war were anathema to him. His colleague, Mr. J. McEwen, accepted in outline the Curtin policy and was critical of the current pessimism concerning the proposed organization. He was, however, somewhat apprehensive about the possible consequences of a logical application of the Atlantic Charter:

> What are to be the implications after the war of the mutual aid agreements and the Atlantic Charter upon our secondary industries which have sprung up under hot house conditions during the war? . . . If the Atlantic Charter is to function in certain directions in anything like a literal sense, it is doubtful whether some of our secondary industries will be able to continue. What has the Government to tell these industries? If Australian manufacturing industries now in existence are to be employed to full capacity in the post-war period, how shall we maintain our export markets for primary products in countries from which, in the circumstances, we shall not purchase anything?[9]

---

[7] The Country party draws its support almost entirely from primary producers. In federal politics, it is normally the junior partner in a coalition with the Liberals.

[8] *C.P.D.*, 19 July 1944, p. 205.

[9] *Ibid.*, 18 July 1944, p. 130.

Back-benchers influence party policies very little, and few of them spoke in the debate. There was general agreement with party leaders that no international organization could succeed without adequate force; there was too an undertone of apprehension that a new body would be no more successful than the League.[10] Only two members, one from each side of the House,[11] were completely pessimistic. They believed that conflicting policies and ideologies made continuing agreement with Russia impossible. Two Labour back-benchers put a strong socialist view that capitalism and imperialism made the satisfactory working of a collective security system improbable.[12]

The first full-scale discussion in the Australian Parliament showed an almost unanimous desire by all parties to build an international security organization around the nucleus of the Big Three. The crux of the problem was the issue of their permanent co-operation, and here a tone of moderate optimism prevailed. The Liberals accepted great power preponderance as inevitable; Labour also accepted it, but emphasized the rights of small nations without foreseeing the possibility of an ultimate dilemma here. Labour's political philosophy gave it a firmer belief in the value of social and economic co-operation as a means of improving world security. The Country party, predominantly sectional in character, emphasized the relationship between war and economic conditions, no doubt seeing advantages for the Australian primary producer in international economic collaboration to raise living standards. Liberals ignored this problem.

On the problem of security there was overall agreement. To the Liberal and Country parties, Commonwealth collaboration had

---

[10] See statements by Senator N. E. McKenna (Labour), Senator B. Sampson (Liberal), and Dame Enid Lyons (Liberal), *ibid.*, 17 July 1944, p. 14; 18 July 1944, pp. 63-65; and 20 July 1944, p. 346.

[11] See speeches by Mr. A. G. Cameron (Country party) and Mr. F. Gaha (Labour), *ibid.*, 20 July 1944, pp. 332-33, and 18 July 1944, p. 123.

[12] See speeches by Mr. D. A. Mountjoy and Mr. J. P. Breen, *ibid.*, 20 July 1944, pp. 340-42 and 320-23.

always had a great emotional appeal. The really significant thing was that the pacifist tendencies and the objections to imperial defence which at one time had characterized the Labour party were no longer in evidence. Three years of war-time office and the proximity of the Pacific War had given it a greater realism and maturity of outlook. Imperial defence had become an integral part of its program and there was now no possibility of substantial conflict between the imperial and international allegiances of Australia. All party leaders agreed to support the world organization but not to rely entirely upon it for defence; collective security and imperial and local defence would become important as conditions should demand.

In the interval between the parliamentary debate in July and the San Francisco Conference, government policy was gradually clarified on a number of points. In July 1944, at the Philadelphia Conference of the International Labour Organisation, the Australian delegate, Mr. J. A. Beasley, vigorously attacked the United States and Great Britain when the former resisted his attempts to commit members to a policy of full employment and the latter refused to discuss any recommendations on social policies in colonies.[13] Both policies were actively pressed by Australia at San Francisco.

On 8 September 1944, Dr. Evatt, discussing the problems of post-war world organization, expressed Australian dissatisfaction with the proposal that international disputes should be settled primarily by a Security Council. Recognising that the united military backing of Great Britain, the United States and the Soviet Union was vital, he felt that non-permanent membership of the Security Council should be increased to at least eight to give representation to some of the middle and smaller powers. In addition, the General Assembly should be given powers and functions which should make it the effective central organ of the world organization. Member nations would be required to affirm the principles they were prepared to

---

[13] See below, pp. 65-66 and 68.

uphold and to enter into specific undertakings as to their duties as members. By November, when the Dumbarton Oaks deliberations had been completed, Australian policy had crystallized sufficiently to permit discussions on matters of common interest with New Zealand at the Wellington Conference. The resolutions of this Conference, adopted by the Australian government on 10 November 1944, became the basis for Australian policy at San Francisco. They read as follows:[14]

> 1. Australia and New Zealand desire to play their full part in the establishment of a General International Organization for the purpose of preserving international peace and security and promoting human welfare.

> 2. In order that such Organization may bring into being an effective and lasting system of collective security, all the members should pledge themselves to co-operate in carrying out, by force if need be, the decisions of the Organization for the preservation of peace.

> 3. The Charter of the Organization should make clear to the peoples of the world the principles on which the action of the Organization is to be based.

> 4. It should be a positive principle of the Organization, openly declared and binding upon all members, that the territorial integrity and political independence of members should be preserved against change by force or threat of force from another power. Provision should be made by the Organization for facilitating the orderly change of situations, the continuance of which might endanger the peace of the world.

> 5. The Charter of the Organization should embody the essential principles of the Atlantic Charter and the Philadelphia Declaration.

> 6. The Organization should be open to all sovereign States subject to approval of their admission by the Assembly.

---

[14] See Parliament of Commonwealth of Australia, *United Nations Conference on International Organization: Report of the Australian Delegates* (Canberra: Commonwealth Govt. Printer, 1945), p. 60.

7. The success of such an Organization will depend upon the leadership of the Greater Powers, but it is essential that all members should actively participate in the general control and direction of its affairs.

To this end, the powers and functions of the Assembly should be such as to enable it at any of its meetings to deal with any matter within the sphere of action of the Organization, subject only to the executive powers of the Security Council in regard to the settlement of disputes and the action to be taken against an aggressor.

8. There should be the maximum employment of the International Court of Justice for the ascertainment of facts which may be in dispute.

9. The Security Council should be limited in numbers, while being as representative as possible, and for the purpose of preserving security should be vested with wide powers.

10. The specialized bodies set up separately for various purposes of international welfare should be brought within the framework of the Organization.

11. Powers responsible for dependent territories should accept the principle of trusteeship, already applicable in the case of mandated territories. In such dependent territories the purpose of the trust is the welfare and advancement of the native peoples. Colonial Powers should undertake to make regular reports to an international body analogous to the Permanent Mandates Commission, set up within the framework of the General Organization. This body should be empowered to publish reports of its deliberations and to inspect dependent territories.

12. For the new Organization to fulfil its task, the condition underlying all others is that the members should fully honour the obligations which they assume.

These general policies were then translated into specific proposals for the amendment of the Dumbarton Oaks draft. The major objectives of the amendments submitted by Australia to the San Francisco Conference were:[15]

1. To include among the purposes of the Organization the promotion of justice, and the rule of law in international affairs and to secure in practice the acceptance of higher moral and ethical standards in the conduct of international relations.

2. To require all members to recognize the compulsory jurisdiction of the International Court of Justice in legal disputes specified in the Court's statute, and to ensure the maximum use of the Court in determining the juridical aspects of international disputes before political actions were taken.

3. To require a pledge from all members to respect the territorial integrity and political independence of other members.

4. To ensure that the wide powers of the Organization could not be used to interfere with matters within a state's domestic jurisdiction, and in particular to require that, if a state were threatened or attacked by reason of a matter within its domestic jurisdiction, the Council, in taking the necessary measures to maintain or restore peace, would not make any recommendations curtailing that state's lawful freedom of action. This involved the extension of the concept of domestic jurisdiction beyond the Dumbarton Oaks draft and the limitation in fact of the overall authority of the new Organization.

5. To give to the General Assembly a wider jurisdiction over, and a full share in, the work of the Organization, and in particular

(a) to vest the Assembly with power to prevent situations from becoming "frozen" in the Security Council by the exercise of the veto by the greater powers;

(b) to exclude the veto of the permanent members of the Security Council from all arrangements relating to the pacific settlement of disputes, the process of conciliation, the amendment of the Charter

---

[15] *Documents of the United Nations Conference on International Organization, San Francisco, 1945* (New York: United Nations Information Organizations, 1945), Vol. III, pp. 543 ff.

itself, and to confine its application to decisions involving enforcement measures, including "sanctions"; and

(c) to remove from the Council control over the expulsion of members and the admission of new members (other than the enemy states).

6. To strengthen the Security Council

(a) by giving it responsibility for initiating and concluding agreements with members on their military contributions; and

(b) by ensuring that its membership be drawn from those powers which had proved themselves able and willing to carry out substantial security responsibilities (e.g., Canada and Australia).

7. To ensure that the failure of the Security Council to act would not prevent the implementation of regional defence measures.

8. To emphasize the importance of social and economic welfare as a major objective of the Organization. This involved:

(a) a pledge from all members to take action, both national and international, for the purpose of securing improved labour standards, economic advancement, full employment, and social security; to take appropriate action through the General Assembly, the Economic and Social Council, and the International Labour Organisation; and to report annually to the Assembly on the actions they have taken;

(b) the elevation of the Economic and Social Council to the rank of a principal organ of the Organization and to give it, under the General Assembly, specific new functions, including the initiation of international conventions on economic and social matters not being dealt with by the specialized agencies; and

(c) the establishing of the principle of trusteeship, that is that the main purpose of administration of dependent territories is the welfare of the dependent peoples and their economic, social, and political development, and to require all members administering such territories to report regularly to an expert advisory commission. (These proposals envisaged the drafting of a new chapter in the Charter to cover the principle of trusteeship.)

chapter three

Australia and the San Francisco Conference

The sixteen volumes of multilithed documents on the San Francisco Conference are useful in showing how the Charter articles took shape, often by slow accretion, like a coral atoll, as a result of the patient amendments by numerous national delegations. The contentious issues were resolved by hard bargaining behind the scenes: at the bar, in the corridors, or in the hotel room. Much of what went on at San Francisco is still the concealed part of the iceberg. Some of it may become known as personal memoirs are published;[1] most of it can only be illuminated from the careful briefs of delegations, briefs which will for long be buried in national archives.

Australia was represented at San Francisco by Mr. F. M. Forde, Deputy Prime Minister and Minister for the Army, and by Dr.

---

[1] See Paul Hasluck, "Australia and the Formation of the United Nations: Some Personal Reminiscences, Part I," *Journal and Proceedings. Royal Australian Historical Society* (Sydney), Vol. 40 (1954), pp. 133-78.

H. V. Evatt, Attorney-General and Minister for External Affairs. Dr. Evatt, a man of great intellect and dominant personality, subsequently emerged as one of the outstanding figures of the Conference, the champion of the smaller powers. A liberal socialist and a former member of the Australian High Court, he brought to the Conference a passionate conviction of the need for morality in international affairs, a sense of mission, and a belief in the need for world government by gradual stages. These were combined with a devotion to legal processes and a humourless determination to establish democratic principles as the basis for the conduct of international relations. The two Labour delegates were accompanied by forty-three assistants and consultants representing a wide variety of shades of opinion within the Labour government and the Opposition. Few Australian delegations have been so carefully briefed as this, but sharp conflicts of opinion developed within the delegation on many points of detail and even of principle.

In accordance with the normal practice of the British Commonwealth, a conference of leading Commonwealth ministers was held in London from 4-13 April 1945, immediately before the San Francisco Conference, to discuss policy and common problems. In 1917 General Smuts had pointed out that an imperial policy, to be a common policy, would have to be a simple policy. "We do not understand finesse in other parts of the Empire. We go by large principles." As the Dominions later became middle powers, conscious of their new stature and increasingly aware of regional interests, they also came to understand finesse. "Large principles" were still important but it became increasingly difficult to formulate a simple policy based upon them. War-time experience had shown the value of finesse in securing agreement and the difficulty of applying "large principles" to complex situations where regional interests tended to diverge.

The purpose of the London meeting, attended by the two leaders of the Australian delegation, was to enlarge the area of agreement among members of the Commonwealth and to discuss frankly the major points of difference and the issues to be faced at San Francisco. There was no attempt to "gang up" on the other powers, no attempt to prepare to exert regional or group pressure at the Conference. From a Commonwealth point of view, a somewhat new situation had developed. Great Britain would occupy an ambivalent position as one of the inner group of sponsoring powers at San Francisco and as the senior member of the Commonwealth. With the Australian insistence that the "middle powers" or "security powers" be given a special role in the new organization, and the division which could emerge from a conflict between the greater and lesser powers, an internal line of cleavage quickly appeared within the Commonwealth. In the discussion of problems of colonial trusteeship during the two preceding years, sharp differences had developed between Great Britain, on the one hand, and Australia and New Zealand on the other. The ANZAC pact had attached great importance to the welfare of native peoples: Great Britain distrusted extensive international supervision of colonial peoples and disliked proposals for the submission of regular reports to an expert advisory body. The London meeting failed to secure agreement on some important issues: this left to the Dominions a good deal of freedom of policy on contentious problems. At San Francisco itself, there were some formal conferences among Commonwealth representatives, but there was far less collaboration and no pretence at hammering out common policies as there had been at the Paris Peace Conference in 1919. Commonwealth consultation appears to have been of an informal kind, at the bar and in the hotel room, with an occasional formal interview between key members of delegations, but often marred by sharp personal conflicts.

THE VETO

From the beginning of the San Francisco Conference, a sharp cleavage developed over the role of the Security Council. The Big Three had been unable to reach a final decision at Dumbarton Oaks on voting procedures in the Security Council: they got no further than an agreement that the veto should apply on all matters which might affect world peace. Britain and the United States subsequently urged that in cases of peaceful settlement an exception be made: that a permanent member should not vote if it were a party to the dispute. After some initial resistance, the Soviet Union accepted the Yalta formula on 7 February 1945. Each of the eleven members of the Council should have one vote; decisions on procedural matters should be made by an affirmative vote of seven members including the concurring votes of the permanent members (except that a party to a dispute should abstain from voting on decisions relating to the procedures for the peaceful settlement of the dispute). The position of Great Britain and the other sponsoring powers was crystal clear: "In view of the primary responsibilities of the permanent members, they could not be expected, in the present condition of the world, to assume the obligation to act in so serious a matter as the maintenance of international peace and security in consequence of a decision in which they had not concurred."[2] Equality of stature rather than of status was the crucial point: the heart of the argument was the burden of responsibility. As Mr. Eden put it in the House of Commons debate, "the conception of democracy in international affairs led people to think—falsely as I believe—that the League [of Nations] was constituted so that every nation must be regarded as exactly equal and that there was no relation between power and responsibility."[3] Britain was determined in 1945 to prevent a repetition of this error.

Anxious to limit the influence of the great powers and so reduce the relative authority of the Security Council, Australia nevertheless accepted, reluctantly and of necessity, a veto in questions involving enforcement action: the great powers would obviously provide the

---

[2] *Documents of the United Nations Conference on International Organization, San Francisco, 1945* (New York: United Nations Information Organizations, 1945), Vol. XI, p. 713. Hereinafter cited as *UNCIO Documents.*

[3] *Great Britain: Parliamentary Debates (Hansard): House of Commons* (London: H. M. Stationery Office, 1945), Fifth Series, Vol. 413, 22 Aug. 1945, p. 674.

bulk of the forces. With the large majority of the other powers, it supported the abridgement or abolition of great power voting privileges on decisions of other kinds. The Australian delegation sought to draw a clear distinction between enforcement and conciliation, and to confine the veto to enforcement measures only.[4]

The Australian view was that "conciliation, or peaceful means of settling a dispute, should be regarded not as a power of the Council but as the duty of the Council because by such means the dispute may be composed and the use of force prevented."[5] The sponsoring powers pointed out that once the Council takes any step beyond preliminary discussion, once it decides to carry out an investigation or makes recommendations, its decisions and actions "may well have major political consequences and may even initiate a chain of events which might, in the end, require the Council under its responsibilities to invoke measures of enforcement."[6] Dr. Evatt claimed that, by preventing the dispute from being settled by conciliation, the veto could result in a chain of events ending in a breach of the peace. He reiterated his demand that the veto should not apply to conciliation and peaceful settlement.[7]

The Yalta voting formula aroused considerable opposition from the smaller powers, and the Conference developed into a fierce and heated battle over the veto. In this most important dispute, the great powers were in a minority and were not prepared to compromise. If the majority did not give way, then it appeared probable that there would be no Charter and no United Nations. In an attempt to clarify the Yalta formula, Peter Fraser, Prime Minister of New Zealand, invited the great powers to interpret it. Sub-

---

[4] Australia's interest in avoiding paralysis of regional defence actions by the Security Council's veto on motions to authorize enforcement actions under regional arrangements was met by the statement, in Article 51 of the Charter, of the individual and collective right to self-defence irrespective of a Security Council decision.

[5] *UNCIO Documents*, Vol. XI, p. 123.

[6] *Ibid.*, p. 712.

[7] *Ibid.*, p. 126.

e

sequently the Australian delegation, on 22 May, sought to pinpoint the problem by submitting a twenty-two section questionnaire. Sixteen days later, the sponsoring powers in a joint statement specifically answered one of the questions and rigidly interpreted the phrase "procedural matters." A broader definition would have given some elasticity to the functioning of the Security Council. In effect, the statement flatly rejected the Australian point of view. Britain alone appears to have taken some initiative in seeking clarification on this point, but it too was quite adamant on the question of retaining the veto. The decision was effected in the penthouse of the Fairmont Hotel, where the great powers held their meetings. A personal interview by Dr. Evatt failed to shake the Big Four although there are grounds for suspecting that there was considerable disagreement among them.

In a vigorous three-day debate, Australia and New Zealand led the attack to exclude the veto from decisions relating to peaceful settlement by regarding them as procedural matters. The representative of Great Britain brushed aside the distinction: "He did not know what the Delegate of Australia meant by a 'veto' on conciliation."[8] In a dramatic roll call, the Australian amendment, redrafted but unchanged in substance, was rejected by 10 votes to 20 with 15 abstentions.[9] It is clear that all those who abstained, and even several who voted against the Australian proposal, favoured the amendment, in principle. When the final vote was taken on the Yalta formula, it was adopted by 30 to 2 with 15 abstentions. Australia and New Zealand were among the abstainers, Cuba and Colombia alone persisting in their opposition. It is equally clear that what Sir Carl Berendson of New Zealand called the "shotgun

[8] *Ibid.*, p. 435.

[9] *Ibid.*, pp. 494-95. *For:* Australia, Brazil, Chile, Colombia, Cuba, Iran, Mexico, the Netherlands, New Zealand, and Panama. *Against:* Byelorussian SSR, China, Costa Rica, Czechoslovakia, Denmark, Dominican Republic, France, Honduras, Lebanon, Liberia, Nicaragua, Norway, Philippines, South Africa, Ukrainian SSR, United Kingdom, United States, USSR, Uruguay, and Yugoslavia. *Abstentions:* Argentina, Belgium, Bolivia, Canada, Ethiopia, Greece, Guatemala, India, Iraq, Luxembourg, Peru, Saudi Arabia, Syria, Turkey, and Venezuela.

wedding" was the result of a plain ultimatum from the Soviet Union (backed by the United States and Great Britain): no veto, no Charter.

The protracted and masterly battle put up by Dr. Evatt did result in an assurance from the sponsoring powers (on 7 June 1945) that the veto would not be used to block discussion of a situation by the Council. The United States announced that the veto would not be used capriciously; the Soviet Union issued a press statement that the five powers would rarely exercise the veto. The suspicions raised by the bitter battle over the veto may well have contributed to subsequent Soviet intransigence in the United Nations. As one observer has remarked, "Article 27 was stiffened and toughened by the blasts of small power eloquence."[10]

On one other issue affecting the Security Council, Australia and Canada obtained, with Commonwealth co-operation, a modification of the Dumbarton Oaks draft. They urged that in the election of non-permanent members to the Security Council, special weight should be given to the "middle" or "security" powers. These were the powers "which, by their past military contribution to the cause of world security, have proved able and willing to assume substantial security responsibilities, or which are willing, and by virtue of their geographical position in relation to regions of primary strategical importance are able, to make a substantial contribution to the maintenance of international peace and security."[11] The substance of the proposal, backed by Great Britain in the Big Four meetings and in committee sessions, was incorporated in Article 23 of the Charter. In practice, however, the drafting victory of San Francisco has proved a hollow one, and the principle established has been subsequently ignored. In the first election of non-permanent members, Australia and Canada, both important from a security point of view, tied for last place. Australia was subsequently elected when

---

[10] Paul Hasluck, *Workshop of Security* (Melbourne: F. W. Cheshire, 1948), p. 131.

[11] *UNCIO Documents*, Vol. III, p. 550.

Canada generously withdrew. Brazil, Mexico, and Egypt were elected to satisfy regional ambitions rather than to add strength to the Security Council.

In retrospect, neither the hopes nor the fears of participants in the veto controversy have been completely fulfilled. The use of the veto to block peaceful settlement has never yet converted a dispute into an armed dispute, despite Dr. Evatt's fears. On the other hand, hopes such as those expressed in the following statement by a United States representative have hardly been fulfilled:

> It is our theory that they [the Permanent Members] will . . . discharge the duties of their office not as representatives of their governments . . . but as representatives of the whole Organization in behalf of world peace and in behalf of world security. Any other course . . . would over a period of time, cause the disintegration of the Organization. Fifty nations would not permit the arbitrary or willful use of the powers of the Security Council when it was adverse to the interests of all of the Organization or of world peace. And so I do not believe that that can occur. Let me say, furthermore, that if there should be one recalcitrant member of the Security Council, with four other members sitting by his side and counseling him and warning him as to the course that they thought he was going to pursue, and with six other members elected by the Assembly, the moral influence, the pressure, and the prestige of these other members would make him think many times before that power should be used arbitrarily or willfully.[12]

How can the Australian stand on the veto be explained? It is patently inadequate to argue that the veto was unreasonable: several small powers did not oppose it and many others opposed it with less vigour than Australia. In the League of Nations, Australia had supported the great powers when the smaller nations sought to weaken their predominance in the Council.[13] Yet at San Francisco,

---

[12] Senator Tom Connally (United States), *ibid.*, Vol. XI, pp. 131-32.
[13] See above, pp. 16-17.

Australia led the attack on the veto even at the expense of sacrificing Commonwealth unity on a major issue.

In discussing the direction of the war and the peace settlement, Dr. Evatt had repeatedly insisted that Australia should participate as the equal of the great powers. He may not, of course, have pressed his claim to the point of demanding an equal voice in *decisions* on these matters. The attack on the veto is not a necessary corollary; yet it is consistent with such views and consistent with the Australian attempt to enhance the role and enlarge the powers of the General Assembly. Moreover, in the past, great power predominance had been acceptable because Australia had been reluctant to assume the responsibilities of equality of status with Great Britain and so had accepted British foreign policy with little demur. The enhancement of Australia's stature during the Second World War and a realization that Britain had global, and not merely regional, interests and commitments produced a willingness to formulate independent policies. Even although the Australian Labour party still leaned heavily on British assistance in its plans for post-war defence, it was normally sensitive to questions of status. San Francisco was the first international conference at which Australia openly attacked a policy that Britain regarded as vital. The intimate discussions among members of the British Commonwealth delegations were replaced, in Australia's case, by a cold aloofness.

Rifts had appeared among Commonwealth members at the London conference in April. Great Britain had rejected Dr. Evatt's proposals for non-self-governing territories, proposals that he held with enthusiasm and considered vital to world peace. The abnormal dual position of Britain as a sponsoring power as well as the senior member of the Commonwealth was unhappily reminiscent of the late nineteenth century relationship between the colonies and the metropolitan power. In 1919 Britain had been committed to support Japanese claims to the former German Pacific territories north of the equator. Although this affected Australian security more directly than did the veto issue at San Francisco, W. M. Hughes had reluctantly accepted Britain's position. Dr. Evatt's policy was a measure of the rapid constitutional evolution of the Commonwealth since the Balfour Report and the Statute of Westminster. It was also indicative of his intense ambition, his sensitivity to opposition, and his realization that Australian leadership of the forty-five smaller nations against the five greater powers could pay dividends in the "horse-trading" on other articles of the Charter.

THE GENERAL ASSEMBLY

A logical corollary to the battle over the veto and the composition of the Security Council was the question of the role and powers of the General Assembly. To Dr. Evatt, the enlargement of the limited powers envisaged for the Assembly in the Dumbarton Oaks draft was "one of the major issues" at San Francisco.[14]

The Dumbarton Oaks proposals outlined the powers of the Assembly as follows:

> The General Assembly should have the right to consider the general principles of cooperation in the maintenance of international peace and security, including the principles governing disarmament and the regulation of armaments; to discuss any questions relating to the maintenance of international peace and security brought before it by any member or members of the Organization or by the Security Council; and to make recommendations with regard to any such principles or questions. Any such questions on which action is necessary should be referred to the Security Council by the General Assembly either before or after discussion. The General Assembly should not on its own initiative make recommendations on any matter relating to the maintenance of international peace and security which is being dealt with by the Security Council.[15]

---

[14] Parliament of the Commonwealth of Australia, *United Nations Conference on International Organization: Report by the Australian Delegates* (Canberra: Commonwealth Govt. Printer, 1945), p. 20. Hereinafter cited as *Australian Report on UNCIO.*

[15] *UNCIO Documents*, Vol. III, p. 4.

Before the San Francisco Conference the sponsoring powers themselves proposed to extend these powers to include the recommending of "measures for the peaceful adjustment of any situations, regardless of origin, which it deems likely to impair the general welfare or friendly relations among nations . . ."[16] Australia pressed for an amendment to establish explicitly the power of the Assembly to consider and make recommendations on "any matter affecting international relations"[17] with the exception that the Assembly would be prohibited from making recommendations on any security question actually being dealt with by the Security Council.

It is evident from the record that Australia was one of the many countries supporting the enlargement of the Assembly's powers. It is equally evident that leadership in this struggle fell to Dr. Evatt. The Soviet Union alone vigorously opposed the move and only accepted the amendment in the closing stages of the Conference when the issue had been thrashed out in a special committee consisting of Gromyko, Stettinius, and Evatt.

The substance of the original Australian amendment was adopted by a substantial majority of the committee considering the powers of the General Assembly. The committee proposed that, except in the case of matters being considered by the Security Council, the Assembly should have the right to consider and to make recommendations on "any matter within the sphere of international relations."[18]

Mr. Gromyko opposed this amendment because he believed that this would circumvent the prohibition of interference in domestic affairs contained elsewhere in the Charter. It would enable any member who disliked any action of its neighbour, even a normal and domestic action such as immigration or customs laws, to bring the matter before the Assembly for its consideration. To Mr. Gromyko this would directly infringe the sovereignty of the state

---

[16] *Ibid.*, p. 629.
[17] *Ibid.*, p. 544.
[18] *Ibid.*, Vol. IX, p. 109.

concerned. Even if no recommendation were made, discussion could strain the relations between the states concerned. He felt that every member had the right to expect the Organization not to interfere in its domestic matters until its actions created a situation threatening international peace and security. Until then, a member could act without restriction not only in the field of its domestic policy but in the field of international policy as well.[19]

To Dr. Evatt, these were groundless fears because he was "convinced that the prohibition against intervention in matters of domestic jurisdiction overrides all other powers granted to the General Assembly."[20] He was prepared, if necessary, to repeat the prohibition specifically in connection with the Chapter under discussion. He considered that the General Assembly, as well as the Security Council, should be trusted not to abuse its powers. In the final compromise, Australia accepted a narrower phrase, "any matters within the scope of the . . . Charter" instead of "any matter within the sphere of international relations."

What was the object of the Australian amendment and why did Australia reject the view of the sponsoring powers that their own amendment to the original proposals rendered the Australian amendment unnecessary? Dr. Evatt's statement of his conviction that "the prohibition against intervention in matters of domestic jurisdiction overrides all other powers granted to the General Assembly" made it clear that his objective was not to widen in any general fashion the powers of the Organization. In its report, the Australian delegation claimed that the Australian amendments were aimed at removing the limiting phrases "general principles" and "maintenance of international peace and security."

> It was the view of the Australian Delegation . . . that if additions to the text were made purporting to remove limitations on the General Assembly's field of discussion and recommendation in relation to security matters, there should be an over-

---

[19] *Ibid.*, Vol. V, pp. 264-65.
[20] *Ibid.*, p. 525.

all clause expressing beyond doubt the wide powers of the General Assembly over all matters of real international concern whether relating to security or welfare and whether particular or general in character.[21]

In fact, the original and subsequent proposals of the sponsoring powers adequately safeguarded the Assembly's right fully to discuss security matters with the reservation (in which Australia concurred) excluding Assembly recommendations on matters under consideration by the Council.

The real purpose behind the Australian amendment was to put beyond dispute the Assembly's right fully to discuss and to make recommendations on two subjects for which Australia at the time considered international co-operation and General Assembly recommendations to be essential: dependent peoples and full employment. Australia considered that the formula it advocated was more likely to enhance the dignity of the Assembly than the draft submitted by the sponsoring powers. As a middle power, conscious of its role in the war, Australia was anxious to enhance the importance of the Assembly vis-a-vis the Security Council. Dr. Evatt had pointed out in 1944 the danger of great power predominance. His championing of the Assembly, in which the smaller powers were all represented, was the logical consequence of his concern at their exclusion from the direction of the Allied war effort. His criticisms of big power control had been largely responsible for the establishment of the Pacific War Council in 1942 as a body in which the smaller belligerents could meet on equal terms with the United States and Great Britain. He had deplored Australia's exclusion from the combined United States-United Kingdom Chiefs of Staff Committee and had insisted upon Australia's right to participate in the Peace Conference on a basis of equality. His championship of the middle and smaller powers came out in his concern at great power predominance in the Security Council. Australia was particularly anxious to establish the right of the Assembly to criticize the capricious

---

[21] *Australian Report on UNCIO, op. cit.,* p. 20.

use by any great power of its right of veto to prevent United Nations action on particular issues.

Australia pressed for an enlargement of the powers of the General Assembly, subject to the qualification that the Security Council had unfettered powers to deal with breaches of the peace. Unlike some of the Latin American republics (e.g., Mexico), Australia refused to accept the view that, except in questions calling for immediate action, Security Council decisions should be subject to review by the Assembly. It hoped rather that the middle powers would be able to exert their influence through their membership in the Security Council.

MEMBERSHIP

On the question of membership in the United Nations, Australia's attitude was somewhat ambivalent. Australia felt that if the United Nations were to function effectively, membership should be universal: this had been the Achilles' heel of the League of Nations. Yet there was a reluctance to admit to membership states whose conduct was not consonant with the principles and essential purposes of the United Nations: this could compromise the Organization's prestige. Speaking to the question of the admission of Spain, Dr. Evatt pointed out that Australia had proposed the inclusion of a provision in the Charter expressly excluding from membership not only enemy countries but also countries which had since 1939 given military assistance to enemy countries.[22]

On the question of inviting Argentina to attend the Conference, his position was more equivocal. When the matter was discussed at the first meeting of the Executive Committee of the Conference, Molotov indicated his intention of opposing the invitation. Dr. Evatt said flatly that if the question stood alone, Australia would oppose the immediate admission of Argentina because of its war record.

---

[22] *UNCIO Documents*, Vol. VI, pp. 130-31.

At the same time, in view of the attitude of the Latin American countries, permanent exclusion of Argentina would be impossible.[23] He therefore proposed the postponement of the question unless Argentina should, on its own initiative, apply for admission: then the Conference might take favourable action.[24] Dr. Evatt did not, however, press his motion and the committee decided in favour of the invitation.

DOMESTIC JURISDICTION

The Dumbarton Oaks proposals as amended by the sponsoring powers contained, among the enumeration of the principles of the organization, the following:

> Nothing contained in this Charter shall authorize the Organization to intervene in matters which are essentially within the domestic jurisdiction of the State concerned or shall require the members to submit such matters to settlement under this Charter; but this principle shall not prejudice the application of Chapter VIII, Section B [Determination of Threats to the Peace or Acts of Aggression and Action with Respect Thereto].[25]

Dr. Evatt, although demanding that the General Assembly have the right to consider and make recommendations on "any matter within the sphere of international relations,"[26] nevertheless considered that this right was subject to the principle "really implicit in any organisation that is genuinely *international* in character" that "no such organisation should be permitted to intervene in those domestic matters in which, by definition, international law permits each state

---

[23] These countries believed there was a moral obligation to admit Argentina since the latter had accepted their terms for reinstatement in the community of American nations, viz., a declaration of war against the Axis, the signature of the Act of Chapultepec, and the acceptance of the principles embodied therein.

[24] *UNCIO Documents*, Vol. V, p. 379.

[25] *Ibid.*, Vol. III, p. 623.

[26] See above, p. 57.

entire liberty of action."[27] The phrase "essentially within the domestic jurisdiction" in the proposals of the sponsoring powers was
preferable to the phrase "solely within the domestic jurisdiction"
which appeared in the Covenant of the League of Nations, since
matters solely within domestic jurisdiction were constantly con-
tracting. The promotion of full employment, for example, a few
years previously would not have been considered a proper subject
for international action. Now, although not "solely" within domestic
jurisdiction, it was still "essentially" within domestic jurisdiction.[28]
This statement, made on 16 June 1945, after the committee debate
had indicated that the full employment pledge would be incorporated
in the Charter, made it clear that Dr. Evatt considered that despite
this pledge full employment was still a matter of domestic jurisdiction. On the question of the determination of what matters were
essentially within domestic jurisdiction, Australia denied the right
of the Organization itself to determine the question, but felt that
where a delay were permissible, an advisory opinion should be
sought from the International Court.[29]

Dr. Evatt also desired to narrow the scope of the proviso that
the domestic jurisdiction principle should not prejudice the application of what was to become Chapter VII of the Charter. He claimed
that as it stood, it would enable the Security Council, in cases where
a state was threatened or attacked by reason of some matter within
its domestic jurisdiction, to intervene by making recommendations
to that state. He contended that the proviso in the paragraph proposed by the sponsoring powers, by permitting the Council to make
recommendations to the attacked or threatened state on certain
questions within domestic jurisdiction, constituted "almost an invitation to use or threaten force, in any dispute arising out of a
matter of domestic jurisdiction, in the hope of inducing the Security

---

[27] *UNCIO Documents*, Vol. VI, p. 437.
[28] *Ibid.*, pp. 511-12.
[29] *Ibid.*, p. 511.

Council to extort concessions from the state that is threatened."[30] Therefore, while emphasizing the continuing responsibility of the Security Council to resist aggression and maintain or restore peace, the Australian amendment sought to prevent the Council from making recommendations to the attacked state on matters within its domestic jurisdiction. The Australian proposal accordingly was to limit the scope of the proviso to "the application of *enforcement measures*" (i.e., those measures which the Council may take under Articles 41 and 42 of the Charter).[31] This amendment was accepted by 31 votes to 3 with 5 abstentions. The Big Three supported the amendment. China opposed it and argued that *preventive* measures might be necessary to maintain peace and security. France abstained, explaining that intervention would be justified if a clear violation of essential liberties constituted a threat to the peace. To the argument that this wide authority was necessary in order to enable the Council to deal with grave infringements of basic rights, Dr. Evatt argued that the correct method to achieve this result was either to make a declaration that the protection of minorities, for example, was "a matter of legitimate 'international,' and not merely of 'domestic' concern," or to make a formal international convention providing for the proper treatment of minorities.[32] Evidently, he did not consider that the statement in the Charter that the United Nations shall promote "universal respect for, and observance of, human rights and fundamental freedoms" was sufficient to make the subject "a matter of legitimate international concern."

As the Australian report on the Conference pointed out, "The extent to which the new Organization will be precluded from dealing with matters of domestic jurisdiction turned out to be, from Australia's point of view, one of the major issues of the San Francisco Conference."[33] While there is no reason to doubt that the restriction

---

[30] *Ibid.*, p. 438.

[31] *Ibid.*, p. 440.

[32] *Ibid.*, p. 439.

[33] *Australian Report on UNCIO, op. cit.*, p. 28.

of intervention was considered desirable on general grounds, it is perhaps significant that in the Australian speeches at the Conference and in the report on the Conference, immigration is taken as an example of a subject on which the Organization would have been able to intervene if the charter had not been amended.

INTERNATIONAL COURT OF JUSTICE

Australia proposed that the Charter should require all members to accept the obligations contained in the "optional clause" of the Statute of the former Permanent Court of International Justice. This meant acceptance of the compulsory jurisdiction of the Court in all legal disputes between members concerning the interpretation of a treaty, any question of international law, the existence of any fact which, if established, would constitute a breach of international obligation, and the nature or extent of the reparation to be made for the breach of an international obligation. Since compulsory jurisdiction was unacceptable to some states (e.g., the United States, USSR), the majority (including Australia) did not press the proposal for fear that these nations would have refused to join the Organization. Australia, by accepting the "optional clause," has acknowledged the jurisdiction of the International Court in disputes with those countries similarly committed.

FULL EMPLOYMENT AND THE ROLE
OF THE ECONOMIC AND SOCIAL COUNCIL

One of the most strenuously pursued objectives of Australia was the conversion of the social and economic chapters of the Dumbarton Oaks draft from a "frigid" into a "full-blooded" document. This involved:

> the inclusion of a statement of purposes far more precise and covering a wider field . . . particularly in the really important field of full employment; the inclusion of a pledge to carry out these purposes; the inclusion of specific functions of the

Economic and Social Council sufficient to enable it to carry out the purposes as stated, and to assist Governments in carrying out their pledge. . . .[34]

The theoretical basis of Australian policy came in part out of an intellectual kinship with those British currents of thought which culminated in Beveridge's *Full Employment in a Free Society*. The empirical basis was to be found in policies evolved by Mr. E. G. Theodore, Labour Premier in New South Wales, to deal with the depression of 1931-32, policies which foreshadowed the Keynesian analysis. The depression had left behind an indelible impression on the minds of all Labour politicians; it reinforced their suspicion of overseas financial and trading interests. With its socialist heritage and vague acceptance of the Hobsonian analysis of economic imperialism went a firm belief in the primacy of economic causes of war. Field Marshal Smuts was stealing Dr. Evatt's thunder when he claimed that "the approach of the Covenant [of the League of Nations] was almost entirely political, and the effort there made was to deal by political methods with the prevention of war . . . We have seen that social and economic unrest is one of the most prolific causes of war."[35]

The Labour government, conscious also of Australia's vulnerable position through dependence on export markets, advanced a theory of full employment to prevent depression. Mr. J. A. Beasley put the argument at the Philadelphia meeting of the International Labour Organisation in 1944.

It is our attitude, and it must be the attitude of every country greatly dependent upon overseas trade, that we cannot possibly restrict our freedom of action with regard to monetary and commercial policy without some assurance that high levels of employment and consumption will be maintained particularly in the main consuming areas. . . . If the United States Government is unwilling to undertake some employment

---

[34] *Ibid.*, p. 21.
[35] *UNCIO Documents*, Vol. VIII, p. 52. See also H. V. Evatt, *Australia in World Affairs* (Sydney: Angus and Robertson, 1946), p. 60.

obligations, we must hesitate before entering into discussions on other aspects of international economic collaboration, and we could not feel ourselves obliged to undertake any commitments which limited our freedom of action to protect our economy against depressed conditions overseas.[36]

The argument was put in greater detail by one of the government's technical advisers:

The growth of unemployment in any major industrial country or group of countries depresses the export incomes and economic activity of other countries, and makes it extremely difficult to maintain high employment. Any individual country that persists in a high employment policy in the face of declining employment elsewhere soon finds that its balance of payments is adversely affected. It is then faced with the choice of either abandoning its own domestic policy of high employment or of turning away from international collaboration toward import restrictions, export subsidies, or exchange depreciation. In other words, if other countries fail to maintain high employment any country may find international economic collaboration incompatible with the maintenance of its own employment.[37]

The policy of full employment was first formulated when it appeared that freedom to maintain tariffs might be restricted in the post-war period. In 1942 Great Britain began discussions with the United States on how it could, after the war, discharge its obligations under Article 7 of the Master Lend-Lease agreement between the two countries. This provided that after the war Great Britain was to provide benefits for the United States in a manner advantageous to world economic relations. To this end there was to be an agreed international action directed towards policies of economic expansion, the elimination of all forms of discriminatory treatment in international commerce, and the reduction of tariffs and other trade

[36] See *Reports of the Australian Delegates to the 26th ILO Conference, Philadelphia, 20 April-13 May 1944*, in Commonwealth of Australia, Parliamentary Papers for the 1943-44 and 1944-45 Sessions, Vol. II, p. 1536.

[37] *Draft Proposal for an International Agreement Concerning Employment Policies* (Canberra: Dept. of External Affairs, 15 Jan. 1945), pp. 1-2.

barriers. The Australian Labour party had a vivid recollection of the depression and the sharp fall in international demand for Australia's staple products that had touched it off. It regarded the countermeasures of the depression government, which included a reduction of works expenditure, as a profound and avoidable mistake. Its leaders were strongly influenced by the economic theories of Keynes and Beveridge. During the war, its advisers were impressed by the possibility of a depression commencing in the United States after demobilization. In such a situation, to prevent unemployment in Australia, it would be necessary either to devalue currency or restrict imports. The international agreements likely to be fostered by the United States would hinder Australia's freedom to adopt these measures, and would still fail to attack the problem where it began, in demand. Unemployment in the United States would inevitably result in a vital drop in world demand.

Australia vigorously asserted the need for a full employment pledge at the United Nations Food and Agriculture Conference at Hot Springs, Virginia, in May 1943. Mr. Bruce, the Australian representative at the League of Nations, had in one sense pioneered the way by securing the acceptance of nutrition as a matter of international concern.

At Bretton Woods in the same year the International Monetary Fund was projected. By the terms of its constitution, a member would be restrained from devaluing its currency by more than 10 per cent without the consent of the Fund. Given a fall in demand for exports, devaluation might be a necessary means to maintain employment in Australia. It was likely that the United States would sponsor an international trade organization, which would limit the right of members to impose import restrictions. The full employment policy also had the practical value of simplicity which made possible the slogan "the employment criteria the test for all economic policy." Internal divisions within the Australian cabinet made the securing of the full employment pledge a valuable weapon for the cabinet group desiring Australian participation in the International

f

Monetary Fund. So deep were these divisions that the decision to participate in the International Monetary Fund was delayed until 1947.

The battle over full employment began at the International Labour Conference held in Philadelphia in 1944. Australia unsuccessfully proposed a draft international employment agreement binding each signatory "to take all measures in its power" to maintain a high level of employment, to collaborate in the exchange of statistical information, and to participate in an international conference whenever a serious decline in employment was developing anywhere. Australia refused to accept as adequate the United States proposal which was described as "merely a declaration that Governments should maintain high levels of employment." United States reluctance to go further arose partly out of increasing conservative, anti-New Deal pressures in the Democratic party, partly out of the impending presidential election. Australian delegates at Philadelphia pressed their views with vigour, tenacity, and with an eye for publicity because the policy was believed to be demonstrably sound and vital to Australian and world prosperity. Publicity in the United States would perhaps win support for the Murray-Wagner-Thomas Bill which sought to commit the United States government to a policy of full employment.

The contest was joined again at San Francisco. In committee, the Australian representatives secured the substitution of "full employment" for "high and stable levels of employment," the phraseology advocated by the United States. American officials pointed out that the United States Senate would not accept a Charter including such a provision and secured the insertion in the minutes of a statement to the effect that all members were "in full agreement that nothing contained in Chapter IX of the Charter could be construed as giving authority to the Organization to intervene in the domestic affairs of member states."[38] The battle narrowed to

---

[38] See *UNCIO Documents*, Vol. VII, pp. 81-82.

the question of implementation, and the gap between the two countries was finally bridged through the good offices of the Soviet delegate. The contentious draft finally became Article 56: "All Members pledge themselves to take joint and separate action in cooperation with the Organization for the achievement of the purposes set forth in Article 55" (i.e., ". . . the United Nations shall promote . . . full employment . . ."). Both sides claimed to have won their point. Canada, supported by the Latin American states, sought to act as an honest broker between the United States and Australia, leaning, however, to the former's view; Australia received support from the United Kingdom, Belgium, and New Zealand as well as from several of the middle and smaller powers. In Chapter X of the Charter, the Economic and Social Council was constituted with powers to carry out the functions for which at Philadelphia Australia had proposed an international organization. (These functions were the exchange of information and statistics and the summoning of a conference whenever unemployment threatened.)

The full employment victory by Australia was in fact a somewhat hollow one. There appears to be no significant difference between a pledge on a matter admitted to be essentially within domestic jurisdiction and so completely unenforceable, and a mere declaration that "governments shall maintain high levels of employment."

TRUSTEESHIP AND THE COLONIAL QUESTION

For several years before the San Francisco Conference assembled, discussions had been taking place between Great Britain and the Dominions on problems of colonial trusteeship. Sharp differences of opinion were also developing between Britain and the United States. The sudden collapse of British rule in Burma and Malaya in the early stages of the Pacific War had created a feeling of shocked surprise in the United States. It confirmed the traditional American suspicion of British imperialism and strengthened the conviction that there were some inherent weaknesses in British colonial policy.

A demand arose for the immediate liberation of "colonies," particularly as colonial empires appeared to contradict the principles of the Atlantic Charter. As early as 1942, Cordell Hull had stated: "We have always believed—and we believe today—that all peoples, without distinction of race, color, or religion, who are prepared and willing to accept the responsibilities of liberty are entitled to its enjoyment."[39] A growing body of United States opinion was in favour of extending the mandates system to all colonial dependencies.

In March 1943, Mr. Hull submitted to Mr. Anthony Eden proposals for a general declaration on dependent territories. These sought to apply to all colonies a system of full reporting on administration to an international authority and to fix target dates for the granting of full independence by the metropolitan powers. Specific pledges were to be given to further native welfare and self-government and to develop and market the natural resources in the interests of the inhabitants and of the world as a whole. The draft was circulated by Great Britain to the Dominions.

The Hull draft revealed the deep differences of view between Britain and the United States over the nature of trusteeship. To the United States, trustees must be held accountable to a third party; to Britain, a colonial trustee was answerable only to its own conscience, perhaps to a vague world conscience. The question of accountability appeared to the former to be the acid test of Britain's attitude to its colonies. In the initial discussions of the colonial problem, many Americans favoured international control of colonial territories, possibly through a condominium. (Later, when it became evident that the United States Navy would press on strategic grounds for occupation of former Japanese territories, it was felt that "condominium" could only mean "pandemonium.") To many Americans, moreover, the principle of the open door appeared a necessary corollary of the mandates system: only in this way would it be

---

[39] Quoted in U.S. Dept. of State, *Postwar Foreign Policy Preparation*, Publication 3580, General Foreign Policy Series 15 (Washington: U.S. Govt. Printing Office, 1950), p. 109.

possible to prevent a colonial power from securing unfair advantages.[40]

British views were at first sharply divided. Early war-time disillusionment with colonies produced considerable support for the extension of international supervision of all colonies, with regular inspection and the encouragement of petitions from subject peoples. But opinion hardened in the Labour and Liberal parties and in the Fabian Society against international control. The war had brought a swift reassessment of British colonial policies and a willingness to define in general terms the fundamental freedoms of colonies. There was a moving away from the Churchillian concept ("What we have we hold") to an extension of trusteeship into partnership. There was a growing acceptance of the view that "we have to transform the Empire into a society where the dependencies . . . will feel themselves to be willing partners, not slaves or servants."[41] Official British policy was moving in the direction of regional collaboration, partly as a result of Lord Hailey's *African Survey* and of the report of the West India Royal Commission of 1939, and partly as a result of war-time experience of functional organizations of a regional kind. The Caribbean and South Pacific Commissions were to be the first fruits of this approach. The latter included not only states with colonial territories in the area but also other states which had a "major strategic or economic interest in it." There was, too, in Britain a growing dissatisfaction with the mandatory system on a variety of grounds: the Permanent Mandates Commission of the League of Nations had had no power to initiate or press colonial powers to introduce welfare policies, and the doctrine of the open door did not necessarily operate for the benefit of colonial peoples. Mr. Oliver Stanley, Colonial Secretary, "flew a kite" in a New York speech in January 1945, suggesting Britain's

---

[40] "The International Interest in Colonies," *The Round Table*, Vol. 35 (1944), pp. 25, 27-28.

[41] See Sir W. K. Hancock in "Colonial Future," *The New Statesman and Nation*, Vol. XXIII (1942), p. 241.

determination to scrap the mandates system. United States reaction was swift and to the point, condemning this attempt to abandon international supervision and scrap the doctrine of accountability. Stanley's proposals were then jettisoned.

The Australian Labour government, influenced by Dr. Evatt, held strong views on the colonial problem. It felt that the principles of trusteeship should be extended to all colonies whether or not they were held as mandates; that non-mandated territories could be placed under trusteeship by the metropolitan powers; and that an expert United Nations commission should be established to exercise general supervision over administration. These proposals stemmed from a conviction that general principles, embodied in a colonial charter, should be applied to all territories regardless of whether, like mandated territories, they contained "peoples not yet able to stand by themselves under the strenuous conditions of the modern world," or whether the peoples of the colonies were more advanced.[42] The ANZAC Agreement of January 1944 declared that ". . . the doctrine of trusteeship (already applicable in the case of the mandated territories . . .) is applicable in broad principles to all colonial territories in the Pacific and elsewhere." The idealism behind Article 22 of the League of Nations Covenant apparently influenced Australian Labour opinion. With it went a strong socialist distrust of European imperialism combined with an awareness of the nationalist aspirations of colonial peoples. Australia was close geographically to many of the emerging nations of Southeast Asia.

The Yalta Conference (February 1945) made little progress in bridging the gap between the American and British proposals. The United Kingdom would not fully accept the Hull draft and the United States had not yet clarified its views about the future of the Pacific Islands. It was agreed at Yalta to include the subject on the agenda at San Francisco and to define the limits of discussion. The future of the mandated territories was left in the air, the fate of the

---

[42] Evatt, *Australia in World Affairs, op. cit.*, pp. 31-32.

Italian colonies and Japanese mandates was unresolved, and no provision was made in the Dumbarton Oaks draft for colonial administration or the future of trust territories. With Australia and New Zealand adopting the substance of the Hull proposals, no agreement was reached at the British Commonwealth Conference in London (April 1945). Further discussions between Britain and the United States on the eve of San Francisco produced a compromise: the United States abandoned its proposals for reporting on colonies, while Britain agreed to accept a declaration of enlightened principles which the metropolitan powers were to undertake to apply in *all* their dependent territories. The changed British attitude may well have been the result of Australian pressure at the London talks and subsequently at San Francisco after private discussions with the American delegation.

The initiative at San Francisco in proposing the addition of new chapters to the Dumbarton Oaks came from Australia and Great Britain. France and China subsequently submitted drafts and the United States representative, Commander Stassen, prepared a working paper as a basis for discussion after a careful analysis of the different schemes had been made by conference officials.[43] Australian dissatisfaction with the British draft led to the submission of more radical proposals to be embodied in a new chapter on dependent peoples.

> (1) All members of the United Nations responsible for the administration of dependent territories recognize in relation to them the principle of trusteeship—viz., that the main purpose of administration is the welfare of the dependent peoples, and their economic, social and political development.

> (2) A member of the United Nations administering any dependent territory to which this paragraph applies undertakes to make reports upon its administration of that territory to an expert commission with advisory functions, to be established by or under the authority of the General Assembly. The Com-

---

[43] *UNCIO Documents*, Vol. X, pp. 641 ff.

mission shall keep the United Nations informed, through the Economic and Social Council, as to the welfare and development of the peoples of the territories to which this paragraph applies.

(3) The territories to which paragraph (2) applies shall be declared either by the voluntary action of the member administering the territory or by the General Assembly, after consideration of the recommendations of a conference or conferences, specially convened by the United Nations, of members responsible for the administration of dependent territories.

(4) The General Assembly may authorize the acceptance of mandates on behalf of the United Nations for the administration of particular territories, in each case by a specified member.

(5) The terms of the mandate shall in each case be defined by agreement between the General Assembly and the mandatory State, and shall include the principle of trusteeship as defined in paragraph (1) and the obligation to report provided for in paragraph (2).

(6) Paragraph (2) shall not apply to such bases or areas in dependent territories as the General Assembly on the recommendation of the Security Council declares to be of special importance for the maintenance of international peace and security.

(7) The General Assembly on the recommendation of the Security Council may remove from existing mandates such military restrictions as are in its opinion prejudicial to the security of the mandated territory or of the United Nations generally.[44]

The obligation in paragraph (1) was to be assumed by all metropolitan powers and not merely by those administering trust territories. The Australian government had firmly stated its view that the advancement of all colonial peoples was a matter of international concern on grounds of justice and world security. Dr. Evatt pointed

---

[44] *Ibid.*, Vol. III, pp. 548-49.

out that the inhabitants of the dependent territories of the victors should in justice receive no less a guarantee than that accorded the inhabitants of the territories detached from the enemy.

> But the conditions of security in this area will not exist unless the peoples are prepared to co-operate with stronger states. To secure this co-operation, it must be made clear that the purpose of administration is their welfare and advancement, and their security as well as ours. A solemn declaration in this Charter would give meaning to the co-operation of East and West in this region. The principle of trusteeship would thus contribute to security.[45]

Great Britain also proposed to write such an obligation into the Charter.

Paragraphs (4) and (5) of the Australian proposal reiterated the safeguards provided for the mandatory powers under the League mandates system. The administration must be vested solely in the hands of the mandatory power with no encroachments by the Organization. No trusteeship agreement may be *imposed* on the administering authority; it could only be bound by what it chose to consent to. It was doubtless these principles that Mr. F. Forde (Australian Deputy Prime Minister) had in mind when he denied that the system could correctly be described as one of "international direction" or "international supervision": it entailed "no interference with sovereignty."[46]

The gap between the Australian and British views had narrowed perceptibly up to this point. The Australian proposals contained no revolutionary elements although they went beyond the League system in imposing obligations on all metropolitan powers. Paragraph (3) of the Australian draft empowered the General Assembly to place a territory under trusteeship, should a metropolitan power refuse to do so (presumably to be then administered by any member willing to accept a trusteeship agreement approved by the Assembly).

---

[45] *Australian Report on UNCIO, op. cit.,* p. 75.
[46] See *UNCIO Documents,* Vol. I, p. 178.

The Assembly could so act only after considering the recommendations of a specially convened conference of all the colonial powers.
The drafting of the section made it clear that these recommendations
would not bind the Assembly. Australia appears to have considered
that flagrant colonial maladministration would be checked by the
threat of transfer by the Assembly of such colonial territories to the
trusteeship system. It is impossible to determine whether Australia
was really prepared to concede such power to the Assembly, or
whether, realizing that it would not be adopted, Australia was using
this as a tactical manoeuvre to win the support of the anti-colonial
powers on other issues.

Great Britain adhered to a distinction between the principle of
trusteeship and the "creation of a special system of international
machinery to apply to certain specified territories." In the British
view, "the fact that a particular territory is not placed under such
special machinery does not mean that the parent state is not being
guided, or that it is absolved from being guided, by the general
policy of trusteeship in its administration of territories outside the
system."[47] Britain opposed the too rigid definition of policy on the
ground that changing circumstances would render it outmoded and
necessitate the difficult task of Charter revision. It did accept in
general terms the United States and Australian concept of accountability, i.e., that "this tutelage should be exercised . . . on behalf
of the United Nations." A clearer appreciation of the wide diversity
of status of native peoples led to British insistence that "the character
of the trust" must differ "according to the stage of development
of the people, the geographical situation of the territory, its economic
condition, and other similar circumstances."[48]

Britain's initial proposals were more comprehensive in analysis
of principle than the much briefer Australian draft, which ignored
the important distinction Britain made in defining the objectives of
a trusteeship system as self-government rather than independence.

---

[47] *Ibid.*, Vol. III, p. 611.
[48] *Ibid.*, Vol. X, pp. 647-49.

The final declaration of principles in Chapter XI of the Charter reduced to concrete form the general objective of British colonial policy with self-government as the goal. Australia urged that the obligations of colonial powers proposed by Great Britain be made explicit and detailed. The specific undertakings in Article (73) paragraphs (a) and (d) were the result of Australian persistence. When it had become clear that none of the colonial powers was prepared to place colonies under trusteeship, Australia unsuccessfully proposed that all metropolitan powers should report annually to the United Nations on the economic, social, and political development of their territories.[49] Agreement was finally secured for the regular transmission under Article 73 (e) of statistical and other technical information.

Australian determination to exercise full control over its own trust territory of New Guinea was evident in the successful resistance to efforts to establish without qualification the principle of the "open door" in trust territories. The Charter stipulates that this principle is to be subordinated to the attainment of the political, economic, and social well being of the inhabitants. This in fact gives the administering authority complete power to ignore the principle. One of the distinguishing features of the old class C mandate under which Australia held New Guinea was that the "open door" principle did not apply. Finally, in concert with Great Britain, Australia successfully established the right to use the resources and manpower of trust territories for defence (Article 84 of the Charter).

In summary, it should be said that under the chairmanship of Mr. P. Fraser of New Zealand, the committee on trusteeship made one of the really notable contributions to the Conference. Its final draft was in large measure based upon the proposals of the experienced colonial powers. Much of the content as well as a great deal of the drafting of Chapters XI-XIII of the Charter was the work of Australia, New Zealand, and Great Britain. Many compromises

---

[49] *Ibid.*, p. 695.

were effected, notably, the adoption of a "hands off" policy towards non-mandated territories. Australia remained adamant and sponsored until a late stage the initial Hull proposal to extend the trusteeship system to include colonies without the consent of the metropolitan powers. Yet in the last analysis it is extremely doubtful whether Australia would ever have consented to place its own colony of Papua under the trusteeship system; to have done so would have been political suicide for an Australian government.

CONCLUSION

The issues discussed in this chapter by no means cover the whole range of Australian interests and proposed amendments to the Dumbarton Oaks draft. Australia filed thirty-eight distinct amendments of substance; of these, twenty-six were "adopted without material change, adopted in principle or made unnecessary by other alterations."[50] It would be absurd to claim for Australia an exclusive or even a primary share in the adoption of specific proposals: some of them had been accepted before the Conference by the great powers, and others had been advanced in slightly different form by the delegations of the smaller powers. Yet the Australian initiative had been an important one both in the drafting process and in the organizing of support for particular amendments: Dr. Evatt's personal influence was very considerable. Australia's major contributions, primarily in the field of full employment, trusteeship, the respective roles of the Security Council and the General Assembly, are not explicable merely in terms of small power versus great power rights. Its attitude on these issues reflected the impact of particular experiences rather than of continuously felt needs: the recollection of the depression of the 1930's, the prediction of a postwar slump, the belief that the military collapse of colonial empires in Asia was the consequence of misrule, the shifting balance of power within the "grand alliance." Yet these experiences were inter-

---

[50] *Australian Report on UNCIO, op. cit.,* p. 15.

preted in the context of a social democratic tradition and a quickening national consciousness and national pride.

The most significant aspect of Australia's action at San Francisco was its pursuit of an independent policy as a small power. This was in contrast to Australian policy previously and subsequently. During the period after 1939, the Dominions became increasingly conscious of their new stature and the older concept of a centralized Commonwealth largely disappeared. The balance of economic power was shifting within the British Commonwealth, the changing role of Great Britain was making regional rather than metropolitan defence arrangements a necessary supplement, and Dominion nationalism was becoming more aggressive and yet more mature. The old Asquithian concept of the conduct of foreign policy became outmoded. No uniform Commonwealth policy could be formulated for a major conference: all that could be done was to narrow the areas of disagreement and perhaps do some hard "horse trading" behind the scenes. Australia consistently followed an independent approach. As Dr. Evatt put it:

> We did not belong to any bloc of nations. For instance, the debate over the powers of the Assembly was mainly with the sponsoring powers led by Russia, with nearly all the other Powers supporting our view. On the other hand, on the full employment question, the Soviet supported us. On regionalism it was necessary to join issue with certain Latin-American Republics who were attempting to secure for their regional group an almost complete independence from the Security Council.[51]

On those sections of the Charter where there was disagreement between the small and the great powers, Australian views were similar to those of the unsuccessful majority, although often put in a less extreme form. Australia consistently championed the role of the middle and smaller powers, often deliberately seeking leadership. Only on one major issue did Australia fail to attain its objective:

---

[51] Evatt, *Australia in World Affairs, op. cit.,* p. 54.

the limitation of the great power veto ultimately provided for in Article 27(3).

The policies supported and proposed by Australia at San Francisco involved no surrender of sovereignty or freedom of action by the Australian government. The New Guinea mandate could be amended only with its consent. The full employment pledge represented its freely adopted policy and excluded United Nations intervention. Australia accepted certain principles to be applied in the administration of Papua, but these too, required no change in current Australian policy and therefore were accepted willingly. On vital questions such as immigration, tariffs, and territorial integrity, Australia maintained every safeguard. By the establishment of the right to defend trust territories and the right of regional defence, Australia's freedom of action in defence was, if anything, extended.

Dr. Evatt's achievement at San Francisco, then, was a considerable one, yet one with odd contradictions. With a clearer view than most of the need for an organic international structure, he nevertheless imposed few new limitations on national sovereignty and carefully safeguarded the principle of domestic jurisdiction. With his experience of judicial conservatism in the Australian High Court, he was reluctant to extend too far the jurisdiction of the International Court. As the champion of the smaller powers, he nevertheless contrived to protect, perhaps unwittingly, the interests of some of the great powers through his emphasis upon the authority of the General Assembly under Article 10 of the Charter. His greatest successes were in drafting procedures rather than in communicating to the smaller powers an understanding of the essential purposes behind proposed amendments. His short-term achievements were substantial. The subsequent shift in the balance of power between the Security Council and the General Assembly has largely vindicated his stand at San Francisco.[52]

---

[52] See G. Sawer, "The United Nations," in Gordon Greenwood and Norman Harper, eds., *Australia in World Affairs 1950-55* (Melbourne: F. W. Cheshire, 1957), pp. 98-102.

chapter four

The Australian Reaction
to the San Francisco Conference

THE PARLIAMENTARY DEBATE,
AUGUST-SEPTEMBER 1945

The parliamentary debate on the ratification of the Charter (Charter of the United Nations Bill) in September 1945[1] took place in the initial flush of enthusiasm following the San Francisco Conference. The Australian delegation believed that it had made a substantial contribution to the success of the Conference. "Australia's greatest contribution was in helping to establish during the period of the Conference . . . a democratic and progressive spirit among very many nations. This spirit was present from the outset, but it was most gratifying to see it translated into practical action after Australia had given a lead on almost every important question."

---

[1] All quotations in this chapter, unless otherwise indicated, are from this debate, which appears in Commonwealth of Australia, *Parliamentary Debates*, Vol. 184, pp. 5016-5451, *passim;* and Vol. 185, pp. 5542-61.

Dr. Evatt felt that the two decisive contributions were the extension of the powers of the Assembly to "prevent the Organization from becoming, in Mr. Churchill's phrase, 'a shield for the strong and a mockery for the weak'" and in "breathing life into the original unsatisfactory chapter of the Dumbarton Oaks draft dealing with economic matters."[2]

These achievements Dr. Evatt stressed in introducing the Bill on 30 August 1945.[3] He was concerned less with a defence of the principles of collective security, which he took for granted, than with an explanation of the Charter as a whole and the amendments proposed to it by Australia. The real centre of power in the United Nations should be the democratic General Assembly: it had been given the fullest powers of discussion and recommendation on practically every subject within the very broad scope of the Charter. One of the striking features of the Conference had been the knowledge and independent attitude of the small nations; these would now be able in the Assembly to "help to balance and compensate the greater power vested in the permanent members of the Security Council." The Assembly would be the creative agency of the United Nations. He deplored the retention of the veto on questions involving the peaceful settlement of disputes and amendments to the Charter. The veto on enforcement he accepted as inevitable, and because of it no member could rely completely on the United Nations, but might have to "fall back on regional arrangements, and ultimately upon its own defences and those of its Allies."

A really significant contribution by Australia lay in the amendments embodied in Article 55 of the Charter. These amendments, carried "against the strongest preliminary opposition," achieved the Labour government's long-standing objective of making an inter-

---

[2] Statement by Dr. H. V. Evatt on the United Nations Conference on International Organization. See *Current Notes on International Affairs* (Dept. of External Affairs, Canberra), Vol. 16 (1945), pp. 177-78.

[3] For Dr. Evatt's detailed defence of his policy, see his speech of 30 Aug. 1945, pp. 5016-39.

national pledge to pursue full employment a fundamental basis of international economic co-operation. If members carried out their obligations, the United Nations would be able to "stamp out any resurgence of Fascist aggression and also set in motion practical steps for achieving freedom from want as well as freedom from fear." This was a broader interpretation of both the meaning and the consequences of full employment than that adopted by the other Australian delegate, Mr. F. M. Forde, who felt that full employment meant "full employment in all the countries according to their own standards . . . of wages and conditions."[4]

Another important Australian principle was also written into the Charter: members responsible for non-self-governing territories were now pledged to accept specific obligations. At the same time Australian interests in New Guinea were carefully safeguarded; New Guinea could not be placed under any trusteeship agreement not approved by the Australian Parliament. The trusteeship system differed from the mandates system in the sanction it gave to the administering authority to defend trust territories. This meant that Australia could include New Guinea in its defence arrangements. In the light of historical experience, this was of vital importance to the defence of the Commonwealth.

The other major point which emerged in the Labour defence of the Charter was that Australian sovereignty would not be seriously curtailed. The vigilance and persistence of the small nations had closed "the dangerous gap" in the Charter on domestic jurisdiction, thus effectively safeguarding the "White Australia" policy. Although members were required to supply military forces to the Security Council, they would have a voice in determining the manner of their use. In any case, the United Nations itself lacked the power to provide adequate protection for members; Australia and the other members of the Commonwealth would still be compelled to maintain powerful defence forces.

---

[4] Mr. Forde was then Deputy Prime Minister. For his speech of 5 Sept. 1945, see pp. 5119-26.

The Opposition attack upon government policy was centred not so much on principles as on the Evatt diplomacy at San Francisco.[5] The hard fact was that there had been frequent and extreme disagreements with the United Kingdom. "Whilst a new world charter may have a value which is as yet untried, our relationship with the British Empire has a value which has been proved in circumstances of very great trial over many generations" (Mr. R. G. Menzies). The Labour attempt to rally the small powers behind Australia in an effort to follow an "independent" policy had seriously impaired Commonwealth relations. Dr. Evatt had reluctantly accepted great power predominance (and the veto as the price of their participation) as a realistic assessment of the situation; he had pressed for an extension of the powers and prestige of the Assembly believing in its efficiency as a forum of world opinion to restrain the evildoer.

The Opposition, with its readier acceptance of the validity of power politics, adopted a very different approach. The "essential difference" between the League of Nations and the United Nations lay, Mr. Menzies believed, in the fact that the "essence" of the latter was that its "nucleus" consisted of the great powers.

> We have here in this Charter a provision for a species of alliance between the United States, the United Kingdom, Russia, China and France, to which there is attached for many useful purposes of discussion and co-operation a great number of smaller powers. The function of these smaller powers will be to influence, so far as they can, the Great Powers; and when the Great Powers have unanimously decided upon a certain course, to play their part in its enforcement.

Accordingly, the role of the Assembly should be a secondary one,

---

[5] The attack was led by the leader of the Liberal party opposition, Mr. R. G. Menzies. See his speech of 5 Sept. 1945, pp. 5111-19. For other statements by Liberal members referred to in this chapter, see Mr. H. E. Holt (subsequently Minister for Immigration), pp. 5174-80; Senator J. W. Leckie (who, although former Deputy Leader of the Opposition, no longer exerted a major influence on policy), pp. 5344-51; Senator G. McLeay (Opposition Senate Leader), pp. 5348-49; Mr. R. S. Ryan, pp. 5169-74; Senator B. Sampson, pp. 5550-54; and Mr. P. C. Spender, pp. 5132-38.

and the "very significant widening" of its powers, to which Labour attached such importance, was of no moment.

The important thing was to ensure that Australian influence be effective in the Security Council; this was possible because of Australia's special relationship with Great Britain as the real head of the Commonwealth. This meant consistent support for British policies and thus a strengthening of British prestige. "Our strength arises from the fact that we can mould the policy of one of the three Great Powers of the world . . ." (Mr. H. E. Holt). (This view of Australia's role in world affairs was of course not inconsistent with that expressed by Mr. Curtin in the debate in July 1944[6] and was in fact the view acted upon consistently by Australian governments in the past.)

Given the Opposition view of the nature both of the United Nations and of the British Commonwealth, the veto appeared less distasteful and less inconsistent with the fundamental principles of the United Nations than it did to the government. Mr. A. W. Fadden, the Country party leader, remarked that the Charter lost "very little in value as a working instrument because . . . of [the] veto."[7] To Mr. Menzies, Dr. Evatt's attack upon the veto, while in "pure theory, completely correct," was unrealistic, since, veto or no veto, "if those five Great Powers understand each other and concur in the action that they are going to take, world peace will be kept; but if any one of them finds its interest running counter to that of the other four and adheres to that so strongly that it is going to fight about it, then world war becomes inevitable." On such premises, it could be argued that in Australia's relations with the United Nations it was unnecessary to consider nations other than the great powers since those without power could be discounted. This was made explicit by some of the Opposition speakers in the debate (for

---

[6] See above, pp. 37-38.

[7] See his speech of 5 Sept. 1945, p. 5127. For other statements by members of the Country party, see Mr. H. L. Anthony, pp. 5164-67; Mr. J. McEwen (who attended the San Francisco Conference as a consultant to the Australian delegation), pp. 5156-62; and Sir Earle Page (5 Sept. 1945), pp. 5139-44.

example, Senator J. W. Leckie and Mr. H. L. Anthony). From this, it was but a short step to the view that the United Nations, with its "unwieldy organization" was inappropriate to its task, since peace depended primarily upon the friendly co-operation of the Big Three (Senator B. Sampson). Such pessimism was then exceptional; subsequently, much stronger support for this view developed.

The Opposition was more sceptical than the government of the value of the contracts and pledges of the Charter, both those relating to security and those relating to welfare. These were, Mr. Menzies claimed, by their nature unenforceable except by war, and there were in fact powerful political forces which could lead nations to break them. Nations not parties to a particular dispute would generally not interfere except in defence of a major interest. What was really required was the development of an international outlook rather than "carefully considered and meticulously drafted written agreements. If the spirit of peace prevails among the nations those writings will not matter very much; but if the spirit of peace be absent, then I believe that no writing will prevent war. Consequently, we do well to put the weight on the spirit that is to be created among the nations, rather than persuade ourselves that the letter of some agreement will prevent further wars." In the same way pledges relating to economic and social policies were of doubtful value because international commitments would be ineffective if internal political pressures were inadequate to promote such objectives. Mr. Menzies was thus in complete disagreement with Mr. Forde's view that the full employment pledge would mean a better prospect of "securing full employment for the mass of the people." He was less pessimistic, however, about the possibility of a progressive development and acceptance of international law even though it lacked a sanction. The International Court could well perform the function of building up a body of common law.

Although Dr. Evatt and Mr. Forde stressed the need for national and regional defence in the event of a Security Council deadlock, they expressed Labour's greater confidence in continued great power agreement.[8] This was influenced by their belief that the fundamental cause of war was a pursuit of national economic advantage; the economic and social clauses of the Charter would eliminate differential conditions and so prevent war. These views were categorically rejected by several Opposition speakers. Yet there was some Opposition enthusiasm especially in the Country party for the Charter's social and economic provisions. On the whole, the Opposition welcomed the setting up of machinery for international negotiation on economic matters; their doubts arose out of their belief that members would not use it to achieve the desired results. Mr. Percy Spender expressed some concern that Labour enthusiasm for full employment arose primarily out of an attempt to use the "external affairs" power in the Australian Constitution to legislate on industrial matters and so to circumvent the refusal of electors at a recent referendum to grant these powers to the federal government. To many Liberal members, the urgent problem was that of creating more effective machinery for imperial economic co-operation: Australia's continued prosperity appeared to depend on the rehabilitation of British industry and the expansion of British markets. As Mr. Menzies observed, this would not, of course, be a primary function of the Economic and Social Council.

Much of the Opposition criticism of the functions of the Economic and Social Council and its concern over the maintenance of national prosperity arose out of the national belief that international consideration of problems of world economic stability might ignore the special problems of Australia. Support for a world conference on economic problems was conditioned by an insistence that there must be "no dictation of our economic policy by the representatives of 50 nations, most of whom have no conception of our conditions" (Senator Leckie). Similar doubts qualified support for full employ-

---

[8] See statements by Senators R. H. Nash and W. J. Large, pp. 5352-61 and 5448-53. Opinion on this point was not completely divided on party lines: cf. Senator W. E. Aylett (Labour) and Mr. R. S. Ryan (Liberal), pp. 5445 and 5172. See also Mr. Spender's statement drawing attention to Russia's violation of the Charter in Eastern Europe (p. 5133).

ment, since Australian employment depended primarily on protection which was not necessarily conducive to employment overseas. Senator Leckie queried, "Are we to be subjected to dictation by the Security Council as to the protective duties that we may impose?" Two rank-and-file Labour Senators, D. M. Grant and W. J. Large, were prepared to accept this as a logical consequence of membership in the United Nations, but the Labour cabinet emphatically repudiated it.

Country party leaders were more hopeful about international co-operation to raise living standards by a greater consumption of foodstuffs. Sir Earle Page believed that the failure of the League of Nations was partly the consequence of the delay in feeding starving Europe in 1919. Peace depended, ultimately, upon "raised standards of living throughout the world, the highest universal factor of employment and continually expanding international trade." Mr. J. McEwen emphasized the Economic and Social Council's function to provide for the "discussion of social and economic problems, upon the solution of which so much depends if we are to achieve that world-wide content without which there can never be any real confidence that war can be avoided." The Country party's attitude toward economic co-operation through the United Nations was, however, significantly different from Dr. Evatt's. To Dr. Evatt and his advisers, full employment provided the only solution, and a sufficient solution, to the fundamental economic problem, the prevention of depression. A high level of international trade would be a consequence, not a cause of full employment. The Economic and Social Council was important chiefly as machinery for facilitating full employment. To the Country party trade was the key, international consultation and commodity agreements merely the means. This policy Dr. Evatt had attacked as manifestly inadequate and outmoded.

Since the trusteeship agreement for New Guinea had not yet been drafted, there was no party debate on trusteeship. There was individual criticism by Senator Leckie of Dr. Evatt's strictures on the colonial powers, and of suggestions that the United Nations should dictate to the United States what bases it should control in the Pacific and that Great Britain's colonial policies should be subjected to international control. There was also a concern expressed by Mr. McEwen lest the trusteeship system should place power in the hands of nations with no experience in the administration of dependent territories. Mr. Spender doubted whether the Charter provisions on non-self-governing territories afforded adequate security for Australia. It was not likely that Timor and New Caledonia would be adequately defended by their traditional and legal owners, Portugal and France. In view of the inadequacy of Dr. Evatt's regional defence scheme and in the absence of a world security plan permitting direct Australian participation in the defence of the two territories, he felt that Australia should vigorously assert its claim to a predominant part in their control.

The Bill to approve the Charter was passed without division and with surprisingly little pessimism as to its successful functioning. The debate reiterated and elaborated the attitudes expressed in 1944 before the San Francisco Conference. Labour was not prepared to rely solely upon collective security and stressed the need for imperial, regional, and national defence. While there was general acceptance of the fact of great power predominance, the Opposition frankly accepted the power basis of the organization; the Labour government emphasized a concern for the rights of the small nations and a belief in the value of the discussion of all problems by the General Assembly. Out of this stemmed Labour's dissatisfaction with the veto and the Opposition's frank acceptance of it. Dr. Evatt's idealism came out in his enthusiasm for pledges; the Opposition, seeing no enforcing authority, was frankly sceptical. Alongside the Liberal suspicion of dictation by an international body on matters of economic policy and of Labour's demand for full employment as an international obligation stood the Country party's enthusiasm for international consultation and negotiation. Labour was more confident of the success of the United Nations, but here there was no clear-cut division on party lines. There was agreement that the Charter adequately safeguarded matters within domestic jurisdiction. The Opposition was more inclined than the government to see the United Nations as an unsubstantial substitute for the British Commonwealth in Australian foreign policy.

PUBLIC OPINION

The problem of gauging "public opinion" on any matter of importance is a difficult one. There are perhaps two major sources, public opinion polls and the leading articles in the Australian metropolitan press.[9] These are rather inadequate bases on which to base firm conclusions. The public opinion polls, taking a stratified cross-section rather than a random sample, give a rough indication of the nature of "background" opinion. These polls have been exceptionally accurate in Australia in measuring opinion on major political issues; on the other hand, if the question asked is a hypothetical one, or if there has been little public discussion about it, then it cannot be assumed that were the issue to become a real one, the public would behave in the way indicated by the poll. Leading articles on the other hand indicate expressed and, to a degree, formative opinion. There is however no device for measuring the extent or influence of opinions so expressed.

In the months preceding the San Francisco Conference polls were taken on several questions relative to an international organization. In June 1944, 67% of the public supported proposals for giving armed forces to the League of Nations after the war; 15% were opposed.[10] Parliamentary opinion at this stage was uniformly in favour of collective security with emphasis on the need for military power as its basis. There was a greater public than parliamentary pessimism over the possibility of the Big Three working together:

[9] For additional information on the Australian press, see Appendix B.

[10] *Australian Gallup Polls*, Nos. 205-12, July 1944 (Melbourne: Australian Public Opinion Polls). A similar poll in Great Britain showed the percentages to be 77% and 15%, respectively.

49% were optimistic as against 39% pessimistic. As in Parliament, a greater degree of pessimism was evident in non-Labour voters: the latter were almost evenly divided, while of Labour supporters 53% were optimistic as against 35% who were dubious of success.[11]

As the San Francisco Conference drew close, there was keen discussion in the press on the question of the desirability of an independent foreign policy for Australia. Public opinion appears to have been extremely critical of government policy, favouring instead a united Empire foreign policy. In reply to the question, whether they would "like Australia to . . . join with Britain and the other Dominions in a common foreign policy or decide for herself how she will deal with foreign countries," 64% favoured the former as opposed to 30% favouring an independent foreign policy. The Labour government appears to have been considerably at variance with public opinion: the poll showed that 54% of those questioned opposed government policy as compared with 39% who supported it. A break down of non-Labour people polled showed that 80% preferred a common imperial policy and that only 16% favoured an independent Australian policy.[12]

In the closing stages of the Conference, a poll showed that Australian interest in the discussions had been slight; of the sample interviewed, two out of every three women and every second man had failed to follow the press or radio reports of the Conference. Only a small minority of the Australian public had formed definite opinions about it. Another 10% of the sample claimed to have followed the reports, but had not been able to form a firm conclusion about the Conference. A later poll indicated that there was considerable interest in the outcome of the Conference. Among those who had followed the reports about the Charter, there was an overwhelming support for the broad principles of the United Nations and for Australian ratification of the Charter. In general, on grounds of sentiment, and with a vague hope for international security as

[11] *Ibid.*, Nos. 314-26, Dec. 1945-Jan. 1946.
[12] *Ibid.*, Nos. 264-71, May 1945.

the outcome, a very substantial proportion favoured Australian ratification.[13] A question not submitted to Parliament was taken up by the polls in September 1945. A survey at that time indicated that 34% favoured joint British and American control of the former Japanese mandated territories while 52% favoured United Nations control, the course consistently advocated by the Australian government.[14] In general there was little public interest in international organization or collective security. People were prepared to concede the need for some form of armed international authority while at the same time being dubious about its success. They were prepared to entrust the United Nations with the control of the Japanese mandates, which were considered vital for Australian defence.

Of the metropolitan newspapers, the *Sydney Morning Herald* has for many years given the fullest reports on international news, and its leading articles are probably as near to being influential as those of any Australian papers. During the months from March to June 1945, thirteen leading articles were concerned primarily with the San Francisco Conference or the question of international co-operation.[15] Eight of these dealt with problems of co-operation among the Big Three and with the need for continued agreement if the United Nations were to achieve its objectives. Each of these voiced anxiety at USSR'S policy in Poland. Five dealt solely with trusteeship and non-self-governing territories. The newspaper was prepared to accept a system of accountability similar to the mandates system but only for former mandated territories and captured enemy territories. The doctrine of international accountability for all colonies was repudiated. The articles called for the return of colonies to the countries from which they had been seized, the granting of unfettered control of the former Japanese mandated territories to the United States, and the amending of the New Guinea mandate

---

[13] *Ibid.*, Nos. 272-83, June-July 1945, and Nos. 284-93, Aug. 1945.
[14] *Ibid.*, Nos. 294-303, Sept.-Oct. 1945.
[15] See *Sydney Morning Herald*, 31 March; 24, 27, and 28 April; 1, 7, 10, and 15 May; 1, 5, and 11 June 1945.

to give Australia full power to defend that territory. They re-affirmed the traditional Australian stand, that the "open door" principle must not extend to New Guinea. Labour proposals for the extension of international accountability, it was pointed out, would win no support and at the same time would embarrass Britain and other allies. Self-determination was a wholly desirable objective, but the inhabitants of Poland were in greater need of United Nations assistance in this matter than those of Papua. Finally, it was suggested that neither Cabinet nor Parliament had considered this aspect of Australian policy, and that some proposals had been advanced irresponsibly by the Australian delegates themselves.

Since peace depended on agreement among the great powers, and without such agreement no organization could guarantee the continuance of peace, the veto appeared to be a realistic recognition of the facts of power. The Soviet attempt to extend the veto to discussion as well as to action was to be deplored. However, it was considered unwise for the small powers to press too strongly for the deletion of the veto provision.

While recognizing that Dr. Evatt had considerably enhanced Australia's reputation at San Francisco, the *Sydney Morning Herald* was strongly critical of his policy in detail. His claim to speak for the British Commonwealth in the Pacific was considered arrogant and his failure to maintain a Commonwealth policy on colonial questions was criticized. The newspaper also opposed his stand on the veto. While regarding the maintenance of full employment as a legitimate objective of the Organization, it considered reprehensible any attempt to extend Parliament's legislative powers by including in the Charter a reference to full employment.

Perhaps the two most influential and widely circulating dailies, apart from the *Sydney Morning Herald*, are the Melbourne *Age* and the Melbourne *Herald*. Over the four months' period, the *Herald* published nine leaders[16] dealing either with the Conference or the

---

[16] See Melbourne *Herald*, 2 and 19 March; 9, 23, and 24 April; 4, 14, 23, and 27 June 1945.

larger issue of international co-operation. Of these, two were devoted solely to trusteeship and the Pacific. The *Herald* vigorously asserted that control over the Japanese mandated territories must be vested in the United States, subject to the latter's acceptance of inspection. Complete internationalization was unthinkable. The remaining *Herald* leaders consisted chiefly of explanations of the United Nations security system which contrasted markedly with the League's system in that it possessed force and was based on realism. One leader noted that Soviet action in Eastern Europe and French action in Damascus were contrary to United Nations declarations and threatened that great power agreement which was the basis for the Organization's existence. Despite detailed criticisms, the *Herald* regarded the Conference as a success and the Charter as being grounded on strength and experience.

During the same period, the *Age* published six editorials on the subject.[17] These were mostly serious and rather sombre explanations of the system and the moral qualities necessary to make it work. The *Age* stressed the need for unity of policy with Great Britain and criticized the failure of the government to have the subject of the Conference debated in Parliament. It considered that agreement with the Soviet claim for three seats in the Assembly would weaken Commonwealth influence. It stated with criticism Dr. Evatt's arguments in favour of preference for middle power representation on the non-permanent seats on the Council. Its general attitude to the completed Charter can best be described as one of cautious optimism.

On the principal issues, the rest of the Australian press agreed substantially with these three dailies. The veto was accepted; the need for United States control of the Japanese mandates was emphasized; full employment was either ignored or treated as a constitutional fraud; events in Poland were viewed with temperate concern. The *Labor Call* was unusually laudatory of Dr. Evatt's policies, while the Communist *Guardian* gave strong support to

---

17 See Melbourne *Age*, 1 March; 4 and 24 April; 21, 25, and 28 June 1945.

Soviet policies. Australia's only widely read weekly political magazine, the Sydney *Bulletin*, anti-Labour and anti-Communist, was critical of Dr. Evatt and trenchantly attacked Soviet imperialism. Although accepting the veto, it concluded that "an organization in which Russia . . . has so much veto power, is no present matter for enthusiasm, and its treatment of Poland, unrepresented and avoided as a subject at San Francisco, will remain the acid test."[18]

The sense of satisfaction over a considerable achievement of the Australian delegation found no echo in the Australian press: its comments were sober and discreetly favourable. It emphasized the need for close and friendly contact with the United States, and waxed sentimental about the British Commonwealth. It provided for that interested minority of citizens following the Conference debates thoughtful editorials and informative special articles. But there was no sense of belonging to a new epoch; rather, cynical memories of a dead League.

---

[18] Sydney *Bulletin*, 25 April and 30 June 1945.

PART TWO

chapter five

Australian Security and the United Nations

National security is a function of power, and power the resultant of a complex interrelationship of geographical position, logistics, and of resources in the broadest sense. Combinations of states in alliance or in an international organization affect the relative effectiveness of national power in achieving security against aggression. Australia, as a small Pacific power, is incapable of defending itself against attack from any major power except through alliance with a great power or a combination of powers. Its strategic problems can only be considered in relation to the strategy of the major powers, and its security rests ultimately upon the results of conflicts between major powers, the decisive battles of which may be fought in Europe, the Middle East, or East Asia. In the absence of an international organization with effective military strength, Australia has no other alternative.

As a two-ocean country, an island continent at the Pacific end

h

of the vital line of imperial communications from London through Suez, Australia has been traditionally dependent for security on British naval power. Australian troops have fought in two world wars in defence of the imperial axis which runs through the Middle East with its great oil reserves. Britain's withdrawal from India, Burma, Pakistan, and Ceylon, the loss of Ceylonese bases, and the nationalization of the Suez Canal, have removed the shield of British protection from the northern rim of the Indian Ocean.

The external factors that most directly affect Australian security today lie in the Pacific region. The most important of these is the basic shift in the power position within the area. The serious decline in effective British strength in the Far East and the modification of the balance of industrial power within the Commonwealth, the steady contraction of British military strength in the Middle East, and the withdrawal of Britain from the Suez Canal Zone: all these have reduced the defensive strength of the United Kingdom in the Pacific. The effective limits of British naval, military, and air power closely coincide with immediate British interests and commitments in Western Europe and the Mediterranean. This has been more than offset by the emergence of the United States as the predominant force in the Pacific. With the greatest industrial potential in history, powerful naval forces, massive air power, and great ground strength, the United States can operate effectively in almost any part of the Pacific region. Of the other European powers actively interested in the Far East, two—the Netherlands and France—have virtually withdrawn from the area. On the other hand, the Soviet Union has strengthened its defensive position and offensive power in the North Pacific. The development of transport facilities in Siberia (particularly the expansion of internal air networks and the improvement in trans-polar flying), the construction of a string of heavy industrial plants from the Urals to Lake Baikal, and the shift of population east of the Urals have all increased Russia's power potential. The Yalta agreements have converted the Sea of Okhotsk into a Russian lake; the building up of the Far Eastern submarine fleet based at Vladivostok has introduced a formidable offensive naval power into the region.

The other post-war power shifts can be noted briefly: the temporary disappearance of Japan as a major factor in the balance, and the emergence of a new massive Chinese power. The initial process of Japanese demilitarization and geographical disarmament through the loss of potential springboards for aggression against its neighbours was accompanied by long term plans to destroy or seriously to modify the economic basis of Japanese military strength. This represented an attempt to prevent the revival of an aggressive militaristic Japan. With the development of the "cold war" and the ensuing drastic revision of United States Far Eastern policy, however, Japan has again become a strategic area, and Japan's rearmament is going forward despite qualms as to the effectiveness of its defensive power in a Pacific war. The revision of post-war policies towards Japan indicated in the Peace Treaty of 1951 and the rapid recovery of Japanese industrial power created in Australia a deep concern over the possibility of a resurgence of Japanese military aggression.

From the point of view of general analysis, the most striking feature of the power change has been the emergence of a unified Communist China capable of successful resistance to the United Nations. China has become the real centre of gravity in the Far East after decades of political and economic instability. The construction of the Trans-Siberian Railway had ended the dominant role of sea-power in the Far East. Manchuria, Outer Mongolia, and Sinkiang have become the major points of ingress to China, replacing the old sea ports of Hong Kong and Shanghai. As a massive land power, China could become a stabilizing force in the area or a disruptive influence should it resort to a policy of landwards expansion in Southeast Asia. The vital strategic problem is whether the West can successfully challenge a land-based Chinese air-power. Commonwealth bases in the Far East have become increasingly insecure. The Korean War showed that the loosely knit unstable

Chinese armies have become tightly disciplined, well-armed forces capable of holding their own in the field with the most modernly equipped Western armies. With this has come the mushroom growth, with Russian assistance, of a Chinese air force of considerable striking power.

The most significant development of all in the Pacific region has been the changed political climate following the decline of Western European influence in Asia and the rapid growth of Asian nationalism. Nationalist movements developed in the initial stages as movements directed against Western imperialism. India, Pakistan, Burma, Ceylon, and Indonesia have achieved independence; the autonomy of Laos, Cambodia, and Vietnam has been recognized; but an understandable and pervasive suspicion of colonialism in general remains. There is a legacy of latent distrust of Western policies making collaboration difficult, for it is feared that it may revive the old colonial dependence; there is an extraordinary sensitiveness to the possibilities of the re-establishment of a dependent status. While European political and economic control helped to create the material and psychological conditions necessary for the elimination of mediaeval social structures, it had a profoundly disrupting effect on the social, intellectual, and political life of Asia. The programs of nationalist movements are not only anti-Western in content but are revolutionary in their social implications and objectives. The social and economic policies of the Western powers have contributed to internal tensions by their effect upon population growth. The national governments are concerned with problems of land reform and land tenure, the elimination of rural indebtedness, improvement in agricultural productivity, the multiplication of transport to convert isolated village markets into regional and then national markets, the provision of social services, and the expansion of industry. The primary interests of most of the borderland peoples of Asia are primarily economic and social, secondarily military and strategic. This cannot be reiterated too strongly in considering problems of Pacific security.

Such then is the geopolitical backdrop for the formulation of Australian policies of security. What are the specific assumptions upon which Australian defence planning must be based?

The first assumption is that, with the development of the "cold war," it is essential to check the form of aggression which has occurred in Korea, in Malaya, and elsewhere in Asia. As Mr. McBride, the Australian Minister for Defence, pointed out in February 1952, it is essential for Australia to make an adequate contribution to the fighting of the "cold war," "essential both to our relations with our powerful friends and to the Allied strategic starting point, should war occur."[1] Soon after this statement, pressure in Indochina reached a new peak. There was a growing concern that what the *Economist* called "a long red tongue of menace" might thrust itself through the island archipelago to Australia. The Minister for External Affairs, Mr. Casey, has concluded that "the Communist advances in the region constitute the greatest menace to Australia at any time since the war."[2]

Secondly, it must be assumed that, should a global war break out, it would be won or lost outside Australia. An invasion of Australia of the pre-1945 type is highly unlikely for perhaps two decades. In these circumstances, local security would depend on the control of sea and air communications in the Pacific and Indian oceans and the adjoining seas. The most serious and likely danger to Australia would result from the defeat of the United Kingdom and the United States: only this could result in invasion and occupation, probably the latter because of the victor's superiority in power. Australia's primary objective, therefore, must be to prevent such a defeat by providing military assistance where it is most urgently needed. Australian defence must be planned in relation to general allied strategy. Since the allies would, for the foreseeable future, retain naval supremacy, Australian troops could be moved overseas

---

[1] Commonwealth of Australia, *Parliamentary Debates* (*C.P.D.*), Vol. 216, 21 Feb. 1952, p. 181.

[2] Melbourne *Age*, 28 June 1954.

in time of war. Air forces would be located at key points as part of a unified command.

The third assumption is that the long-term possibilities of aggression lie with an expanding China or a resurgent militaristic Japan. Australian defence planning has always assumed the possible renewal of a threat from Japan: both diplomatic and military pressures have been directed toward preventing such a revival. An invasion of an island continent like Australia could only be mounted by an oceanic power.

Japanese expansion in the past has arisen partly out of population pressure and partly out of broad militarist schemes of aggrandizement following in outline the pattern of the Tanaka Memorial. There is the continuing fact that a sparsely populated Australia lives cheek by jowl with the densely populated countries of Southeast and East Asia. As the late Leader of the Opposition, Mr. Chifley, put it, "the simple fact is that at its present rate of increase the population of the world will be doubled within the next 70 years and the greater proportion of that increase will be in Asian and Pacific countries . . . With from 200,000 to 300,000 soldiers in the country, and a population of from 20,000,000 to 30,000,000, our position would be completely hopeless if the people to the north of this continent were hostile to us."[3]

The specific fear of Japan is primarily a matter of observation and of experience: the Japanese occupation of Manchuria in 1931, the "special undeclared war" against China in 1937, and then the Pacific War itself when Australia was for the first time threatened with physical invasion. The traditional fears of half a century materialized as Japanese bombs fell on Darwin. At the close of the war Australia sought both retribution and protection from Japan. Only by destruction of Japan's armament industries and the imposition of drastic limitations on post-war military forces, and by the drastic social reorganization of Japan and the creation of

---

[3] *C.P.D.*, Vol. 212, 7 March 1951, p. 84.

a government which was at once responsible and democratic, did Australia believe that the long-term danger from Japan could be reduced. Feeling in Australia towards Japan resembled somewhat the traditional antagonism felt by France towards Germany. Australian policy was largely brushed to one side by the United States, the chief occupying power in Japan. Japan was steadily converted into "the workshop of East Asia," the pace of social reform was drastically slowed down, and Japan's police forces expanded. Democratic government appeared increasingly to be a mere facade. American attempts to woo Japan, a coveted ally, posed awkward problems alike for Australian foreign policy and Australian defence.

The dilemma had to be resolved in 1951 when the peace settlement with Japan was drafted and the tougher preliminary draft of 1947 was jettisoned. Australia persisted in the view that the treaty should effectively limit Japan's rearmament, explicitly restrict naval construction, and control the import of strategic materials. But when the chips were down, only New Zealand and the Philippines were prepared to support the Australian policy of restricted rearmament. The Japanese Peace Treaty was finally accepted with the ANZUS Pact as a *quid pro quo:* it was an unpalatable but necessary step with no alternative but the absurd one of a continued Australian occupation of Japan. The Prime Minister recognized the wisdom of a policy of generosity:

> We should be foolish to force a hard and bitter peace upon Japan because we feared that in 15 or 20 years' time Japan might once more become an aggressor, when the real and deadly and present question is whether, inside the next two years, we shall between us be strong enough to resist (and therefore deter) a vast Communist aggression against one manifestation of which we are actually now fighting in Korea.[4]

Mr. Casey, Minister for External Affairs, made a similar point in the parliamentary debate:

---

[4] R. G. Menzies, "The Pacific Settlement Seen from Australia," *Foreign Affairs*, Vol. 30 (1952), p. 193.

> The simple fact is that as things are today, Japan is quite in-
> capable of threatening anybody—indeed the Japanese are in-
> capable of defending themselves—and, meanwhile the whole
> of Asia is subject to strong and immediate pressure . . . from
> Communist aggression. . . . The immediate problem that we
> have to consider . . . is the security of Japan, even more than
> security against Japan.[5]

A disarmed Japan could easily fall under Communist control and
an embittered Japan would be more likely to align itself with China
than one to which full sovereignty had been generously restored.

Yet Australia's decision to accept the 1951 Treaty was regarded
as the lesser of two evils, and as involving a deliberate preference
for short-term as distinct from long-term security. The Labour
Opposition voted against ratification of the Japanese Peace Treaty
on the ground that it endangered Australia by permitting unlimited
Japanese rearmament on sea, on land, and in the air. This, together
with assistance from the United States for such rearmament, would
give to Japan, the only power in Asia that in the foreseeable future
could have the industrial capacity to launch an invasion of Australia,
the means to launch such an invasion. Moreover, rearmament of
Japan, far from improving the Western position in the "cold war,"
might well endanger it, since an armed nation may dictate terms
in a way that an unarmed vassal can never attempt. In a rearmed
Japan, it would be primarily the Japanese government which would
determine how its forces should be used to promote Japanese
interests. Dr. Evatt contended that, "Should a war occur between
the Western democracies on the one hand, and Russia and China
on the other, Japan might remain neutral; or it might be prepared
to enter the conflict on the side on which its interests would best
be served in the long run."[6]

Australian distrust of Japan subsided slowly, and long-term defence
plans envisage the possibility of a renewal of attack. The constant

---

[5] *C.P.D.*, Vol. 216, 6 Feb. 1952, pp. 20 and 24.
[6] *Ibid.*, 21 Feb. 1952, p. 234.

suspicion of Japanese activities near Australian waters was evidenced by the public concern over the revival of Japanese pearling activities and the plans for a survey by the United States of the waters around New Britain. In 1947 the Chifley government made plans for mapping by the United States of Pacific areas of mutual interest. These came to a head in 1954. The United States proposed to use a number of Japanese technicians and seamen, perhaps one hundred in all. The Australian reaction was immediate and bitter, with the press almost unanimous. Fearing that the survey would pave the way for fresh Japanese spying on the approaches to North Australia, the Leader of the Opposition pointed out that "the basis of the objection is not sentimental but rests on the ground of defence security."[7] This was only partly true because sentiment reached a high pitch. It was necessary to withdraw the Japanese teams and to substitute Filipinos. The incident reflects the intensity of Australian feeling on the subject and the important role that Japan plays in Australia's defence planning.

These, then, are the kind of practical assumptions, short-term and long-term, upon which Australian policy has to be based. Apart from the primary function of local defence of Australian territories and waters, Australia's role would appear to be one of collaboration with other democratic powers to contain communism while the "cold war" continues. This would help deny to communism strategic positions in Southeast Asia which would facilitate victory in a global conflict. Such collaboration would carry with it mutual security responsibilities, namely, that in the unlikely event of Australia being attacked independently of its major allies, the United Kingdom and the United States, they would immediately provide military assistance. Accordingly, the Minister of Defence in 1952 described the function of the Royal Australian Navy as follows: "to make an adequate and effective contribution to the naval defences of the

[7] See statement by Dr. Evatt in Melbourne *Herald*, 1 Feb. 1954; see also Gordon Greenwood and Norman Harper, eds., *Australia in World Affairs 1950-55* (Melbourne: F. W. Cheshire, 1957), pp. 166-67.

British Commonwealth." He stated that the role of the army was

> first, to provide such forces as may be required for possible
> commitments under the United Nations Organization, in-
> cluding regional arrangements in the Pacific; secondly, to par-
> ticipate in British Commonwealth defence; thirdly, to provide
> for the basic organization for expansion in time of war; and
> fourthly, to provide for the local defence of Australia and its
> territories.[8]

Such an analysis, it should be pointed out, is essentially a pre-atomic one which assumes a protracted war using all the traditional forces rather than sudden press button war in which atomic projectiles might be launched on Sydney from Hanoi.

To fulfil Australia's obligations, the government introduced a three-year defence plan in July 1950, involving an expenditure of approximately £885 million. By June 1952, £577.3m. had been allocated: army, £220.2m.; navy, £147.5m.; air force, £138.1m. In March 1951, the government revived compulsory military training whereby all medically fit males were obliged to perform 176 days' service over a period of three years commencing at the age of eighteen. Under this scheme, by 1954, 82,000 men were scheduled to have completed their initial period of three months' continuous training. In 1952 two infantry battalions and two air force squadrons together with naval forces were in action in Korea, two additional air force squadrons were on war service in Malaya, and one air force wing was serving with the Royal Air Force as part of the United Kingdom's peace-time garrison in the Middle East. In the same year, regular political and staff conferences under the ANZUS Treaty began. In 1953-54 Australia made available surplus war stores for use by the French government in Indochina.

The completion of the three year defence program required a transition in planning from "preparedness by a critical date" to

---

[8] *C.P.D.*, Vol. 216, 21 Feb. 1952, pp. 184-85. There is considerable controversy about Australian defence policy. An opposing viewpoint is given in "Australia: The Dilemma of Defence," *The Round Table*, Vol. 42 (1952), pp. 274-81.

sustaining a "long haul." It necessitated a rebalancing of the whole program for 1954-55. The army, with a mobilization target of 115,500 men, was to be more carefully proportioned between a small permanent force and a predominantly citizen army. More important was the shift in planning emphasis to the air force at the expense of the other two services. For 1953-54, within the overall defence allocation of £200 millions, 32.1 per cent was allowed for the air force as compared with 26 per cent for the navy and 41.9 per cent for the army. The justification for the shift lay in a clear appreciation of the strategic role of air power in Southeast Asia. "While South East Asia is held, defence in depth is provided to Australia and there will be no direct threat, except to sea communications."[9] A year later the Prime Minister, Mr. Menzies, announced the important decision to despatch troops to Malaya as part of a Commonwealth strategic reserve. This involved the stationing of sea, land, and air forces outside Australian territorial limits for the first time in peace. There was no basic change in defence planning or in general strategy: defence in depth, with adequate local defence, remained the cardinal features of Australian planning.[10]

Security for a middle or small power like Australia is a function much more of foreign policy than of military planning. From necessity rather than choice, Australian Ministers for External Affairs since 1945 have sought to surpass Bismarck as a juggler, keeping five balls in the air simultaneously: the cultivation of Commonwealth ties to strengthen it as a system of mutual security; the establishing of the closest possible relations with the United States as the major Pacific power; efforts to establish friendly relations with Australia's

---

[9] Statement by the Minister for Defence, Sir Philip McBride, in *Current Notes on International Affairs* (Dept. of External Affairs, Canberra), Vol. 25 (1954), 11 April 1954, p. 290.

[10] *Ibid.*, Vol. 26 (1955), pp. 278-91. In 1957 the National Service Training scheme was revised, and service was confined to the army with a limited annual intake of 12,000. By 1957, 180,000 men had been given partial training. This decision was made so that the nucleus of regular army troops could be expanded. See *ibid.*, Vol. 28 (1957), pp. 319-27.

Asian neighbours in the Pacific; the promotion of plans for regional collaboration through a specific security pact; and finally, support for the United Nations and the use of the United Nations as a forum for the expression of Australia's views as an independent sovereign state. Different ministers have attached a varying importance to these five policies; none would deny the necessity for arduous juggling, and all have paid more than lip service to the task.

In the changed circumstances of the post-war world, some of the perennial problems of Australian policy were re-posed. Was not in fact the cultivation of Commonwealth ties of crucial importance? In the inter-war period, Australia had sought security through the pursuit of the two closely integrated policies, collaboration with the British Commonwealth of Nations and support for the League of Nations. But sentiment had always given preference to the first. The inability of the League to prevent or to quarantine military conflicts added the weight of experience to sentiment. Australia's defence policy was made increasingly to dovetail with imperial defence policy. The Australian Labour party gave the most guarded support to League of Nations security policies and opposed "war camouflaged as sanctions." The Pacific War showed clearly that British commitments had outstripped resources and that the revival of considerable British power in the region was improbable. It was a realization of this shift in power that led the Australian Labour government after 1945 to make its own assessments of the problems of the Pacific.

It was for these reasons that Labour began to turn to international collaboration as a solution to the problem of Pacific security. The San Francisco Conference engendered a spirit of quiet optimism about the possibilities of collective security. This was reinforced by the belief that the rewriting of Article 55 of the Charter would help cut at the economic roots of war. But this sober enthusiasm was not shared by the Liberal Opposition whose predilections were for closer collaboration with the British Commonwealth. Both parties firmly endorsed the United Nations in principle; each moved increasingly even before 1950 to achieve security independently of the United Nations. The interesting thing was the frank recognition by the Labour party of the need for Empire solidarity, the increasing caution about the value of the United Nations. Amplifying Labour's post-war policy announced in the Governor-General's speech of 6 November 1946, Mr. J. Dedman, Minister for Defence, admitted that:

> we have only to look at the history of the constitutional evolution of the British Commonwealth to realize that the growth of a system of collective security under the United Nations will necessarily be slow. . . . In the meantime, reliance must primarily be placed on co-operation in Empire defence and, in the last resort, on the forces that can be raised in an emergency to provide for the inherent right of individual self-defence under the charter.[11]

Labour recognized the need to provide forces which could be "placed at the disposal of the United Nations for the maintenance of international peace and security, including regional arrangements in the Pacific."[12] This was at least given paper primacy, but ranked little above the commitments for Commonwealth co-operation. During the war, Mr. Curtin had worked out detailed plans for Empire defence. At the 1946 Conference of Commonwealth Prime Ministers, Mr. Chifley had argued for imperial co-operation on a regional basis, with the United Kingdom, New Zealand, and Australia assuming primary responsibility. But he did add, as a footnote to the scheme, that "the United States of America, and perhaps later . . . other countries with possessions in that area" should be consulted.[13] At all technical levels there has been continuing and close consultation among Commonwealth members, the dovetailing of strategic plans, the training of staff officers, and the provision of weapons and equipment. Commonwealth collaboration alone

---

[11] *C.P.D.*, Vol. 192, 4 June 1947, p. 3336.
[12] *Idem.*
[13] *C.P.D.*, Vol. 198, 23 Sept. 1948, p. 832.

could not provide security in the Pacific: the Pax Britannica was a relic of the past.

The most important change in Australian foreign policy since the war has been the expansion of contacts and the cultivation of a special relationship with the United States. The basic dilemma of Australian policy was posed in an editorial in the Melbourne *Argus* (16 October 1953):

> Australia's geographical position as a sparsely populated white outpost in the Pacific draws her ever more closely into the orbit of American power. Most Australians recognise instinctively that with Britain weakened and impoverished by the Second World War, Australia is more dependent than ever on American protection—Australia needs the moral courage to face the full implications of her dependence on American power in relation to her ties with Britain. It is vital that the two should be reconciled, and that Australia at the same time should retain her integrity and independence as a nation.

The early stages of the Pacific War showed the frailty of Commonwealth power there. Mr. Curtin's dramatic appeal for United States aid in 1942 was followed by an effective and successful partnership between the two countries. A conviction that the Australian and American ways of life had much in common was reinforced by feelings of warm gratitude for United States aid in checking the Japanese threat of invasion. Yet despite the importance of close ties between the two countries, the war ended with no permanent links established. Extreme national sensitiveness in Canberra over the continued use by the United States of a base in the Admiralty Islands contributed to the northward shift in the new American defensive perimeter. No mutual obligations of a military kind were entered into until the ANZUS Pact was concluded in 1951. This helped sharpen the dilemma: sentimental ties to Britain were reinforced by an awareness of positive military commitments and diplomatic support. Yet "precedent and sentimental doubts must not be allowed to obscure the truth that the effective defence of

Australia now depends largely on comradeship with the United States."[14] The crucial problem came to be not one of choice between the two powerful attracting forces but rather how to prevent friction from developing between them. Would Australia be compelled to become a satellite of the United States, or could Australia, like Canada, follow an independent policy and perform a useful role as mediator or interpreter between the United Kingdom and the United States?

The chief divergences between Australia and the United States in military and diplomatic policy prior to the conclusion of the ANZUS Pact arose out of differing assessments of the role of Japan in the new Pacific power balance. Australian influence in the Allied Council for Japan and in the Commonwealth of Nations was insufficient to prevent the United States from framing the generous Japanese Peace Treaty of 1951. This did much to determine the structure and pattern of security in the northern Pacific, perhaps in the whole Pacific as well.

Where did the United Nations fit into the Pacific pattern? In the early stages scarcely at all. There had been much talk, prior to the San Francisco Conference, of the need for giving "teeth" to the new international organization. But despite the attempts to create a procedure for military collaboration, this did not produce military consultation or provide the United Nations with a single battalion. Australian defence estimates made provision for "forces to be placed at the disposal of the United Nations for the maintenance of international peace and security," but collective security appeared a remote dream until 1950. When the Security Council condemned North Korean aggression, however, Australia immediately placed military forces at the disposal of the United Nations.

The outbreak of the Korean War led to the introduction of the "Uniting for Peace" resolution at the fifth session of the General Assembly. Section D of the draft resolution provided for the establishment of a Collective Measures Committee which was

---

[14] Melbourne *Herald*, 12 June 1953.

in consultation with the Secretary-General, to study and make a report to the Security Council and the General Assembly . . . on methods which might be used and resources, including armed force, which are or might be made available to the United Nations in order to maintain international peace and security in accordance with the Purposes and Principles of the Charter, taking account of collective self-defence and regional arrangements (Articles 51 and 52 of the Charter).[15]

The Australian view was that the powers proposed for the Committee were far too wide and positively dangerous in that the estimate of national resources could assist a potential aggressor and "military planning . . . against some unarmed enemy . . . would either be a waste of time or, if it were realistic, playing with fire."[16] This section of the proposal was finally amended to meet some of the Australian objections, and the reference to "resources" was deleted.

There would appear to have been a difference of purpose between Australia and the sponsors of the proposal, notably the United States. Neither the final draft nor the speeches on it contained any reference to would-be aggressors by name. By implication the Committee appears to have been envisaged as an anti-Soviet instrument. Australia appears to have been rather reluctant to regard the Committee as having a specific political function. Mr. Spender, during the initial discussions, emphasized the importance not merely of dealing with military actions but of incorporating "a constructive economic policy for peace and security. It was not only a question of providing technical assistance for under-developed countries but also of seeing that the economically strong gave aid to the economically weak."[17]

The Collective Measures Committee, on which Australia was represented, dealt mainly with military matters: the Spender proposal

---

[15] For the text of the original proposal, see General Assembly, Official Records (G.A.O.R.): 5th Sess., Annexes, Vol. 2: Agenda item 68, p. 5. For the text as adopted, see General Assembly Resolution 377(V), 3 Nov. 1950.

[16] *Ibid.*, 1st Ctte., 356th Mtg., 10 Oct. 1950, pp. 73-74.

[17] *Idem.*

was ignored. Its reports were useful as clarifying possible action in the future and suggesting procedures to facilitate action, but, as the Australian delegate pointed out, such "action under the collective security system could not be made automatic. The Security Council or the General Assembly would have to decide in each case what particular measures were to be recommended to governments. The measures proposed . . . implied no prior commitments on the part of Member States."[18] The Australian delegate made it clear that his country was prepared to give full support to United Nations proposals. Australian troops were serving in Korea and further contributions could be considered. Two Australian generals had been appointed to the panel of military experts set up under the "Uniting for Peace" resolution. Furthermore, the Australian delegate pledged that "within the limits of the country's resources and within the framework of the constitutional provisions in force," Australia would "grant all assistance and facilities to armed forces participating in United Nations collective measures."[19] So far as economic measures were concerned, the Australian government would be prepared to comply with any recommendations by the Security Council or the General Assembly. The Australian government was prepared to support United Nations decisions on particular issues by force if necessary. This was a far cry from the hesitations over League of Nations sanctions against Italy.

REGIONAL PACTS AND SECURITY: ANZUS AND SEATO

Despite the promise of full support for the schemes of collective security envisaged in the "Uniting for Peace" resolution and elaborated by the Collective Measures Committee, Australia has always felt that it would gain a far greater measure of security through a regional pact to be negotiated if possible in terms of Article 52(1) of the Charter. In discussing the initial draft resolution, Mr. Spender

[18] G.A.O.R., 7th Sess., 1st Ctte., 573rd Mtg., 12 March 1953, p. 439.
[19] *Idem.*

i

had preferred the formation of regional security pacts to the creation of a United Nations force with a skeleton command as a means to greater security.

The need for special regional arrangements to ensure security in the Pacific has been an important part of Australian foreign policy.[20] Regional security for Australia has been closely linked with the attempt to establish closer relations with the United States as the predominant power in the Pacific. The original Lyons proposal for a Pacific Pact put forward in May 1937 after the collapse of the Washington Treaties of 1921-22 had been given such a chilly reception by the other Pacific powers that it had remained stillborn. The ANZAC Pact of 1944 between Australia and New Zealand was a bilateral attempt to create the nucleus of a wider regional agreement, but it attracted no wider support.

In 1945 the Labour government's move to negotiate a pact with the United States as a deterrent against a resurgent Japan was equally unsuccessful. At San Francisco the Australian delegates collaborated with Senator Vandenberg in drafting Chapter VIII of the United Nations Charter dealing with regional security. In March 1950 the Australian Minister for External Affairs, Mr. Spender, pressed for the creation of "a defensive military arrangement . . . between countries that have a vital interest in the stability of Asia and the Pacific, and which are at the same time capable of undertaking military commitments."[21] The Canberra conversations in February 1951 with Mr. Dulles resulted in the initialling on 12 July 1951 of the ANZUS Pact. The United States then concluded bilateral treaties with Japan and the Philippines. These three pacts provided an un-coordinated system of regional defence, an initial step in the consolidation of peace in the area.

The ANZUS Pact came into existence primarily as a result of divergences between Australia and New Zealand on the one hand and the United States on the other over the terms of the Japanese

---

[20] See Greenwood and Harper, *op. cit.*, pp. 157 ff.
[21] Statement by Mr. Spender, *Current Notes*, *op. cit.*, Vol. 21 (1950), p. 163.

Peace Treaty. The ultimate condition for acceptance of the treaty by Australia, New Zealand, and for that matter, the Philippines, was the simultaneous conclusion of military pacts between these countries and the United States. The ANZUS Pact, however, was limited in membership and its obligations were rather vaguer than many Australians had hoped for. Article IV provided that "each Party recognises that an armed attack in the Pacific area on any of the Parties would be dangerous to its own peace and safety and declares that it would act to meet the common danger in accordance with its constitutional processes." This is in many ways a more diluted commitment than the corresponding commitment under the North Atlantic Pact—whereby the "parties agree that an armed attack against one or more of them shall be considered an attack against them all" and that each will assist the party so attacked by taking "such action as it deems necessary including the use of armed force to restore and maintain the security of the area." Both treaties constitute "a declaration of intent" by the parties proclaiming "publicly and formally their sense of unity, so that no potential aggressor could be under the illusion that any of them [stood] alone," either in Europe or in the Pacific.[22] The careful drafting of the ANZUS Treaty was designed to avoid reopening the bitter debate in the United States Congress over the ratification of NATO and Monroe Doctrine phraseology was deliberately used.[23] The general satisfaction in Australia with the conclusion of the pact and the apparent underwriting of Australian security by the United States was so general that the possible limitations in commitments passed

[22] Preamble of the ANZUS Pact. For text, see *Current Notes, op. cit.*, Vol. 22 (1951), p. 404. For more extensive critical analyses of the pact as it affects Australia's security, see W. Macmahon Ball, "The Peace Treaty with Japan," *The Australian Outlook*, Vol. 5 (1951), pp. 138-39; Norman D. Harper, "Security in the South West Pacific," *Pacific Affairs*, Vol. XXIV (1951), pp. 170-76; and D. C. S. Sissons, "The Pacific Pact," *The Australian Outlook*, Vol. 6 (1952), pp. 20-26.

[23] R. G. Casey, *Friends and Neighbours: Australia and the World* (Melbourne: F. W. Cheshire, 1954), pp. 80-82; cf. J. F. Dulles, "Security in the Pacific," *Foreign Affairs*, Vol. 30 (1952), pp. 180-81.

virtually unnoticed. There are still sharp divisions of opinion within Australia about the relatively binding force of the ANZUS and NATO formulae.

There are obvious defects from the point of view of Australian security in the ANZUS Pact, defects which have led to a considerable measure of doubt as to its value. Part of the criticism rests upon the assumption that Australia could or would remain neutral in a Pacific war: such an assumption would be repudiated by most Australians. The most serious defect of the pact lies in its restricted membership. The original Australian proposals envisaged the participation of the United Kingdom and other Commonwealth countries as a nucleus, and "such other countries as might wish to do so . . . providing . . . that they are capable of contributing military commitments" (Spender).[24] Pressure to include the United Kingdom was strongly resisted by a United States suspicious of British imperialism and colonialism and reluctant to underwrite the defence of any British colonies even on reciprocal terms. The United States was at this stage anxious to limit its Pacific commitments and felt that the inclusion of Britain would necessitate at least the simultaneous inclusion of France. Consequently, no British delegate attended the first meeting of the ANZUS Council at Honolulu in September 1952, even as an observer, and Britain is still rigorously excluded. Despite exceedingly sharp British criticisms on this point, criticisms echoed vigorously in Australia, there was never any intention of weakening normal Commonwealth ties, of veering permanently into the United States orbit or of providing any substitute for the already close military consultation among members of the Commonwealth.[25] The British view is that Britain has an absolute moral obligation to come to Australia's assistance in the event of an attack. There is a remote possibility that British exclusion from

---

[24] *Current Notes, op. cit.*, Vol. 21 (1950), p. 164.

[25] Norman D. Harper, "Australia and U.S. Pacific Policy 1951-54," in G. Greenwood, ed., *Australian Policies Toward Asia*, Australian Papers, Institute of Pacific Relations Conference, 1954 (Melbourne: Australian Institute of International Affairs), Part III, pp. 9-11.

ANZUS might mean the weakening of this sense of obligation, and that from a long-term Australian point of view the vital question may well be not who has the resources to contribute to Australia's defence, but rather who has the will.

A more serious danger was that ANZUS might be interpreted in Asia as a Western pact designed to safeguard white national interests to the exclusion of those of the region as a whole. A broadening of the basis of the pact to include Asian states appeared to be a necessary condition for its success. In the early stages of negotiations Washington proposed the creation of a Pacific security council which could subsequently include the Philippines, India, and other countries, possibly even Japan. Australia was equally aware of the danger, but the inclusion of Japan in a Pacific council which would arrange secret military staff discussions among members was regarded with considerable alarm and scepticism.[26]

Much of the criticism of the ANZUS Pact arose out of a belief that effective United States commitments to Australia would in fact be very limited, and that Australia could easily be involved in a military conflict touched off by United States policies of which Australia disapproved. To many Americans, the Pact appeared as "a mutually-approved Monroe Doctrine for the South Pacific,"[27] and indeed the ANZUS formula follows closely the form of wording of the Monroe Doctrine. The pact was furthermore viewed as an alignment of Australia and New Zealand with the United States against communism. There was some doubt in Australia whether the United States realized that Australia saw the pact as a re-insurance against Japan and whether the United States would regard the treaty as creating an obligation to defend Australia against Japan. Sceptics felt, further, that the treaty would be invoked only in the case of a general war when the United States would already be involved and would be compelled to dispose of its forces on a

---

[26] See Sissons, "The Pacific Pact," *op. cit.*, p. 25.
[27] *Christian Science Monitor*, 13 July 1951.

global basis rather than in accordance with the pact. Finally, the pact created at least the theoretical possibility that, should an incident be created in Chinese waters by trigger-happy American pilots or naval commanders, Australia would be automatically involved in the ensuing conflict despite overwhelming dislike of the policies which provided the *casus foederis* for the outbreak of war.

A careful appraisal of the ANZUS Pact would show it to be an imperfect but realistic guarantee of Australian security at the time it was concluded. The disadvantages are the inevitable ones arising out of collaboration or alliance between a great and a small power. The effective contribution of the latter is so limited as to be of marginal value; the former will more probably be embroiled in any major conflict and so will have little strength available for regional action.

The conclusion of the Korean armistice in July 1953, and the increasing Chinese pressure in Southeast Asia, particularly in Indochina, underlined the imperfections of ANZUS. Preoccupied with the potential threat from a resurgent Japan, Australia was slow to realize the shift in the power structure in East Asia. The real threat in this area, both to British communities and to the broad strategic interests of the United States, clearly came from an expanding China rather than from a new militant Japan. The network of United States treaties in the Pacific, that *tour de force* of the Dulles diplomacy, did not in fact seal off the Pacific from the Asian mainland: a defence gap existed from Indochina through Indonesia to Ceylon. The pacts were not really integrated and all members depended heavily upon the United States for vital military assistance. Despite, perhaps because of, the United States threat of "massive retaliation" against aggression, there was little Asian enthusiasm for regional defence pacts. Support for neutralism of the Indian type steadily increased.

Australia, in fact, lies on the natural line of Communist advance through Southeast Asia. In the crucial sector from Manila to Calcutta there were no effective defence arrangements: the tenuous and fragile

British defence line rested precariously on Singapore and made no contact with the American defence perimeter terminating at Manila. It was a realization of the vulnerability of this southeastern gap that led Australia to contribute a fighter squadron to the British forces in Malaya. The Indochina crisis created on the one hand a frank reluctance in Australia to underwrite French policy in 1954, and on the other, an increasing sensitivity to the implications of a Communist victory. Maps published in China indicated a long-term desire to extend Chinese boundaries through the whole of Southeast Asia to the Celebes. To the Australian government, the west Pacific area—the offshore island chain as well as the mainland of Southeast Asia—appeared to be in jeopardy from direct and indirect pressures from Peiping. The Geneva settlement of July 1954, with the partition of Vietnam, meant that the southernmost frontier of communism was no further from Darwin than the east coast of Australia is from the west.

The development of the Indochina crisis coincided with an Australian federal election, but Australian diplomatic activity was directed towards the achievement of long-term collective defence of the region. A meeting of the ANZUS Council at Washington in June 1954 took steps to form a Southeast Asia collective defence system.[28] It was an appreciation of the deterioration of the situation in Indochina that produced the sense of urgency in Washington to create the South East Asia Treaty Organization (SEATO) to complement NATO. It also produced the historic decision of the Australian government on 5 August 1954 to commit itself in advance in Southeast Asia. Australia had pressed consistently for a tighter Pacific pact:

> ANZUS should be the cornerstone of a comprehensive alliance, open to all colonial powers as well as Asian countries which have major interests in the area and are determined to defend them against communism. The Pacific cannot be de-

---

[28] See Greenwood and Harper, *op. cit.*, pp. 172-80.

tached from East Asia. The problems of both should be dealt with as parts of a whole; they need central direction.[29]

The collapse of French power in Indochina merely enhanced the urgency of speedy action. A month before the conference of the SEATO powers at Manila, the Australian Prime Minister, Mr. R. G. Menzies, announced full Australian support for the new organization and the abandonment of Australia's traditional policy of making no treaty commitments in advance of war.

> In the two great world wars, Australia had an opportunity to decide what it was going to do and enough time to assemble, train, equip and despatch armed forces. We cannot gamble upon this being our position any longer . . . We have decided that in any great defence organization of the kind envisaged, we must accept military commitments.[30]

The United States proposals for a regional umbrella against expanding communism immediately raised the question of the role of the Asian countries. As Mr. Casey pointed out, "no country can be saved from communism unless its government and people want to be saved."[31] He fully realized that without Asian support there could be no effective security pact. Yet there were grave doubts among the peoples of Asia as to the value of new military agreements as a means of saving them from communism. Burma refused to participate in the United States scheme. The conference of the Colombo powers (28 April—2 May) while strongly opposed to colonialism, was sharply divided over regional pacts. India distrusted a proposal which threatened neutralism and might involve positive action to check communist aggression. Indonesia declined the invitation to attend the proposed discussions. Thailand, the Philippines, and Pakistan agreed to co-operate. The inclusion of these three states was important because there was the danger that SEATO would become primarily a European grouping, and "a white man's

[29] Hobart *Mercury*, 17 Dec. 1952.
[30] *C.P.D.* (House of Representatives), Vol. 4, 5 Aug. 1954, pp. 66-67.
[31] Melbourne *Age*, 13 May 1954.

SEATO would be an effective fighting body, but it would not be an effective political body. Military resistance must have a firm political basis."[32] At the same time, it was clear that the effective military power of both the Philippines and Thailand was exceptionally limited, and that, in the eyes of some Asian states, they were so closely tied to the United States that they were occasionally referred to as American satellites. Pakistan's adherence, which arose largely out of a concern over the potential threat of India, meant an enormous enlargement of the geographical area covered by the pact.

The South East Asia Collective Defence Treaty,[33] signed by eight Pacific powers (Australia, France, New Zealand, Pakistan, the Philippines, Thailand, the United Kingdom, and the United States) at Manila on 8 September 1954, represented a partial but incomplete realization of the Australian desire for an effective regional pact. It was a very different document from that envisaged in April. Attempts to secure a tighter agreement, to give more effective teeth to the treaty, were unsuccessful. The preamble to the Manila Treaty specifically brings it within the ambit of the United Nations Charter. In Article I the parties undertake to "settle any international disputes in which they may be involved by peaceful means . . . and to refrain in their international relations from the threat or use of force in any manner inconsistent with the purposes of the United Nations." The defence obligations under Article IV(1) are defined in terms similar to those used in the ANZUS Pact: there is no automatic commitment to use force but agreement "to meet the common danger in accordance with . . . constitutional processes." Article IV(3) makes it clear that the treaty is not designed to stabilize or re-

---

[32] *The Economist* (London), cited in Sydney *Bulletin*, 2 June 1954. See also Melbourne *Herald*, 7 June 1954 and Melbourne *Age*, 8 June 1954.

[33] For text of the treaty, see U.S. Dept. of State *Bulletin*, Vol. XXXI (20 Sept. 1954), pp. 393-96, or *Current Notes*, *op. cit.*, Vol. 25 (1954), pp. 671-75. For a fuller discussion of Australian attitudes to it, see Greenwood and Harper, *op. cit.*, pp. 180-84; Norman Harper, "Australia and Regional Pacts 1950-1957," *The Australian Outlook*, Vol. 12 (1958), pp. 11-18.

establish colonialism in any form. One of the most significant features is the emphasis upon collaboration to "promote economic progress and social well-being"; this is reiterated in the Pacific Charter signed simultaneously with the treaty. The SEATO countries are pledged not merely to uphold rights of self-determination but to "cooperate in the economic, social and cultural fields in order to promote higher living standards, economic progress and social well-being in this region."

To Australia, the value of the treaty lay more perhaps in its moral implications than in the degree of military power that could be deployed in the event of aggression. The lukewarm Asian support for SEATO and an increasing American reluctance to assume further military commitments in Southeast Asia largely determined the shape of the Manila Treaty and made it a vastly different document from the tight treaty envisaged earlier. It added little to military security in Southeast Asia despite the suggestion of Sir John Slessor that long-range bomber fleets and atomic bombs provided effective back teeth.

Australian policy since the signature of the Manila Treaty has been largely directed toward putting flesh and blood on the military skeleton, to converting "an insurance policy and a deterrent into an effective shield to protect northern Australia" (R. G. Casey). These attempts to build an effective security arrangement in Southeast Asia were intensified with the development of the Formosan crisis at the end of 1954. Discussions in London at the Commonwealth Prime Ministers Conference in January 1955 were followed by conversations between Mr. Menzies, President Eisenhower, and Mr. John Foster Dulles in Washington. The extent to which Washington was prepared to commit itself is revealed in the following statement which was issued by Mr. Menzies after these talks:

> In the general task of preventing further Communist aggression, the United States considered the defence of South-East Asia, of which Malaya is an integral part, to be of very great importance . . . I was informed that though the tactical em-

ployment of forces was a matter . . . to be worked out in detail on the Services level, the United States considered that such effective co-operation was implicit in the Manila Pact.[34]

The Australian decision to station troops in Malaya (announced on 1 April 1955) was a significant departure in Australian defence and foreign policy. It was an attempt to give teeth to the Manila Treaty and to make specific the general defence commitments that Australia had pressed at the Bangkok meeting of the Manila powers (23-25 February 1955). Strategically, it involved an important switch in Australian policy. It meant the peace-time commitment of Australian ground troops outside Australia's territorial limits, a significant departure in defence planning. In the last two world wars, Australian troops fought as part of a British force in the Middle East. Now Malaya, an area of crucial importance to Australia, had tacitly, with British consent, also become an Australian responsibility.

In the post-war period, the old dilemma of the relative importance of sentiment and realism reared its head with renewed vigour. Australian policy has been based upon a frank acceptance of the crucial importance of the United States to the defence of Australia. While recognizing that Britain has "massive, specific and traditional commitments" in the Pacific, there is the equally strong recognition of the fact that Britain is heavily committed in Europe and the Middle East. The value of ANZUS and SEATO lies in the fact that they keep Australia in continuous touch with United States strategy; Australia is thus better able both to influence policy and to assert its own contributions. At the same time, as the Prime Minister pointed out, "We were neither isolationists nor purely regional in our outlook. We were simply saying that we would fit into the pattern of world defence in those places and respects which our geographical position and our limited resources rendered most

---

[34] See statement by Mr. Menzies to the House of Representatives, *Current Notes, op. cit.*, Vol. 26 (1955), pp. 281-91. The text of the agreed statement drafted in Washington is on pp. 289-90.

swift and effective."[35] The post-war record indicates that Australian defence and foreign policies have been framed with a perceptible swing towards support for the Pacific policies of the United States, at times at the expense of raising intra-Commonwealth difficulties. Yet this has never involved an uncritical acceptance of United States policies or a tendency to become an American satellite. Australia has consistently sought to pin down the United States to more precise military commitments in Southeast Asia. Australia has also been a friendly critic of American policies and has attempted to build a bridge between the United States, the United Kingdom, and Asia.

THE SUEZ CRISIS[36]

Although Australian defence policies in the Pacific have been increasingly orientated towards those of the United States, in the Middle East Australian interests have largely coincided with those of the United Kingdom. Traditionally, Australian defence planning before 1939 had been closely geared to British global and regional policies. It had rested on the assumption that Britain could, in the last analysis, provide the naval and air strength necessary to repel attacks upon Australia after Australia had perhaps borne the brunt of the initial attacks. This necessitated a string of imperial bases between London and Singapore to make effective imperial and Commonwealth defence plans in the Mediterranean and Indian Oceans. Gibraltar, Malta, Suez, Aden, Colombo, and Singapore were the key strategic bases along what had come to be described as the jugular vein of the Commonwealth. Australian forces served

---

[35] *C.P.D.* (House of Representatives), Vol. 4, 5 Aug. 1954, p. 68.

[36] For a full discussion of Australia and Suez, see Greenwood and Harper, *op. cit.*, pp. 341-56. Some of the economic conclusions on p. 341 need to be modified in the light of later research (see n. 37 below). See also W. Macmahon Ball, "The Australian Reaction to the Suez Crisis: July-December, 1956," *Australian Journal of Politics and History*, Vol. II (1957), pp. 129-50.

in the Middle East in two world wars to safeguard this vital line of communications.

The Middle East and Suez are of considerable economic importance to Australia. The oil reserves upon which Australia could draw are mainly located there. In recent years, refineries have been established at Kwinana (W. Australia), at Geelong and Altona (Victoria) and at Kurnell, Clyde and Matraville (New South Wales). These are capable of handling about four-fifths of Australia's refined petroleum needs. About 60 per cent of Australia's crude oil is imported from the Persian Gulf area so Suez is of no importance so far as Australian oil supplies are concerned. On the other hand, the volume of Australian trade through Suez (£900 millions) is considerable: it exceeds in volume and value the combined trade of India, Pakistan, and Ceylon and has been steadily increasing in volume. As an exporter of wool, wheat, meat, fruit, and other primary products, Australia has routed most of these exports to the United Kingdom, Germany, and France through Suez. In 1955, approximately 43 per cent of total exports went through the Canal. Canal traffic northward from Australia, although steadily increasing, has been declining relatively because of the sharp rise in tanker traffic from the Gulf ports to Europe. Imports via Suez have been much smaller. The machinery, textiles and other consumer goods imported from the United Kingdom have been shipped mainly via the Cape: Although the Cape route is 800 miles longer than the Suez run and adds perhaps 3-4 days to the length of a voyage, this has been largely offset by the heavy Canal charges. Approximately 12 per cent of Australia's imports passed through Suez in 1955. The Suez Canal, then, handled approximately 23 per cent of Australia's total trade. Canal tolls, freedom of navigation and the ability of the Canal to handle large passenger and cargo vessels are important issues for the Australian economy. The closing of the Canal could have a serious impact on that economy by raising freight costs which could gradually squeeze Australian goods out of export markets in Europe. But although valuable for passenger traffic, and more important for Australian exports than imports, "Suez is not vital to the Australian economy."[37]

The contraction of British influence in the Middle East and British recognition of the independence of India, Pakistan, Burma, and Ceylon left the northern top of the Indian Ocean as a weak and relatively exposed sector in the imperial system of defence. Britain's decision in July 1954 to withdraw its troops from the Suez Canal Zone meant a further weakening of the main line of strategic communications between London and Australia. This change brought a re-examination of Australian defence needs, and on 1 April 1955 Mr. Menzies announced the decision to station Australian troops in Malaya. This brought under more direct Australian control military forces operating outside Australia; it involved some small-scale assumption of responsibility by Australia for Asian defence. It meant the tacit abandonment of the Middle East as a sector to be defended by Australian troops. At the same time, Australian sentimental attachment to the Middle East remained deep, largely because soldiers had fought there in two wars, and Australian passenger traffic and ocean commerce still used Suez.

The nationalization of the Suez Canal Company by President Nasser on 26 July 1956 touched off the crisis which culminated in the armed intervention of Britain and France in Egypt on 31 October. The nationalization of the Canal threatened a breach of the 1888 Constantinople Convention guaranteeing free navigation of the Canal. It also raised a series of legal and political problems of compensation for the Canal Company, efficient operation of the Canal, the adoption of reasonable transit charges, and the provision of adequate safeguards for the improvement of Canal facilities. The Australian cabinet adopted as a basic principle of policy "freedom of passage through the Canal for all countries at all times without

---

[37] W. Woodruff & L. McGregor, *The Suez Canal and the Australian Economy* (Melbourne: Melbourne University Press, 1957), pp. 10, 18, 19-20; *Year Book of the Commonwealth of Australia, 1953* (Canberra: Govt. Printer, 1954), pp. 478-81.

discrimination, reasonable charges, and efficient operation."[38] In the absence of the Prime Minister, who was abroad, the cabinet decided upon a firm policy of action. There was no desire to use force, but no suggestion for action through the United Nations to settle a dispute in a sensitive strategic area. Dr. Evatt, leader of the Labour Opposition, was almost alone in insisting that the dispute be taken to the United Nations and in condemning threats of force against Egypt.[39]

The Australian government fully supported the attempts to resolve the Suez crisis outside the framework of the United Nations. Mr. Menzies, in a broadcast from London (13 August), insisted upon the need for negotiating "some new international agreement ensuring the continued use of the Suez Canal as an international waterway." He deprecated proposals for associating such an agreement with the United Nations. It was only after the breakdown of the first London Conference, attended by twenty-two interested nations, and failure of the Menzies mission to Cairo (3-9 September), that Great Britain and France brought the Suez situation to the attention of the Security Council (12 September). In a joint letter to the President of the Council, they said that the refusal of the Egyptian government to negotiate on the basis of the majority proposals made by the London Conference was "an aggravation of the situation which, if allowed to continue, would constitute a manifest danger to peace and security."[40] At the same time, discussions at the second London Conference (19-21 September) led to the formation of the Suez Canal Users' Association. When Egypt refused to recognize the new Association, Britain and France requested that the situation be considered by the Security Council.

Two days later (25 September) Mr. Menzies outlined Australian policy to the House of Representatives. To him, the economic

---

[38] *Current Notes, op. cit.*, Vol. 27 (1956), p. 489.

[39] Melbourne *Sun*, 9 Aug. 1956. He was supported a week later by the executive of the Federal Parliamentary Labour party.

[40] Security Council, Official Records (S.C.O.R.): 11th Year, *Supple. for July, August and September 1956*, pp. 28-29.

implications of a threat to the Canal were the most serious. "An open canal is essential to British prosperity, and . . . a closed canal could mean mass unemployment in Great Britain, a financial collapse there, a grievous blow at the central power of our Commonwealth, and the crippling of our greatest market and our greatest supplier." He vigorously defended Anglo-French action and repudiated the view that the dispute should have been immediately referred to the United Nations. The crucial problem was the use of force as a solution. Mr. Menzies argued that "we must avoid the use of force if we can. But we should not, by theoretical reasoning in advance of the facts and circumstances, contract ourselves out of its use *whatever those facts and circumstances may be*." Should the Security Council be deadlocked by a Russian veto,

> we can organize a full-blooded programme of economic sanctions against Egypt, *or* we can use force to restore international control of the Canal, *or* we can have further negotiations provided we do not abandon vital principles, *or* we can "call it a day," leave Egypt in command of the Canal, and resign ourselves to the total collapse of our position and interests in the Middle East. . . .[41]

The significant thing was that he insisted that force might properly be used for purposes other than self-defence or to enforce a decision of the United Nations, a view that was inconsistent with Australian obligations under the United Nations Charter.

Dr. Evatt bitterly attacked this view in a speech punctuated by heated interjections (from both sides). As the leader of a party accepting the principle of nationalization of public utilities he was anxious to ensure that the setting up of any kind of international control of the Canal should not restore the power of private shareholders. He was less concerned with the economic and strategic consequences of any interruption of Canal traffic than with the international consequences of action by the Canal users against

---

[41] *C.P.D.* (House of Representatives), Vol. 12, 25 Sept. 1956, pp. 824, 825. (Italics in press release of speech.)

Egypt. Resort to power politics in preference to mediation through the United Nations enhanced rather than diminished the risks of international conflict. Economic sanctions, the alternative proposed by Mr. Menzies, were not only provocative: they were also a form of warfare.[42]

Australian policy since July had been directed towards the settlement of the Canal dispute by an agreement providing for "free and open transit through the Canal without discrimination, overt or covert—this covers both political and technical aspects" and ensuring that "the operation of the Canal should be insulated from the politics of any country." These conditions were included in a six-point agreement on basic principles between the British, Egyptian, and French representatives approved by the Security Council on 13 October.[43] The Australian government's view was that the only effective way in which these principles could be implemented was to establish by a new international convention a body "charged with the operation, maintenance and development of the Canal." Egypt, as a member of such a body, would have a voice—but not a controlling voice—in its decisions.[44] In fact, no provision was made for implementing these principles. The Anglo-French draft resolution requesting Security Council endorsement of the London proposals was supported by nine members in the Council but was vetoed by the Soviet Union.

The Israeli invasion of Egypt and the Anglo-French ultimatum to Egypt on 30 October took the Australian government completely by surprise in spite of their knowledge that Israel was mobilizing. This was reflected in the initial uncertainty as to Australia's policy in the Security Council, an uncertainty arising out of sharp divisions within the Australian cabinet. On 30 October, the United States introduced a resolution calling upon Israel "immediately to withdraw its armed forces behind the established armistice lines"; it

---

[42] *Ibid.*, pp. 826-27.
[43] S.C.O.R., 11th Yr., 743rd Mtg., 13 Oct. 1956, p. 18.
[44] *Ibid.*, 737th Mtg., 8 Oct. 1956, p. 18.

k

called upon all members "to refrain from the use of force or threat of force in the area in any manner inconsistent with the purposes of the United Nations. . . ."[45] Australia abstained from voting on this resolution, but then supported the Russian resolution which omitted the provision calling on all members to refrain from the use or threat of force and from supplying arms or assistance to Israel. This was vetoed by Britain and France, with the United States abstaining.[46] Australia abstained again on the Yugoslav resolution calling for an emergency session of the General Assembly under the "Uniting for Peace" resolution of 1950.

The Australian government reacted swiftly and almost instinctively to support the British government as it had in 1914 and 1939. Mr. Menzies, in his statement to Parliament on 1 November, accepted at its face value the British assurance that the purpose of the intervention was to localize the conflict and to protect the Canal; as soon as the Security Council had dealt with the situation, British forces would be withdrawn. The action of the British government was "proper. . . . It seems to us to be quite realistic and to pay due regard to the moving and inexorable facts of life."[47] The British decision was a unilateral one without any consultation of the Dominions. In the earlier stages of the crisis, there had been direct discussions between Mr. Menzies and Sir Anthony Eden in London, but consultation with Canberra had been irregular since Mr. Menzies' Cairo mission.[48] Mr. Menzies' defence of Britain's failure to follow constitutional custom, on the grounds of emergency, was not a wholly convincing one, and it evoked strong criticism from Dr. Evatt.[49]

---

[45] *Ibid.*, 749th Mtg., 30 Oct. 1956, p. 31.

[46] *Ibid.*, 750th Mtg., 30 Oct. 1956, p. 5.

[47] *C.P.D.* (House of Representatives), Vol. 12, 1 Nov. 1956, p. 2059.

[48] Sir Arthur Fadden admitted on 13 September that Australia had been neither consulted nor informed about the Canal Users' Association. Melbourne *Herald* and Melbourne *Age*, 14 Sept. 1956.

[49] *C.P.D.* (House of Representatives), Vol. 12, 1 Nov. 1956, pp. 2064-66 and 8 Nov. 1956, pp. 2120-26.

The swift Australian official support for the British government resulted partly from the strong sentimental ties between Britain and Australia, partly from a conviction that Commonwealth unity should be preserved on what appeared to be a vital security matter, and partly from a strong disapproval of Egyptian action in nationalizing the Canal by unilateral action. When the General Assembly was hastily convened for its first emergency session under the 1950 "Uniting for Peace" resolution, it passed on 2 November a United States resolution (64 votes to 5, with 6 abstentions), urging "as a matter of priority" an immediate cease-fire and the halting of the movement of all military forces and arms to the area.[50] Australia was in a minority which included the three belligerent powers and New Zealand. Australia abstained both on the Canadian resolution (3 November) requesting the Secretary-General to submit within 48 hours a plan for the creation of a United Nations emergency force and on the second Canadian resolution the following day establishing a United Nations Command and authorizing the recruitment of officers from states other than permanent members of the Security Council.

Australian policy of support for Great Britain brought virtual isolation in the United Nations. The policy itself was adopted in spite of criticisms in the cabinet itself and in face of strong opposition in Parliament and from public opinion. A significant minority in the cabinet, led by Mr. Casey, opposed the use of force because it could split the Commonwealth by antagonizing the Asian members and antagonize the United States. Dr. Evatt repudiated what he described as "gun-boat diplomacy" and repeated his earlier attack upon the "new theory about . . . force in international affairs . . . that you can use force without the authority of the United Nations if you think it is right that it should be used. . . . That is an absolutely intolerable and illegal doctrine. . . . Military force can be

---

[50] G.A.O.R., 1st Emerg. Special Sess., 561st and 562nd Plenary Mtgs., 1 Nov. 1956, pp. 11-12 and 34-35. For statements by the Australian delegate, see *ibid.*, pp. 27-29, and 563rd Plenary Mtg., 3 Nov. 1956, p. 72.

used only with the authorization of the United Nations, or in self-defence in the case of armed attack against one's nation."[51] Public opinion hardened over the wisdom of British policy and split deeply when bombing attacks on Port Said commenced.[52]

For ten days in November, Australia and New Zealand were isolated in company with the three "aggressors" in the United Nations. On 6 November, Egypt severed diplomatic relations with Australia as a means of retaliation for the Australian endorsement of British action. The acceptance of a cease-fire and the Assembly decision to create a United Nations Emergency Force eased the tension and helped end Australian isolation in an international body which had expressed by overwhelming vote its moral disapproval of Anglo-French action. Australia offered military forces for UNEF, but their exclusion was a wise decision by the United Nations commander. The first task of Australian diplomacy was now to secure through the United Nations a general settlement of the Suez problem and to try to re-establish stability in an area which threatened to become a political vacuum.

So far as Australian strategic policies were concerned, the Suez episode was less serious than it would have been had Australian troops been involved. Relations with the United States were not impaired, but the crisis underlined the importance of relying on United States rather than British support east of Suez. "The practicalities of to-day indicate that if Australia is to have a continuing Western ally occupying the [Pacific] region that ally must be the United States."[53] More serious immediately was the jolt that Australian policy gave to the Asian members of the Commonwealth and to the SEATO powers. India had advanced its own proposals for a compromise mainly favourable to Egypt, and Mr. Nehru had condemned the Canal Users' Association as "full of dangerous

---

[51] *C.P.D.* (House of Representatives), Vol. 12, 1 Nov. 1956, p. 2062.

[52] For further discussion of reactions in Parliament, the press, and public opinion, see below pp. 292-95 and 307-12.

[53] E. H. Cox in Melbourne *Herald*, 3 Nov. 1956.

possibilities and far-reaching consequences." To India, the British-French attack upon Egypt was "naked aggression," "a flagrant violation of the U.N. Charter" which could not be tolerated by "the self-respecting and independent nations of Asia and Africa." Pakistan, a member of the SEATO and Baghdad Pacts, condemned the "aggression" which "constitutes a threat to the entire Moslem world."[54] Thailand and the Philippines joined the other Asian powers in demanding a cease-fire and United Nations action to deal with the crisis. Mr. Casey's assessment of Asian reactions to British and Australian policy was painfully accurate. Australia's stand on Suez aligned it with "colonialist powers" and appeared likely both to weaken SEATO and to threaten much of the work accomplished through the Colombo Plan to establish friendly relations between Australia and the countries of Asia. In the months following Suez, Mr. Casey had a great deal of fence-mending to do in Asia.

ECONOMIC POLICIES AND SECURITY

Australian short-term security has been sought primarily in military terms; long-term security is a matter of politics and economics as well as of military power. Yet Australian governments have been fully aware that the short-term problem is an economic as well as a military one, that in dealing with both short- and long-term problems a primarily military approach is far too limited, and that it is necessary to divorce economic from military considerations as far as this is practicable. This is clear from consistent Australian support for the United Nations Economic Commission for Asia and the Far East (ECAFE). It is equally clear from Australian support for the United Nations technical assistance program and for the Colombo Plan.

Australia's sponsorship of the Colombo Plan reflected a complex of motives and interests: the idealism of the early post-war period,

---

[54] *Keesing's Contemporary Archives* (London), Vol. X, 1955-1956, p. 15209; *The New York Times*, 4 Nov. 1956. For Asian reactions, see *Asian Recorder*, Vol. I (1956), pp. 1138-43, 1152-55.

the real humanitarian interest in the welfare of underdeveloped communities, and the belief that Australian security, long-term and short-term, depended upon the preservation of political stability through economic action. The belief that full employment would help to remove the economic and social causes of war was reiterated in the Colombo Plan. In its origin, the plan reflected no great originality on the part of Mr. Spender, the Minister for External Affairs, or the Australian government. The significant thing is that at the first Commonwealth Conference held in Asia, political problems proved too intractable for agreement. To Asians, the primary issues were, as Mr. Senanayake of Ceylon pointed out, the economic needs of Asia. "The degree of success which followed [the Spender Resolution] is perhaps the measure of the failure to achieve any political or defence agreement designed to buttress anti-communist defences."[55]

In the particular context of security policies, there is a danger that the humanitarian aspects of the Colombo Plan may be lost sight of. The purpose of the plan was essentially to assist governments in the area to mobilize their productive resources in accordance with plans they drafted themselves; the sponsoring governments, including Australia, were to make capital available to accelerate this process and to provide experts to administer, or to advise upon, any developmental plans approved. The comprehensive developmental programs drafted in the initial stages provided for a total capital investment of £1,868 millions, primarily to promote agriculture, transport, and communications. The Australian contribution was to be £A31.25 million, together with £A3.5 million for technical assistance over a six-year period. A permanent Consultative Committee was set up by the Colombo Conference, and the first meeting

---

[55] R. G. Neale, "Australian Interests In and Attitudes Towards Economic Assistance to Asia," in *Australian Policies Toward Asia, op. cit.*, Part V, p. 4. This is by far the best analysis of Australian policy and attitudes towards the Colombo Plan. See also E. E. Ward, "The Colombo Plan," *The Australian Outlook*, Vol. 5 (1951), pp. 191-202, and Greenwood and Harper, *op. cit.*, pp. 143-47.

was held in May 1950 in Sydney. The Australian government in 1952 set up an Economic and Technical Assistance Section in the Department of External Affairs "to expedite the procurement of supplies against contributions in the light of requests from recipient governments and Australian availabilities."[56] It was realized from the beginning that it was desirable to include non-Commonwealth countries in the plan: the United States, Cambodia, Laos, and Vietnam joined the group of Colombo Plan countries in 1951, Burma and Nepal in 1952, Indonesia in 1953, and Japan, the Philippines and Thailand in 1954.

The Colombo Plan was based upon the assumption that for the countries of South and Southeast Asia, "economic improvement is indispensable to social stability and necessary to strengthen their free institutions." The real problems were population pressure and poverty rather than self-government. At the same time, Australia realized that poverty invites communism and that by preventing the spread of poverty, the spread of communism could be checked. The political significance of measures of economic reconstruction had to be emphasized in Australia for reasons of domestic politics as well as for security purposes: purely humanitarian policies stand little chance of success if they involve increased taxation. The political objects behind the Colombo Plan were frankly recognized by Mr. Spender.

> Our policy must be to ensure . . . that these new States [i.e. Pakistan, Ceylon, India, Indonesia, Vietnam, Laos, and Cambodia] co-operate with each other and with us in meeting positively and actively the new problems created in this area by the emergence of Communist China and by the ever-increasing thrust of communism which endeavours to ally itself, in the pursuit of its ends, with the millions of people of South-East Asia.

[56] United Kingdom, Command Paper 8529, *The Colombo Plan: The First Annual Report of the Consultative Ctte. on Economic Development in South and South-East Asia*, Karachi, March 1952 (London: H. M. Stationery Office, 1952), pp. 55-56.

We live side by side with the countries of South and South-East Asia, and we desire to be on good-neighbour terms with them. Above all, it is in our interest to foster commercial and other contacts with them and give them what help we can in maintaining stable and democratic governments in power, and increasing the material welfare of their people. In doing so we take the long view. We will be helping to provide them and ourselves with the best defence against the effective penetration of Communist imperialism.[57]

The object of the plan and of government policy was succinctly described by Mr. Spender as "to draw the teeth of Communist imperialism by carefully applied measures of economic assistance." Continued support for the plan was due partly to the hard fact that "we feel the hot breath of international communism on our necks in Australia."[58] It was also due to an appreciation of the fact that economic well-being, like peace, is indivisible. It was perfectly clear that the Australian contribution would be no more than a "drop in the bucket" in terms of Asian needs. Australia itself was an underdeveloped country, importing capital, and with only a limited supply of capital for use outside the country. Australian policy involved, up to a point, a deliberate preference for overseas investment for economic, political, and strategic purposes as compared with national developmental projects. The plan would, from an Australian point of view, be a token of goodwill, a means of establishing a closer working relationship among the participating countries, a method of increasing stability. It was, as Mr. Casey (Minister for External Affairs since 1950) put it, a potent weapon in that "contest for the minds and hearts of the peoples of Asia that lies at the heart of the power conflict in Asia." Much more important, Australia could use its initiative to obtain the effective economic collaboration in Asia of the United Kingdom and the United States.

---

[57] *C.P.D.*, Vol. 206, 9 March 1950, pp. 623 and 628.
[58] R. G. Casey, Brisbane *Telegraph*, 13 July 1954.

Economic aid is a major instrument of national foreign and security policies today. The danger lies in attaching either economic or political strings, and in direct interference in the domestic affairs of the recipient countries. Australian aid under the Colombo Plan has never had any strings at all. "There are no conditions attached to what we are seeking to do other than what we are glad to provide will be applied towards the broad purpose that both you and we have in mind." Aid has been given only in response to requests which are examined by the Minister and his staff as to "the nature of the project, the end use of the goods . . . , and their cost and availability in Australia."[59] The recipient governments formally report periodically on the manner in which the aid has been used. The requests for assistance are dealt with on their merits regardless of the social or political institutions of the country concerned; where a number of similar requests have been made, priority may have to be given because of the limits of Australian resources rather than because of political considerations. In the final analysis, aid is based on Australia's own interests in the area; this is no way retards social and economic progress in the recipient countries or imposes political strings.

Foreign economic policy performs as vital a role for security in this area as purely military agreements, perhaps in the long run a more important one. The signature of the Pacific Charter at Manila, on 8 September 1954, was a recognition of this fact. "It must be a constructive political document which will help the Colombo governments in their fight against local Communists."[60] The Australian government realizes the vital importance of economic policies and the danger of confusing economic and military programs; for this reason it has attempted to keep the Colombo Plan distinct from the ANZUS and SEATO Pacts. This view is based on the hard fact that "to the north of Australia, excluding the 460 million

---

[59] R. G. Casey, in *Current Notes, op. cit.*, Vol. 25 (1954), p. 14.
[60] *The Economist* (London), cited in Sydney *Bulletin*, 15 Sept. 1954.

Chinese, there are approximately 700,000,000 or 800,000,000 Eastern peoples. If this country cannot be on friendly terms with the people of the East, irrespective of the forms of government that they have, the outlook for future Australian generations will be very bad" (Mr. J. B. Chifley, 1950).[61]

CONCLUSION

There is general agreement among Australian political parties in their assessment of the potential threats to Australian security. Undue importance is perhaps attached to the view that Australia would be the primary target of a resurgent militarist Japan: this arises possibly more out of Australia's feeling of self-importance than from a realistic appraisal of the power situation in the Pacific. It also arises because Australian immigration policy is criticized by the overpopulated countries of Asia, such as Japan and India, as well as by all Asian nations which feel that the policy is based on racial discrimination. Most Australians feel that "our immigration policy is not based on colour prejudice or on an assumption of racial superiority."[62]

Given Australia's geographical position and resources, there is little effective choice in matters of security if one discards, as the vast majority of Australians do, the alternative of isolationism and neutrality. The means to security lie in the five alternatives which must in fact be pursued simultaneously.[63] In the last resort Australia must depend on external assistance from the United Kingdom and the United States. Despite Australia's sentimental and traditional attachments to the Commonwealth, it has become clear that the United States is the only democratic power capable of concentrating massive force in the Pacific area. This is why so much importance

---

[61] *C.P.D.*, Vol. 209, 27 Sept. 1950, p. 24.

[62] *Brisbane Courier-Mail*, 9 July 1954.

[63] See above, pp. 109-10.

has been attached by Australia to the ANZUS and SEATO Pacts. The advances in nuclear weapons since 1954 have merely confirmed the Australian view.

What part does the United Nations play in providing security for Australia, and hence in Australian foreign and defence policies? How can Asian goodwill towards Australia be enhanced in the political battle for the mind and soul of Asia? The problem resolves itself into two parts: military and economic. At the military level, all political parties in Australia accept the proposition that any improvement in the international situation permits a reduction of defence effort. This is of course equally true of every peaceful country in the world. The Australian view in 1950 was that at present the United Nations "is manifestly unable to protect Australian interests" and that it is therefore the duty of the government to "follow simultaneously a policy of making supplementary arrangements among those whom we know to be our friends."[64] Australian pressure to conclude a Pacific pact and its defence policies reflect the failure of the United Nations to maintain international harmony and its lack of power to maintain peace.

The fact that the United Nations does not play a primary role in Australia's security calculations did not prevent Australia from giving the strongest possible support to the United Nations in Korea. Participation in the Korean action enabled Australia to act in support of the United States through international channels. The argument of international duty influenced the decision. But as Sir Horace Robertson (formerly Commander of British Commonwealth Forces in Korea) pointed out, Australia was also fighting in Korea to ensure that it would receive assistance from other countries if it became the victim of aggression. The Suez episode confirmed the Australian belief that the United Nations lacked military power despite the creation of the United Nations Emergency Force, "a fragmentary . . . force which is pretty clearly not designed

---

[64] *C.P.D.*, Vol. 206, 9 March 1950, p. 638 (Mr. Spender).

to be a fighting body."[65] In a general way, the United Nations can contribute to Australian security by improving relations between the protagonists in the "cold war," and by promoting Asian welfare. But the direct contribution of the United Nations is felt to be small compared with that offered by regional pacts within the ambit of the United Nations and by the direct cultivation of Commonwealth and Asian friendship. Suez showed that overwhelming pressure of public opinion could make the United Nations an effective force in dealing with aggression by democratic states; Hungary demonstrated the impotence of the United Nations in handling totalitarian aggression.

At the economic level, Australia works closely with the United Nations, operating through ECAFE and the specialized agencies. Yet while supporting the United Nations economic and technical assistance programs, Australia has made its main contribution to the development of Asian welfare outside this framework. The Colombo Plan, conceived as a Commonwealth rather than a United Nations project, was designed to improve relations between Australia and its Asian neighbours. Australia's long-term and short-term interests in this vital strategic area tie Australia with Asia more closely than do the interests of any other Western member of the United Nations. Australia felt it important to receive credit and goodwill for capital investment and technical assistance it contributed. The Colombo Plan and United Nations economic policies complement one another; the significant thing is that Australia felt it necessary to operate outside rather than inside the ambit of the United Nations.

---

[65] Mr. R. G. Menzies, 30 Nov. 1956. *Current Notes, op. cit.*, Vol. 27 (1956), p. 748.

chapter six

The Problem of Domestic Jurisdiction

> Nothing contained in the present Charter shall authorize the United Nations to intervene in matters which are essentially within the domestic jurisdiction of any state or shall require the Members to submit such matters to settlement under the present Charter; but this principle shall not prejudice the application of enforcement measures under Chapter VII. (Article 2(7))

To countries accepting the Austinian or similar theories of sovereignty, one of the major difficulties to be faced in joining an international organization has been the question of how far national sovereignty would be impaired. Apart from the juristic problem, there has always been the pragmatic political question: how far will membership of such an organization impinge upon, or impair control of, matters regarded as of vital importance by the governments or nationals of the member states? Traditionally, states have been peculiarly sensitive to matters affecting their national honour, their economics, and their social systems. Accordingly, international law has come to recognize certain matters as of purely domestic concern unless regulated explicitly by treaty provisions. The questions of tariffs, of immigration policies, of the maintenance of living standards, and of the granting of citizenship, for example, have come by custom and precedent to be so regarded. To Australia the establishment and preservation of secondary industries and the maintenance of living standards and ethnic homogeneity by control of immigration have come to be regarded as sacrosanct: no government prepared seriously to jeopardize these could secure popular support. Unrestricted national controls over such matters has always been a necessary condition of Australian membership of any international body. Australia is not unique in this respect.

In recognition of the reluctance of states to permit any interference in their internal affairs, the Covenant of the League of Nations provided (Article 15(8)) that:

> if the dispute between the parties is claimed by one of them, and is found by the Council, to arise out of a matter which by international law is solely within the domestic jurisdiction of that party, the Council shall so report, and shall make no recommendation as to its settlement.

It was, for example, because of Australia's desire to safeguard its freedom of action on matters normally recognized by international law as being within the domestic jurisdiction of a state that W. M. Hughes in 1919 had pressed for the creation of a special class C mandate permitting the application of Australian tariff and migration policies to New Guinea. Recognizing that the increasing interdependence of nations made the nineteenth century concept of domestic jurisdiction less than adequate to twentieth century conditions, the governments in drawing up the Dumbarton Oaks proposals for the creation of the United Nations accorded the domestic jurisdiction principle a relatively unimportant position: it was merely an exception to those provisions relating to the pacific settlement of disputes. However, at San Francisco the "domestic jurisdiction" clause was inserted in Article 2 as one of the basic principles of the United Nations.

This was an issue upon which Australia had clear-cut opinions. Dr. Evatt took a prominent part in the successful attempts to enlarge those sections of the Charter relating to human rights, economic and social activities, and the competence of the Assembly to consider and make recommendations on all matters within the scope of the Charter. Yet at the same time, he played an equally prominent part in attempting to strengthen the provision in Article 2(7) limiting the scope of authority of the Organization. The Australian delegation at San Francisco supported the view that the United Nations should be prohibited from interfering in matters "essentially" (as opposed to "solely") within the domestic jurisdiction of a state. It opposed the view that the Organization should itself decide what matters came within the scope of domestic jurisdiction (although agreeing that the advice of the International Court of Justice on this point might in some case be useful), and fought a successful battle to amend the Dumbarton Oaks proposals to ensure that even in connection with threats to the peace and acts of aggression the Organization would not be permitted to make recommendations concerning matters essentially within the domestic jurisdiction of a state.[1]

Despite the Evatt amendments to Article 2(7), it still remained ambiguous and appeared to conflict with Articles 10, 14, 55, and 56 of the Charter. The word "essentially" is "a piece of philosophical and legal jargon, tracing back to Aristotelian distinctions between essentials and accidents, and like most such words, is very indeterminate."[2] Its meaning may be clarified either by political debate involving value judgments, or by a judicial decision as to its "true" meaning. In consequence, there has been considerable disagreement

---

[1] See above, pp. 62-63. The substitution of the word "essentially" for "solely" in the final draft of Article 2(7) was the work primarily of Dr. Evatt.

[2] G. Sawer in Gordon Greenwood and Norman Harper, eds., *Australia in World Affairs, 1950-55* (Melbourne: F. W. Cheshire, 1957), p. 99.

within the United Nations whether the Security Council, the General Assembly, or the International Court of Justice was the appropriate body to define the meaning of the phrase and so the competence of the United Nations. What has been Australia's attitude and what have been the attitudes of those powers with which Australia has been broadly in agreement, e.g., the United States, the United Kingdom, the non-Asian British Dominions, France, and the Netherlands? (These states are referred to in this chapter as the "domestic jurisdiction group" although, as will be evident, they have taken varied positions concerning the application of Article 2(7) to some of the specific issues which have come before the United Nations.)

THE LABOUR GOVERNMENT AND
DOMESTIC JURISDICTION 1946-49

In 1946, India, under Articles 10 and 14, brought before the United Nations General Assembly charges that the policies of the Union of South Africa, particularly the Asian Land Tenure and Indian Representation Act of 1946, contravened both the Charter and the Capetown agreement between the two governments. An Assembly resolution adopted in December of that year declared that the treatment of persons of Indian origin in South Africa had impaired friendly relations between the two states and that such treatment should be in conformity with the international obligations accepted by the two governments. It requested the two governments to report to the next session of the Assembly on the measures adopted to achieve this objective. Australia did not take part in the long committee discussion concerning the competence of the United Nations. Along with twenty-three other members, including Canada, the Netherlands, South Africa, the United Kingdom, and the United States, Australia opposed the proposal adopted in committee.[3] When

---

[3] France supported the proposal; New Zealand abstained. For the vote, see General Assembly, Official Records (G.A.O.R.): 1st Sess., 2nd Part, Joint 1st and 6th Cttes., 6th Mtg., 30 Nov. 1946, p. 51.

the proposal was voted upon in plenary session, Australia shifted its position slightly and abstained, after having supported an alternative but unsuccessful proposal to request an advisory opinion from the International Court of Justice concerning the application of Article 2(7) in this instance.[4]

A year later the question was raised again by India, which had meanwhile imposed economic sanctions on the ground that South Africa had refused to negotiate on the basis of the Assembly resolution. A draft resolution reaffirming the 1946 resolution and requesting both governments to hold round-table discussions on the basis of that resolution and to report to the Assembly thereon, was supported by a majority but lapsed because it lacked the requisite two-thirds majority. Again Australia did not take part in the debate. Along with other members of the "domestic jurisdiction group," Australia voted against the proposal.[5] Much of the opposition to the draft resolution probably arose from the belief that South Africa would refuse to co-operate if the resolution were passed rather than from any doubt as to the Assembly's competence in the matter.

A further debate on the issue took place in the Assembly in May 1949. New Zealand and the United Kingdom expressed grave doubts as to the powers of the Assembly and were reluctant to proceed to a resolution. Canada and France considered that the Assembly could discuss the situation but not intervene. The United States considered it permissible for the Assembly to express an opinion "in the form of a recommendation designed to assist the parties in reaching a decision."[6] Australia ignored the question of competence and abstained on a South African proposal that the Assembly declare that the question was completely within the domestic juris-

---

[4] The Netherlands, New Zealand, South Africa, the United Kingdom, and the United States all voted in favour of the request for an advisory opinion and voted against the proposal adopted. See *ibid.*, 52nd Plenary Mtg., 8 Dec. 1946, p. 1061.

[5] France, however, voted in favour of the proposal. G.A.O.R., 2nd Sess., 120th Plenary Mtg., 20 Nov. 1947, pp. 1169-70.

[6] G.A.O.R., 3rd Sess., 2nd Part, 1st Ctte., 266 Mtg., 10 May 1949, p. 294.

diction of South Africa. This proposal was defeated, securing only five votes in its favour.[7]

During the discussion at this session on other proposals, Australia objected to the adoption of any condemnatory resolution, considering that the only hope of a solution lay in mutual agreement between the parties. Accordingly, Australia opposed an Indian suggestion that a committee be appointed to study the problem and report to the Assembly, and in committee opposed a French-Mexican proposal that India, Pakistan, and South Africa be invited "to enter into discussion at a round-table conference taking into consideration the purposes and principles of the Charter of the United Nations and the Declaration of Human Rights." Australia then proposed, unsuccessfully, a resolution omitting all reference to the Charter and the Declaration, and merely calling on the governments to "renew their efforts to reach an agreement . . . through round-table conference or by other means such as mediation and conciliation." In the plenary session, however, Australia voted for the French-Mexican proposal, which was passed by a vote of 47 in favour, 10 abstentions, with only South Africa opposing.[8]

Australian policy on the question of treatment of Indians in South Africa[9] was both cautious and fluid. To a greater degree than the other powers sensitive to questions of domestic jurisdiction, Australia refused to commit itself on the specific issue of domestic

---

[7] *Ibid.*, 268th Mtg., 11 May 1949, p. 321. South Africa was supported only by Argentina, Brazil, Greece, and the Netherlands; Canada, France, New Zealand, and the United Kingdom all abstained.

[8] As for the votes of the other members of the "domestic jurisdiction group," South Africa voted against the proposals; the United Kingdom abstained except to vote against the Indian proposal; France and the United States also voted against the Indian proposal with Canada, the Netherlands, and New Zealand abstaining. All five of these countries voted with the majority in favour of the French-Mexican proposal. For the voting in committee and plenary meetings, see G.A.O.R., 3rd Sess., 2nd Part, 1st Ctte., 11 May 1949, pp. 321-24, and 212th Plenary Mtg., 14 May 1949, p. 455. For the text of the various proposals, see *ibid.*, Annexes to 1st Ctte., p. 23, and General Assembly Resolution 265(III), 14 May 1949.

[9] For the Australian attitude after 1949, when the Liberal government replaced the Labour government, see below, pp. 170-71.

jurisdiction; at the same time, Australia preferred to avoid any reference to general Charter obligations as justifying a General Assembly resolution. Although abstaining when South Africa sought to claim the issue as one completely within its domestic jurisdiction, Australia did vote with the majority in favour of the French-Mexican proposal in 1949. Australia's only inexplicable and inconsistent vote occurred in 1946, when Australia abstained instead of joining forces with Canada, New Zealand, and the United Kingdom in opposition to the original resolution on the question.

On several occasions, the Australian Labour government was in the unusual position of opposing those states attempting to prevent United Nations action on an issue by relying on the "domestic jurisdiction" clause. Among these issues were the questions of Indonesia, Spain, the Russian wives, and the violation of human rights in Hungary, Bulgaria, and Romania. The first two issues came before the Security Council; the latter two arose in the Assembly, and here Australia took a leading role, even parting company in some degree with those countries with which it usually agreed on the application of Article 2(7).

In March 1949 Australia and several Latin American countries took the initiative in bringing before the General Assembly the general question of the observance of fundamental freedoms in Bulgaria and Hungary, and the specific question of the recent trials of church leaders in those countries. From the outset Australia's views on the application of Article 2(7) to the issues differed from those of the countries with whom Australia was generally in agreement. When at the very outset of the discussions the question of jurisdiction arose, Dr. Evatt expressed the view that "the right of discussion provided for in Article 10 of the Charter was one of its most important provisions." He went on to state:

> There was no question or problem which came within the scope of the Charter and which concerned its aims, its principles or any one of its provisions, which could not be discussed by the General Assembly. If any question could be

covered by an Article of the Charter, that question could no longer be held to be a matter essentially within the domestic jurisdiction of a State.[10]

The United States view came close to Dr. Evatt's but stopped short of it: the discussion was justified by various articles of the Charter (10, 14, 55, and 56), but "any action by the General Assembly beyond a debate of the issue involved would have to be examined on its merits and in the light of all relevant Articles . . .", including presumably Article 2(7).[11]

The United Kingdom, however, adopted a different approach: the fact that in the peace treaties Hungary and Bulgaria had specifically undertaken the obligation to ensure the free exercise of human rights was sufficient to place the question outside the scope of Article 2(7). There was no incompatibility here with the usual British argument which on other occasions Australia had supported, namely, that the United Nations could only intervene where there was a breach of specific obligations. However, in this case Australia refused to base United Nations competence on the treaties. Dr. Evatt argued that "the provisions of a treaty between different countries did not affect the jurisdiction of the United Nations if such jurisdiction already existed."[12] Accordingly, Australia sponsored a proposal which noted "the violation of the principles set forth in the Preamble and in the Purposes of the United Nations Charter" and sought to establish an eleven-member committee to study the situation in the two countries concerned.[13] This proposal was supported only by Chile, Cuba, Lebanon, and New Zealand. Thus Australia, for no apparent reason, parted company with most of the "domestic jurisdiction group," basing a claim for United Nations intervention on Article 55 and urging relatively strong measures. After its own

---

[10] G.A.O.R., 3rd Sess., 2nd Part, General Ctte., 58th Mtg., 6 April 1949, pp. 15-16.

[11] *Ibid.*, 189th Plenary Mtg., 12 April 1949, p. 12.

[12] *Ibid.*, General Ctte., 58th Mtg., 6 April 1949, p. 16.

[13] *Ibid.*, *Ad Hoc* Pol. Ctte., Annexes: p. 9.

proposal was defeated, however, Australia joined with the other members of the group[14] and voted in favour of the resolution adopted by the Assembly. The preamble of this resolution stated that Bulgaria and Hungary had acted contrary to the purposes of the Charter but stressed the obligations of the two countries under the peace treaties. It is significant that the resolution contained no reference to the Charter provisions relating to human rights. It merely noted the accusations, expressed the hope that measures would be taken in accordance with the treaties, and "most urgently" drew the attention of Bulgaria and Hungary "to their obligations under the Peace Treaties."[15]

At the next session of the Assembly the same differences recurred on this issue. Australia again based the competence of the United Nations solely on Article 55 and unsuccessfully attempted to set up an investigating committee. Australia, however, along with the other members of the "domestic jurisdiction group," voted in favour of the resolution finally adopted by the Assembly, which requested opinions from the International Court of Justice as to whether a dispute of the nature provided for in the treaties existed, and whether the dispute could be settled in accordance with the procedure provided in the treaties if Hungary, Bulgaria, and Romania refused to appoint representatives to the commissions as required by the treaties. An initiative by the Netherlands secured the insertion in the preamble of a reference to Article 55 of the Charter and the moral responsibility of the United Nations to promote the observance of human rights.[16]

The basis for the opposition to the Australian proposal was not that it was "illegal" or inconsistent with Article 2(7), but rather that it was regarded as premature and too drastic. The significant

---

[14] South Africa did not take part in the voting but the South African delegate had previously denied the competence of the Assembly to intervene.

[15] General Assembly Resolution 272(III), 30 April 1949.

[16] General Assembly Resolution 294(IV), 22 Oct. 1949. For the Australian proposal, see G.A.O.R., 4th Sess., *Ad Hoc* Pol. Ctte., 7th Mtg., 4 Oct. 1949, pp. 25-27.

thing was that the majority of members saw no reason to take advantage of a means whereby they could avoid claiming that the Charter *per se* permitted intervention on questions involving alleged violations of human rights in general.

On the Russian wives question, also discussed for the first time at the third session of the General Assembly, Australia virtually reversed its position vis-a-vis the rest of the "domestic jurisdiction group." On this occasion, Australia was more eager than the others to base United Nations consideration on something firmer than general Charter principles. The question arose out of an allegation that the USSR was violating fundamental human rights, traditional diplomatic practices, and the principles of the Charter by preventing the Soviet wives of foreign nationals from leaving Russia to join their husbands. The final resolution, introduced by Chile and supported by Australia, contained references to the Preamble and Articles 1(3) and 55(c) of the Charter, declared that such measures as were complained of were not in conformity with the Charter, and recommended that the Soviet government withdraw such measures.[17] All the members of the "domestic jurisdiction group" supported the resolution except that South Africa abstained. Australia's approach to the problem, however, seems to have been somewhat different from that of the United Kingdom and the United States. Australia suggested that the International Court be asked for an advisory opinion on the subsidiary point, whether restriction on the movements of members of the families of foreign diplomats was contrary to international law. Apparently, Australia would have preferred to deal solely with the narrower questions in order to avoid reliance on the provisions of the Charter. Canada, the United Kingdom, and the United States had fewer misgivings in supporting the Chilean proposal, presumably because the interests of some of their nationals, husbands of Soviet wives, were involved.

Another specific case of alleged violation of human rights arose

---

[17] General Assembly Resolution 285(III), 25 April 1949.

in October 1949 during the consideration of the relations between Greece and its northern neighbours. The USSR proposed that the First Committee of the General Assembly call upon the Greek government to suspend and rescind death sentences imposed on eight persons accused of political offenses. The committee (with all of the members of the "domestic jurisdiction group" voting with the majority) decided that it was not competent to vote on the Soviet proposal. At the same time, however, the committee decided that it was competent to request the President of the General Assembly to negotiate with the Greek government for the suspension of the sentences, while the Conciliation Commission on the Balkans was carrying out its efforts to bring about a settlement of the issues in dispute. The "domestic jurisdiction group" was divided on the question of the competence of the committee to entertain this latter proposal. France, the Netherlands, and New Zealand voted in favour of the committee's competence; Canada and the United Kingdom were opposed; Australia, South Africa, and the United States abstained.[18] Australia's abstention may have arisen out of anxiety at the action of the Greek government without any intention of creating a precedent for intervention. The existence of the Conciliation Committee made this position possible, since the death sentences could be considered relevant to the issues before that Committee.

While Australia was a member of the Security Council in 1946-47 there was considerable discussion concerning the application of Article 2(7). One of the first of these discussions arose over the Spanish question which was brought before the Council in April 1946. Communist opposition to the Franco regime had long been evident, but with the development of the "cold war" some of the Western powers were becoming less critical of the Spanish government. Poland claimed that the existence and activities of the Franco government had led to international friction and endangered inter-

[18] See G.A.O.R., 4th Sess., 1st Ctte., 297th Mtg., 26 Oct. 1949, p. 112.

national peace, and that the Security Council should therefore take action under Chapter VII of the Charter and call upon member states to sever diplomatic relations with Spain.

Preliminary discussions in the Security Council produced agreement that the Council had the power to study the situation to consider what action should be taken. An Australian proposal to establish a sub-committee of enquiry was adopted without opposition; it had the political advantage of providing a period during which tempers might cool. The USSR abstained on the ground that the facts were self-evident and that such an investigation was unnecessary.

The Australian delegate adopted a judicial approach. *Prima facie*, the question was one of domestic jurisdiction. The mere existence of a fascist government did not give the United Nations the right to intervene. However, if on investigation there was proof that this government's policy and activities were of international concern, the subject would be within the ambit of the Charter. The argument suggested that there was evidence from previous multilateral resolutions and declarations condemning the Franco regime that the matter was of international concern. Further evidence would be required before the Council could properly decide that it was a source of international friction or a danger to international peace and security. The evidence so far presented was contradictory. He pointed out in conclusion that if it were decided after investigation that United Nations action were justified, then stronger action than the severence of diplomatic relations would be necessary.[19]

Australia chaired a sub-committee (including Brazil, China, France, and Poland) which, after a month of detailed study, presented a unanimous report, subject to certain Polish reservations. The substance of the report was that: (1) The Council could not, on the existing evidence, determine that there existed a "threat to the peace" and consequently could not give any directions under

---

[19] Security Council, Official Records (S.C.O.R.): 1st Year, 1st Series, No. 2, 35th Mtg., 18 April 1946, pp. 194-98.

Articles 41 and 42. (Poland's reservation claimed that such action could be taken.) (2) The situation was one "likely to endanger the maintenance of international peace and security" (Chapter VI, Article 34). (3) The Council accordingly under Chapter VI, Article 36, should "recommend appropriate procedures or methods of adjustment." (4) The appropriate procedure was for the Council to endorse the Three Power Declaration of 4 March 1946, and to transmit to the General Assembly a recommendation that it should recommend that members sever diplomatic relations with Spain.[20]

Dr. Evatt made a detailed defence of the report. He pointed out that Article 2(7) did not say that the United Nations should not intervene in any matter which did not fall within Chapter VII. What it did say was that it should not intervene in a matter essentially within the domestic jurisdiction of a state. "When considering this point we can forget about Chapter VII. We should concern ourselves only with the terms of Article 2, paragraph 7, and ask ourselves whether or not this question is essentially within the domestic jurisdiction of Spain." He then quoted from his delegation's memorandum at the San Francisco Conference. "Once a matter is recognised as one of legitimate international concern, no exception to the general rule is needed to bring it within the powers of the Organization." The nature of the situation, the action proposed, and the objective of that action were all international in character and in no way essentially domestic. The various multilateral resolutions and declarations occasioned by the regime, the fact that many governments had already broken off international relations with Spain—all these things established the international character of the situation.

---

[20] *Ibid.*, Special Supple.: Rev. Ed., *Report of the Sub-Ctte. on the Spanish Question*, pp. 1-12. The Three Power Declaration of France, Great Britain, and the United States expressed the hope "that leading patriotic and liberal-minded Spaniards may soon find means to bring about a peaceful withdrawal of Franco" and set up an interim government. Such a government, if "dedicated" to "political amnesty, return of exiled Spaniards, freedom of assembly and political association and provision for free public election . . ." should be accorded recognition.

That situation has already led to strong expressions of concern and disapproval by various Governments and to the closing of a frontier. There is a record of past participation in the Second World War and of recent action hindering the victorious Allies in removing vestiges of Nazism. Various Governments, Members of the United Nations, have already broken off diplomatic relations and recognised a rival Government. All this is a matter of vital international concern. The situation, I submit, is the complete antithesis of an essentially domestic situation.[21]

The action proposed (the breaking off of diplomatic relations) was international since "this is a form of action completely within the control of the various nations and it is within their sole discretion to adopt this measure." How the change within Spain was to be brought about was left entirely to the Spaniards. The purpose of the action was international since it was simply to remove a danger to international peace and a cause of international friction. That the international objective might be served by a withdrawal of the Franco regime was incidental.

The United Kingdom delegate was opposed to the part of the recommendation which advocated breaking diplomatic relations, but rather than exercise a veto against the majority, he voted for it. He felt that the Council could intervene in the internal affairs of a country only where there was a clear threat to the maintenance of international peace and security (i.e., the kind of situation covered by Chapter VII, Article 39). His government disliked the Franco regime and stood by the Declaration of March 1946. "What is now proposed is that the United Nations, as such, should take corporate action, or bring corporate pressure to bear on Spain in order to force the present regime from power." It was undeniable that the form of the regime in any particular country is a matter of domestic jurisdiction. The sub-committee had decided that there was insufficient evidence to establish a threat to the peace, yet its operative

---

[21] For Dr. Evatt's statement, see S.C.O.R., 1st Year, 1st Series, No. 2, 44th Mtg., 10 June 1946, pp. 312-21.

recommendation was that members should break off diplomatic relations. This was one of the sanctions mentioned in the Charter not as appropriate for application under Chapter VI, but under Chapter VII. "It really would be tragic," he remarked, "if the principal victim in this case were to be the Charter itself."[22] He suggested that an advisory opinion be sought from the International Court, a procedure similar to that proposed for such cases by the Australian delegation at San Francisco.

Dr. Evatt showed, for the first time, a willingness to adopt a more elastic interpretation of Article 2(7) and to deal with an issue on political rather than the juristic grounds he had suggested in 1945. He opposed the British proposal because it would cause lengthy delay and was unnecessary. "We must not, in my opinion, refer matters to the Court unless there is some overriding necessity for doing so."[23] France and the United States supported the action recommended by the sub-committee. The USSR vetoed all proposals for action on the sub-committee's report as inadequate and unacceptable. Finally, the Council removed the question from its agenda and the matter was taken up by the General Assembly. Australia's firm stand on this issue was surprising in view of its usual caution on matters of domestic jurisdiction.

During the conflict in Indonesia the question of domestic jurisdiction was raised at various stages, although it was largely irrelevant since a disturbance of the peace had already occurred. Australia interpreted Article 2(7) more narrowly than either the United Kingdom or the United States. Australia and India brought the matter before the Council following the first "police action" by the Dutch in July 1947. Australia proposed that the Security Council "note with concern the hostilities in progress between the armed forces of the Netherlands and of the Republic of Indonesia," and determine that these hostilities constituted a "breach of the peace under Article 39 of the Charter." Australia proposed that the Council

---

[22] *Ibid.*, 46th Mtg., 17 June 1946, pp. 344-49.
[23] *Ibid.*, p. 353.

call upon the Netherlands and the Republic of Indonesia, "under Article 40 of the Charter of the United Nations ... to cease hostilities forthwith," and "settle their disputes by arbitration" in accordance with the Linggadjati Agreement, which the two parties had signed a few months previous.[24]

The resolution which the Security Council adopted, however, contained no reference to either Article 39 or 40 of the Charter. It merely noted the hostilities with concern and called upon the parties to cease hostilities forthwith, settle their dispute "by arbitration or by other peaceful means," and keep the Council "informed" about the progress of the settlement.[25] No reference was made to Articles 39 and 40 because certain members (particularly Belgium, France, and the United Kingdom) doubted whether Article 39 covered the situation. They felt that a breach of the peace required war between two states, and they were unwilling to regard Indonesia as a state. Australia argued that the large scale of military operations and the *de facto* recognition of Indonesia by the Netherlands and other governments permitted recourse by the Council to Article 39.[26] Even in its amended form, the resolution was passed with Belgium, France, and the United Kingdom abstaining. The United Kingdom considered that the resolution prejudged the legal position "because to call on parties to cease fighting is definitely to imply that Article 2, paragraph 7, of the Charter, does not apply."[27]

On the question of the procedure to be adopted by the Security Council to facilitate a political settlement between the parties as distinct from the mere cease-fire, Australia proposed a more positive role for the Council than did the United States, which offered its good offices outside the Organization. Australia did not go so far

---

[24] S.C.O.R., 2nd Year, No. 67, 171st Mtg., 31 July 1947, p. 1626.

[25] *Ibid.*, No. 68, 173rd Mtg., 1 Aug. 1947, pp. 1700-03. Australia's position was more consistent with the Charter than that adopted by the Council. On this point, see Hans Kelsen, *The Law of the United Nations* (New York: Frederick A. Praeger Inc., 1950), p. 443n.

[26] S.C.O.R., 2nd Year, No. 74, 181st Mtg., 12 Aug. 1947, pp. 1930-31.

[27] *Ibid.*, No. 68, 173rd Mtg., 1 Aug. 1947, p. 1674.

as Poland in attempting to impose a method of settlement on the parties.[28] Poland proposed that the Council itself establish a commission to "act in the capacity of mediator and arbitrator between the Government of the Netherlands and the Government of the Republic of Indonesia." Australia proposed a procedure whereby each party would select one arbitrator, the Security Council selecting the third. The Australian delegate pointed out that, while under the Linggadjati Agreement the parties had voluntarily agreed to settle their disputes by arbitration, it was doubtful whether the Council should force arbitration on them. After its offer of good offices was rejected, the United States continued to oppose any suggestion for arbitration by the Council and proposed that the Council offer its good offices to the parties, a procedure which it was hoped would avoid further debate on the controversial issue of competence. The United States proposal was adopted by eight votes, with Poland, Syria, and the USSR abstaining.[29]

Australia was chosen by Indonesia as its nominee on the Council's Committee of Good Offices and played an important role in the work of the Committee. When hostilities were resumed in Indonesia in December 1948, the Australian representative in the Security Council strongly condemned the action of the Dutch, accusing them of bad faith. He stressed the right of the Indonesian people to independence and mentioned the possibility of expelling the Netherlands from the United Nations for violating Article 25.[30]

In the Indonesian dispute, the merits of the legal arguments may well have been subordinated to other issues. The sympathies of the Australian Labour government were clearly with the Indonesians

---

[28] For the text of the Polish and Australian proposals, see *ibid.*, No. 77, 185th Mtg., 15 Aug. 1947, p. 2017, and No. 82, 193rd Mtg., 22 Aug. 1947, p. 2174.

[29] *Ibid.*, No. 83, 194th Mtg., 25 Aug. 1947, p. 2209. Poland, Syria, and the USSR voted in favour of the Polish proposal; Belgium, France, the United Kingdom, and the United States voted against; Australia, Brazil, China, and Colombia abstained. On the Australian proposal, Australia, Colombia, and Syria voted in favour, with the rest of the Council members abstaining.

[30] S.C.O.R., 3rd Year, No. 133, 390th Mtg., 23 Dec. 1948, pp. 5-17.

on ideological and strategic grounds. The members of the Opposition were much more sympathetic to the Dutch whom they considered a more useful potential ally than the Indonesians. They were also somewhat apprehensive of the wide powers of the United Nations. In addition, they saw some merits in the colonial system in Asia. In February 1949, Mr. Menzies, in criticizing the government's handling of the dispute, warned against the confusion of self-government with the "abject abandonment of legitimate material interests and administrative responsibilities of which many millions of colonial peoples still warmly approve," adding that "we have been assisting to put the Dutch out of the East Indies. If we continue to do that the same process will no doubt, in due course, eject the British from Malaya and the Australians from Papua and New Guinea."[31] He pointed out that the dispute was one essentially within the domestic jurisdiction of the Netherlands, and that in a similar fashion the "White Australia" policy could be made a subject of international intervention.

Three other issues which came before the Security Council during this period while Australia was a member of the Council deserve mention: the question of the statute for the Free Territory of Trieste; the Greek frontier incidents question; and the dispute between the United Kingdom and Albania concerning incidents in the Corfu Channel. In none of these cases was the application of Article 2(7) of the Charter a central issue. However, the stand which Australia took concerning the extent of the powers of the Security Council, while of marginal relevance to the domestic jurisdiction principle, is ultimately directly related to it, for the narrower the powers of the Security Council, the less danger there is of interference in each member's jurisdiction.

In December 1946 the Security Council was asked by France, the USSR, the United Kingdom, and the United States to guarantee the independence and integrity of the Free Territory of Trieste as

---

[31] Commonwealth of Australia, *Parliamentary Debates*, Vol. 201, 15 Feb. 1949, pp. 269-70 and 274-75.

established by them in the Italian Peace Treaty. Their claim that the Security Council was competent to do this was supported by a legal opinion from the Secretary-General concerning the interpretation of Article 24(1) of the Charter. In this article the members of the United Nations "confer on the Security Council primary responsibility for the maintenance of international peace and security, and agree that in carrying out its duties under this responsibility the Security Council acts on their behalf." The Secretary-General interpreted this as a substantive grant of power additional to the specific powers referred to in Article 24, paragraph 2 (that is, the powers granted in Chapters VI, VII, VIII, and XII of the Charter).

Australia rejected this interpretation on the ground that only in the particular circumstances referred to in Chapters VI and VII of the Charter could the Council acquire jurisdiction. "Before the Council may act, there must be a dispute or a situation which might lead to international friction or give rise to a dispute or a threat to the peace . . ."[32] Alternatively, Australia argued that even if it were assumed that Article 24(1) conferred duties over and above the specific powers listed in Chapters VI, VII, VIII, and XII, any action taken by the Council under such power must not go further than was warranted by "the purposes and principles of the United Nations" since under Article 24(2) the Council was specifically required to act in accordance with the latter. The action proposed regarding Trieste could not be directly related to such purposes and principles. Australia therefore abstained.

It is impossible to determine how far any particular interpretation of the Charter is advanced out of sincere conviction, in accordance with long term policy, or as an opportunistic move in a particular case. In this instance both conviction and opportunism coincided. If one accepts as an important factor in Australian policy at San Francisco (and previously at Geneva) a desire to prevent Council interference in domestic issues, then the Australian attitude to Trieste can be similarly explained. Furthermore, Australia's contention that

[32] S.C.O.R., 2nd Year, No. 1, 89th Mtg., 7 Jan. 1947, p. 6.

that proposed action would extend the function of the Security Council beyond the maintenance of international security becomes significant when it is noted that the guarantee of Trieste's territorial integrity was accompanied by functions which related to "the ordinary good government of the Territory, and not to the maintenance of peace and security."[33] Australia suggested that this was a dangerous precedent. "The question is not whether a particular situation now existing is of concern to the Security Council, but whether the Security Council has power to act in a certain way in the future."[34]

There is an alternative hypothesis for Australia's attitude. The solution proposed had been decided upon at the Paris Peace Conference by the foreign ministers of the great powers who had systematically rejected all the proposals made there by Dr. Evatt. Accordingly, in the Trieste debate in the Security Council, Australia made clear that it still preferred its own Paris proposals. Since the foreign ministers had ignored the advice of the smaller powers, they should now handle the Trieste problem without the assistance of the non-permanent members of the Council, which should not be bound to commitments that the great powers could evade at will by use of the veto.

In the Greek frontiers incident question, there was a lengthy discussion during the summer of 1947 concerning the competence of the Security Council to establish a commission to investigate frontier violations and to assist the countries concerned in settling their disputes. Poland and the USSR argued that a decision of this nature could be taken only under Chapter VII, when there had been a "breach of the peace," and that if made under Chapter VI, it would merely be a recommendation and not a decision which members were compelled to "accept and carry out" under Article 25.

The United States justified the establishment of the commission under the reserve powers allegedly provided in Article 24(1). Australia, as in the Trieste case, rejected this argument but accepted

---

[33] *Ibid.*, p. 7.

[34] *Ibid.*, No. 3, 91st Mtg., 10 Jan. 1947, p. 56.

the action proposed on other grounds. Before taking action under Chapter VI, the Security Council was bound by Article 34 to investigate the dispute or situation. Thus, the absence of power adequately to investigate or to demand co-operation from members in such investigation would prevent the Council from using the Charter procedures for the pacific settlement of disputes in any circumstances. The grant of a certain power connoted the grant of authority to exercise that power. Incidental to the power of investigation was the power to move freely and examine witnesses in the countries concerned. A decision to investigate was accordingly more than a recommendation.[35] Australia thus advanced an interpretation which would enable the Council to function on an issue in which Australia desired it to function. The Australian delegation apparently thought its arguments less capable of extension to permit intervention in domestic matters than the "reserve power" argument advanced by the United States.

This restrictive trend was not apparent in the Australian arguments in the dispute between the United Kingdom and Albania over the incidents in the Corfu Channel. The Australian position appeared to attribute to the Security Council extensive and compulsory powers to impose methods of settlement. In this dispute Albania, although not a member of the United Nations, had, as a condition of its participation in the Council's discussion of the dispute, voluntarily accepted "all the obligations which a Member of the United Nations would have to assume . . ."[36] The Council on 9 April 1947 recommended that "the United Kingdom and the Albanian Governments should immediately refer the dispute to the International Court of Justice in accordance with the provisions of the Statute of the Court."[37] Albania was not a party to the Statute and had not accepted the compulsory jurisdiction of the Court in such matters.

---

[35] For the Australian position, see *ibid.*, No. 61, 162nd Mtg., 22 July 1947, pp. 1418-20.

[36] *Ibid.*, No. 7, 96th Mtg., 28 Jan. 1947, p. 131.

[37] *Ibid.*, No. 34, 127th Mtg., 9 April 1947, p. 726.

m

Australia argued that the Council resolution, a recommendation of "appropriate procedures or methods of adjustment" under Chapter VI (Article 36), was a decision of the Council. Albania, having accepted a member's obligations, was obliged under Article 25 to accept and carry out this recommendation. Should Albania refuse to appear before the Court, the Court legally could give judgment.[38] The United Kingdom subsequently adopted this argument before the Court. Although the Court did not decide the point, seven of its judges in separate opinions rejected this contention that a recommendation under Article 36(3) was binding.

The implications of the Australian argument are extensive: the Security Council could impose on any member the binding obligation, in any situation "likely to endanger the maintenance of peace," to accept any "appropriate procedures or methods of adjustment." In the hypothetical case of such a situation arising out of Australia's immigration policy, it would be open to the Council to arrive at a decision binding Australia to resort to arbitration. This is a situation very similar to that which Dr. Evatt sought so hard to avert by his proposed amendment to the Dumbarton Oaks draft.[39]

Reviewing the policy of the Australian Labour government generally on the matter of domestic jurisdiction, it is difficult to find a basic consistency. At San Francisco, Australia claimed that inclusion of the promotion of human rights and the full employment pledge as principles of the United Nations did not withdraw such matters from domestic jurisdiction. In the next two or three years Australia tended to support the reference of issues of competence to the International Court; but such support was often hesitant and unenthusiastic. Yet in the Indonesian, Spanish, and religious trials issues, Australia actively attacked the claim of domestic jurisdiction. On the Spanish case, Dr. Evatt argued if the facts indicated that the Franco regime, by its nature and conduct, "is likely to interfere with international peace and likely to be a menace to its neighbours,

---

[38] *Ibid.*, pp. 722-23.

[39] See above, pp. 61-64.

then the existence of that regime is no longer a matter of essentially domestic concern."[40] There was no such inconsistency in the Australian argument on the Indonesian issue: it was based on the claim that the Republic of Indonesia, in virtue of its *de facto* recognition, was a state, and that its relations with the Netherlands were accordingly international. In the Greek trade union leaders case, however, Australia supported the majority in favour of a decision that the Assembly was not competent to call on the Greek government to take steps to see that the execution of certain trade union leaders who had been sentenced to death was not carried out.

The Australian delegates tended at times to give varying and elastic definitions of domestic jurisdiction which caused confusion as to Australia's basic attitude. In the religious trials case, Australia did not rely on the provisions in the peace treaties but claimed the issue to be an international one because of the human rights provision of the Charter, combined with the power of the Assembly under Article 10 to discuss any matters coming within the scope of the Charter. Australia tended to note the actions of individual governments which did not directly affect international security and to support resolutions inviting peaceful settlement by the parties involved. In this case, Dr. Evatt said that:

> the right of discussion provided for in Article 10 of the Charter was one of its most important provisions. There was no question or problem which came within the scope of the Charter and which concerned its aims, its principles or any one of its provisions, which could not be discussed by the General Assembly. If any question could be covered by an Article of the Charter, that question could no longer be held to be a matter essentially within the domestic jurisdiction of a State.[41]

This represents one of the most sweeping statements made by an

---

[40] S.C.O.R., 1st Year, 1st Series, No. 2, 46th Mtg., 17 June 1946, p. 352.
[41] G.A.O.R., 3rd Sess., 2nd Part, General Ctte., 58th Mtg., 6 April 1949, pp. 15-16.

Australian representative. It appears to be fundamentally inconsistent with the position taken by Australia at San Francisco.

Similarly Dr. Evatt's argument in the Spanish case, that even in circumstances not amounting to a threat to peace the Security Council had power to recommend such measures as the breaking off of diplomatic relations, was contrary to the main current of Australian interpretation. Such reasoning could embarrass Australia in just that kind of situation in which Dr. Evatt claimed he had at San Francisco successfully prevented United Nations intervention—namely, a situation in which an Asian country might desire such intervention in matters concerning Australian immigration or tariff policies. His argument in the Spanish case was virtually that anything which evokes consideration by other countries is international in character. The logical extension of this would be that should two Asian countries express concern at Australian immigration policy, and should relations thus become strained, the subject would then be suitable for United Nations action under Chapter VI. Although the Security Council could not *direct* members to take any action and could not direct Australia to take specific measures, it could on the analogy of Australia's proposals on the Spanish question *recommend* that all members take action hostile to Australia with a view to removing the cause of the situation. The measures recommended could be the severance of diplomatic relations or even an economic embargo.

THE LIBERAL GOVERNMENT AND
DOMESTIC JURISDICTION 1949-57

With the change of government in Australia in December 1949, came a shift in emphasis in Australian foreign policies, and with it a stiffening of the Australian attitude to the application of the principle of domestic jurisdiction. Instead of the somewhat elastic interpretation given on occasion during the Evatt period, the Australian government adopted the unvarying view that Article 2(7) has a "simple, explicit and unmistakable" meaning. This view has been that it prohibits discussion as constituting intervention and that the phrase "nothing contained in the present Charter . . ." must be given its full effect. This interpretation has not been fully shared by Canada, New Zealand, and the United States; it does accord with that of the United Kingdom.

The adoption of this stronger line may be partly the result of the differing theoretical basis of the Australian political parties. It was principally due to a changing assessment of the international situation and a reliance upon regional pacts as a means of defending Australia. The new foreign policy developed by Mr. Spender and Mr. Casey gave priority to power relations rather than to the United Nations. This shift in emphasis was confirmed by the intensified attack upon the colonial powers by the anti-colonial bloc in the Trusteeship Council and other organs of the United Nations. The favourable climate of opinion at the end of the war facilitated a remarkable degree of agreement on the powers and procedures of an international organization. With the deterioration in East-West relationships after the war, a more rigid interpretation of Article 2(7) was perhaps a necessary recognition of the real limitations on any workable international organization.

The seventh session of the General Assembly (1952-53) was the occasion for a series of statements by Australian delegates in support of a narrow interpretation of the powers of the United Nations to intervene in domestic affairs. The Australian position on the *apartheid* question (the question of the racial policies of the Union of South Africa) clearly indicated this changed approach to Article 2(7) of the Charter. In the earlier discussions on the related question of the treatment of Indians in South Africa, Australia had finally supported the 1949 resolution inviting the parties to confer. At the seventh session, however, Australia explicitly denied the right of the Assembly even to discuss such matters. The argument on *apartheid*— that the United Nations could intervene in such a case only if it decided upon enforcement measures under Chapter VII—was very

similar to the United Kingdom argument on Spain, an argument
that Dr. Evatt had vigorously repudiated.[42]

Australia gave a detailed interpretation of Article 2(7) and the
powers of the Assembly on the Tunisian question. The Australian
delegate (Mr. Percy Spender) opposed the Arab-Asian draft resolution which urged France to establish normal conditions and civil
liberties in Tunisia and recommended that negotiations be resumed
with the aid of a commission of good offices to implement the right
of self-determination and the fulfilment of the national aspirations
of the Tunisian people. The Australian view was that this action
in fact constituted intervention as prohibited by Article 2(7). The
sole exception to this prohibition—enforcement measures under
Chapter VII—was inapplicable since the application of such measures was solely a function of the Security Council. Even if there
were a threat to peace, and on this issue no one believed that there
was, intervention was not within the competence of the General
Assembly. The Security Council alone possessed such power.
Furthermore, the domestic jurisdiction of a state was not restricted
to its metropolitan area. Tunisia did not possess complete sovereignty
and therefore the question was one of domestic jurisdiction.

> The fallacy of the argument that the mere existence of a treaty
> between France and Tunisia placed the Franco-Tunisian dis-
> pute beyond the scope of paragraph 7 of Article 2, was that
> the word "essentially" was given the same meaning as "solely".
> . . . [At San Francisco] the general desire to limit the com-
> petence of the United Nations had been clearly shown. If the
> word "solely" had been used, the competence of the United
> Nations would have been so widened that it would have been
> difficult to find any treaty that could not be submitted to
> the consideration of the General Assembly. The presence of
> the word "essentially" destroyed any argument based on com-
> parisons with the old Covenant of the League of Nations or

[42] See above, pp. 155-57. In the Spanish case, Evatt was justifying action under
Chapter VI which appears to sanction United Nations action more explicitly
than do Articles 55 and 56, the articles relied upon in the later stages of the
South African question.

with the decisions of the old Permanent Court of International Justice, which, it should be remembered, were based on words different from those of paragraph 7 of Article 2.[43]

It was impossible to justify intervention by reference to other provisions of the Charter such as Article 73 in view of the opening words of Article 2(7): "Nothing contained in the present Charter shall authorize the United Nations to intervene . . ." Mr. Spender stated:

> Article 103 . . . gave no competence to the United Nations and merely stated that the Charter should prevail over agreements concluded earlier or subsequently. It referred to "obligations," and applied only in cases of conflict of obligations . . . which would presumably be clear and precisely defined, [and] should not be confused with objectives, aims or purposes which did not amount to obligations. In the present case there was no conflict of obligations within the meaning of Article 103; yet even assuming that there were, that fact would not confer competence upon the General Assembly . . ."[44]

The same arguments were put forward by the Minister for External Affairs, Mr. R. G. Casey, in the general debate at the opening of the session:

> To my mind, the Charter must be regarded and considered as a whole. At San Francisco, the document would not have been acceptable to many of us had not its various provisions been interrelated. In this connexion, I refer to Article 2, paragraph 7, *which prohibits the discussion* of matters of domestic jurisdiction. By stating broad humanitarian principles in the Charter, I do not think that the nations at San Francisco had in mind that the Organization would thereby be permitted to discuss or to intervene in questions of domestic economic or social legislation.[45]

---

[43] G.A.O.R., 7th Sess., 1st Ctte., 545th Mtg., 11 Dec. 1952, p. 258.

[44] *Ibid.* The draft resolution was defeated: 24 in favour, 27 against, 7 abstentions. Australia, Belgium, Canada, the Netherlands, New Zealand, South Africa, United Kingdom, and the United States were among those opposed.

[45] G.A.O.R., 7th Sess., 384th Plenary Mtg., 20 Oct. 1952, p. 107. (Italics added.)

Later, speaking on the question of the treatment of Indians in South Africa, Mr. Casey stated:

> I believe that the meaning of Article 2(7) is simple, explicit and unmistakable. "Nothing"—that is to say nothing else included in the Charter—"nothing contained in the present charter shall authorise the United Nations to intervene in matters which are essentially within the domestic jurisdiction of any State". . . . In my view it is not sufficient to point to other articles of the Charter to justify discussion on a wide range of other matters essentially of domestic concern. All such provisions must be read subject to Article 2(7) which explicitly in its wording, and by reason of its position at the forefront of the Charter, governs the whole of the application of the Charter.[46]

The argument was put even more explicitly by another Australian delegate on the question of *apartheid*:

> The words "nothing contained in this Charter" mean what they say, and it is difficult to see how provisions such as those of Articles 55 and 56 can be held to create over-riding obligations. The fact that the single and special exception mentioned in Article 2(7) concerned enforcement measures should dispel any doubt as to the Article's intention or meaning. . . . We are firmly of the belief that Article 2(7) . . . overrides all other Articles of the Charter. But in any case, are we to agree that any aspect of the very wide range of topics mentioned in Article 55, which are claimed to be a matter of international concern or even moral indignation, can become a proper subject for intervention by the United Nations? Again let all members of the Committee consider the implications of such a doctrine. As we see it, the word "intervene" in Article 2(7) means what it says. Its simple Latin derivation means "to come between." It has been claimed here that mere discussion or perhaps even the passage of a resolution does not constitute intervention. I think that we need only cast our minds back over the progress of this debate so far to

[46] See statement by R. G. Casey in *Current Notes on International Affairs* (Dept. of External Affairs, Canberra), Vol. 23 (1952), p. 664. For summary, see G.A.O.R., 7th Sess., *Ad Hoc* Pol. Ctte., 10th Mtg., 5 Nov. 1952. p. 46.

see that discussion in itself is intervention. . . . The whole purpose of bringing forward an item or a resolution is to modify or change an existing situation, which is "ipso facto" intervention.[47]

From an analysis of the voting at the seventh session, it can be seen that the "domestic jurisdiction group" was comparatively united in opposing the more far-reaching proposals for United Nations intervention. On many of the "compromise" proposals that were actually adopted by the Assembly, the members of the group were split with South Africa voting against, Australia and the United Kingdom usually abstaining, while the United States tended to vote in favour of the resolutions. Thus on the Tunisian question all the members of the domestic jurisdiction group voted in committee against the Arab-Asian proposal. The resolution adopted by the Assembly, appealing to the parties and expressing the hope that negotiations would continue, was supported by Canada, New Zealand, and the United States, with Australia, the Netherlands, and the United Kingdom abstaining.[48]

Except for the United States, all the members of the "domestic jurisdiction group" abstained from voting on the resolution adopted on the question of the treatment of Indians in South Africa which established a United Nations Good Offices Commission to assist the parties in negotiating a solution in accordance with the purposes and principles of the Charter and the Universal Declaration on Human Rights.[49]

On the *apartheid* question the South African proposal that the General Assembly declare that it was not competent to adopt either

---

[47] For this statement by P. Shaw in the *Ad Hoc* Pol. Ctte., 16th Mtg., 14 Nov. 1952, see *Current Notes, op. cit.*, p. 666. For a contrary view, see H. Lauterpacht, *International Law and Human Rights* (London: Stevens & Sons, 1950), Ch. 10, especially pp. 213-14.

[48] For the vote, see G.A.O.R., 7th Sess., 1st Ctte., 546th Mtg., 12 Dec. 1952, pp. 270-71. A vote taken on a similar resolution on the Moroccan question revealed the same split. *Ibid.*, 407th Plenary Mtg., 19 Dec. 1952, p. 426.

[49] See General Assembly Resolution 615(VII), 5 Dec. 1952, p. 8, and G.A.O.R., 7th Sess., 401st Plenary Mtg., 5 Dec. 1952, p. 330.

of the draft resolutions recommended by the Political Committee
was defeated. Australia, France, and the United Kingdom supported
the South African position; the United States was opposed; and
Canada, the Netherlands, and New Zealand abstained. On the
resolution establishing a commission to study the question, the
entire "domestic jurisdiction group" abstained. (In an earlier vote
on the terms of reference of the commission, Canada and the United
States had abstained and the other members of the group had voted
against.) A second resolution calling on all members to bring their
policies into conformity with their Charter obligations to promote
the observance of human rights and fundamental freedoms was
supported by Canada, the Netherlands, and the United States with
the other members of the group abstaining.[50]

At the seventh session of the General Assembly, then, Australia
clearly defined its policy of broad construction of domestic jurisdiction. Australia then and subsequently disavowed any intention
of approving of *apartheid* itself: the issue was a legal not a political
one. At the ninth and eleventh sessions of the Assembly, Australia
reiterated this view when the *apartheid* and Algerian questions were
again raised and when the issues of Cyprus and West Irian were
placed on the agenda. At the ninth session, an Australian delegate,
in denying jurisdiction to the General Assembly, pointed out that
"the United Nations held no legislative power; it was not a world
government."[51] Two years later, Sir Percy Spender, an eminent
constitutional lawyer who subsequently was elevated to the International Court, made no attempt to suggest that the question of
the meaning of Article 2(7) be referred to the International Court.
He denied the competence of the General Assembly "to give an
interpretation of the United Nations Charter which would have any

---

[50] See General Assembly Resolution 616A & B(VII), 5 Dec. 1952, pp. 8-9, and
G.A.O.R., 7th Sess., 401st Plenary Mtg., 5 Dec. 1952, pp. 331-34. See also the
voting at the outset of the session in connection with the South African proposal
that the Assembly declare itself not competent to consider the question. *Ibid.*,
381st Plenary Mtg., 17 Oct. 1952, p. 67.

[51] G.A.O.R., 9th Sess., *Ad Hoc* Pol. Ctte., 44th Mtg., 6 Dec. 1954, p. 211.

legal validity," but refrained from proposing that the Court be asked for an advisory opinion on the scope and validity of Article 2(7).[52] On the West Irian question, he claimed that the real issue was that of Dutch sovereignty in the area; this was a legal question which could be submitted to the International Court of Justice by either party.[53]

The issue of domestic jurisdiction was also raised in another context when the United Nations and the International Labour Organisation (ILO) proposed to establish a joint Fact-Finding and Conciliation Commission on Freedom of Association. The initiative for setting up this Commission came from the Economic and Social Council (ECOSOC) in August 1949. At the 110th Session (January 1950) of the Governing Body of the ILO, the question was raised whether cases should be referred to the Commission irrespective of the consent of the government concerned. The Australian delegate strongly supported the view that consent was necessary. Australia was also concerned with the possibility that governments could be held accountable for their conduct in fields where they had never accepted international obligations.[54] The terms of reference of the Commission as ultimately determined by the ILO and ECOSOC did not completely satisfy the Australian objection. Although it was stated that "no complaint shall be referred to the Commission without the consent of the Government concerned," the terms of reference contained the provision that if consent was not forthcoming, the Governing Body should consider "taking any appropriate alternative action designed to safeguard rights relating to freedom of association involved in the case, including measures to give full publicity to charges made, together with any comments by the Government concerned, and to that Government's refusal to co-

---

[52] G.A.O.R., 11th Sess., 1st Ctte., 844th Mtg., 12 Feb. 1957, p. 196.

[53] *Ibid.*, 858th Mtg., 25 Feb. 1957, pp. 285-87.

[54] See ILO, Minutes of the 110th Sess. of the Governing Body, 6th Sitting, 6 Jan. 1950, pp. 82-83 and ECOSOC, Official Records: 10th Sess., 355th Mtg., 17 Feb. 1950, pp. 71-72.

operate in ascertaining the facts and in measures of conciliation."[55]

Australia subsequently supported South Africa in suggesting that the Governing Body of the ILO had exceeded its powers in establishing the Commission. Australia sought to limit the jurisdiction of the Commission to allegations against a country of infringements of trade union rights embodied in international conventions or other agreements to which the country was a party.[56] At the 1950 session of the International Labour Conference, the Australian view was stated as follows:

> No State is internationally obliged to accord trade union rights unless it is bound by a Convention to do so; . . . if it is not so bound, trade union questions are, so far as it is concerned, matters of domestic jurisdiction. Any machinery to investigate infringements of these rights should therefore have jurisdiction only as regards States bound by the Conventions concerning trade union rights which the Organisation has adopted.[57]

The issue raised far-reaching questions of principle. "The Organisation must not become involved in matters of purely domestic concern nor in the internal politics of individual members. There are certain issues which rightly belong within the competence of national Governments only, and the Organisation must be very, very careful not to intrude."[58] Australia was concerned at the tendency, of which the Commission was but one illustration, for international bodies to exceed the limits imposed by their constitutions. Like South Africa, Australia had no desire to prevent the establishment of such a commission. This did not mean that Australia accepted the con-

---

[55] See ILO, Minutes of the 110th Sess. of the Governing Body, 7th Sitting, 6 Jan. 1950, pp. 91-92. See also ECOSOC Resolution 277(X) (c) i-iii, 17 Feb. 1950.

[56] See United Nations Doc. E/AC.7/L.13, 14 Feb. 1950, for text of the Australian amendment proposed in the Social Ctte. of ECOSOC.

[57] ILO, Record of Proceedings of the International Labour Conference, 33rd Sess., 17th Sitting, 28 June 1950, p. 272.

[58] *Ibid.*, 5th Sitting, 13 June 1950, p. 59.

stitutionality of such activities except in so far as they related to ratified conventions or were undertaken at the request of a member state. Australia objected to the fact that the Commission in effect would make judgments and that the Governing Body could use coercive power against states refusing to permit investigations of allegations.

Any other attitude to the Commission would have been inconsistent with the wider domestic jurisdiction argument so frequently asserted by Australia. Australia's attitude was also influenced by an issue in domestic politics. The Labour government had supported the 1948 International Labour Convention on Freedom of Association and Protection of the Right to Organize although it realized the difficulty it would face in ratifying the convention. The distribution of powers between the federal government and the states would delay ratification, since ratification by the federal government could only follow action by all states. A Liberal government introduced in 1950 a Communist Party Dissolution bill which would have excluded former members of the Communist party from office in trade unions. An investigation and a hostile report by an international body on this proposal would naturally have been most unwelcome.

CONCLUSION

The whole problem of domestic jurisdiction is bedevilled by the difficulty of judicial interpretation and perhaps by loose drafting. The Australian sponsors of the revised draft of Article 2(7) at San Francisco successfully supported the inclusion of the word "essentially," wider in meaning than "solely." By so doing they hoped to broaden the field of domestic jurisdiction: the United Nations should not intervene in matters which were "in their essence" within domestic jurisdiction and did not have significant international implications. In fact, this amendment has failed to achieve its purpose.

Real difficulties arise over the interpretation of the word "intervention." Professor Lauterpacht defines it as "a peremptory demand or an attempt at interference accompanied by enforcement or threat of enforcement in case of non-compliance."[59] He argues that a "recommendation," in so far as it is calculated to exercise direct pressure likely to be followed by measures of enforcement, constitutes intervention but other recommendations, even if addressed to individual states, do not. Yet the very glare of publicity surrounding discussions at the United Nations itself involves very real pressure on the parties concerned, especially if a pointed recommendation emerges. Goodrich and Hambro consider that

> while discussion does not amount to intervention, the creation of a commission of inquiry, the making of a recommendation of a procedural or a substantive nature, or the taking of a binding decision constitutes intervention under the terms of [Article 2(7)] . . . To limit intervention to coercive measures would have the result of largely limiting the application of the paragraph to the field of the exception which obviously could not have been intended.[60]

This amounts to saying that "intervention" must, as a matter of interpretation, cover a broader range of activities than the taking of enforcement measures to meet threats to the peace, breaches of the peace, and acts of aggression. There is, therefore, still room for the application of Article 2(7) to a wide field of measures to which the exception specifically stated in the Article does not apply.

The crux of the matter is that few governments have attempted to adopt a purely legal interpretation of Article 2(7), even if this were possible in view of the conflicts of judicial opinion. The attitude of governments on the meaning of the Article has been governed primarily by political considerations, based on the particular government's interest in giving a wide or a narrow meaning to the Article

---

[59] Lauterpacht, *op. cit.*, p. 168.
[60] Leland M. Goodrich and Edvard Hambro, *Charter of the United Nations*, 2nd Rev. Ed. (Boston: World Peace Foundation, 1949), p. 120.

according to whether or not it wished to focus international attention on particular issues. Consistency of policy on, or interpretation of, Article 2(7) has been somewhat exceptional.

Australia's attitude has been dominated by its assessment of the extent to which its fundamental interests at a given time will be affected by the meaning given to this Article. At San Francisco it appeared that Australia was attempting to give a traditional interpretation to the word "intervention"; that is, that it should be narrowly interpreted as covering only a definite and tangible interference in a particular situation. Shortly after the ratification of the Charter, it became clear that Australia intended to adopt a "loose construction" of the sphere of domestic jurisdiction. After 1949 there was a steady move to the view that "discussion in itself is intervention. . . . The whole purpose of bringing forward an item or a resolution is to modify or change an existing situation, which is, 'ipso facto,' intervention."

The Labour government was from the outset prepared to interpret the Charter restrictively in the case of South Africa, primarily because to have done otherwise would have meant embarrassing another member of the Commonwealth. That government was also disinclined to take or support any action which suggested that the mere inclusion of a subject among the principles of the United Nations withdrew it from domestic jurisdiction.

Australia has, in recent years, validly stressed the argument that an alleged violation of human rights by another government was in itself insufficient to rebut a plea of domestic jurisdiction. There are some difficulties arising out of the relationship of Article 2(7) to Articles 55 and 56. But these refer to the *promotion* by the United Nations of full employment and respect for and observance of human rights and fundamental freedoms, and contain a pledge by all members of the United Nations "to take joint and separate action in cooperation with the Organization for the achievement of [these] purposes. . . ." The mere mention of desirable ends does not place all international action relevant to those ends outside the scope of the domestic jurisdiction limitation. Any member nation alleging a violation of human rights could demonstrate that these rights were the subject of an international obligation stemming from a treaty commitment or a recognized international custom. It could also demonstrate that the violation of these rights involved an actual or potential threat to international peace and security. Yet in the religious trials case, Australia felt that the basis for international action arose not out of peace treaty obligations but from the Charter itself. At the same time it seems clear that Australia was also inclined in this case, as well as in the Spanish question and the Russian wives issue, to favour a particular construction of the Charter with a view to discomforting its political enemies.

The shift in Australian attitudes since 1949 cannot be interpreted solely in terms of party differences. When the Liberals were in opposition, they did not criticize the government's stand on the Russian wives and religious trials questions, nor were the desultory attacks on the Labour government's Spanish policy related to the issue of domestic jurisdiction. Since coming into power, the Liberals have been forced to examine the whole problem more closely. The intensification of the "cold war" and the concerted attacks on the colonial powers have both contributed to the hardening of the Australian interpretation of Article 2(7).

In one sense the steady move to a strict rather than a loose interpretation of domestic jurisdiction is of little real consequence. As Sir John Latham has pointed out:

> The exclusion of matters of domestic jurisdiction is of little practical significance because of the absence of any generally accepted criterion of domestic jurisdiction, and for the further reason that a discussion as to whether a matter is or is not one of domestic jurisdiction will open up the whole matter. In practice, Article 2, paragraph 7, has had little real operation except in increasing possibilities of argument.[61]

---

[61] Sir John Latham, *Open Diplomacy* (Sydney: Australian Institute of International Affairs, 1953), p. 18.

On the other hand, the growing acceptance of the view that discussion in fact constitutes intervention is based on the firmly held belief that intervention in matters of domestic jurisdiction threatens vital Australian interests. It is also based on the belief that such intervention may in the end destroy the United Nations itself.

n

chapter seven

Trusteeship and
Non-Self-Governing Territories

Australia's attitude to the problems of trusteeship and non-self-governing territories is determined primarily by its own experiences in colonial administration and secondarily by general theories of trusteeship and colonial policy. Australia became involved in the problems of governing dependent territories as a consequence of an extreme but perfectly natural preoccupation with the problem of security. It was clamorous pressure from the then unfederated Australian colonies, alarmed by German imperial designs in the Pacific, that pushed a reluctant British government into establishing a protectorate over southeastern New Guinea in 1884, shortly after Germany had declared a protectorate over the northeastern part of the island. Concern with the strategic importance of the island had already led to Queensland's precipitate and unconstitutional attempt to annex eastern New Guinea. The British crown colony of New Guinea was administered through the Governor of Queensland from

1888 to 1900 and then by the Governor-General of the Common-wealth of Australia. In 1906 the colony was renamed the territory of Papua and became a territory of the Commonwealth of Australia.

The same strategic interests motivated the Australian govern-ment's concern with the future status of the German colony of New Guinea at the Peace Conference in 1919. Annexation "in the interests of Australian security" was discarded by a bellicose Aus-tralian Prime Minister only when the Conference reluctantly agreed to the special class C mandate, devised by his own staff to give Australia virtual sovereignty over the territory. It should be pointed out, however, that Australian administrative policy in Papua, first under William McGregor and then under Sir Hubert Murray, was profoundly influenced by the principles of the "dual mandate" as propounded by Lord Lugard and applied for example by William Temple in Nigeria.[1]

Acting on the principle that there should be "a barred and closed door with Australia as the guardian of the door," Australia made full use of its powers under the mandate agreement to apply its immigration and trade policies to New Guinea. Throughout the period of the mandate, the Permanent Mandates Commission of the League of Nations generally commended the Australian administra-tion. A growing Australian opinion had become concerned with the rate of progress of the peoples of New Guinea.[2] On the other hand, the Australian administrators were often subjected to considerable pressure by the planters, many of them returned soldiers of the

---

[1] For annexation, see J. D. Legge, "Australia and New Guinea to the Establish-ment of the British Protectorate," *Historical Studies: Australia and New Zealand* (University of Melbourne). Vol. IV (1949), pp. 34-47; Marjorie Jacobs, "Bismarck and the Annexation of New Guinea" and "The Colonial Office and New Guinea, 1874-84," *ibid.,* Vol. V (1951-52), pp. 14-26 and 106-18; J. D. Legge, *Australian Colonial Policy* (Sydney: Angus and Robertson, 1956), Ch. 2. For administration under Murray, see *ibid.,* Ch. 9 *et seq.* and Lewis Lett, *Sir Hubert Murray of Papua* (London: Collins, 1949).

[2] See F. W. Eggleston, ed., *The Australian Mandate for New Guinea*, in the "Pacific Relations Series," No. 2 (League of Nations Union and Melbourne University Press, 1928).

First World War. The planters, concerned primarily with the rapid economic development of the territory, were impatient and critical of regulations framed to protect native labour and to preserve native land ownership. The authorities were more than willing to rely upon the Mandates Commission for support of their policie conceived according to trusteeship principles. The most eloquent testimony to both the quality and the success of the Australian policy was later provided by the many instances of devoted service by the natives during the Second World War.

The major criticisms of the mandates system were twofold. In the first place, the shortage of both trained personnel and funds suggested the desirability of unifying the administration of the colony of Papua and the mandated territory of New Guinea. The terms of the mandate made this difficult. Secondly, and far more important from an Australian point of view, was the problem of defence. The terms of the mandate specifically prohibited the use of the mandated territory as a military base. Yet in Australian eyes, New Guinea was a vital strategic base, for offence or defence. The most Australia had been able to do at the Versailles Conference was to prevent the application of the "open door" principle to mandated territories. Australia's worst fears were realized when some of the decisive battles for the defence of Australia during the Second World War were fought in New Guinea.

At the San Francisco Conference the Australian delegation at first oscillated between two extremes: a real awareness of the vital strategic importance of New Guinea as a defensive unit, and an ideological distrust of colonial capitalism in general.[3] Australia's, or perhaps Dr. Evatt's, distrust of imperialism was indicated by the Australian proposal to place all colonial territories under international supervision and apply trusteeship principles to them. This, it was believed, would be an important factor in lessening international tensions, and so ensuring world peace. On this point the

---

[3] See above, pp. 72 and 77-78.

Australian position seemed closer to that of some of the "non-administering" powers than that of the colonial powers. There was widespread opposition at the Conference to placing all colonies under the supervision of the United Nations Trusteeship Council. Australia did, however, secure the insertion in the declaration concerning non-self-governing territories of provisions for the regular transmission of information to the Secretary-General. Australia also supported the successful proposal of China and the United States providing for periodic visits of United Nations missions to the trust territories.

THE TRUSTEESHIP AGREEMENTS
FOR NEW GUINEA AND NAURU

The change in Australia's attitude to trusteeship became very clear in the discussions in the United Nations General Assembly in the autumn of 1946 on the trusteeship agreement for New Guinea. There was a basic disagreement in principle on the question how the League of Nations mandates could be converted into United Nations trusteeships. Should the trusteeship agreements limit the rights and extend the obligations of the administering authorities or should they confirm existing rights to enable these authorities to carry out the new Charter obligations? This broad issue resolved into three specific questions: Were the mandatories obliged to place their mandates under trusteeship? Were trusteeships to be administered by individual members or by the United Nations itself? Which were the "states directly concerned" that must agree upon the terms of the individual trusteeship agreements?[4]

On each of these questions Australia supported the preservation of the rights of the administering authority. Australia denied the Soviet claim that it was obligatory to place mandated territories

---

[4] See Article 79 of the Charter.

under trusteeship,[5] and refused to support the Indian proposal that trust territories should be administered by the Organization as a whole. On the third question (despite the fact that Australia had already consulted with France, New Zealand, the United Kingdom, and the United States on a draft trusteeship agreement for New Guinea),[6] Australia stated that "only those states which had in international law a recognizable interest in the sovereignty, control or disposition of a territory could claim to be 'directly concerned'."[7] Obviously the only state that could fulfill these requirements was the mandatory power itself.

In considering a draft trusteeship agreement, Australia was anxious to preserve the rights it had enjoyed under the class C mandate from the League of Nations. Article 84 of the Charter permits the administering authority to "make use of volunteer forces, facilities, and assistance from the trust territory" in providing for the defence of the territory. To carry out Charter obligations to promote the welfare and advancement of New Guinea, Australia needed powers to regulate social, economic, and commercial developments: these are provided under Articles 76(d) and 80 of the Charter, and give Australia the right to control immigration and trade. These rights were further safeguarded under Article 4 of the draft agreement which stipulated that Australia had "the same powers of legislation, administration and jurisdiction in and over the Territory as if it were an integral part of Australia": this merely reiterated the position as it had existed under the mandate.

The draft trusteeship agreement for New Guinea submitted by Australia was discussed at length in the Fourth (Trusteeship) Com-

---

[5] Debate on this question arose out of the compromise reached at San Francisco on the wording of Article 80. The first paragraph states that the terms of existing mandates will be modified only by the new agreements. The second paragraph states that this shall "not be interpreted as giving grounds for delay or postponement of the negotiation and conclusion of [such] agreements . . ."

[6] Clive Parry, "The Legal Nature of the Trusteeship Agreements," *The British Year Book of International Law, 1950* (London: Oxford University Press, 1951), Vol. XXVII, p. 172.

[7] See Commonwealth of Australia, *Parliamentary Papers*, 1945, No. 49, p. 18.

mittee of the General Assembly and in the special sub-committee established to study all the draft agreements in detail. The Australian case for the draft was put by the Australian delegate, Prof. K. H. Bailey who argued strongly for giving to the administering power the sole authority in the territory.[8] New Guinea differed from other mandated territories both in its complex ethnic composition and its strategic geographic position. Furthermore, its economy and social system had been seriously dislocated by the Japanese invasion during the war. The primitive character of the New Guinea people made difficult the achievement of Charter objectives even if authority were undivided and clearly recognized; the task would be impossible should authority be divided and the prestige of the administering authority diminished. It was therefore essential to draw a clear line between the functions of administration and the advisory functions of supervision assigned in the Charter to the Trusteeship Council to which the administering authority was ultimately accountable. Australia was unwilling to administer the territory "on behalf of the United Nations." The inclusion of this phrase would suggest the concept of an agency and open the way to possible interference in administration by members of the Trusteeship Council. As in common law, a trustee was more than an agent; although he was legally accountable for exercising the trust in the interest of the ward, he did not act as a principal as had the mandatories.

The Australian government was proposing to bring about an administrative union of the trust territory with Papua in the interests of the inhabitants. Article 5 of the draft agreement provided for such a union. The administering authority's discretion on this matter had been made explicit "in order to preserve a clear distinction between the functions of administration and of supervision" and, while the application of this provision would be subject to discussion

---

[8] See General Assembly, Official Records (G.A.O.R.): 1st Sess., 2nd Part, 4th Ctte., 18th Mtg., 11 Nov. 1946, pp. 92-95, and 26th Mtg., 11 Dec. 1946, p. 163. See also records of Sub-Ctte. 1 of 4th Ctte., 4th Mtg., 21 Nov. 1946, pp. 20-22.

and supervision by the Trusteeship Council, it was not subject to the latter's approval.

Australia was reluctant to accept any of the proposed amendments to the draft.[9] It was explained that the brevity of the draft agreement was the consequence of the full statement of specific obligations in the Charter. Partial restatement could result only in the understandable implication that the subjects omitted were of comparative unimportance. Thus, the Australian delegate explained that a proposed amendment to the draft agreement to safeguard the equal rights of entry, residence, and property of all nationals of United Nations members could not be accepted. If the amendment was intended to give greater rights than those conferred by Article 76 of the Charter, it was unacceptable; if not, it was redundant and unnecessary. Control of immigration and economic activities would continue to be necessary: a regime of strict equality could not be maintained without prejudice to the interests of the inhabitants. The inclusion of further provisions in the trusteeship agreement relating to general education, freedom of conscience, and political advancement was inappropriate in view of the backward condition of the territory. It was possible that "the task of promoting the welfare and the political and social development of New Guinea would still continue for the next twenty or even hundred years." The proposal by the Soviet Union to subject the authority of the administering power to take military measures within the trust territory to the control of the Security Council was also rejected on the ground that, in accordance with the Charter, it was for the state submitting the trusteeship agreement to determine whether the defence of the territory should be brought within the control of the Council.

---

[9] See G.A.O.R., 1st Sess., 2nd Part, 4th Ctte., 18th Mtg., 11 Nov. 1946, pp. 95-96, and 24th Mtg., 24 Oct. 1946, pp. 148-51; *ibid.*, Sub-Ctte. 1 of 4th Ctte., 4th Mtg., 21 Nov. 1946, p. 24; 9th Mtg., 26 Nov. 1946, pp. 59-64; 12th Mtg., 29 Nov. 1946, pp. 88-90; and 16th Mtg., 1 Dec. 1946, p. 115. For texts of the proposed amendments and Australia's comments thereon, see *ibid.*, 4th Ctte., Part II, pp. 240-51.

The draft agreement for New Guinea as proposed by Australia was accepted by the General Assembly without substantial amendment.[10] The agreement approved by the Assembly on 13 December 1946 was identical with the original draft except on one point. To meet criticisms in the Fourth Committee, Australia agreed to the inclusion in Article 8 of the agreement of a more specific statement concerning its obligations under Article 76 of the Charter.

The draft trusteeship agreement for Nauru, to be administered by Australia on behalf of Australia, New Zealand, and the United Kingdom, was not submitted until the 1947 session of the General Assembly. The debate on the draft was similar to the 1946 discussion on the agreement for New Guinea. The draft agreement for Nauru was more specific about the political advancement of the natives, who were described as "culturally advanced and almost all literate."[11] Australia successfully resisted pressure, particularly from China, India, and the USSR, to modify the agreement to resemble more closely the agreements for the "more advanced" territories of Ruanda-Urundi and Western Samoa.[12] A Soviet proposal that the administering authority undertake to promote periodic visits as might be arranged by the Assembly or the Trusteeship Council was also defeated. The only amendment accepted was the inclusion in the provision relating to defence of a reference to Article 84 of the Charter. One proposed amendment was withdrawn in the light of the following declaration by Australia:

> . . . Article 76d of the Charter is accepted by the delegations of Australia, New Zealand, and the United Kingdom as a binding obligation in relation to the trusteeship agreement for Nauru, it being also noted that in accordance with the terms of Article 76d the welfare of the inhabitants of Nauru is the paramount consideration and obligation. . . .

---

[10] See below, Appendix C, pp. 379-81 for text of the New Guinea agreement.

[11] G.A.O.R., 2nd Sess., 4th Ctte., 35th Mtg., 2 Oct. 1947, p. 25.

[12] See below, Appendix C, pp. 382-83, for excerpts of parallel provisions on political advancement included in the trusteeship agreements for Nauru, Western Samoa, and Ruanda-Urundi.

It is recognized that, in the paramount interests of the native
inhabitants the Administering Authority is obliged to maintain
appropriate non-discriminatory controls and restrictions on
non-Nauruan residents of Nauru.[13]

This declaration was included in the Trusteeship Council minutes
but not in the agreement.

One criticism of the New Guinea agreement, that it was concerned primarily with the rights and powers of the administering
authority, applied with almost equal cogency to the Nauru agreement. In each case, the agreement maintained and extended existing
Australian rights. Yet there is little justice in the claim that Australia
sought to circumvent the trusteeship system wherever possible. There
is much logic in the Australian claim that unfettered discretion by
the administering authority was an essential feature of the system
and that it was undesirable to repeat in incomplete form in the
agreement the general obligations of the Charter. At the same time
the debate does indicate a difficulty in the trusteeship system; its
usefulness depends partly on the extent to which the views of the
Council are acceptable to the administering power, partly on the
influence which discussions have on the outlook of the non-administering powers.

All the other trusteeship agreements provide for the submission
to the International Court of Justice of disputes over interpretation
that may arise between the administering authority and other
members of the United Nations. Such a provision was deliberately
omitted from the Australian agreements. Australia argued that the
provision was unnecessary in the light of Australia's acceptance of
the Court's compulsory jurisdiction under the "optional clause."[14]
Although New Zealand and the United Kingdom had similarly
accepted the "optional clause," they provided specifically in their

---

[13] G.A.O.R., 2nd Sess., 4th Ctte., Annexes, p. 133.
[14] G.A.O.R., 1st. Sess., 2nd Part, Sub-Ctte 1 of 4th Ctte., 12th Mtg., 29 Nov.
1946, p. 86.

trusteeship agreements for the reference of disputes to the Court.[15] The acceptance of the "optional clause" by Australia and other Commonwealth countries is not complete; specifically excluded are "disputes with regard to questions which by international law fall exclusively within the jurisdiction of the Commonwealth of Australia."[16] The omission from the Australian trusteeship agreements of a provision for the reference of disputes to the Court would thus exclude from the Court's jurisdiction disputes arising out of the agreements if it were decided that they concerned matters of domestic jurisdiction. The Australian government saw no reason to debar itself in advance from taking advantage of such a decision.

THE SOUTH WEST AFRICA QUESTION

Australia's attitude on the nature of the trusteeship system was further clarified during the discussions on the status of South West Africa. On 14 December 1946 the General Assembly adopted a resolution expressing its refusal to accede to the incorporation of the mandated territory of South West Africa in the Union of South Africa and recommending that the territory be placed under trusteeship. (Australia along with most of the other administering powers abstained from voting on this resolution.)[17] South Africa flatly rejected the recommendation and proceeded with plans to give South West Africa representation in the Union Parliament. South Africa declared its intention of continuing to administer the territory in the spirit of the mandate, but asserted that the right to submit petitions as it had existed under the mandates system could no longer be exercised.[18] The debate at the next session of the General Assembly culminated in an Assembly resolution urging South Africa

---

[15] The same was true of France.

[16] International Court of Justice, *Yearbook 1946-47*, p. 216.

[17] See General Assembly Resolution 65(I), 14 Dec. 1946, and G.A.O.R., 1st Sess., 2nd Part, 64th Plenary Mtg., 14 Dec. 1946, p. 1327.

[18] G.A.O.R., 2nd Sess., 4th Ctte., 33rd Mtg., 27 Sept. 1947, pp. 15-16.

to submit a trusteeship agreement before its next session. (France and the United States were among the forty-one supporters of the resolution; Australia, Canada, and the United Kingdom voted against it; New Zealand abstained.)[19]

During the debate Dr. Evatt, at length and in uncertain terms, led the defence of South Africa.[20] The Assembly, he claimed, was attempting to coerce South Africa into a course of action which it was not legally obliged to take, and which all delegations at San Francisco had agreed was voluntary. South Africa's action with regard to the 1946 resolution of the General Assembly had been "very reasonable." It behooved the Assembly to accept in good faith what South Africa had done in good faith, especially in view of the outstanding contributions which South Africa and Field Marshal Smuts had made to international co-operation. The relevant objective of the Charter was the betterment of the condition of the natives. "There is nothing in the International Trusteeship System which of and by itself makes the condition of the native peoples better. It depends upon the Administering Power. . . ." The quality of South Africa's administration was not in doubt. Furthermore, despite the absence of a trusteeship agreement, South West Africa would still as a non-self-governing territory be within the purview of the Organization since "the Union Government will have to give, voluntarily [*sic*], reports for the information of the Secretary-General."

Dr. Evatt went on to comment that interference with the discretion of the South African Government was involved. "It is wrong . . . to keep on hammering away at Field Marshal Smuts in order to compel him to do something which, after careful consideration, in his view and in the view of his Government, it is not the proper course to take at the present time." The consequences of the resolution would be unfortunate. By injuring the prestige of the government it could

---

[19] *Ibid.*, 105th Plenary Mtg., 1 Nov. 1947, pp. 650-51, and General Assembly Resolution 140(III), 1 Nov. 1947.

[20] G.A.O.R., 2nd Sess., 104th Plenary Mtg., 1 Nov. 1947, pp. 581-89.

assist people in South Africa who were less liberal than Smuts. This would not help the natives. The very wide powers of the General Assembly should be used wisely; otherwise they might fall into disrepute. The Assembly should not direct its recommendations against a particular power or a particular man unless it had overwhelming proof that such action was in the interests of the United Nations as a whole.

The Australian attitude on the South African question has not changed. Australia opposed the decision taken by the Fourth Committee in 1951 to hear in person the representatives of the Herero, Dama, and Damara tribes on the ground that, since the International Court had stated in an advisory opinion that the peoples of South West Africa retained the right of petition they had acquired under the mandate, the United Nations procedure must conform to that of the mandates system. This required petitions to be transmitted by the mandatory power itself; there was no provision whatever for oral petitions.[21] With the exception of the United States, which abstained, all the administering powers accepted this view. Nor were any of them prepared to support the Fourth Committee's commendation of Reverend Michael Scott's efforts on behalf of the tribes.[22] Similarly, they all abstained from voting on the resolution favoring a trusteeship agreement for South West Africa.[23]

The South West African question has posed some interesting issues of principle as well as of Australian policy. At San Francisco Dr. Evatt proposed that the General Assembly should have the power to determine which particular territories should come within the system of full reporting and inspection.[24] The whole doctrine

[21] G.A.O.R., 6th Sess., 4th Ctte., 204th Mtg., 16 Nov. 1951, pp. 17-18.

[22] See *ibid.*, 248th Mtg., 15 Jan. 1952, p. 321, and Annexes: Agenda item 38, p. 21.

[23] See General Assembly Resolution 570(VI) B, 19 Jan. 1952, and G.A.O.R., 6th Sess., 362nd Plenary Mtg., 19 Jan. 1952, p. 375.

[24] See Australian amendments to the Dumbarton Oaks proposals in *Documents of the United Nations Conference on International Organization, San Francisco, 1945* (New York: United Nations Information Organizations, 1945), Vol. III, pp. 548-49.

of international accountability loomed large in Australian policy at this early stage; it was not supported by the colonial powers, and Australia then tended to shift ground. The final draft of the Charter, although somewhat equivocal on this point, did not definitely require mandatory or other powers to bring colonial or mandated territories under the international trusteeship system. It was made abundantly clear in the subsequent advisory opinion of the International Court on the South West African case that there was no obligation whatever on South Africa to negotiate a trusteeship agreement with the United Nations.

As the pressure on South Africa to submit such an agreement increased, and as South Africa's attitude hardened into a complete unwillingness to meet the United Nations on the issue, the problem became essentially one of keeping the door open to further negotiations, of preventing a complete impasse. Australian policy in the Fourth Committee of the Assembly was directed primarily at maintaining some flexibility in the situation to enable the United Nations on one hand and South Africa on the other to arrive at an agreement through moderating their demands without giving way on any fundamentals. This proved impossible, although both sides later set out their demands in less uncompromising terms.

At the same time, Australian policy appears to have been increasingly affected by the conviction that members of the United Nations must be brought to realize that administering governments are not prepared to undertake obligations beyond those specifically provided for in the Charter and in the trusteeship agreements. Dr. Evatt's arguments—that the discretion of governments not be interfered with and that undesirable political consequences could follow United Nations intervention—in fact go little beyond this, although they do involve a considerable modification of his earlier views on trusteeship as a system.

The behaviour of inexperienced members of the Trusteeship Council in using it primarily as a political forum and the development of the "cold war" partly explain this shift in attitude. At the same time, Australia was showing a clearer appreciation of the United Kingdom's reluctance, clearly evident at San Francisco, to support without serious qualifications the principle of international accountability. A rigid insistence on the legal obligations of the Charter rather than the spirit of its provisions could strengthen the concept of accountability. The peculiarly complex nature of the South African problem and the influence of the idea of Commonwealth solidarity also help to explain Australia's willingness to give a strict rather than a broad construction to Charter obligations.

THE TRUSTEESHIP COUNCIL'S RECOMMENDATIONS

There is no simple way to test the willingness of the administering authorities to pursue the Charter objectives set out in Articles 76, 87, and 88 for trust territories; nor is it simple to assess the effectiveness of their policies in achieving these objectives. The only obligation which can be tested with relative ease is the implied obligation to submit to the Trusteeship Council regular reports and not to obstruct petitions and visiting missions. The function of the Trusteeship Council is merely that of *ex post facto* review since an essential feature of the system is that the administering authority's responsibility for policy and its implementation is complete and unshared. The administering authority will consider the Council's recommendations and implement them only if, in its opinion, they will better achieve Charter objectives. The issues that have arisen concerning the administration of New Guinea and Nauru and the recommendations that the Council has made to Australia in this regard are sketched briefly in the following sections.

New Guinea: The major issue between the Trusteeship Council and Australia arose out of the latter's desire to form an administrative union of the trust territory of New Guinea and the neighbouring Australian territory of Papua. When Australia first accepted the mandate for New Guinea a Royal Commission was appointed to consider whether the mandated territory should be jointly admin-

istered with Papua. Its recommendation in 1919 against unification
was based primarily on contentious and transitory technical grounds;
it ignored the strongly expressed views and the wide experience of
Sir Hubert Murray, who presented a minority report.[25] No serious
attempt at ending the anomaly of separate and parallel administration was made until 1948, when the government submitted to Parliament the Papua and New Guinea Bill. The Bill provided for the
unification of the trust territory and Papua under a single administrator assisted by an executive, a legislative council, and a single
judiciary. The Governor-General of Australia was empowered to
define provinces within the combined territory. The status of the
trust territory was to be protected by two provisions: its annual
expenditure must not be less than the revenue raised therein, and
the administrator was required to reserve for the Governor-General's
assent any ordinance which he believed might not be fully in accord
with Australia's obligations under the trusteeship agreement.[26]
Although Australia claimed that it was not obliged to submit the
proposal to the Trusteeship Council before implementation, the
passage of the bill was delayed to enable the Council to consider
it. Australian policy differed from British policy in this respect: in
1947 the United Kingdom had linked the trust territory of Tanganyika
administratively with Kenya and Uganda without consulting the
Council.

The Trusteeship Council reported that "an administrative union
must remain strictly administrative in nature and scope" and that
it was "not entirely convinced that the proposed union . . . may
not go so far as to compromise the preservation of the separate
identity of the Trust Territory."[27] The Council considered that "the
establishment of a union of the kind proposed imposes an em-

---

[25] See Eggleston, *op. cit.*, pp. 12-13, 113-14, and 124-25.

[26] For text of the Papua and New Guinea Bill 1948, see United Nations Doc. T/
138/Add. 1, 6 July 1948.

[27] G.A.O.R., 3rd Sess., Supple. No. 4, Report of the Trusteeship Council,
pp. 16-17.

barrassing burden on the judgment of the Council, and that it may constitute a difficulty in the way of the discharge by the Council of its responsibilities . . ." It drew attention to the fact that, since the Governor-General could define provinces that included portions of both territories, territorial boundaries might eventually be obliterated. The Council also pointed out that a combined tariff system should not affect the rights of United Nations members and their nationals under Article 76(d) of the Charter. The Council suggested that the International Court of Justice be asked whether the administrative union was compatible with the trusteeship agreement. It finally recommended the review of the proposals in the light of its conclusions and the views expressed in the Council.

To meet some of these objections, the Bill was amended in detail. The Papua-New Guinea Act, which came into force on 1 July 1949, provided that the separate identity and status of New Guinea as a trust territory would be maintained. The provisions of the 1948 Bill permitting the Governor-General to define provinces within both territories by proclamation and allowing the institution of a tariff were deleted. Non-official groups in the trust territory were given representation on the Legislative Council. The Trusteeship Council dislikes administrative unions in general and has persisted in its objections to joint legislatures and joint judiciaries where such unions have been effected. Australia has refused to make further amendments to the Act and the Council has agreed that the existing judicial system "sufficiently safeguards the interests of the inhabitants."[28]

In its annual reports, Australia has furnished separate financial, statistical, and other data relating to the trust territory. The boundaries between the two territories have been maintained in practice and expenditure in the trust territory has exceeded revenue derived from it. This has met with the approval of the Council, and after the visit of the 1953 mission, the Council concluded that, ". . . in

---

[28] G.A.O.R., 6th Sess., Supple. No. 4, Report of the Trusteeship Council, p. 240.

o

considering questions relating to the administrative union affecting
the Trust Territory of New Guinea, it had no information which
might indicate that this union was, at this stage of its development,
not in the interests of the inhabitants of the Trust Territory."[29] The
Council also concluded that "common customs, fiscal and administrative services organized on an inter-territorial basis might have
advantages for the individual Territories participating in such
arrangements, particularly under economic and social conditions
prevailing in territories like Papua and New Guinea."

From the beginning, the Trusteeship Council has urged that there
be greater participation by the native peoples in both central and
local legislation and administration, and that legal status be given
to the traditional native courts. In 1951 Australia established a
Legislative Council for the combined territories; it consisted of
seventeen official and twelve non-official members. Three of the
latter (two from the trust territory) were natives nominated by the
administration; three of the non-official members were elected. The
Council was empowered to make ordinances for the government
of the territory but these required the approval of either the Administrator or the Governor-General of Australia. In practice, the
Council has tended to be an advisory rather than an effective
legislative body since the official majority ensures that only ordinances acceptable to the administration are adopted.

The inclusion of native members was strongly criticized by some
resident Europeans on the ground that the New Guinea natives were
often incapable of grasping territorial as distinct from regional or
village issues. The Trusteeship Council was not satisfied with the
rate of progress, although it became more cautious in its views

---

[29] The report of the visiting mission can be found in Trusteeship Council,
Official Records (T.C.O.R.): 12th Sess., Supple. No. 4, U.N. Visiting Mission
to Trust Territories in the Pacific, 1953: Report on New Guinea, hereinafter
cited as Report of the Visiting Mission (1953). The action taken by the Council
on this report is described in the Council's Report to the General Assembly,
G.A.O.R., 8th Sess., Supple. No. 4, hereinafter cited as Report of the Trusteeship
Council (1953).

after the report of the 1953 visiting mission. Noting that "at the present stage of political development" native representation had "little except educational significance," the Council decided that the "desirable objective of gradually increasing the representation of the indigenous inhabitants on the Legislative Council may at the present stage be most effectively approached by developing its usefulness as a means of political education and preparation for more active participation . . ." Accordingly, it urged that all practicable steps be taken, "including the possible participation of additional indigenous persons in the work of the Council . . . to extend among the indigenous population an understanding of the legislative procedures . . ."[30] The Trusteeship Council suggested that New Guinea observers be appointed to the Legislative Council. The administering authority made several appointments and this has been of considerable educative value. The 1956 visiting mission pointed out that "an arrangement which denies voting power to persons attending a legislature cannot satisfy the people for long nor give them a feeling of active participation in the management of the affairs of the Territory."[31] It recommended the nomination of additional New Guinea members as a means of satisfying the growing desire of the people of New Guinea to participate in their own political development. It also suggested the addition of New Guinea representatives to the town and district advisory councils which are at present wholly European.

---

[30] Report of the Trusteeship Council (1953), *op. cit.*, p. 87. The Papua and New Guinea Bill was amended in 1957 to remove certain technical flaws in the provisions for representation. After six years' experience, the Opposition urged greater representation of missionary groups and the native population. The Minister for Territories pointed out that "at the present stage, it is not possible to form a comprehensive electorate by which the natives could choose their representatives" (Mr. P. Hasluck). See Commonwealth of Australia, *Parliamentary Debates* (*C.P.D.*) (House of Representatives), Vol. 15 (New Series), 15 May 1957, p. 1420.

[31] The report of the visiting mission can be found in T.C.O.R., 18th Sess., Supple. No. 5, U.N. Visiting Mission to Trust Territories in the Pacific, 1956: Report on New Guinea, hereinafter cited as Report of the Visiting Mission (1956).

A more effective means of political education could be found in native participation in government at the local and regional levels. The Papua and New Guinea Bill of 1948 had envisaged the establishment of democratic native village councils with "such functions as may be provided by ordinance in relation to the peace, order and welfare of the inhabitants in the areas in respect of which they may be established."[32] The Trusteeship Council recommended the review of these powers to give natives greater initiative in the conduct of their own affairs and to train them in the essentials of public finance by giving some measure of financial responsibility to the councils.[33] These recommendations were partly met by the establishment of four native village councils in 1951 and two more in 1952 under the Native Village Councils Ordinance 1949-52, mainly in the Rabaul and Manus areas. The councils were set up after the local people had expressed a desire for them: in one instance, the Raluana people have firmly refused to form a council despite a mixture of government persuasion and proclamation. The 1953 visiting mission was impressed by the fact that the councils were successfully carrying out business and government activities necessitating the imposition of taxes. Accordingly, the Trusteeship Council endorsed the mission's view that "a rapid development of this system of local government would do much to hasten political advancement . . ."[34] and welcomed Australia's proposal to make available more specialist officers for this purpose.

No further progress was made in setting up village councils between 1953 and 1956. The continued hostility of the Raluana people seemed to have crystallized in a direct hostility to the whole idea of a village council, and this had a discouraging effect on the administration. The 1956 visiting mission, while recognizing the

[32] G.A.O.R., 3rd Sess., Supple. No. 4, Report of the Trusteeship Council, p. 12.

[33] G.A.O.R., 4th Sess., Supple. No. 4, Report of the Trusteeship Council, p. 65.

[34] Report of the Trusteeship Council (1953), *op. cit.*, p. 89, and Report of the Visiting Mission (1953), *op. cit.*, pp. 13-14.

difficulties in the way of extending the system, felt that the administering authority had become somewhat timid in its approach and was delaying action until exceptionally favourable circumstances had been created for the establishing of new councils. It urged a speeding up of the program, even if it meant taking some risks: "any failure to accelerate their development at this critical stage would be a threat to the whole programme of advancement . . . and much of the present good-will towards the Administration will be lost."[35]

Criticism of Australian progress has developed in the Trusteeship Council, chiefly among members of the Soviet and Latin American blocs who considered that attempts were being made to perpetuate a colonial status in the territory.[36] Comparisons with village government in India and other parts of Asia are misleading because of the more advanced social forms which exist in these countries. In the atomized society of New Guinea-Papua, the difficulties of integration are very considerable; slow but steady progress is being made in the creation of clusters of villages to be governed by a village council. These councils do fit in with New Guinea traditions in many parts of the territory where community rather than individual opinion is the decisive force in village life. They will be the basis upon which a more advanced political structure of a regional and territorial kind will ultimately be built.

The Trusteeship Council had also proposed that statutory recognition be given to existing indigenous courts and that they be increased in number. The 1953 visiting mission agreed with the Australian view that this "would be quite impossible with the many varying levels of development which now exist."[37] However, "since there is nothing to prevent people who are conducting a village council satisfactorily from maintaining also their own court with specified

[35] Report of the Visiting Mission (1956), *op. cit.*, p. 29.
[36] See, for example, the statement by the Soviet delegate in T.C.O.R., 18th Sess., 723rd Mtg., 10 July 1956, p. 191.
[37] Report of the Visiting Mission (1953), *op. cit.*, pp. 10-11.

statutory powers," the mission felt that statutory recognition might be given to the courts in certain advanced areas. Similar views were expressed by the 1956 visiting mission, which also urged that minor matters, particularly those concerned with native law and custom, be dealt with by New Guinea court members.

In the economic field, the Council has noted the interdependence of social progress and economic development. It urged Australia to survey the resources of the territory, to draw up a comprehensive plan for development, and to provide the indigenous inhabitants with "the means of participating to an ever-increasing extent in developing the wealth of the Territory."[38] It commended the efforts to foster native co-operatives. Australia is handicapped in part by the lack of detailed knowledge of geological and forest resources and of soil fertility. Full-scale surveys are gradually being carried out as part of long-term policy. Detailed planning has, however, not gone further ahead than three years and long-term objectives exist mainly in broad terms. The Council has always favoured the greater use of direct taxation, particularly of gold-mining profits. The 1953 visiting mission partly endorsed the administering authority's view that this was impracticable when it reported that "the imposition of direct taxes may fall short of a solution of the Territory's financial problems . . . [since] many of the indigenous people have no money income . . . nor could the few Europeans . . . make a major contribution in direct revenue."[39] Three years later, the visiting mission proposed the imposition of direct taxes but at the same time pointed out that "in view of the tremendous difficulties due largely to the geographical features of New Guinea the task of an Administering Authority could be a challenge to any nation, even the richest and most technically advanced." It suggested that "the international community has a special responsibility to help

---

[38] G.A.O.R., 5th Sess., Supple. No. 4, Report of the Trusteeship Council, p. 124.

[39] Report of the Visiting Mission (1953), *op. cit.*, p. 19.

the Administering Authority in all possible ways to meet this challenging task . . ."[40]

In the social field, the Council has continually pointed out the inadequacy of medical facilities, deficient both in personnel and hospitals. The 1953 visiting mission, although "not unaware of the great financial contribution which the Administering Authority is making to the improvement of the Territory's health services," pointed out these inadequacies, and contrasted many of the native hospitals, "in urgent need of improvement," with many of the European hospitals in which equipment and facilities were "more than adequate."[41] The Council endorsed this view. The next visiting mission expressed concern both at the shortage of trained doctors and at the lag in hospital construction despite plans for the establishing of regional hospitals.[42]

The problem of corporal punishment in native territories is a universal one. Corporal punishment has always been illegal in New Guinea except by court sentence, and the Council has repeatedly urged its complete abolition. Australia's initial reaction was that in fact no sentences of corporal punishment had been imposed since the resumption of civil administration. In 1952 such punishments were abolished for all offences except certain misdemeanors by juveniles, sexual offences against females, certain crimes of violence, and prison offences relating to mutiny and gross personal violence. (These crimes are so punishable in Australia itself.) Although Australia expressed in principle its support for the complete abolition of corporal punishment, this did not satisfy the Council, which has continued to press for total abolition.[43]

The Trusteeship Council has continually pressed the administration to push forward with its plans for the general improvement of education despite the shortage of funds, since the high rate of

---

[40] Report of the Visiting Mission (1956), *op. cit.*, pp. 25-26.

[41] Report of the Visiting Mission (1953), *op. cit.*, p. 21.

[42] Report of the Visiting Mission (1956), *op. cit.*, pp. 36-37.

[43] Report of the Trusteeship Council (1953), *op. cit.*, p. 104.

illiteracy hinders political advancement. It has contrasted the facilities for secondary education afforded to European and Asian students with the absence of such facilities for New Guinea natives. On the very controversial matter of the use of "pidgin English" in education and administration, the Council has been most critical of Australian policy. The 1953 visiting mission took the view that

> Pidgin is not only not a suitable language for instruction, but . . . it has characteristics derived from the circumstances in which it was invented which reflect now outmoded concepts of the relationship between indigenous inhabitants and immigrant groups. Therefore, it believes that the most energetic steps should be taken to eradicate this jargon from all instruction given within the Territory, and that plans be urgently developed to eliminate it from the Territory completely.[44]

Because of the immense diversity in native dialect, the absence of any other *lingua franca*, and the conflict of opinion among linguistic specialists, "pidgin English" has continued to be widely used. There has been some suspicion of "pidgin" among the anti-colonial powers as a vestige of colonialism. In 1956, the visiting mission, while recognizing its value as a *lingua franca*, pointed out that it handicapped both the political and educational advancement of the people: "Regardless of how satisfactory Pidgin may have been for the purposes it served in the past, it is now inadequate and completely unsatisfactory as a means of communication for any people who expect to take their place in the modern world in the future."[45] The Australian government has now developed plans for the extension of the teaching of English as the *lingua franca* in the territory.

One aspect of education was the subject of a resolution adopted at the sixth session of the Assembly, recommending that the administering authorities take "all appropriate steps to disseminate information on the United Nations, and on the International Trustee-

---

[44] Report of the Visiting Mission (1953), *op. cit.*, p. 25.
[45] Report of the Visiting Mission (1956), *op. cit.*, p. 40.

ship System in particular, among the population and in the schools."[46]
This is a peculiarly difficult task in tribal areas where a cluster of
villages normally represents the limit of geographical awareness:
broader organizational concepts are almost beyond the limits of
understanding of primitive peoples. Australia was criticized both
in the Trusteeship Council and by the 1953 visiting mission for the
general ignorance of the United Nations found in New Guinea and
Nauru.[47] At the eighth session of the General Assembly, a resolution
was passed asking the administering authorities to supply the
Secretary-General with suggestions concerning the appropriate channels of information through which United Nations information
might be sent direct to the territories.[48] Australia abstained from
the vote on the ground that this involved a usurpation of the administrative authority exercised by Australia under Article 2 of the
trusteeship agreement.

The whole problem of administering a large and substantially
unexplored territory with a scattered and heterogeneous population,
much of it at Stone Age levels of culture, is a far more complex
one than that of governing more advanced and homogeneous peoples.
The development of New Guinea requires a considerable investment
of capital. This has always constituted a difficulty for Australia; a
country itself in need of extensive capital investment for developmental purposes. When the mandate for New Guinea was originally
accepted, Sir Joseph Cook, Acting Prime Minister, said that Australia would expect the territory to pay for itself. British experience,
and the experience of other European powers, has shown that this
is impossible for at least a generation. Australia at first rather
reluctantly moved to an acceptance of the need for subsidy. Efficient
administration and social development must depend on revenue;
this depends on production, which is impossible without investment.

---

[46] General Assembly Resolution 556(VI), 18 Jan. 1952.
[47] See below, pp. 384 ff., Appendix D, "Attitudes of the Native Peoples of
Papua and New Guinea to the United Nations 1945-54."
[48] General Assembly Resolution 754(VIII), 9 Dec. 1953.

Present Australian policy lays great stress on attracting capital and at the same time safeguarding native rights and welfare. These have been the factors limiting the more rapid development of New Guinea and Papua, and more speedy realization of the trusteeship objectives.

The Australian administration has been aware of the criticisms by experts in colonial administration[49] and the Trusteeship Council. The visiting missions of 1950, 1953, and 1956 contained ex-colonial administrators of wide experience. But there has been a tendency to national self-assertion and some impatience at a great deal of uninformed and inexpert political criticism from the anti-colonial bloc. The visiting missions have shown an increasing awareness of the problems: the 1953 mission praised the administration for its efforts to bring wider areas under control through a policy of "peaceful penetration." The Trusteeship Council endorsed this report and noted the arduous nature of the duties of officers entrusted with the task of penetrating uncontrolled areas.[50]

As the Trusteeship Council, with the exception of two or three members, became milder in its comments on Australian policies, Australian administrators and officials became more adamant in their refusal to give effect to some of the criticisms. As the concept of domestic jurisdiction was being given a broad construction with a view to limiting the competence of the United Nations, so in the Trusteeship Council, Australian delegates increasingly insisted that the authority of the Trusteeship Council was a limited one.

> The responsibility for administrative decisions and action was the Administering Authority's alone. All Administering Authorities gave attention to the Council's suggestions, but it was for each Administering Authority to decide whether such suggestions were useful, practicable and wise. If that were not so, the Administering Authority would have abandoned its

---

[49] See Lucy Mair, *Australia in New Guinea* (London: Christophers, 1948), *passim;* and M. Groves, "The History of Papua," in *Historical Studies: Australia and New Zealand*, Vol. V (1953), pp. 386-401.

[50] Report of the Visiting Mission (1953), *op. cit.*, p. 8, and Report of the Trusteeship Council (1953), *op. cit.*, p. 85.

responsibility, an attitude which would not be consonant with the Charter and the Trusteeship Agreements. It was from that standpoint that the Australian Government regarded the recommendations 'and suggestions of the Trusteeship Council. In its view, the fact that an Administering Authority had failed to comply with a recommendation of the Council did not necessarily lay it open to criticism. . . . It was rather a question of the Administering Authorities giving attention to the Council's suggestions than of compliance with the Council's recommendations being demanded.[51]

Nauru: Nauru is a trust territory administered by Australia on behalf of itself, New Zealand, and the United Kingdom. The Trusteeship Council has made a series of recommendations to the administering authority covering a variety of matters. As in New Guinea, it has urged greater participation by the natives both in administration and in legislation. The Council of Chiefs was replaced in 1951 by a Local Government Council elected by universal suffrage but this, according to the Trusteeship Council, "does not fully satisfy the persons directly concerned."[52]

Repeated and unsuccessful attempts have been made by the Trusteeship Council to obtain full financial information from the British Phosphate Commissioners about their operations, so that the Council can determine whether the Commissioners are paying reasonable wages and providing adequate revenue for the administration. The Commissioners have substantially increased the royalties payable to the administration and to various trust funds for the natives. The question not yet decided is whether they are as large as the Commissioners can afford. The Council has repeatedly requested Australia to give careful consideration to the problem of livelihood of the inhabitants of Nauru when the phosphate deposits

---

[51] T.C.O.R., 16th Sess., 626th Mtg., 29 June 1955, p. 118. Cf. *South Pacific* (Sydney), Vol. 8 (1955), p. 81. For an excellent survey of Australian policy in Papua-New Guinea, see J. Andrews, "New Guinea and Papua" in Gordon Greenwood and Norman Harper, eds., *Australia in World Affairs, 1950-55* (Melbourne: F. W. Cheshire, 1957), pp. 323-40.

[52] Report of the Trusteeship Council (1953), *op. cit.*, p. 115.

become exhausted, some sixty years from now. Mr. Krishna Menon (India) has proposed the sending of soil and manure so that the island can provide a living for its people after the phosphate deposits have been exhausted. Another proposed solution is the transfer of the present population (after retraining) to another island, but this could not take place without the free consent of the islanders. In fact, the Australian government has been studying the problem in consultation with the Nauruans.[53]

The Council has commended the social achievements of the administration, which has introduced a comprehensive modern housing program and increased medical facilities. To meet the criticisms of the 1953 visiting mission, the administration approved the construction of a new hospital. The major educational problem has been to restore facilities for secondary education destroyed during the war. This was completed in 1951. Education is compulsory between the ages of six and sixteen, and in 1952 thirty-five Nauruans were studying abroad. The practice of subjecting contract laborers to penal sanctions has been abolished. The Movement of Natives Ordinance, whereby the movement of indigenous and Chinese inhabitants is restricted after dark by a pass system, has evoked continuous criticism from the Council, criticism which the administration has resisted. Immigration policy has however been partly relaxed to allow Chinese workers to bring their families into Nauru, subject to certain safeguards.

TRANSMISSION OF INFORMATION
ON NON-SELF-GOVERNING TERRITORIES

The adoption of the Australian proposals at San Francisco (Article 73(e) of the Charter) has imposed on all members responsible for non-self-governing territories the obligation

---

[53] *Sydney Morning Herald*, 23 June 1954. See also T.C.O.R., 715-18th Mtgs., 28 June — 2 July 1956, pp. 129-31, 141-45.

> to transmit regularly to the Secretary-General for information purposes, subject to such limitation as security and constitutional considerations may require, statistical and other information of a technical nature relating to economic, social, and educational conditions in the territories for which they are respectively responsible. . . .

At the first session of the General Assembly a proposal was made to set up a committee to receive and consider such information. It was also proposed to make compulsory the submission of political information. Australia's view was that such a committee was superfluous since the Secretary General was the appropriate repository of information, and that, although the transmission of political information was desirable, it was nevertheless optional. The Assembly set up an *ad hoc* committee to examine the Secretary-General's summary and analysis of the information, but it was agreed that the transmission of information about political progress was voluntary.[54] Similar committees were set up for temporary periods at subsequent sessions of the Assembly. At the seventh session (1952) it was proposed to establish such a committee on a permanent basis. Australia, unlike some of the other colonial powers, had co-operated in regularly forwarding political information. Yet Australia demurred at anything more than a three-year tenure for the committee. The proposal met with a frigid reception by the other administering powers, and the committee was extended for only three years.[55]

At the same session the Assembly adopted a resolution, in the face of the unanimous opposition of the administering powers, inviting the latter to facilitate the participation of indigenous representatives from the non-self-governing territories in the work of the committee and to provide the executive and legislative bodies in the territories with copies of the reports of the committee and relevant resolutions of the Assembly.[56] The Australian delegate felt

---

[54] G.A.O.R., 1st Sess., 2nd Part, Sub-Ctte. 2 of 4th Ctte., 2nd Mtg., 18 Nov. 1946, p. 13, and General Assembly Resolution 66(I), 14 Dec. 1946.

[55] General Assembly Resolution 646(VII), 10 Dec. 1952.

[56] General Assembly Resolution 647(VII), 10 Dec. 1952.

that any "dual representation" was "entirely unacceptable" and
would lead to "chaotic situations." While considering that the
problem might be met by the inclusion of "competent indigenous
representatives of the territories in the delegations of the Member
States," he stressed that "the composition of their delegations was
the exclusive prerogative of the Member States."[57] Commenting
on these resolutions, Mr. R. G. Casey, the Australian Minister for
External Affairs, declared that they represented part of a continued
drive to take the determination of policy out of the hands of the
countries responsible. "This we cannot agree to, and we will strenuously resist this tendency."[58] This statement came on top of a sharp
Australian rejoinder that unless the Assembly accepted the view
that the transmission of political information was voluntary, those
administering powers which were submitting such information might
have to reconsider their position.[59]

THE AUSTRALIAN PARLIAMENT AND TRUSTEESHIP

Trusteeship has been discussed only on three occasions in the
Australian Parliament, one of them very briefly. The first important
debate took place in connection with the ratification of the United
Nations Charter.[60] Trusteeship was considered again during the
debate on the Papua and New Guinea Bill 1948-49. In this debate,
the Labour government vigorously defended the trusteeship agreement for New Guinea both on the grounds of security and of native
welfare. The strong Opposition attack[61] centred around the power

---

[57] G.A.O.R., 7th Sess., 4th Ctte., 269th Mtg., 11 Nov. 1952, p. 140.

[58] For summary of statement by Mr. Casey, see *Current Notes on International
Affairs* (Dept. of External Affairs, Canberra), Vol. 23 (1952), p. 741.

[59] G.A.O.R., 7th Sess., 4th Ctte., 258th Mtg., 29 Oct. 1952, p. 70.

[60] See above, pp. 69 ff. and 88-89.

[61] For the major criticisms by the Opposition, see *C.P.D.*, Vol. 201, 1 March
1949, p. 741 (Mr. T. White), p. 769 (Mr. J. McEwen), and p. 777 (Mr. O. H. Beale);
and *ibid.*, 2 March 1949, pp. 843-44 (Mr. H. Holt), p. 850 (Mr. C. W. Davidson),
and p. 856 (Mr. P. C. Spender).

of the United Nations to carry out inspections which, it was felt, could facilitate espionage. This led to proposals for either annexation of the type being attempted in South West Africa, or a strategic trusteeship on the United States pattern with the right to close certain areas for security reasons and so prevent inspection. Further grounds for criticism were the equality clause in the Charter which might allow unrestricted immigration, and the alleged limitation of the defence power of the administering government to local defence. The co-operative procedure of the government in delaying and then modifying the Bill in accordance with the recommendations of the Trusteeship Council was openly attacked. Liberal opinion was exceptionally sensitive; it resented as humiliating Australia's being held accountable to the representatives of peoples with appalling records with regard to administration and the observance of human rights. Such criticisms in no way affected Liberal policy after the election of 1949. While individual Liberal and Country party speakers have violently attacked the Council, the Liberal government has attacked neither the terms of the trusteeship agreements nor the principles of the trusteeship system.

The continuing criticisms of the anti-colonial powers despite the general commendation of Australian administration by the 1956 visiting mission evoked mild resentment in the Parliament during the debate on the estimates for 1956-57. Although the Trusteeship Council in its reports has made no reference to it, individual members of the Trusteeship Council have alleged that racial discrimination was being practised by segregation of Papuans.[62] The differing levels of education achieved at the primary stage of education have necessitated the adoption of different curricula and teaching methods as the best means of narrowing the cultural gap between Papuan and European children. A real problem will develop when a small elite of educated Papuans is created as a result of secondary and university

---

[62] *C.P.D.* (House of Representatives), Vol. 13 (New Series), 11 Oct. 1956, pp. 1418-19 (Mr. P. E. Joske).

training given on the mainland of Australia; it will be temporarily difficult for them to adapt themselves to conditions existing in Papua-New Guinea during the transition period.

The second point of criticism was the pressure of Afro-Asian powers for the setting of a date when the territory will be fit for self-government. Several of the newly independent countries of Asia, exceptionally sensitive to the survival of colonialism in any form, have pressed with enthusiasm and little knowledge for such a decision. The difficulties here are very great indeed and parliamentarians of both major political parties were in complete agreement that this would be premature. The cultural backwardness of the peoples of New Guinea, a backwardness that the visiting missions fully appreciate, makes it impossible to set a target date for self-government. One of the Papuan members of the Legislative Council suggested that he and his colleague "be sent to the United Nations, where we could tell those people to mind their own business. We are perfectly satisfied with what is being done for us."[63]

The press makes little comment on trusteeship questions and rarely reports Council recommendations. The criticism of the use of "pidgin English" did arouse a controversy that found echoes in the press. The Australian public is badly informed about the trusteeship system and its application to New Guinea and Nauru. Even informed opinion has found it difficult to keep up to date because of the paucity of information. Unofficial European opinion in New Guinea appears extremely critical of trusteeship, and the visiting mission was vigorously attacked in the local press. One of the three elected European members of the Legislative Council has demanded repudiation of the agreement and outright annexation, claiming that development has been delayed principally because of "Lake Success tomfoolery."[64]

---

[63] See *ibid.*, p. 1427 (Mr. A. A. Calwell).
[64] Melbourne *Herald*, 13 Aug. 1953.

CONCLUSION

At San Francisco Australian enthusiasm for the doctrine of international "accountability" arose in part out of the socialist heritage of the Australian Labour party. There was a genuine desire to assist the nascent and vocal nationalist movements in Asia as well as a consciousness of the need to establish friendly relations with new countries close to Australia. Dr. Evatt was fully aware of the need to retain popular support in Australia and to find formulas which would appeal to the emerging Asian nations. His personal enthusiasm for the doctrine of accountability had no permanent foundations in public or political attitudes in Australia. He was far in advance of his own party and found little support in public opinion. Concern for general international accountability was thus little more than a passing phase in Australian policy. In a sense this was reflected in Australia's insistence upon the free exercise of its full powers to determine policy in its own trust territory of New Guinea. In no other way did Australia conceive it possible to achieve the enlightened doctrines of trusteeship, doctrines of specific accountability which were regarded as desirable and to which Australia has attempted to adhere.

Australia has aligned itself with the other administering states on almost every issue in the Trusteeship Council. On only one occasion, at the first session of the Council, did an Australian delegate adopt a policy disconcerting to another administering power: he pressed the United Kingdom delegate for information on a petition from Tanganyika which the latter was disinclined to give.[65] Even earlier Australia had begun to move into the administering camp and has since been subjected to criticism by the non-administering powers, especially the Soviet bloc, some of the Latin American and Middle Eastern states, and the Afro-Asian bloc.

Is there any real justification for the assumption that a system of international "accountability" is both desirable and valid? Due

---

[65] See T.C.O.R., 1st Sess., 20th Mtg., 21 April 1947, pp. 527-32.

P

weight must be given to those who stress the lack of knowledge of many critics of governments administering trust or non-self-governing territories. Failure to appreciate the social and economic conditions in any particular territory can result in the advocacy of courses of action in such territories that are unrealistic, if not harmful to the interests of the inhabitants. Yet there would appear to be certain useful consequences flowing from a system of international accountability which more than balance any adverse effects of ill-informed criticism. The primary and most significant benefit to be derived arises from the effect on governments administering trust territories of the realization that their actions are subject to regular and frequent review at an international level. This produces a greater alertness on the part of the government and administrators and an increased readiness to consider changes in established practices, if not revisions in laws and ordinances.

This factor of international review is especially important for countries like Australia and New Zealand which possess few dependent territories. Their officials, whose experience has usually been confined to one area, can benefit from the wider experience of the representatives of other administering governments with broader responsibilities in the colonial field. Developments which would normally occur may be accelerated through the process of international review. Changes in the government of Western Samoa were, for example, obviously hastened by the prospect of a review of the administration by the Trusteeship Council in 1947 and some clauses of Papua-New Guinea Act 1949 reflected criticisms in the Trusteeship Council.

It is also important that senior administrative officers are forced to justify at an international level their actions, or lack of them. In the absence of any such accountability they might well take the view that any outside critic was ill-informed and that it was a waste of time for them, as experts, to concern themselves with public discussion. Field officials, endeavouring to secure a reconsideration of established policies, might find it useful to refer to possible

criticism at the international level as a means of securing governmental action on particular problems. The very existence of the international trusteeship system lessens political extremism, particularly in the older established territories. Reference to the United Nations provides a safety valve to local leaders who need not rely on a single channel of protest.

The particular form of international "accountability" represented in the United Nations trusteeship system is based upon two basic principles. Firstly, the trustee government exercises complete and exclusive powers of administration in the trust territory: there is no suggestion of subordination in the sense that these governments could be described as agents of the United Nations. Secondly, the function of review is exercised by the United Nations through its Trusteeship Council and ultimately through the General Assembly. The function of review, of advisory supervision, is in fact exercised primarily by the Trusteeship Council, a body which by its composition does not possess sufficient knowledge of conditions in trust territories to ensure that recommendations will be constructive and realistic. Special opportunities are available to the Trusteeship Council to acquire local knowledge of particular trust territories: the annual reporting procedure, the technique of the triennial visiting mission, the attendance each year at the Trusteeship Council of special field representatives from each of the territories. The real danger arises when political and ideological considerations give rise to ill-informed *post hoc* criticisms which are unrelated to the specialized and often technical needs of the inhabitants of the territories. When the Trusteeship Council becomes a political forum, it ceases to be a valuable organ of review.

As to New Guinea and Nauru, the Trusteeship Council has cast its recommendations in permissive forms which do not face the administering authority with the odium of refusing to accept them. This very desirable practice has focussed attention upon specific Charter obligations and particular local problems. This has in fact accelerated government action in several instances. The system of

visiting missions has aroused some criticism in Australia. The effectiveness and capacity of such missions must, of course, depend
greatly upon the personalities and capacities of the members of the
missions themselves. They depend perhaps even more upon the
quality of the accompanying Secretariat officials. From a purely
technical point of view, there is much to be commended in the
suggestion that the missions be composed entirely of Secretariat
officials, trained to gather and assess vital information. Yet the
benefits to be derived from such a change are more than offset
by the major advantage of the present technique: the opportunity
it provides to representatives of non-administering governments to
educate themselves in the problems of administration in the field.
On the whole, Australia has profited considerably from the system
in so far as it has made the Trusteeship Council much more conscious
of the peculiar problems of New Guinea and Nauruan administration. The 1953 visiting mission pointed out that "there was no real
parallel between physical conditions in New Guinea and those in
the other Trust Territories." The mission could not "help but feel
that some of the discussions which had taken place on the political
advancement of the indigenous people had been premature." The
mission performed a similar valuable service to Australia in pointing
out that "the Nauruan people cannot be regarded as more than a
small community, and in no case as a potential State; moreover,
this community, isolated as it is and a small island in the Pacific,
has services exceeding by far those of any other community of
similar size."[66] The present composition of the Trusteeship Council
(half of the seats are allocated to the administering powers) and the
system of visiting missions does make possible realistic and constructive recommendations.

The Declaration Regarding Non-Self-Governing Territories (Chapter XI of the Charter) appears to have accomplished very little.
There is some value in a solemn declaration of this type. It not

---

[66] Report of the Trusteeship Council (1953), *op. cit.*, pp. 81 and 112.

only establishes general principles; it also brings within the purview of the United Nations the question of the degree to which colonial powers generally are discharging their "sacred trust" to promote the welfare of colonial territories. Yet its practical effect has been almost negligible. The discussions in the General Assembly on these problems have developed into procedural wrangles—for example, over the committee to receive reports submitted by the colonial powers. There has been little real discussion of the substantive problems—economic, social, and educational—of colonial territories. Somewhat optimistically, Australia at San Francisco had pressed for the declaration in Chapter XI because it felt the exchange of information would assist the various administrations. The ensuing discussions in the United Nations may have had some educative value for any members open to conviction. In fact, however, a deadlock developed when the critics of administering governments directed the discussion to political developments in sensitive areas, such as West Africa, and most administering governments were not prepared to support any political discussion whatever.

Finally, it cannot be emphasized too strongly that, from an Australian point of view, New Guinea is a sensitive area. It occupies a unique position as compared with other trust territories. No other trust territory is so intimately related from a security point of view to its administering government. The most important threat to Australian security was in fact checked there in 1942-43. Awareness of the Australian public's apprehension on that score directly conditions attitudes taken by Australian representatives in the United Nations and its organs when problems directly or indirectly affecting New Guinea are discussed. Any action taken by an Australian government must reflect this basic fact. The development of atomic weapons which may make possible attacks on Melbourne from a base at Saigon or Hanoi in no way affects the political reality of the physical proximity of New Guinea to Australia.

chapter eight

Economic and Social Co-operation

FULL EMPLOYMENT

Haunted by the spectre of the depression and conscious of its exceptionally vulnerable position of dependence on export markets, Australia fought vehemently at San Francisco to commit the United Nations firmly to the ideal of full employment. As an objective this commanded the unanimous support of all Australian political parties: disavowal of such a policy would have been tantamount to political suicide. Australian policy at the post-war conferences, culminating with San Francisco, was directed towards obtaining a pledge from other countries, particularly the great industrial countries, to maintain a high and stable level of employment which would in turn help to support stable export markets. While this aim was not fully achieved, some measure of success was accomplished by the insertion in Article 55 of the Charter of the provision that the United Nations "shall promote . . . full employment." To achieve the purposes listed in Article 55, "all Members pledge themselves to take joint and separate action in cooperation with the Organization" (Article 56). The Economic and Social Council (ECOSOC) was empowered to make studies and recommendations and to hold international conferences on subjects within its competence, including full employment (Article 62).

These Charter provisions represented the maximum that could be achieved at the time. The Australian proposals for co-ordinated international action to prevent the recurrence of depression included the full employment pledge, the continuous exchange and collation of statistical information on economic conditions, and agreement to meet in conference should unemployment develop. Internal policies were embodied in concrete form in the Australian White Paper of May 1945;[1] external policies had already been outlined at a series of international conferences. There was little international opposition to the general principles behind these policies; the differences arose chiefly over the desirability of using the term "full employment."

The appropriate organ for the regular review of economic trends appeared to be the United Nations Economic and Social Council. In 1948 the first of a series of annual questionnaires was despatched by the Council to governments. These require a comprehensive analysis of employment conditions and payments positions, an estimate of probable trends in both of these spheres, and a survey of plans for combating declining employment should it appear. The replies are collated and reviewed annually by ECOSOC. The functional commissions set up by ECOSOC and concerned with reports on specific problems usually consist of representatives of governments rather than of independent experts. This tends to make the discussions mainly political in character, and in consequence the commissions submit very general recommendations rather than

---

[1] Commonwealth of Australia, *Parliamentary Papers, Full Employment in Australia*, 1945, No. 11 (Canberra: Commonwealth Govt. Printer), pp. 1193-1212.

technical advice. These do little more than urge governments to consider their responsibilities under Articles 55 and 56, to intensify their efforts to maintain full employment, and to keep international trade at the maximum level. Since 1951 the questionnaires have improved in quality as trained economists have played a greater part in drafting them; fuller and more detailed information has been obtained and this has made the collated replies more useful to members.

A more constructive step was the appointment of a group of experts in 1949 to consider the measures required to achieve full employment. Their report, *National and International Measures for Full Employment*, emphasized adequacy of demand as the vital factor, and recommended a number of concrete measures, domestic and international. With regard to the former, the experts recommended that governments annually determine and publish employment targets and draw up stabilization plans. These plans were to include details of proposed fiscal, credit, money investment, and wage and price policies to promote expansion. They were also to contain provisions for automatic compensatory action under which governments bound themselves in advance to set their enumerated countermeasures in operation within a stated time should employment levels fall below prescribed limits. These domestic measures were to be supplemented by international action to achieve an expansion of world trade. One of the methods proposed was to enlarge the functions and activities of both the International Bank and the International Monetary Fund. The recommendations of the committee of experts were adopted by ECOSOC on 15 August 1950,[2] with one major amendment: automatic compensatory action was not recommended to governments.

Another expert committee presented a report on *Measures for International Economic Stability* in 1951. The committee suggested that international commodity agreements on raw materials similar

---

[2] ECOSOC Resolution 290(XI), 15 Aug. 1950.

to the International Wheat Agreement were more satisfactory than financial grants or loans. It advocated a steady flow of international capital to keep the flow of goods steady, and the development of adequate international monetary reserves to maintain imports during a recession. During the discussion of the report in ECOSOC, the underdeveloped countries drew attention to the omission of any analysis of the relationship between prices of primary products and the prices of manufactured goods, and of the importance to under-developed countries of the pursuit of stable economic policies by the industrialized countries. These concerns were reflected in the resolution adopted by the General Assembly in December 1952 which recommended that governments co-operate in establishing international primary commodity agreements and that they consider, when adopting measures affecting the price of primary commodities, the effect of such measures on the terms of trade of newly-developed countries.[3]

The real effect of the recommendations of ECOSOC and the Assembly has been remarkably limited. Great Britain alone has adopted a specific, numerical, full employment target. Governments have demurred for a variety of reasons: primarily, because the measures appeared superfluous or unreal while levels of employment were high, or alternatively, because action was neither desirable, possible, nor constitutional in those states where the powers of governments were limited. Some government answers to questionnaires indicated too that advance planning to maintain full employment was difficult because the problem was so intimately bound up with their balance of payments. The general acceptance of the principle of full employment has, however, been accompanied by active co-operation in the pooling of information, potentially valuable as a basis for countermeasures against depression. The creation of machinery for collating and distributing information has been an important function of the United Nations. The immediate value

---

[3] General Assembly Resolution 623(VII), 21 Dec. 1952.

of ECOSOC's methods of handling the problem may be seen in the continuous consultation among experts; ideally, the effectiveness of these methods will become apparent when "every Government succeeds in implementing all of the measures announced [to promote full employment and economic stability] despite the political and other difficulties that may be encountered."[4]

Despite its vehement insistence on the full employment pledge at San Francisco and the inclusion of an Australian member in each of ECOSOC's small groups of experts, there has been little public discussion and fewer public statements by the Australian government or its officials. In 1950, during the discussion in ECOSOC on the report on *National and International Measures for Full Employment*, Dr. E. R. Walker, the Australian member of the group of experts, remarked that the government had not yet had time to "make commitments regarding some of the experts' recommendations," but that "concrete proposals would in due course be submitted to Parliament."[5] At about this time the Australian government set up an inter-departmental committee to consider the experts' report, but the results of this study have never been made public.

In their annual answers to the questionnaires, Australian governments have indicated their inability to fix the specific level of unemployment which would require the application of countermeasures. Their view has been that "if any significant change [i.e. in the employment situation] occurs, appropriate measures will be taken, but these can only be determined after full examination of the factors involved."[6] There is in fact a very real difficulty in finding domestic measures to fit each country. The crucial and critical action must be taken in the international field. Australia felt that effective

---

[4] A. A. P. Dawson, "The United Nations and Full Employment," *International Labour Review*, Vol. LXVII (1953), p. 417.

[5] ECOSOC O.R. (Official Records), 11th Sess., 391st Mtg., 18 July 1950, p. 136.

[6] See United Nations Doc. E/2565/Add. 1, 18 May 1954, p. 14. This document and E/2408/Add. 3, 12 June 1953, contain the Australian reply to the full employment questionnaire for 1953.

action was possible only by joint efforts to establish a new equilibrium in world trade and by its stabilization through the provision of additional monetary reserves for a country where export income had declined with a falling off of overseas demand. The flow of international private lending must be supplemented by public foreign investment by governments with a surplus balance of payments. The special problems arising out of the rapid growth of the Australian economy has forced Australia to adopt a highly flexible policy: discretionary rather than automatic measures would be needed to combat a fall in employment. In fact, circumstances limit the extent to which uniform internationally agreed policies are either practicable or desirable: a flexible domestic plan has been essential.

As a country in which prosperity depends principally upon the price for its exports, especially wool, Australia has stressed the need for joint efforts to establish a new and high equilibrium in world trade. The only safeguard for Australian prosperity lies, objectively, in international planning and co-operation together with the adoption by other countries of expansionist domestic economic policies. Hence, too, the need for the stabilization of international trade through the provision by international means of additional monetary reserves for any country where export income declines following a contraction of overseas demand. During the 1953 discussions in ECOSOC on measures to check the deflationary consequences of reduced defence expenditure, the Australian delegate urged that the United Nations maintain a careful scrutiny of consumer demand and aim at the abolition of import restrictions and the stabilization of prices for primary commodities. Australia has also urged the industrialized countries to supply their less developed neighbours with capital goods as well as capital. In common with other countries Australia has pointed out that it is impossible to determine at an international level the appropriate domestic methods for maintaining full employment; these would depend for success on co-operation among states, each of which was pledged to full employment at home.

Certain basic assumptions are common to all Australian political parties: the need for full employment, the repudiation of deflation as a solution to depression, the injurious effect on the country's economy of a falling overseas demand for Australian products. Both the Labour and Liberal-Country party governments have consistently attempted to prevent sudden falls in export prices by concluding long-term commodity agreements. The point of disagreement is whether full employment means employment of, for example, 97 or 100 per cent of the labour force. Labour, with grim memories of the 1931 depression, is perhaps more prone to predict and diagnose the advent of unemployment, while the non-Labour parties and management are more concerned with the rapid labour turnover and the half-hearted achievements of "over-full" employment. But here the disagreement, or rather the difference of emphasis, ends. The fundamental agreement between the parties was demonstrated in January 1950 when, immediately after the change-over from the Labour to the Liberal government, the Australian delegate on the UN Economic and Employment Commission was at first very critical of the Dutch, Danish, and Belgian representatives when they suggested that the report on *National and International Measures for Full Employment* concentrated unduly on the objective of full employment. The discussion on this report, however, illustrated the change in attitude in Australia and other countries since the optimistic but distant days of 1945 when it was believed that full employment would cure all economic ills.

In a sense there has been no opportunity since the San Francisco Conference to test the "full employment" doctrine as a proposed panacea. The planners of Australia's future in 1945 expected a brief demobilization depression to be followed by a boom for two or three years with rising export prices. This in turn would be followed by a collapse of the 1930 type, with a contraction of spending and consequent unemployment of both labour and capital. Such a pattern did not develop for reasons beyond the ability of the 1945 experts to predict. Marshall Plan aid was used to revitalize the Australian economy,

and the outbreak of war in Korea produced a further boom, especially in raw material prices. In fact there was no post-war depression of the type anticipated in the light of previous major wars. There was a progressive inflation from 1945 to 1951, and for Australia a phenomenal expansion of export income and a considerable influx of capital. A deflationary Australian budget in 1950 was followed in 1951-52 by a steep fall in export income due to external factors. This resulted in a "slight fall in total employment and an emergence of some unemployment"[7] which reached its peak of 41,633 in January 1953. This had no immediate effect on the upward trend in prices and the total volume of personal incomes. The government promptly eased credit and promoted investment with a view to immediate restoration of full employment. Its objective was "full employment without inflation," a much more elusive goal than the "full employment" of 1945.

The established policy of the present Liberal government, with which the Opposition would not disagree, is indicated in its reply to the 1953 ECOSOC questionnaire:

> In Australia at the present time the policy of maintaining full employment is an essential element of a comprehensive framework of policy aimed at maintaining the stability of the economy and expanding the basic productive facilities of the country. An important aspect of this broad policy is that it is designed to provide the conditions under which full productive employment for an expanding population may be continuously realized. Not only does it aim to protect the economy, as far as practicable, from developments which could endanger the level of employment by leading to a general deficiency of effective demand, but it also implies an expansion in the economy so that the growing labour force may be used effectively in increasing the real national product.[8]

The arguments for full employment had become more sophisticated and more complex than in 1945.

---

[7] United Nations Doc. E/2408/Add. 3, 12 June 1953, p. 5.

[8] United Nations Doc. E/2565/Add. 1, 18 May 1954, p. 2.

There can be no question that Australian domestic policies would be materially assisted by the use of international credit and investment to counteract impending or actual depression. The United Nations is obviously the appropriate medium for the fostering and execution of such arrangements. In other words, succeeding Australian governments have agreed that the way to safeguard the country's prosperity is through international planning and co-operation together with the adoption of expansionist domestic policies by other nations. This is the one type of international economic co-operation which, all parties agree, is essential to Australia. A particular international organization, i.e., the United Nations, is not a *sine qua non* of such co-operation. If, for political reasons, it should disintegrate, then an international conference to deal with this specific problem could be convened without great difficulty and could set up machinery for consultation between subsequent conferences. The political feuding arising out of the East-West conflict and out of the divisions between colonial and non-colonial powers has had a less disruptive effect upon the discussions in ECOSOC than has been evident in discussions in other United Nations organs. The evidence is overwhelmingly in favour of co-operation inside rather than outside the United Nations.

Did the much-publicized Australian fight to obtain United Nations support for "full employment" achieve anything? The Australian delegation at San Francisco played an important part in closely associating the United Nations with this doctrine and in enhancing the importance of ECOSOC. The whole issue of "full employment," however, has been rather academic in view of world trends in the decade since 1945. Yet it does appear that the only two measures that member nations might adopt to ensure stability under conditions less favourable than those which have existed since 1945 are the maintenance of full employment and the control of inflation. Under conditions of instability and perhaps world economic crisis, domestic policies tend to accentuate depression: a drop in American demand for imports, especially of raw materials, has an immediate impact both on world trade and on employment. International regularization of import controls is as important as domestic full employment. The United States, with its experience of widespread unemployment during the depression, has been moving towards a policy of full employment since the San Francisco Conference. Domestic pressures rather than the influence of bodies like the United Nations and ECOSOC have been mainly responsible. A United States economist, in discussing the report on *Measures for International Economic Stability*, commented that

> . . . in terms of fluctuations, the United States might be inclined to accept a moderate amount of irregularity, and rely on its social-security system to provide for the resulting unemployment. But the impact of our fluctuations on other countries will not allow us, as good citizens of an interdependent world, to decide the question in the same terms that might govern us if we were isolated.[9]

THE GENERAL AGREEMENT ON TARIFFS AND TRADE

So far as Australia is concerned the problem of import controls is intimately related to the question of the regularization of international trade. A comparison of amount of trade per capita shows the dependence of Australia on international trade to preserve both living standards and prosperity. In terms of U.S. dollars, the comparative figures for 1953 and 1956 were: Australia 371 and 382, Canada 585 and 668, United Kingdom 321 and 376, the United States 166 and 187.[10] Australian trade shows an excess of imports from the United Kingdom, largely compensated for by an excess of exports to continental Europe. Wool constitutes more than half the value of exports and foodstuffs approximately one-third.

---

[9] Quoted in "Rx for World Slumps," *United Nations World*, Vol. 6, No. 9 (1952), p. 39.

[10] Estimates based on import and export figures in *Statistical Yearbook 1957* (New York: United Nations, 1957), table 1, pp. 23-28 and table 152, pp. 426-27, 430-31.

In 1939 the Australian tariff (in accordance with the Ottawa agreements) provided for reciprocal preferences among members of the British Commonwealth. British products were thus given preference over other foreign goods in the Australian market; in return, Australian primary products, with the chief exception of wool and wheat, enjoyed preferential treatment in the British market. Separate trade agreements concluded in the 1930's with Belgium, Czechoslovakia, France, and Switzerland, and later with Brazil and Greece, gave these countries a more limited preferential treatment. Underlying all these agreements is the agreed policy of protection for Australian industries which is considered essential in order to maintain existing living standards, to increase the population, and to achieve a considerable measure of self-sufficiency in key defence industries. Protection is afforded partly by tariffs, partly by subsidies, and by the fixing of domestic prices for certain agricultural products above world prices.

One of the major objectives of the Atlantic Charter was the promotion of freer international trade, "the enjoyment by all States, great or small, victor or vanquished, of access, on equal terms, to the trade and to the raw materials of the world which are needed for their economic prosperity" (Clause 4). The Bretton Woods Conference had urged the reduction of obstacles to international trade and attempts were subsequently made to set up an International Trade Organization. In 1947 a series of tariff concessions were negotiated at Geneva on the basis of most-favoured-nation treatment. Australian negotiations with the United States centred chiefly round the tariff on wool imports and, after protracted discussions, the Truman administration over-rode Congress and granted a 25 per cent reduction in wool duties. Bilateral agreements with a number of other countries covered a wide range of Australian commodities. The agreements were consolidated in the General Agreement on Tariffs and Trade (GATT) concluded among twenty-three countries. GATT in general protected the tariff concessions already negotiated, but it required the extension of individual concessions to all members.

From an Australian point of view, the significant thing was that GATT reduced some imperial preferences and froze the rest at their 1947 level.

The Australian Parliament debated at length Australia's adherence to GATT and finally made it conditional upon ratification by both the United States and the United Kingdom. The Liberal and Country parties were highly critical because they felt that GATT represented a foreign attempt to shatter imperial preference and that the multilateral principle was unwieldy, hindering rather than assisting the negotiation of future tariff concessions. Sentiment, strategy, and economic self-interest appeared to support the Ottawa system of preferences instead of the dubious advantages of an international system.

Labour support for GATT was not unanimous. The Minister for Postwar Reconstruction, Mr. J. Dedman, supported it because the concessions reduced United States duties on wool and so strengthened the position of Australian primary producers in one of the world's expanding markets.[11] He argued that any concessions made by Australia were justified by the recent improvements in the relative cost structure of Australian industries. The Prime Minister, Mr. J. B. Chifley, made it clear, however, that support for GATT arose primarily out of a sense of moral obligation to assist in liberalizing international trade, an obligation Australia had explicitly assumed under Article 7 of the Lend-Lease agreement. Australia also supported GATT because the British government believed that GATT was essential to its economic existence. His comment is illuminating: "Of course, if the matter had been left to us, we should not have initiated a conference to discuss the lowering of world tariff barriers."[12] Labour's defence was in terms of the specific gains made in the bargaining at Geneva and tended to gloss over the partial surrender of tariff autonomy.

---

[11] Commonwealth of Australia, *Parliamentary Debates* (*C.P.D.*), Vol. 194, 11 Nov. 1947, pp. 1882-84.

[12] *Ibid.*, Vol. 196, 26 Feb. 1948, pp. 254-55.

q

GATT has been a shuttlecock in the battle among the vested interests in Australia. The pastoralists, selling in world markets, cannot pass on their costs; they prefer cheap rather than domestic manufactures. GATT appears to them as "a trade agreement which has undoubtedly done much to restrain tariff barriers and to expand world trade."[13] Manufacturers, sheltered behind a high tariff, regard GATT as "the most dangerous and vexatious agreement ever foisted on Australian industry."[14] Chambers of Commerce, concerned primarily with the volume of trade and therefore with low tariffs, are supporters of GATT.[15]

Since 1947 Australia has benefited less than was anticipated from GATT. The preferences Australia enjoys, frozen by GATT at the 1947 level, are specific and not ad valorem. Price rises since 1947 have proportionately reduced these advantages, leading to a demand for a general upward revision of imperial preference. The lowering of the specific United States duty on wool which accompanied GATT has been of relatively little value to Australia with the substantial rise in wool prices. Hopes for an expansion of Australian exports to the United States were not realized: the shift from Democratic to Republican control of Congress brought with it a restriction of imports of primary products as part of a general price support program for domestic agriculture. This was not accompanied by restrictions on domestic production, and the accumulation of surplus stocks of dairy products and wheat led to attempts to dispose of them abroad, thus increasing competition in traditional Australian markets. Over the same period the relative cost advantage of Australian manufactures has declined; this has evoked importunate pressures for increased protection. The steady and continued shift

---

[13] Statement by the President of the Graziers' Federal Council, *Sydney Morning Herald*, 15 July 1954.

[14] Statement by the Federal Tariff Office of Associated Chamber of Manufactures, Melbourne *Age*, 5 May 1953

[15] See statement by the President of Victorian Chamber of Commerce, Melbourne *Age*, 2 Aug. 1954. See also C. W. James, "Foreign Economic Policy of Australia," *The Australian Outlook*, Vol. 7 (1953), pp. 153-63.

in the Australian economy from primary to secondary industry has increased the relative lobbying power of the Australian manufacturer. The rapid increase in Australia's adverse trade balance in 1952 led to the adoption of drastic import controls and a licensing system which sharply cut imports. Australian dissatisfaction with GATT led to strong pressure for revision of the agreements.

This demand for revision has been intensified by Japan's admission to GATT. The Japanese peace treaty of 1951 (Article 12) had provided for the extension of most-favoured-nation treatment on reciprocal basis for a period of four years. Australia had ceased to grant most-favoured-nation treatment to Japanese imports in 1937 and strongly opposed proposals by the United States to apply such treatment to Japan under GATT in 1948. The fear of competition from cheap Japanese manufactured goods produced extreme apprehension in Australian and British manufacturing circles. Considerable damage had been done to Australian industry by the sudden flooding of the Australian market by Japanese imports in the 'thirties and, when tariffs had proved an inadequate means of protection, a policy of outright discrimination had been adopted. Japan was admitted to associate membership in GATT in 1953 by 26 votes to 0, with 7 abstentions (these included the United Kingdom, New Zealand, South Africa, and Australia). India and Pakistan, anxious to reduce living costs and feeling that domestic industries were not threatened, supported Japan's admission.[16]

Japan's accession to GATT inevitably affected the network of tariff agreements worked out at Geneva in 1947. These did not adequately prevent a sudden disruption of trade by Japanese exports of the pre-war type. In September 1953, the members of GATT agreed, under Australian and British pressure, to carry out a comprehensive review of the agreements. This was done at discussions in Geneva between October 1954 and March 1955. The revised

[16] D. F. Nicholson, *Australia's Trade Relations* (Melbourne: F. W. Cheshire, 1955), Chs. 8-10 and 12, especially pp. 245-55. See also W. Prest in Gordon Greenwood and Norman Harper, eds., *Australia in World Affairs, 1950-55* (Melbourne: F. W. Cheshire, 1957), pp. 130-36.

agreements made concessions to Australia in the use of tariffs and import restrictions to protect its balance of payments, and discouraged the dumping of export surpluses in world markets. At the same time, no revision of preferences was adopted and so the advantage enjoyed by Australian primary products in the British market narrowed with the general inflationary pressures which increased prices. In June 1955 Japan became a full member of GATT, but Australia refused to extend most-favoured-nation treatment to Japanese goods. New trade treaties were negotiated between Australia and the United Kingdom in November 1956 and between Australia and Japan in July 1957.[17]

Australian support for GATT in 1947 appears to have been a reluctant modification of the set pattern of trade policy made possible by exceptional but temporary circumstances. Australian support for tariffs, consistently expressed during the League of Nations era, is more insistent today as the demand for full employment is allied with a policy of substantial immigration and of industrial expansion. As an exporter of primary products and raw materials, dependent for about half of its export income upon wool, and at the same time rapidly shifting the balance of its economy towards industralization, Australia has found itself in something of a dilemma. Traditionally relying heavily on preferences in imperial markets, Australia has found GATT's rule against new preferences irksome because it debars the United Kingdom from increasing its preferences on Australian goods. Increased protection of Australian goods by the reduction of preferences on British goods involves a consequent reduction of duties on imports from other countries.

INTERNATIONAL LABOUR ORGANISATION

Of all the major international organs, the International Labour Organisation (ILO) is the one with which Australia has been asso-

---

[17] See *Current Notes on International Affairs* (Dept. of External Affairs, Canberra), Vol. 27 (1956), pp. 785-93; Vol. 28 (1957), pp. 580-84.

ciated for the longest period. The ILO was established along with the League of Nations in 1919 under the provisions of the Versailles Treaty, and Australia as a signatory to that treaty became a founding member. Because it is concerned with labour and related social matters which are the subject of much domestic political controversy, the ILO has a greater political significance within Australia than do the other specialized agencies of the United Nations. In the early stages it evoked from governments and organizations in Australia few opinions of a contentious kind. Since the admission of the USSR in 1954, discussions of ILO problems have aroused keen interest.

Australian association with the ILO raises the question of the peculiar difficulties which most federal states have to face when specific international conventions have to be implemented internally. This does in practice debar federal states like Canada, the United States, and Australia from active participation in many of the important activities of the ILO. The ILO is of special interest because of its tripartite structure (employer, employee, and government): it is the only international body under government auspices in which decisions are subject to the approval of two of the most important non-governmental groups in society, groups which in Australia have direct political links both at the federal and state level. This tripartite structure is the clearest source of strength for the ILO. The ILO is of interest, too, because of its possible impact on non-metropolitan territories. It is for these reasons that the ILO rather than the Food and Agriculture Organization or the United Nations Educational, Scientific and Cultural Organization was selected as the specialized agency of most interest for this study.

The impact of the activities of the ILO is largely intangible in the sense that it cannot be accurately measured or assessed even when it can be clearly observed. The organization is concerned partly with carrying out technical studies. The 1953 program, for example, included analyses of productivity, wages, housing, and the condition of workers in underdeveloped regions; the 1957 program covered analyses of productivity (including the social effects of automation), labour management relations, workers' education, and freedom of association.

Australia, with extensive experience in industrial relations and with a reputation for social experiment, has been exceptionally interested in labour problems and has been anxious to share its experience with other countries. A mixture of genuine humanitarianism and of hard-headed realism lies behind Australian policies of collaboration with its Asian neighbours. Rising living standards are a matter of mutual interest to all countries in this region. Australian insistence upon the legalizing and strengthening of trade unions in post-war Japan had political and economic objectives. The raising of living standards and an increase in purchasing power would promote production and expand international trade; democratic trade unions would be a useful buttress against the revival of totalitarianism and the growth of communism. Australian foreign policy is vitally concerned with the improvement in living conditions in South and East Asia: support for the Colombo Plan, for United Nations technical assistance programs and for the work of all the United Nations specialized agencies indicates this. Yet these are intangibles that cannot be documented or measured. A documented study of Australian relations with the ILO tends to concentrate upon the conventions, the products of international co-operation. This tends to obscure important humanitarian considerations and particularly Australia's willingness to pool experience and give assistance to the less highly developed countries in improving labour conditions. It obscures, too, the important indirect influence that the ILO is constantly exerting on industrial relations in Australia.

The obligations of member governments towards International Labour conventions are laid down in Article 19 of the Constitution of the ILO. After a convention is adopted at a session of the International Labour Conference, it is forwarded to all members to consider. Each member government is required, within eighteen months from the closing of the session, to bring the convention before the competent authority or authorities for legislative or other action. The government must inform the Director-General of the International Labour Office when this has been done and what action has been taken. If the competent authorities adopt the convention, the government must communicate the formal ratification to the Director-General and take the necessary steps to make the convention effective. When consent is not given, the only obligation resting upon the government is to report to the Director-General at appropriate intervals as requested by the Governing Body "the position of its law and practice in regard to the matters dealt with in the Convention, showing the extent to which effect has been given, or is proposed to be given, to any of the provisions of the Convention by legislation, administrative action, collective agreement or otherwise and stating the difficulties which prevent or delay the ratification of such Convention" (Article 19, Section 5(c)).

For countries with a federal constitution many of the matters dealt with by International Labour Conferences are ordinarily the concern of the state legislatures. Where a federal government regards a convention as appropriate for federal action under its constitutional system, its obligations are the same as those of non-federal governments: the procedures outlined above are followed. In the case of conventions that the federal government regards as more appropriate for state rather than federal action, a slightly different procedure is adopted. The federal government must bring the conventions to the notice of the appropriate state authorities for action not later than eighteen months after the closing of the session of the Conference. The ILO Constitution also provides that the federal government may "arrange, subject to the concurrence of the state, provincial or cantonal governments concerned, for periodical consultations between the federal and the state, provincial or cantonal authorities with a view to promoting within the federal state coordinated action to give effect to the provisions of such Conventions and Recommendations" (Article 19, Section 7(b)(ii)).

The written Constitution of the Commonwealth of Australia gives
to the federal Parliament the power to legislate on enumerated
subjects; the residue of power is left to the states. The federal
Parliament, under Section 51 (XXXV), is empowered to deal with
"conciliation and arbitration for the prevention and settlement of
industrial disputes extending beyond the limits of any one State."
While no other powers specifically relating to labour and industry
are enumerated, the federal trade power (which covers navigation
and stevedoring) and control over territories and public servants
gives considerable scope for federal action in these fields.[18] Where
no direct federal power exists, a great deal can be accomplished
by informal co-operation between the Commonwealth and state
governments. This, of course, is limited by the strength of states'
rights sentiment and by the extent of bureaucratic rivalry: vested
interests may well prevent effective collaboration. An alternative
lies in the enlargement of the federal industrial powers by amendment to the Constitution: on each occasion that the Commonwealth government has sought such amendment by referenda it has
failed.

The external affairs power, another of the powers enumerated in
Section 51 of the Constitution, is potentially of the utmost importance in determining the scope of federal power for the implementing of obligations arising from international treaties or conventions. No international agreement can itself "create legal rights
or duties or alter any existing law within Australia. Hence an international undertaking which requires for its performance any such
act in the law can be carried out only by legislation of an appropriate
Australian parliament."[19] The Commonwealth Parliament has the
power to "make laws for the peace, order, and good government

---

[18] See O. de R. Foenander, *Studies in Australian Labour Law and Relations*
(Melbourne: Melbourne University Press, 1952), pp. 6-7.
[19] G. Sawer, "Execution of Treaties by Legislation in the Commonwealth of
Australia," *University of Queensland Law Journal*, Vol. 2 (1955), p. 298. See
also K. H. Bailey, "Fifty Years of the Australian Constitution," *Australian Law
Journal*, Vol. 25 (1951), pp. 321-22.

of the Commonwealth with respect to ... external affairs." If this power extends to legislation to give effect to any international agreement, then the distribution of powers between the Commonwealth and state governments may be drastically altered. Initially, a strict construction of the external affairs power by the High Court appeared to circumscribe the authority of the federal government. A broader construction was later adopted, particularly by Evatt and McTiernan J. J. in *Ex parte Henry* (1936).[20]

Since 1908, however, the states have accepted the doctrine that the Royal Prerogative with respect to international affairs is vested solely in the federal government and is not shared by the states. The federal government therefore has the exclusive power of adopting or ratifying a convention; most conventions, however, can only be implemented with the co-operation of the states.

The Commonwealth will as a rule ratify a convention if it is convinced, firstly, that the standards embodied in the legislation of each of the six states are precisely (and not merely generally) in accordance with the standards of the convention, and secondly, that the states have no objection to the ratification of the convention (i.e., that they are prepared not to repeal their legislation during the period the convention is in force). It has, of course, to be satisfied that standards in the fields for which it has power to legislate (e.g., aborigines, territories) also conform to those of the convention. The comment made in 1942 by the Commonwealth Attorney General (then Dr. Evatt) is still a valid one:

> The Commonwealth has promptly submitted draft Conventions to the States immediately after receipt of the text thereof from the International Labour Organisation. It has been difficult to obtain their views with any degree of despatch, and practically impossible to secure unanimous action.[21]

He drew attention to the conclusion reached by the sub-committee of the Conference of State Premiers in 1936 that the provisions of

---

[20] *Commonwealth Law Reports*, Vol. 55 (1936), p. 608.

[21] Cited in K. H. Bailey, "Australia and the International Labour Conventions," *International Labour Review*, Vol. LIV (1946), p. 290.

nine conventions submitted to the states appeared substantially to be covered by existing state legislation or practice and that in eight other cases only minor amendments to state laws seemed to be required. He pointed out, however, that none of these seventeen conventions had in fact been ratified, one state (South Australia) consistently refusing to communicate its views to the federal government.

A meeting of Commonwealth and State Ministers of Labour in April 1947 considered the amended Constitution of the ILO and the implementation of its obligations by Australia. It was clear that part of the difficulty lay in the fact that the states were not consulted in the formulation of International Labour conventions and that they were not able to participate in the proceedings of conference sessions when the conventions were adopted. The meeting adopted procedures to resolve these difficulties and the Commonwealth government then agreed to include state representatives in the Commonwealth delegations to those sessions of the International Labour Conference where matters concerning the states would be discussed.

In spite of the new procedures, the situation in 1958 is still essentially the same as it was in 1942. The Commonwealth has, for example, requested the views of the states about ratifying two conventions adopted at the 1951 International Labour Conference: Queensland and Tasmania, both with Labour governments, have never replied. States' rights feeling against the Commonwealth appears to be stronger than Labour enthusiasm for the ILO. South Australia opposed ratification of the first of these conventions (dealing with minimum wage-fixing machinery in agriculture) and both South Australia and Western Australia opposed the ratification of the other convention concerning equal remuneration for men and women workers.[22] In 1952 Victoria failed to express its views

---

[22] Commonwealth of Australia, Dept. of Labour and National Service, *Statement in Relation to the Conventions and Recommendations Adopted by the Thirty-Fourth Session of the International Labour Conference, June, 1951*, pp. 3-5.

on other conventions referred to it. Since Australia joined the ILO, there have been only four instances where the states have been unanimous in not objecting to the ratification of conventions, the subject matter of which was within their legislative competence; in two of these instances, although the laws of the states were already in accord with the convention, it took the states thirty-four years to agree to ratification.

How effective are International Labour conventions in stimulating Australian legislation? The amendment of the Commonwealth Navigation Act in 1935 and again in 1952 and in 1958 to bring it into conformity with conventions appears to be the major instance of direct response. When existing legislation is being amended, provisions in conformity with conventions may be incorporated. Thus, for example, in 1952 the minimum age for employment at sea was raised in connection with the revision of federal legislation in this field.

At the state level, conventions would appear to exert little direct influence despite occasional attempts to amend legislation. Shortly after the adoption of the International Labour convention on minimum wage-fixing machinery in agriculture, the Labour leader of the Opposition in South Australia attempted, without success, to amend the state's industrial code to give rural workers the right to approach the state Industrial Court.[23] Although the attention of the party was directed to the issue by a member who had attended the International Labour Conference, it was perhaps significant that the case for amendment was based upon the injustice of the rural workers' special position and on the need to prevent them from transferring to other occupations. Reference to the adoption by the International Labour Conference of the principle of wage-fixing for rural work was incidental and peripheral. The debate took place within the context of local party politics and centred around the problem of fixing wages in a field where income depends on fluc-

---

[23] South Australia, *Parliamentary Debates* (Adelaide: Govt. Printer), 1951, pp. 534 ff.

tuating external prices. At the same time, in Victoria, New South Wales, and Tasmania, Labour governments amended existing legislation to extend wage-fixing machinery to rural workers and thus incidentally achieved the objectives of the International Labour convention. This reform had been part of Labour policy; international adoption of this convention while Labour was in office stimulated state action.

Commonwealth action in 1952 to abolish penal sanctions in labour contracts in Nauru may be attributed in part to ILO activity. Abolition followed vigorous criticism in the United Nations Trusteeship Council and the expectation of a hostile report on the question by the Joint ILO-United Nations *Ad Hoc* Committee on Forced Labour. In that section of its report dealing with Nauru, the Committee stated its opinion that "the risk of heavy penal sanctions for breach of contract constitutes a serious restriction on the personal liberty of the worker. Legislation of this kind, if abused or vigorously implemented, might lead to a system of forced labour for economic purposes."[24] The committee noted that the Australian government had announced its intention of abolishing penal sanctions and was accordingly amending the relevant legislation.

The influence of ILO standards is not limited to subjects governed by ratified conventions. The indirect influence on various industrial tribunals in Australia is considerable. These Commonwealth tribunals and state tribunals (whose titles vary from state to state) are responsible (subject to legislative direction in the case of some of the state tribunals) for determining conditions of work in those industries over which they have jurisdiction. This includes state employees. In many cases, especially on hours of work, the tribunals lay down standards in Australia which in general equal or exceed those provided for in International Labour conventions. Commonwealth and state governments often prefer not to ratify these con-

---

[24] ECOSOC O.R., 16th Sess., Supple. No. 13, Report of the *Ad Hoc* Ctte. on Forced Labour, p. 22.

ventions lest ratification interfere with the work of these tribunals. Accordingly, Commonwealth and state governments are not solely responsible for implementing International Labour conventions. State-created industrial tribunals often share this responsibility informally by considering relevant conventions in determining industrial conditions.

The importance of state action can be judged from the total number of International Labour conventions for which the assent of the states would be needed for ratification. By 1957 the ILO had adopted 107 conventions; of these Australia ratified 20, including only 4 for which the assent of the states was obtained. Of the unratified conventions, 6 had been revised and so were no longer open for ratification; of the remaining 81 the Commonwealth has power to ratify only 14 without first obtaining the consent of each of the states. In other words, the effective authorities in a majority of cases are not responsible to the ILO. Although a state representative has been included in every delegation to the sessions of the International Labour Conference since 1949, the Australian states have not adopted one of the 17 new conventions requiring their support before the federal government could ratify them.[25]

The 14 unratified conventions that deal with matters solely within the ambit of Commonwealth legislation fall into several categories. Eleven relate to social security matters, a subject that did not come within the Commonwealth's legislative powers until the constitutional referendum of 1946. Ratification of these conventions is probably impossible at the moment because they are inapplicable to an Australian system: they are all based on the concept of insurance whereas in Australia social security is financed primarily through taxation. The remaining three conventions apply only to non-metropolitan territories.

---

[25] In practice, representatives from the state attend International Labour Conferences, but as representatives and agents of the Commonwealth. Where such representatives have participated in and approved of the conclusions of the Conference, the record of state ratification has in no way been improved.

Before the war, there may have been some substance in the frequently repeated argument that, since Australian labour standards were generally in advance of ILO requirements, failure to ratify conventions was of little domestic consequence. Today such an argument is no longer true. Of the 81 conventions still open to ratification by Australia, probably 65 prescribe standards in advance of those laid down in Australia *taken as a whole*.[26] This lag is particularly marked with the post-war conventions. Of the 40 conventions adopted by the ILO between 1945 and 1957, Australia has ratified only 5; the other 35 set standards which are in advance of those so far achieved in one or more Australian states. It is not without significance that not one of the 9 conventions adopted since 1950 has been ratified: all are in advance of Australian standards.

Members are normally obliged to apply conventions they ratify to their non-metropolitan territories (including trust territories) "except where the subject matter of the Convention is within the self-governing powers of the territory or the Convention is inapplicable to the local conditions or subject to such modification as may be necessary to adapt the Convention to local conditions" (Article 35 of the ILO Constitution). The obligation to report on progress towards ratification and on the difficulties therein encountered is substantially the same as for self-governing countries.

Australia has extended to its non-metropolitan territories only five of the relevant conventions it has ratified. The ILO Committee on the Application of Conventions criticized Australia for failing to submit sufficient information about developments in its territories. The criticism produced a number of legislative and ad-

---

[26] These include: Nos. 68, *Food and Catering* (*Ships' Crews*); 69, *Certification of Ships' Cooks;* 74, *Certification of Able Seamen;* 77 and 78, *Medical Examination of Young Persons;* 79, 89, 90, *Night Work of Women and Young Persons;* 87, *Freedom of Association and Protection of the Right to Organise;* 96, *Fee-Charging Employment Agencies;* 99, *Minimum Wage-Fixing Machinery* (*Agriculture*); 100, *Equal Remuneration for Men and Women Workers;* 101, *Holidays with Pay* (*Agriculture*). (Of these, Nos. 68, 69, 74, and 87 have been ratified by the United Kingdom.)

ministrative changes which met most of the criticisms. Of the four conventions dealing specifically with non-metropolitan territories adopted at the thirtieth session of the International Labour Conference (1947), one envisages conditions far in advance of those existing at present in Australian territories. Another is being considered but, because of its complicated nature, administrative difficulties may delay action for some time. A third convention requires legislative protection of the right of association. There are no legislative prohibitions on associations of workers and employers in the territories, but such organizations have not yet developed to any extent. The administrations in the territories consider that the interests of the native peoples are better served by official supervision of employer-employee relations. The recently organized Workers' Association in Nauru, the only such association yet formed, appears to have been, at least in part, a direct result of the International Labour convention. In the case of the fourth convention concerning labour inspection in non-metropolitan territories, both law and practice substantially conform to the convention; it has now been ratified with minor modifications in administrative detail. Local European unofficial opinion in the territories seems opposed to the ratification of any of the conventions. The strength of such pressure is impossible to predict; it has to be weighed on each occasion when government action becomes necessary.

At the International Labour Conference of 1951 the Australian government delegate commented about proposals for new conventions and recommendations: "We [Australia] are reaching the stage when we must say 'pause and let us get our breath: let us put into effect the good resolutions of the Conference lest we legislate in vacuo.'"[27] In view of the rather complicated situation in which Australia finds itself in relation to the hundred conventions already adopted by the International Labour Conference, this seems a reasonable plea. The Commonwealth government is devoting much

[27] ILO Conference, Record of Proceedings, 34th Sess., 1951 (Geneva, 1952), p. 292. Mr. W. Funnell (Government representative).

more attention to the study of ILO matters than at any time in the past. The tabling in the Australian Parliament of a report on the various conventions and recommendations adopted at the 1951-54 sessions of the International Labour Conference[28] was apparently an attempt to force the states into activity.

The present method of voluntary ratification by each member government of the ILO appears to be functioning with considerable success. This is supplemented by the practice of reporting on the implementation of conventions, ratified or unratified, to an ILO committee of experienced experts. These practices have not created political feuds or aroused any general exasperation in Australia. Discussions at ILO meetings have usually been temperate where non-political issues were involved. The need to win support from all three classes of representative—the government representative and the independent employer and employee delegates—contributes to this.

In the early stages there was a great deal of apathy in Australia towards the ILO. It was rarely mentioned in parliamentary debate. The appointment of a delegation or a discussion of the world economic situation by the ILO would rate a paragraph in the press; the list of conventions adopted at a conference was rarely regarded as newsworthy. Since 1954 much more attention has been given to ILO decisions, especially those which appear to impinge upon Australian interests. The vigorously expressed opinions of Mr. A. Monk, President of the Australian Council of Trade Unions and a member of the Governing Body of the ILO, were widely discussed. The views of Mr. L. Byrne (President of the Australian Council of the Employers' Federation, and from 1957 also a member of the ILO Governing Body) on the relationship between the ILO, Australia and Asia, and the activities of the ILO Asian Advisory Committee attracted considerable attention. The ILO vocational training institute held in Australia in February-March 1953 aroused

---

[28] *Statement in Relation to Conventions* . . . , *op. cit.*, p. 4.

interest. Parliamentary discussion of issues raised by International Labour conventions has become much more frequent, especially since the re-entry of the USSR has raised a number of contentious political matters.

Among trade unionists there is often only a faint ripple of interest except when representatives are appointed to attend sessions of the International Labour Conference. The Australian Council of Trade Unions, the executive council of the trade union movement, has always been keenly interested in the work of the ILO and has given active support to its policies. On the other hand, to most Trades and Labour Councils in Australia, the ILO appears to have little practical value for union objectives or problems. This is partly the result of ignorance. There is always the danger that the reports of delegates will be received at a Council meeting when the notice paper is crowded with items of greater immediate importance. Verbal reports tend to be briefly minuted, written reports may be buried in Council archives, and details of conventions transmitted to the appropriate state trade union leaders for discussion and action are likely to be shelved. Only too frequently the urgent demands of local union problems, industrial and political, crowd aside other wider issues. Information rarely percolates through to the rank-and-file members who, although vitally affected by conventions, are often unaware of their existence. There has been in some left-wing union circles a suspicion of federal leadership and a distrust of decisions taken at a rather remote international level by a body on which union representatives are outnumbered.[29] Interest has greatly increased since the USSR was admitted as a member. Left-wing unions revised their attitude and often moderate trade union representatives were politically embarrassed by obtaining Soviet support for their proposals.

The apathy among rank-and-file Australian unionists and among

---

[29] See e. g., Mr. Haylen: The ILO is a "log-rolling organization for right-wing organizations." *C.P.D.* (House of Representatives), Vol. 16 (New Series), 18 Sept. 1957, p. 776.

r

many trade union officials arises in part out of the generation-old assumption of the superiority of Australian working conditions to those prevailing in other parts of the world: there is here a serious time lag between myth and reality. More important is the general reliance upon political action through a parliamentary Labour party to achieve union objectives by legislation. Australian union members consider that their primary objective is to acquire voting strength in the constituencies to give them the power to carry out their policies: no International Labour convention is necessary to define these. The arbitration system is a second, and in some cases the most important, method by which labour attempts to secure improved conditions. This makes International Labour conventions rather less relevant to Australian conditions, especially as Parliament has hesitated to implement conventions concerning matters covered by awards prescribed by industrial tribunals. The federal government accepts this situation. Its view on the ratification of the 1951 convention on equal remuneration for men and women workers was that "The Commonwealth Court of Conciliation and Arbitration is . . . the body empowered to deal with such issues and indeed is generally recognised as the authority appropriate for the purpose. There are powerful reasons for maintaining this attitude."[30]

It would be wrong to assume that Australian trade unions are indifferent to the ILO and its standards. Mr. Monk, as President of the Australian Council of Trade Unions, has an abiding interest in the ILO and relates its principles to ACTU policy as fully as possible. In the ACTU's successful campaign (1946-47) before the federal Arbitration Court for a forty-hour week, one convention was freely cited as providing an international standard. In another case before the court, counsel for the ACTU supported the claim that the rate of remuneration for women employees should not be reduced by pointing out that at the 1951 International Labour Conference the Australian government delegate voted in favour of

---

[30] *Statement in Relation to Conventions . . . , op. cit.,* p. 5.

the recommendation on equal pay, although he had abstained from voting for the convention. In the past too many unionists have felt that union executives could better spend their time in "doing important jobs at home," in discharging their "real functions" instead of "making trips abroad." This attitude has changed considerably since 1952 largely as a result of the distribution of union representation among a larger number of trade unions. Mr. Monk as president of the ACTU has attended most meetings, and an increasing number of union leaders are now familiar with ILO activities. This is having a considerable indirect influence on union attitudes.

The attitude of employers is difficult to ascertain. The kind of administrative problems which trade unions experience at the state and federal levels are also to be found in employers' federations and prevent the widespread dissemination of information about ILO activities. Ignorance and indifference are to be found cheek by jowl with suspicion. To some employers the ILO appears as a dangerous organization with a staff that has a vested interest in the welfare state or even in socialism. Accordingly they feel that they cannot neglect the organization: their attendance might put a brake on socialist policies. Others are concerned at the possible effect of new conventions on the cost structure of particular industries. There has on the whole been little continuity in the membership of the Australian employer delegations to International Labour Conferences despite efforts to achieve it. Australia was elected to deputy membership of the employer group of the Governing Body of ILO in June 1954 and to titular membership in 1957. Australian employers have strongly supported the ILO technical assistance program. A few believe that the raising of Asian labour standards would enhance the competitive capacity of Australian industry in international or domestic markets: the ILO could in fact provide a useful mechanism to accomplish this by indirection.

In the post-war period, there have been few strong pressures within Australia to give positive support to the ILO and so strengthen its authority. Such pressures as have been slowly developing in recent years have had to operate within a constitutional system which makes difficult Australian ratification of the International Labour conventions. The federal structure itself and the existence of a highly developed arbitration system restrict the field of action. The fact that the law and practice of the six states, the Australian Capital Territory of Canberra, the Northern Territory, and the Commonwealth government itself must be in precise accord with the provisions of a convention slows down the whole process of ratification. It would be generally agreed in Australia that amendment of the constitution or an alteration in the arbitration system could not be justified primarily because such changes would make ratification easier. The complicated legal and administrative structure in Australia not infrequently provides an excuse for, rather an explanation of, inaction and delay.

More frequent and regular conferences between state and federal officials, round-table discussions between employers and employees, and the education of public opinion could accomplish much. Steps have been taken to ensure continuous consultation between the states and the federal government at both the political and administrative levels. The Joint Advisory Committee, set up in 1954 under the chairmanship of the federal Minister for Labour (Mr. H. Holt), mirrored the tripartite character of the ILO itself. It discussed all labour, industrial and related matters of concern to Australia, including the ILO; its terms of reference included the examination of successive conventions and the best machinery to expedite ratification. The committee met with only partial success and is now in abeyance because of the withdrawal of the ACTU. While the Labour party itself remains to most trade unions the main instrument for improving labour conditions, interest in the ILO will remain limited. The cumulative effect of direct trade union contacts with the ILO may gradually bring a significant change in attitude as the number of union representatives with a first hand knowledge of the functioning of the ILO increases.

The Australian record for ratification of conventions—20 by 1957—[31] does not compare favourably with that of advanced unitary states, such as France (73), the United Kingdom (58), the Netherlands (44), and New Zealand (39). It is comparable rather to that of some federations faced with similar constitutional problems, such as Canada (18) and the United States (7). The majority of federal states, and these include Argentina, Brazil, West Germany, India, Switzerland, and Yugoslavia, have a better record of ratification. The USSR, which joined the ILO in 1934 but ceased to be a member from 1940-1954, is a federal state with an unusual balance of power between the central and state authorities. Over the past four years it has ratified a considerable number of important International Labour conventions and by so doing has won a considerable propaganda advantage in non-Communist countries, especially in Asia.

This poor record of ratification has weakened Australia's reputation as a socially advanced country. Since the war, the ILO has sought to improve labour conditions in the underdeveloped countries. The Australian government has given strong support to these efforts by active co-operation with the technical assistance programs and by encouraging the development of an independent trade union movement in Asia. The success of this policy is partly jeopardized by the discrepancy between Australian law and practice and ILO standards.

While there is an increasing concern at the delay in Australian ratification of International Labour conventions (as a Labour member has commented, "Australia has the worst reputation in the free world . . . for carrying out its international obligations"[32]), the

---

[31] See *C.P.D.*, Vol. 13, 30 Oct. 1956, pp. 1930-36, for a list of all the conventions and Australia's action upon them. "In many cases, provisions of the convention are in advance of the standards existing in one or more of the States, even if only in minor respects, and until these standards are amended by the States in question, ratification is not possible" (Mr. Holt), *ibid.*, p. 1936.

[32] Mr. E. G. Whitlam, *ibid.* (House of Representatives), 22nd Parliament, 3rd Sess., 14 May 1958, p. 1839.

rising interest in the ILO has developed largely because of the political problems raised when the USSR rejoined the organization early in 1954. This brought to a head an issue which had been raised in a variety of forms over a period of almost twenty years: whether employer and employee representatives from Communist countries could be legally admitted to sessions of the ILO.

The central issue involved is whether it is preferable to retain the essentially tripartite character of the ILO, with its representation of governments, employers, and employees, or to dilute this principle in the attempt to achieve universality of membership. No challenge to the credentials of employer or employee representatives from the USSR was made until 1937, a year after reservations had been made by some employers' representatives. The objection raised was rejected by the Credentials Committee and by the plenary session of the International Labour Conference. In 1953, the "free" employers questioned the credentials of the Czechoslovak employers' delegate, although no challenge was made to the employers' representative from Poland or Yugoslavia or to the workers' delegates from any of these countries. The "free" employers' objection to the seating of delegates from Communist countries on the ground that they were substantially or wholly under the control or influence of their governments threatened the tripartite character of the ILO. Carried to its logical conclusion, it could mean that the status of employer representatives from Socialist as well as Communist countries could be jeopardized and so the effective membership of the ILO would be drastically reduced. The Credentials Committee in 1953 recommended that the Czech employers' delegate be admitted, and Australian government and workers' representatives supported the decision.

The re-admission of the USSR in 1954 was followed by the entry of Byelorussia and the Ukraine and by a renewal of interest in ILO activities and the ratification of its conventions by Albania, Bulgaria, and Hungary. Both the employers' representatives and the International Confederation of Free Trade Unions (ICFTU) renewed their challenge to the seating of employer and employee representatives from Communist countries on the grounds that they were merely mouthpieces of their governments and so would destroy the delicate tripartite balance of the ILO. They argued in fact that there were no free associations of either employers or employees in Communist countries.

In March 1955 the Governing Body of the ILO decided the matter should be referred to an independent committee. The McNair committee, appointed to examine the question, presented a report in 1956. The majority report recognized the fact that while there were differences in degree rather than principle in the extent of government regulation of both employers' and workers' organizations in different countries, trade unions in Communist countries were in fact free, even though they were subject to influence by the Communist party. Employers' organizations however did not exist in the USSR but the majority report felt that "socialized management" had a contribution to make to the ILO and so ought to be represented. The employers' group in 1956 failed to secure support for a proposal to amend the Constitution of the ILO to exclude representatives of both employers and employees who were not freely nominated without government influence.

The Australian government's view has been that this challenge to the credentials of one group of representatives threatened the whole tripartite structure of ILO:

> . . . that the legal position, practice and history of the Organisation appeared to establish the right of Governments to nominate as representatives of employers and workers persons of the type whose credentials had been challenged; . . . that the so-called autonomy of the groups could not be exercised to defeat the Constitution of the Organisation and the rights which it gave to duly accredited delegates and advisers; . . . That the existence of freedom of association could not be considered as a prerequisite to membership any more than any of the other objectives of the I.L.O.; that to accept the employers' viewpoint was to argue that some States could not

appoint any delegates to represent their work people and that in fact some members of Governments (the United Kingdom, France and Australia are some examples), had sent representatives of public authorities to I.L.O. meetings as employers' representatives and that no distinction in principle could be drawn between this approach and that of accepting Soviet employers and workers.[33]

This desire to retain both the tripartite character of the ILO and universality of membership, an attitude shared by most of the other Commonwealth governments, aroused considerable criticism from Associated Chambers of Manufactures in Australia. They had "persistently pressed our Government to change its overseas policy towards the communists but without avail."[34] After the Hungarian revolt in 1956, the Australian government voted with the majority at the International Labour Conference in 1957, in refusing to accept the credentials of both employers' and workers' representatives from Hungary. At the same time, the Australian government delegates abstained on the question of recognizing the credentials of the Hungarian government representatives. (The vote was 94 in favour of barring the representatives, 88 against with 52 abstentions; the necessary two-thirds majority was thus not obtained.) The Australian attitude, in common with most other member governments, has been that the question of such recognition was primarily a matter for decision by the United Nations General Assembly itself rather than the specialized agencies. For this reason Australia at previous International Labour Conferences had not opposed the seating of government delegates from Nationalist China and so abstained in the case of Hungary.[35] This abstention was the subject

---

[33] *Reports of the Australian Government Employees' and Workers' Delegates to the Fortieth Session of the International Labour Conference, Geneva, June 1957.* Introductory Observation by the Rt. Hon. H. E. Holt, Minister of State for Labour and National Service, p. 8.

[34] Quoted in *C.P.D.*, Vol. 16, 18 Sept. 1957, p. 775.

[35] *Report of the . . . Delegates to the 40th Sess., op. cit.*, pp. 13-16; *C.P.D.*, Vol. 16, 12 Sept. 1957, p. 571 (Mr. Holt).

of bitter criticism from the Australian Labour party which regarded abstention as implicit support for the Communist Kadar government.[36] In May 1958, the Australian government decided to review its policy and to vote against accepting the Hungarian government delegates.

---

[36] *Ibid.*, pp. 571 and 579 (Dr. Evatt and Mr. Calwell); and 18 Sept. 1957, pp. 775-76 (Mr. Haylen).

chapter nine

Human Rights

The whole problem of human rights is one in which Australia has been particularly interested. At the Paris Peace Conference in 1946 Australia vigorously pushed a radical proposal to establish a world court of human rights, a judicial body which would be empowered to hand down binding decisions. Australia has been a member of the United Nations Commission on Human Rights ever since it was established in 1947 and has continued to support the proposal for a world court in the face of almost continuous opposition from the great powers. Since 1950, perhaps as a result of greater experience in international co-operation and also as a consequence of the harder realism which has slowly replaced the initial idealism of the San Francisco Conference, Australia has begun to doubt whether judicial enforcement of international legal instruments can at present promote respect for human rights. There has, too, been a clearer appreciation of the difficulties which arise because of the federal structure of certain states and of the special problem created by the position of non-self-governing territories.

The subject of human rights was almost ignored in the Dumbarton Oaks proposals. But pressures for the inclusion of human rights within the ambit of the United Nations Charter steadily mounted. In the first place, the aggressor states in 1939 had been totalitarian states; their governments would have been less likely to seize power and retain it had human rights in these countries been more adequately safeguarded. The establishment of effective safeguards for free election and freedom of speech, and the protection of political critics against imprisonment would have made difficult this seizure and retention of power. The denial of basic political rights, especially in the backward areas, and the failure to establish minimum standards of living, accentuated political instability and contributed to the outbreak of war. The proper safeguarding of human rights would, it was felt, minimize the danger of war. In the second place, democratic leaders had emphasized in key speeches the need for respect for human rights. President Roosevelt's "Four Freedoms" speech of 6 January 1941 and the Atlantic Charter of 14 August 1941 had done precisely this. It was felt that the United Nations must attempt to implement the basic principles of the war-time democratic alliance.

In the drafting of the Charter, the majority of delegates were careful to exclude any suggestion that the United Nations, solely by virtue of the Charter, was competent to take action to impose upon members the observance of human rights. For this reason the Panamanian proposal to include in the Purposes of the Charter reference not only to the promotion but also to the protection of human rights was rejected. A similar proposal by Australia relating to another section of the Charter was more successful, and as a result the Dumbarton Oaks draft was amended to empower the Economic and Social Council (ECOSOC) to promote observance of as well as respect for human rights.[1] The Australian draft proposed

---

[1] The text of the Australian amendment will be found in *Documents of the United Nations Conference on International Organization, San Francisco, 1945* (New York: United Nations Information Organizations, 1945), Vol. III, p. 546.

"observance by all members," which suggests that Australia may have been prepared to countenance discussion by ECOSOC (and hence by the General Assembly) of specific violations by members of human rights. If this is so, then Australian policy was somewhat ambivalent, since in one debate at San Francisco, Australia had declared emphatically that the mere reference in the Charter to human rights did not withdraw that subject from the scope of the domestic jurisdiction of a state and did not empower the United Nations to protect minorities. Such a power could be conferred only by the acceptance by a member of a specific agreement dealing with that subject.[2] This view was much more in accord with Australia's usual approach to the question of domestic jurisdiction and of the scope of power of the United Nations.

Australia's interest in human rights was directed primarily to ensuring the inclusion of the promotion of economic and social rights as a major function of the organization. Full employment was regarded as a prerequisite to the enjoyment of human rights and individual freedoms. This explains the vigorous Australian campaign to secure the recognition of the right of employment and a pledge by all members to implement it.[3]

Considerable difference of opinion developed almost immediately in the Human Rights Commission on the question whether to proceed at once to a universal declaration of human rights or to delay such a declaration until a convention or covenant of human rights could be adopted simultaneously. At its first session (1947) the Human Rights Commission decided, on the initiative of the United States, to adopt the former course. The United States felt it important to formulate such a declaration to cover the interim period during which the various articles of a legally binding covenant were being debated.

Australia, in common with the United Kingdom and New Zealand,

[2] *Ibid.*, Vol. VI, p. 439.
[3] See H. V. Evatt, "Economic Rights in the United Nations Charter," *Annals of the American Academy of Political and Social Science*, Vol. 243 (1946), pp. 4-5.

preferred the simultaneous drafting and promulgation of both the declaration and the covenant. The Australian view was that a declaration was quite inadequate, and that, since it did not entail any legal obligations, it "would not in any way affect the lives of men and women."[4] As a mere declaration, it created no legal obligations. As for the content of the declaration, the government attached "particular importance" to the "right to social security, equitable and satisfactory working conditions, rest and leisure and an adequate standard of living to ensure the health and well-being of every man and his family."[5] There was general agreement with the Australian view that any formula implying obligations should be avoided and that in stating the rights of individuals no reference should be made to the corresponding obligations of states.[6] Yet how could such a declaration, imposing no legal obligations, assist in promoting respect for human rights? One kind of answer came from a United States delegate who suggested that it would serve as "a common standard of achievement for all peoples of all nations." A second kind of answer was provided by Dr. Evatt, the President of the Assembly, shortly after the General Assembly on 10 December 1948 unanimously adopted the Universal Declaration of Human Rights:

> It was the first occasion on which the organized community of nations had made a declaration of human rights and fundamental freedoms. That document was backed by the authority of the body of opinion of the United Nations as a whole and millions of people, men, women and children all over the world, would turn to it for help, guidance and inspiration.[7]

---

[4] United Nations Doc. E/CN.4/SR.27, 3 Dec. 1947, p. 5. The mimeographed records of the Commission on Human Rights of the Economic and Social Council (ECOSOC) can be found in the E/CN.4 document series. Summary records are indicated by the designation "SR."

[5] General Assembly, Official Records (G.A.O.R.): 3rd Sess., 1st Part, 181st Plenary Mtg., 10 Dec. 1948, p. 875.

[6] *Ibid.*, 3rd Ctte., 103rd Mtg., 15 Oct. 1948, p. 151.

[7] *Ibid.*, 183rd Plenary Mtg., 10 Dec. 1948, p. 934; cf. Mr. A. Watt, *ibid.*, 181st Plenary Mtg., 10 Dec. 1948, p. 875.

Throughout the discussions the policy and direction of interest of the Australian delegation was a continuation and development of its San Francisco policy: emphasis upon the primary importance of economic rights and the need for pledges binding members to secure and protect them.

From the beginning Australia has emphasized the need to include in the covenant economic and social articles and has supplied much of the constructive thinking on this question. In June 1949, when a Labour government was in power, Australia proposed the inclusion of articles setting forth the right to work, to social security, to education, and to state supervision of wages and working conditions.[8] The change of government at the end of the year brought no significant change of attitude on this issue. The original proposals were resubmitted by the new government in 1950, stated perhaps in broader terms but without substantial modification. This broadening of terms was necessary to make the provisions of the covenant applicable to states at varying stages of economic and social development, and so acceptable to most members. The decision to tread more circumspectly, to be content "not to go beyond basic prescriptions" in the economic field, and "to allow the work of filling out to be done subsequently," arose out of a more realistic appreciation of the problems facing the Commission on Human Rights. Some members of the Commission did not share Australia's enthusiasm for human rights in the economic and social field, and as work progressed, the complexities of the subject became much clearer. The varying stages of economic and social development of the members of the United Nations made difficult the formulation of specific rights which would be of universal validity.

One feature of the amended Australian proposals can be directly attributed to the new government. After the statement in the draft covenant that "everyone shall have the right to work," Australia suggested the insertion of a new clause, "and correlatively shall be

---

[8] United Nations Doc. E/CN.4/SR.131, 27 June 1949, pp. 3-4.

under the duty to fulfil his obligations with respect to work for which he is voluntarily engaged."[9] In addition, a clause explicitly permitting contributory systems was to be inserted in the proposed article on the right to social security: this was prompted by the partial adoption of such a system in Australia. But amendments in detail involved no basic change in policy. The peroration of the Australian delegate who introduced the changes could as well have been made under the Labour government: he referred to the need for the speedy mastery of "the inequalities arising in human societies from *laissez-faire* policies in relation to modern industrialization . . . if the coherence of present-day society [was] to be preserved."[10]

Australia consistently maintained the view that economic and social rights and personal and political rights should form part of the same covenant. The United Kingdom pressed for a separate covenant on economic and social rights on the ground that the economies of some countries were insufficiently developed to enable them to guarantee such rights. Inclusion of these rights in the original covenant might divide the United Nations into two groups: those that could and those that could not guarantee such rights. On this point Australia disagreed with the United Kingdom and continued to do so as late as 1951. "In view of the wide publicity given to the Universal Declaration of Human Rights and the general feeling that economic, social and cultural rights must receive the same attention as civil liberties," Australia "was convinced that the exclusion of those rights from the Covenant would cause the latter to be regarded as mockery. The Australian government was not prepared to envisage such a possibility."[11] Subsequently, the United States, the United Kingdom, and other governments made clear their adamant opposition to the inclusion of these rights, while other factions, including the underdeveloped countries and the Soviet bloc, were as unyielding in their opposition to the exclusion

---

9 United Nations Doc. E/CN.4/353/Add.10, 22 March 1950, p. 11.

10 United Nations Doc. E/CN.4/SR.184, 9 May 1950, p. 4.

11 United Nations Doc. E/CN.4/SR.203, 24 April 1951, p. 21.

of economic and cultural rights from the covenant. Australia finally modified its position and gave its support to the compromise decision in 1951 to draft two separate covenants, one to cover civil and political rights, the other economic and social rights.

Australia's preference for judicial enforcement of specific obligations in the field of human rights dated from the Paris Peace Conference of 1946. In the peace treaties, the former enemy states had bound themselves to recognize and maintain in their territories specified human rights. However, the organs provided by the treaties to consider violations were *ad hoc* and not judicial. To establish some sufficient sanction and means of enforcement, Australia proposed that an international judicial tribunal be set up whose judgments would be enforceable against both individuals and states. This tribunal might be invoked either by individuals or by groups. Such a proposal was in accordance with Dr. Evatt's firm belief that judicial procedures should be more widely utilized at the international level. The foreign ministers rejected these proposals which were too advanced for general acceptance.

Some countries adopted the view that the Human Rights Commission could examine complaints of violations of human rights. At the first session of the Commission in 1947, a proposal by the Philippines to establish a sub-committee for this purpose was defeated. Australia voted with the majority, following consistently the view that an international obligation binding a member can be created only by that member's formal acceptance of the specific obligation. At a later meeting of the Commission (February 1947) the Australian government proposed the creation of an International Court of Human Rights. This would be open to both individuals and states, and its decisions would be binding on all states ratifying an international covenant of human rights to be drawn up and adopted by the Commission.[12] The Australian proposal was based upon the contention that the Security Council could not adequately

---

[12] See details in United Nations Doc. E/CN.4/SR.15, 5 Feb. 1947, pp. 2-3.

ensure the application of human rights: it could act only if peace were endangered.

Neither the United States nor the United Kingdom was prepared to carry implementation as far as this. The former favoured a system of reporting; the latter preferred a procedure allowing the General Assembly to authorize the Secretary-General to obtain an explanation from a state allegedly violating the covenant. If a state persistently violated the covenant then it could be expelled from the United Nations by resolution of the General Assembly. Both the United States and the United Kingdom consistently opposed the suggestion that individuals be granted the right to petition the implementing organ. The USSR has consistently denied that the Charter permits any international supervision, investigation, or enforcement of a covenant on human rights. The Soviet view is that the implementation of the Declaration of Human Rights and the covenant is a matter solely of domestic jurisdiction.

Most members of the Commission gradually came to favour conciliation rather than judicial procedures. The United Kingdom and the United States, however, proposed a different procedure: the opening of bilateral negotiations between the accusing and the accused state. Should they fail to reach a solution, the matter would be referred to a specially-convened international Human Rights Committee which would report its conclusions to the Secretary-General. The United States delegate insisted that the committees should confine themselves to fact-finding and leave world opinion to exert pressure. He also felt that, since states were free to ratify or reject the covenant, the ratifying states should not be compelled to accept elaborate enforcement machinery.[13] France and India at first favoured in principle judicial enforcement but gradually swung round to support the majority proposals. Both continued to demand

---

[13] See United Nations Doc. E/CN.4/SR.168, 4 May 1950, pp. 6-8, and SR.177, 12 May 1950, p. 9, for the United States and United Kingdom viewpoints. For text of their joint proposal, see United Nations Doc. E/CN.4/444, 22 April 1950.

s

that individuals be granted the right to petition the implementing authority.

Australia argued that any system other than judicial enforcement would be ineffective, and that the United Kingdom-United States proposals, by relying on bilateral negotiations, gave too much free play to the bargaining strength of the great powers. Australian suspicion of the great powers, so marked at San Francisco, still influenced policy as late as 1949. However, while the Labour government was still in office, Australia indicated that if its proposals were unacceptable, it would support the French plan for setting up a permanent implementation committee with power to recommend but not to make binding decisions. Australia still insisted that the right of individuals to petition such an authority was essential.[14] In 1950, after the change in government, Australia still spoke of the necessity for a court but voted for the United Kingdom-United States proposals and thus against those of France. At the sixth session of the General Assembly (1951), Australia modified its view again. The main objective was to secure acceptance of the covenant by as many governments as possible. A covenant which merely recorded the existing law and practice of states would serve little purpose; the inclusion of obligations unacceptable to a substantial number of states would be unwise. Since many states would refuse to ratify it, no covenant should include at present the right of individual petition.[15] Australia had in fact finally arrived at the United States starting point on the question of implementation.

This change in approach was fully apparent in May 1951 when the Australian delegate declared to the Commission that "the weakness of a Covenant without measures of implementation had been emphasised," and to those who argued that such a covenant would remain a dead letter, he replied that "it would have the same value as any treaty and be accompanied by the customary sanctions."[16]

---

14 United Nations Doc. E/CN.4/SR.105, 2 June 1949, pp. 4-5.

15 United Nations Doc. E/CN.4/SR.177, 12 May 1950.

16 United Nations Doc. E/CN.4/SR.211, 7 May 1951, pp. 12-13.

In the past no one had argued more vigorously than Australia that such a covenant would be a dead letter. However, this was not an extreme change of attitude, and Australia continued to support proposals enabling either party to a case which the Human Rights Committee had failed to settle by conciliation to bring the matter before the International Court of Justice. Such a proposal was finally adopted by the Commission in 1953.[17] Since the draft covenants now provide that either state which is a party to a dispute can virtually force the issue before the International Court, Australia's initial preferences for judicial settlement have been substantially met. The change in attitude on the right of individuals to petition the Committee was, however, a complete *volte-face*. Australia now attacked this right on the ground that it would be used by mischief-makers to embarrass the very governments most desirous of promoting human rights. In addition the prestige of national tribunals would be lowered if appeals were allowed to an international body on matters which should be subject in the last resort to domestic jurisdiction.

In 1952 the Human Rights Commission, on instructions from the General Assembly, adopted an article for inclusion in the draft covenant or covenants which declared that

> all peoples and all nations shall have the right of self-determination, namely, the right freely to determine their political, economic, social and cultural status. All states, including those having responsibility for the administration of Non-Self-Governing and Trust Territories and those controlling in whatsoever manner the exercise of that right by another people, shall promote the realization of that right in all their territories . . .[18]

The resolution specified that the right of self-determination included permanent sovereignty over natural wealth and resources, and that

---

[17] United Nations Doc. E/CN.4/SR.390, 21 Oct. 1953, p. 16.
[18] ECOSOC, Official Records: 14th Sess., Supple. No. 4, Report of the 8th Sess. of the Commission on Human Rights, pp. 10-11.

"in no case may a people be deprived of its own means of subsistence on the grounds of any rights that may be claimed by other States."

Australia opposed the inclusion of such an article on the ground that self-determination was a political principle rather than a legal or individual right. It was out of place in the covenants, which dealt only with such rights: "Self-determination is more in the nature of a group political right, not the sort of individual right with which the Commission is competent to deal."[19] As the Australian delegation pointed out in its report to Parliament,

> while the principle of self-determination was an important and valuable one in its proper application, a misapplication of it could . . . play into the hands of world Communism, which would, of course, welcome such a fragmentation since it would facilitate its aggressive designs. The principle of self-determination further should not be confused with the attainment of the self-government or independence by Trust and Non-Self-Governing Territories which is a distinct question otherwise covered . . . by the Charter. Lack of independence did not necessarily entail the denial of human rights: in some countries . . . enjoying forms of sovereign independence there can be found greater injustice and greater oppression than will be found in most, if not all, of the colonies of metropolitan nations of Europe over the last hundred years.[20]

The principle of self-determination, as defined in Article 1 of the draft covenants, was in fact ambiguous in its wording and extensive in its application. The words "peoples" and "nations" were used almost as interchangeable terms in the debate, and the position of minorities was not clearly determined. The whole tradition of Anglo-American law was opposed to the vague concept of rights embodied in the covenants. The framers of the draft tended to confuse sociological claims or aspirations, political and moral principles, with legally enforceable rights, rights which carried no

---

[19] G.A.O.R., 5th Sess., 317th Plenary Mtg., 4 Dec. 1950, p. 555.

[20] *Report of the Australian Delegation to the Seventh Regular Session, First Part, of the United Nations* (mimeo.), New York, 8 Jan. 1953, pp. 154-55.

corresponding obligations. Australia has consistently supported the principle of self-determination, but "could not consider that self-determination was a right that could be expressed in a legally binding international agreement."[21] Accordingly, it opposed the adoption of Article 1 in 1955 and supported the Danish proposal to postpone a decision on the article until governments had constructively examined it.

Australia supported the colonial powers when the question of the application of the covenants to dependent territories was considered during the fifth session (1950) of the General Assembly. The issue had arisen before the change in government in 1949, but the elections brought no change in Australian policy. The Australian government proposed that metropolitan powers should declare to which of their territories the covenants would extend, and should implement the covenant in these areas as soon as possible. These powers should state their reasons for not extending the covenants to all of their territories, if the application was not universal.[22] Both the United States and the United Kingdom submitted similar proposals. The General Assembly, however, on 4 December 1950, instructed the Human Rights Commission to include provisions in the covenants requiring extension to all the territories of a signatory state.

In May 1953 the United States representative on the Commission announced that, under existing circumstances, her government would not ratify the covenants. She felt that the covenants would not be ratified as widely as was first thought; nor would they be as effective as had been anticipated. As was to be expected, the Australian government adopted a similar decision. The Australian delegate, Mr. Whitlam, stated that "in their present form, the draft covenants

---

[21] G.A.O.R., 10th Sess., 3rd Ctte., 669th Mtg., 23 Nov. 1955, p. 226. For a full statement of the Australian position, see *ibid.*, 647th Mtg., 28 Oct. 1955, pp. 114-16.

[22] ECOSOC Official Records: 11th Sess., Supple. No. 5, Report of the 6th Sess. of the Commission on Human Rights, p. 22.

already contained features which, if retained, would prevent a number of States, including Australia, from acceding to them without such reservations as would jeopardise their whole effectiveness, or that such features were also to be found in some of the proposals for additional articles."[23] He pointed out that some of the provisions were such that even the most highly-developed states could not apply them; others posed constitutional problems in their application; some were so vague and imprecise that they were already becoming textually mischievous. Mr. Whitlam drew attention to the Assembly's directive that the right to self-determination must be included. The inclusion of such a right among "human rights and fundamental freedoms" had never been contemplated by any of the Western powers at San Francisco. Since none of the other articles contains principles not already recognized in practice in Australia, the issue of self-determination was the chief stumbling block to Australian ratification. In all probability a fundamental alteration in the colonial application clauses would also be a necessary condition for Australian acceptance of the covenants. Finally, he stated that the subsequent decision of the Commission not to include a federal clause also precluded Australian ratification.

When the Third Committee of the Assembly began voting on the provisions in the proposed covenant on rights in the economic, social, and cultural fields in 1955, Australia opposed the adoption of Article 1, and, in 1956, abstained with the United Kingdom and the United States from the final vote on Articles 6-12 (right to work, right to just and favourable conditions of work, trade union rights, right to social security, right to protection to family life, pregnant mothers, and young children, right to an adequate standard of living). Australia supported Article 13 (right to physical and mental health).

Two legal problems of a general nature have emerged from the discussions on human rights. Minor legal difficulties have constantly

---

[23] United Nations Doc. E/CN.4/SR.341, 9 May 1953, p. 4.

been smoothed out by discussion and compromise. But a recurrent problem has been the difference of function performed by national courts in the different states. This may be seen in the discussions on the right to life itself. To Americans, accustomed to the abstract statements of rights in their Constitution, statements which their courts have defined to meet concrete situations, it was appropriate to state this right in the covenant simply as "no one shall arbitrarily be deprived of life." The British and Australian procedure was entirely different. In the British view, statutes were the counterpart of the covenant, and statutes are designed to cover concrete situations. To entrust a court with the task of deciding the meaning of the term "arbitrarily" in this context would be to give it a power which properly belonged to the legislature. Britain proposed an article stating that "no one shall be deprived of life," but including explicit exceptions. To the United States representative this seemed "rather to authorize killing than to safeguard the right of life."[24] It is likely that the American public would have viewed it as such. A further objection was that the inclusion of specific exceptions might result in unusual courses of action. Moreover, enumeration of exceptions might be construed by the courts as definitive, whereas other exceptions, not yet contemplated by the framers of the covenant, might easily arise. The conflict between particularization and comprehensiveness has been an enduring one, retarding considerably the final drafts, which in some important respects bear the American rather than the British imprint.

The second major legal problem is that posed for federal states: what obligations can the federal government assume? Canada, Australia, and the United States have all been vitally concerned with the inclusion of a federal clause in the covenants. In this they have had the sympathetic support of India. At the eighth session of the Commission these countries and the United Kingdom agreed on a draft federal clause. This provided that the obligations of a

---

[24] United Nations Doc. E/CN.4/SR.139, 30 March 1950, p. 4. For the British amendment, see E/CN.4/365, 22 March 1950.

federal government would be the same as those of any non-federal government in respect of any provisions in the covenants the implementation of which were, under the constitution of the federation, wholly or in part within federal jurisdiction. On the other hand, where implementation was wholly or in part within the jurisdiction of the constituent "states," the obligation of the federal government would be to bring such provisions, with favourable recommendations, to the notice of the appropriate authorities and to inform the Secretary-General as to the situation of the law within the constituent states. In 1954 proposals for the inclusion of a federal clause in the covenants were finally rejected.

So far as the division of powers is concerned, the Australian federal structure was modelled primarily upon that of the United States rather than that of Canada. States' rights are exceedingly important in all three countries, but the constitutions differ in their protection of these rights. Under the Australian federal Constitution, power to implement most of the rights specified in the draft covenants would lie primarily with the constituent states rather than with the federal government. The inclusion of a federal clause is essential if Australia is to ratify the covenants. This view was put firmly before the Third Committee of the General Assembly by the Australian delegate in 1950. He pointed out that the central government could not assume responsibilities which were beyond its competence without endangering the basic compromise of federation and ultimately the federation itself. The people desire the constituent states to retain and exercise their powers. For the federal government unilaterally to accept and ratify the covenants would not only be provocative of state feeling but would be a breach of the whole spirit of the federation. It was a basic function of the Australian High Court to "maintain the balance between the federal government and the governments of the constituent states."[25]

In Australia the constituent states would be responsible for

---

[25] G.A.O.R., 5th Sess., 3rd Ctte., 292nd Mtg., 25 Oct. 1950, p. 134.

implementing the economic, social, and cultural rights as well as the civil and political rights set forth in the present covenants. The right to social security would be an exception, for the Commonwealth government has full legislative power in this field under Section 51 (XXIII and XXIIIA) of the Constitution. Otherwise, it has full power to implement the covenants only in its continental and external territories[26] (i.e., in the Northern Territory, the Australian Capital Territory, and Papua and New Guinea). The states, within their respective territories, have plenary power with respect to most of the matters with which the two draft covenants deal, and these rights are therefore within the legislative field of the states provided the state laws are not inconsistent with Commonwealth laws.[27]

Australian governments, in contrast with the earlier attitude of the United States and the United Kingdom, have accepted since 1944 the basic assumption that progress towards international security and advancement towards higher living standards in underdeveloped countries are ends desirable in themselves and necessary for securing the traditional liberal political rights which both the United States and the United Kingdom stress. Of course the Australian government did not deny the importance of freedom of opinion and the other more traditional rights. Moreover, Australian governments seem to have extended this assumption to include the provision of means, at the international level, for ensuring the observance of individual rights. This should take the form of influence exercised through international machinery and applied to individual governments to persuade them to discharge their freely assumed obligations to observe human rights. Australia has shared in a gradual evolution of thought concerning specific means of implementing these rights. Although at first reluctant to contemplate any means of promoting

---

[26] Sections 51 (XXIX) and 122 of the Australian Constitution.

[27] Sections 109 and 51 of the Australian Constitution. This is a view from which a leading Australian constitutional lawyer, Professor G. Sawer, dissents: see *Australian Journal of Politics and History*, Vol. III (1957-58), p. 9.

human rights except through judicial enforcement, Australia's view matured with experience in the Human Rights Commission. Australia had not anticipated that its motives in supporting the federal and colonial clauses in 1945 would become suspect, and had believed that international agreement on such issues would be relatively simple. Experience with the practical difficulties of international negotiations and its own problems as a colonial power contributed to this changed approach. Idealism became tempered with realism as the "cold war" developed.

On the whole, the Australian and the United Kingdom representatives on the Human Rights Commission have adopted identical approaches. This has been reflected in their common attitude on drafting problems: there have been basic differences of method between British and other countries in the interpretation of texts. They have adopted similar attitudes on questions involving the application of the draft covenants to colonial territories and the right of self-determination. This is not surprising in view of their similar legal and constitutional background and political, legal, and cultural institutions. States with common interests and comparable legal and political traditions inevitably tend to collaborate and so become identified as a group, e.g., the Anglo-Saxon, the Anglo-American, the Brussels Treaty powers, the Middle East, the Latin-American, the Soviet, and the Afro-Asian blocs. The growth of understanding and solidarity among states with common interests, such as the United Kingdom and Australia, has made for frank and relatively continuous discussion between them of controversial issues and has made possible the reconciliation of opinion before formal debates take place. At the same time, it is well to remember that some differences on vital questions have been partly resolved in the Commission: whether economic and social rights should be included in the covenants, whether the members of the proposed Human Rights Committee should be elected by the International Court or by the member states, whether a federal-state clause is justified or not.

The attitudes of Australia and the United States have not been so markedly similar. The Australian representatives have shown no great enthusiasm for the United States program of action in the field of human rights put forward in 1953 following the decision of the United States not to ratify the covenants.

Australian public opinion has been little affected by the discussions at the United Nations on the Declaration or the covenants. Press references have been very scanty and there have been no discussions in Parliament. In the United States, on the other hand, a bitter controversy developed over the possibility of United States adherence to the covenants: it came to a head during discussions on the proposed Bricker Amendment to the United States. Constitution. It would be going too far to suggest that Australian public opinion has been completely indifferent. Special groups, like the Australian Association for the United Nations and various Australian Jewish organizations, have shown a keen interest in the drafting of the covenants. New Australians from Eastern Europe have frequently urged government action through the United Nations against members of the Soviet bloc. These approaches have usually had the support of religious groups. References have also been made to the Declaration of Human Rights by persons or groups interested in using a specific provision as a "prop" to support them in public controversies over the alleged denial of a "right." This was done in New South Wales in 1953 when controversy developed over legislation imposing compulsory unionism and requiring newspapers alleging government corruption to disclose to the authorities the sources of their information. Reference to the Declaration was also made when passports were withdrawn from people proposing to attend "peace" conferences in Communist countries.

It would be easy to exaggerate the importance of these isolated instances. The people concerned had no real interest in upholding the Declaration as a whole; they sought rather to use it as a means to secure a tactical advantage often of a party political kind. It is of course possible that continued references to the Declaration (and subsequently to the covenants when they come into force) could have a cumulative and important effect on public opinion. But that stage is certainly a long way off in Australia. In Australia, as in other parliamentary democracies, the sanction of public opinion should be an adequate safeguard for human rights without the additional buttress of international obligation. This was felt to be true in 1900 when the federal Constitution was finally adopted. Although the provisions of the United States Constitution were carefully studied and often followed, there was no proposal for an Australian bill of rights either then or subsequently.[28] The problem becomes a more complex one in perhaps two kinds of situation. For one thing, it is clear that in any community—democratic or non-democratic—plagued by hysteria, normal human rights of a political nature can be seriously threatened if not wholly jeopardized. Protection of national courts may prove inadequate. Yet any attempt to appeal beyond these to international tribunals would be impracticable and could be met by a plea of domestic jurisdiction. Secondly, in non-democratic states the problem may well be more acute and the fetish of national sovereignty be reinforced by ideological pressures and differing semantic concepts.

The problem is largely one of sincerity of intention and of good faith. Without these, any Declaration of Human Rights is but a frail instrument to protect the individual. Much depends on the constant pressure and diligent example of those countries where fundamental personal rights, political and economic, have been recognized and are firmly established by due processes of law and supported by an overwhelming public opinion. In the international field formal recognition of such rights has a certain practical as well as a theoretical value.

---

[28] A single exception is Section 116 of the Australian Constitution, which prohibits the Commonwealth from establishing any religion or imposing any religious test.

The principal Australian parties and a growing segment of re-sponsible public opinion are coming to feel that Australia's vital interests may well be affected by the extent to which human rights, including the right to an adequate and secure standard of living, are realized. Australia has consistently and patiently pressed in the Commission for international recognition of these basic human rights, believing that in so doing democracy could be strengthened in backward countries. Struggling indigenous peoples could be given the support of an international standard to assist them in protecting human rights against apathy and unenlightened pressure groups. But the attempt to translate general principles into effective covenants has proved exceedingly difficult in practice. Semantic and philo-sophical differences have often prevented agreement in drafting covenants. Covenants themselves tend to assume an unreal quality when, for example, support for self-determination comes from anti-colonialist countries which refuse to recognize minority rights and engage in internal repression and which have as their immediate objec-tive securing political advantage in the "cold war." A sense of practical realities and a feeling of responsibility make Australia reluctant to accept sweeping obligations which would be difficult to enforce. This reluctance is strengthened by a knowledge that some of the staunchest advocates of specific human rights have neither the intention nor the power to enforce them: Poland in supporting freedom for trade unions and Saudi Arabia in advocating women's rights. These attitudes have produced the apparent gap between theory and practice in Australian policy, and the long record of Australia's abstentions in the Third Committee.

PART THREE

chapter ten

The Scope and Utility
of the United Nations:
Parliamentary and Press Attitudes

The first formulation of views on the nature of the world organization to be established after World War II and the effective leadership given the smaller powers at San Francisco by Australia were
the work of a Labour government responding in part to the world
climate of opinion of the war years. It was cautiously optimistic
about the probable success of the United Nations and pledged to
support for its basic principles. That government retained office
until December 1949. It was replaced by a Liberal-Country party
government which is still in office having successfully contested
two more elections.[1] The change in government coincided roughly
with the Korean crisis. How far have there been fairly stable attitudes in Australia toward the United Nations? What has been the
extent of party differences? To what extent has there been a develop-

---

[1] For information on Australian political parties and governments during the
period, see Appendix A, pp. 372 ff. below.

t

ment or modification of attitudes in the light of the functioning of the Organization?

THE LABOUR GOVERNMENT
AND THE UNITED NATIONS
JULY 1945-DECEMBER 1949

In a statement to Parliament in 1948 Dr. Evatt concisely enumerated the principles of his foreign policy, principles consistently followed during his term of office as Minister for External Affairs:

> To support at all times, and faithfully, the principles expressed in the United Nations Charter . . .

> In international disputes, to insist on independent investigation of all the facts with a view to a settlement based upon right and justice, and not upon mere expediency or mere strategical preparation for another war. . . .

> To give every possible assistance to the peoples of the world by way of relief and rehabilitation required because of World War II.

> To maintain and strengthen our ties of kinship with Britain and the Dominions through co-operation in defence and welfare matters. . . .

> To strengthen Pacific security by appropriate regional arrangements in co-operation with the United States of America and other Pacific nations. . . .

> To support democratic principles both in the United Nations and particularly, in the making of peace settlements. . . .

> To emphasize the duty of contributing towards preventing war by actively supporting all welfare organizations such as United Nations organs and agencies . . . and all important international bodies concerned with the welfare of peoples, especially those in the Pacific and South-East Asia region . . .[2]

---

[2] See Commonwealth of Australia, *Parliamentary Debates* (*C.P.D.*), Vol. 196, 8 April 1948, pp. 748-50.

These principles were restated in substantially similar terms at regular intervals[3] until the Labour government was defeated at the polls in December 1949. There is a basic continuity in Labour's war-time and post-war foreign policy objectives and in its views on international organization, despite fluctuating enthusiasm and even inconsistency of action. The changing balance of power, the disintegration of the "Grand Alliance," and the development of the "cold war" produced no significant restatement of policy. The first two and the sixth of Dr. Evatt's points were those most likely to come under fire as of less practical value as the international situation deteriorated. The substance of the debate between the government and the Opposition lay in the relative importance attached to these principles. The phrase "democratic principles" can be interpreted to include the problems of the veto, and the need for open diplomacy and for confidence in the "middle" and "small" powers which exert their main influence in the General Assembly. These "democratic principles" were defended on grounds of morality and equity; it was, moreover, felt that these principles were most likely to achieve and to maintain peace.

Ministerial statements on international affairs repeatedly criticized the principle of the veto, and claimed that its relatively infrequent exercise was the result of Assembly criticism, largely sponsored by Australia.[4] The Opposition regarded this criticism as pointless since without the veto there could have been no United Nations. British and United States support for Australia's attitude did not cause the Opposition leader, Mr. R. G. Menzies, to shift ground; he believed that Australia might find the veto useful should the USSR interfere in Papua or some other territory of vital importance to Australia.[5]

---

[3] *Ibid.*, Vol. 200, 2 Dec. 1948, pp. 3894-904 (Mr. J. B. Chifley); Vol. 201, 9 Feb. 1949, pp. 90-92; and Vol. 202, 21 June 1949, pp. 1212-26 (Dr. H. V. Evatt).

[4] *Ibid.*, Vol. 189, 8 Nov. 1946, pp. 95-96 and 103-04; Vol. 190, 26 Feb. 1947, p. 160; Vol. 192, 5 June 1949, p. 3679; and Vol. 202, 21 June 1949, pp. 1215-20.

[5] *Ibid.*, Vol. 189, 13 Nov. 1946, pp. 159-60; and Vol. 193, 19 Sept. 1947, p. 127.

Dr. Evatt's distrust of great power diplomacy had been evident at San Francisco where he contrasted its underlying expediency with the devotion of the "middle and smaller powers" to high principles. He continued to praise the high standards of Assembly discussions and decisions. His suspicion of the great powers was intensified by their failure to accede to his protracted demand for effective participation by the smaller belligerents in the drafting of the peace treaties. His criticisms were oblique rather than direct. He frequently contrasted the unsatisfactory attempts of the great powers to draw up the treaties with the successful settlement of disputes by the United Nations which, he claimed, had acted solely on the basis of justice. He also compared the existing drift towards war and "power politics dominating the just settlement of many problems" with the sterling work of the Assembly. In its handling of the Palestine dispute, for example, he felt the Assembly had approached the problem not on the basis of expediency but impartially and solely in terms of the best interest of the inhabitants.[6]

This belief in the integrity of the small powers when meeting together in the Assembly was combined with a continuing confidence in the utility of the United Nations as a means of lessening international tension. Dr. Evatt derived some satisfaction from the fact that great power disagreement in the Security Council had in fact given to the Assembly a role far more important than that which was visualized at San Francisco. In the spring of 1948, he stated:

> Time and time again I have seen the arguments put forward by the smaller nations succeed because the meetings are public, and no country whatever its form of government can be indifferent to world opinion, or to the opinion of its own people. Therefore, it has frequently happened that decisions have been reached unanimously, because of the weight of argument put before the assembly by the middle and small nations.[7]

---

[6] *Ibid.*, Vol. 196, 8 April 1948, p. 742. See also Vol. 201, 9 Feb. 1949, pp. 76-92; and Vol. 202, 21 June 1949, pp. 1218-19.

[7] *Ibid.*, Vol. 196, 8 April 1948, p. 741.

Dr. Evatt's confidence in the Assembly rose even higher the following year. It had, he claimed, brought the great powers together in the Berlin deadlock and had thus been instrumental in promoting agreement on Berlin as well as on the Austrian peace treaty; it had made similarly useful contributions to the handling of the Balkan and Korean situations. Its functions had been enhanced far more than had been conceived possible in 1945.

> There is no power in the Assembly so great that it does not attend to the opinion of the majority of the Assembly and the criticisms publicly uttered in the Assembly. Equally, there is no power so small that it cannot influence the decisions of the Assembly. . . . The fact is that the organization is working. Make no mistake about that! It is there to stay. Nothing can stay its progress now that . . . Great Power understanding is gradually being extended. I believe that the United Nations Assembly has rendered a very great contribution to the maintenance of peace, especially during the last two or three most difficult years.

The Assembly was establishing for itself "a position analogous in international affairs to the position that was developed in Great Britain during the long years of struggle by the House of Commons in relation to the executive." Every report came to it. It had the power of the purse. "Gradually each organ is looking to the General Assembly—that is, to world public opinion—for guidance." He pointed out that "all international disputes should be settled by reference to what is just and right and not according to what is expedient" and expressed pride in the fact that at the United Nations Assembly session in Paris, Australia had "endeavoured to act in accordance with those principles."[8] He deprecated the view that Australia should concern itself solely with matters directly concerning its national interests. Peace was indivisible, and the Charter imposed upon all members the unavoidable duty of exerting them-

---

[8] *Ibid.*, Vol. 202, 21 June 1949, pp. 1220-26.

selves on all matters within its scope. "There is not one question [before the United Nations] upon which Australia is not compelled, in the last resort, to express its opinion, either early in the consideration, or, at any rate, by its vote."[9]

Opposition criticism of the Evatt policies in the United Nations arose fundamentally out of a differing assessment of the value of the United Nations and its relationship to the British Commonwealth of Nations. On occasion the Opposition took issue with him on a particular vote in the United Nations. But the burden of its criticism was that Australian foreign policy was being forced out of focus. Dr. Evatt's earnest and voluble support of international idealism had at times led to a neglect of vital Australian interests. The attempt to formulate an independent policy, without proper consultation with the United Kingdom to secure parallel or combined action, had steadily diminished Australian prestige. Undue support had been given to the United Nations' "experiment" to the detriment of the tried and proved British Commonwealth. The success of the United Nations depended on the motives of its members, and if these were wrong, then public debates could prove injurious to world peace, "the delegates becoming the vocal champions of conflicting ideals and interests, and small disputes growing into great ones in the forcing house of publicity and propaganda."[10]

Sharing neither Dr. Evatt's personal attachment to the United Nations nor his distrust of secret diplomacy, the Opposition at an early stage advocated direct negotiations with the USSR outside the United Nations in an attempt to lessen tensions.

> Are the Western democracies going to achieve a common understanding with the people of Russia by well-advertised and bitter wrangles at the Security Council, or by . . . bilateral,

---

[9] *Ibid.*, Vol. 201, 9 Feb. 1949, p. 76.

[10] See Mr. R. G. Menzies' statement, *ibid.*, Vol. 186, 20 March 1946, pp. 437-40. For other Opposition speeches, see also pp. 447-49 (Mr. J. McEwen), and pp. 457-58 (Mr. H. Holt).

> informal discussions and exchanges, not in the glare of publi-
> city, not with limelight effects when the champions enter the
> lists, so that those who are looking on may applaud them,
> but in that quiet, informal, off-stage way in which the best
> results are achieved?[11]

Conflicting estimates of Soviet objectives were more influential in determining party attitudes than ethical convictions, "lessons" of international organization, or beliefs in the importance of the United Nations and its principles. Attitudes on the efficacy of the United Nations were largely the product of differing assessments of the origins and nature of the "cold war."

Although deeply concerned at Soviet action and policies, Dr. Evatt at first regarded Russian policy as defensive. Early in 1946 he took the position that Soviet expansion was primarily in accordance with secret arrangements made with the United States and the United Kingdom "alone and without reference to their allies."

> Having no clear evidence to the contrary and having during
> the last four years come to know some of Russia's greatest
> statesmen, I take the view that the Soviet Union's policy is
> directed towards self-protection and security against future
> attack . . . One must arrive at some conclusion in these matters
> or it is impossible to move ahead with any policy. That is the
> opinion upon which I act.[12]

He believed that the war-time exclusion of the USSR from atomic secrets was one of the root causes of its suspicion of the West in the United Nations; he praised the Soviet contribution to the Allied victory and cautioned that neither side should get tough with the other. In April 1948 he attacked anti-Soviet propaganda and took some comfort from the fact that Russia had sponsored a General Assembly resolution condemning war propaganda. He subsequently

---

[11] *Ibid.*, Vol. 189, 13 Nov. 1946, p. 163 (Mr. Menzies).
[12] *Ibid.*, Vol. 186, 13 March 1946, p. 205.

attacked the "defeatist attitude which would regard war as inevitable or agreement between the powers as impossible of achievement."[13]

Mr. R. G. Menzies from the beginning forthrightly attacked Dr. Evatt's view on Russia as "reminiscent of the case which was made out for Hitler's *Lebensraum* before the war." If Dr. Evatt's theory of defensive motives were accepted "the day will come when the Soviet Union will be able to dictate its own terms to the world." Russia's accessions of territory had upset the balance against the democracies. It was therefore necessary for Australian defence to "cultivate its special friendships with such nations as have common interests with it."[14] With Mr. Winston Churchill's Fulton speech still ringing in his ears, Mr. Menzies pleaded for a United States-British Commonwealth alliance. Since Dr. Evatt and the Labour party were politically committed to open diplomacy and the rejection of alliances, this meant to them a revival of the "hopeless" policy of power politics.[15] In February 1949 Mr. Menzies reiterated his lack of faith in the efficacy of "ideals" as a solution to the "cold war" and justified his pursuit of a policy of expediency.

> The immediate, practical, urgent problem that must be faced in this world so full of danger is not whether we ourselves subscribe to a certain ideal state of affairs, but whether this scheme [i.e. the United Nations] works now or can work now. . . . Expediency matters in this world, and if we are confronted by a state of affairs in which we find things challenging the peace of the world and the security, safety and future of our own people, it is of no use stating airy-fairy legalistic ideals.

He repudiated Dr. Evatt's basic assumption that the United Nations could act as well as talk. Great power aggression could never be restrained by the Security Council; it could be checked only "by

[13] *Ibid.*, Vol. 200, 2 Dec. 1948, p. 3901. For other statements by Dr. Evatt concerning his views on the USSR, see Vol. 186, 13 March 1946, pp. 204-05; Vol. 189, 8 Nov. 1946, pp. 103-04; and Vol. 196, 8 April 1948, pp. 743 and 750-51.

[14] *Ibid.*, Vol. 186, 20 March 1946, pp. 439-44.

[15] *Ibid.*, Vol. 189, 15 Nov. 1946, p. 337.

some other great power or great powers acting together, not under the Charter but in spite of the existence of the Charter."[16]

Opposition criticisms of the government's foreign policy, except on the Indonesian question, were in fact rather desultory and perfunctory. For example, the Opposition questioned whether government support for the partition of Palestine was anti-British; whether the Western powers resented Australia's action in sponsoring Assembly intervention in the Berlin dispute; and whether Australia in voting in the United Nations should follow the lead of the United Kingdom and the United States. To the charge that their policy was inconsistent and confusing, Labour pointed out that in the Security Council, Australia had voted with the USSR on only twenty-three occasions. On eighteen of these, both the United States and the United Kingdom had also voted with the USSR. On the remaining five occasions (mainly concerning Indonesia), Australia was in the same camp as the United States.[17]

The Indonesian question divided the two parties most sharply. The Labour government had brought the dispute before the Security Council partly on general principle, but primarily because of the uncomfortable proximity of Indonesian fighting to Australia.[18] Vigorous Liberal dissent from that action lay in their preference for the Dutch as reliable allies and in their suspicion that the Indonesians were pro-Japanese and Communist. To them the matter was one of domestic jurisdiction. Labour policy was establishing a dangerous precedent which might subsequently lead to an Australian request to Britain to use its veto in defence of Australia's domestic jurisdiction. "Australia, of all countries, has a keen interest in preserving its authority over matters which are within its own domestic jurisdiction, because, to be perfectly plain, that clause was designed to safeguard Australia's right to maintain the White Australia policy."[19]

---

[16] *Ibid.*, Vol. 201, 15 Feb. 1949, pp. 265 and 267.
[17] *Ibid.*, Vol. 193, 24 Sept. 1947, p. 169 (Mr. A. Fraser).
[18] *Ibid.*, Vol. 201, 9 Feb. 1949, p. 80 (Dr. Evatt).
[19] *Ibid.*, Vol. 193, 24 Sept. 1947, p. 176 (Mr. Menzies).

THE LIBERAL GOVERNMENT
AND THE UNITED NATIONS
DECEMBER 1949-JUNE 1957

The first considered Liberal assessment of the United Nations was made by the new Minister for External Affairs, Mr. P. Spender, in March 1950. As usual, foreign policy had not been a major issue at the election of 1949; candidates before the poll had been reluctant to commit themselves on their views about the United Nations.

Liberal support for the United Nations appeared to be conditional upon the Organization's own consistent pursuit of its principles. The role of the United Nations should be a limited one: to bring the pressure of world opinion to bear on the parties rather than to assume responsibility for composing differences which the great powers themselves could not resolve. The United Nations, Mr. Spender stated,

> has shown that it can define areas of agreement and dis-
> agreement, exercise a deterrent to unilateral or violent action,
> and mediate successfully. It has found international solutions
> of problems that have been pressed upon it. In some cases it
> had failed in its attempts, in others it has succeeded. . . . It
> is the only organised mechanism available to us for finding
> agreed solutions of problems that are international in scope.
> Its members should therefore apply the organization to those
> useful tasks that are within its reach at the moment, and try
> as well to extend its authority by seeking to find a basis for
> agreement on major subjects like atomic energy, disarmament
> and the like.[20]

Mr. Spender, in analyzing the actions taken at the 1949 session of the General Assembly, noted with concern the "increasing tend-ency" by the Assembly "to overstep its competence in relation to non-self-governing territories" such as Papua. With a view to con-fining the Assembly's activities within the proper limits, Australia had denied the Assembly's right to demand political information

---

[20] *Ibid.*, Vol. 206, 9 March 1950, p. 637.

on the territories or to make recommendations regarding individual territories. Mr. Spender found a similar tendency towards "exaggerated interpretations" of the Assembly's powers and the duties of members on the question of human rights and fundamental freedoms. Here, a specific covenant defining and limiting these powers and duties was necessary.

A dissipation of the energies of the United Nations over a wide field to the detriment of major questions of security could lead the Organization to ignore its basic objective, the maintenance of peace. There had been an unnecessary proliferation and duplication of agencies and committees, particularly within the Economic and Social Council and the General Assembly; most of these activities were outside the real scope of the United Nations. While pressing for the rationalization of the programs of some of the specialized agencies, he admitted the value and need for economic co-operation.

> The promotion of a healthier world economic situation is fundamental to the maintenance of close political relations among democratic countries, and indeed to the preservation of some countries as democracies. . . . The United Nations and other specialized economic agencies can play an important part in achieving this purpose, and Australia will cooperate with them to that end.[21]

The most significant thing about Mr. Spender's speech was the shift in emphasis in Australian foreign policy. This had been implicit in Liberal criticism while in opposition; it now became explicit. The United Nations was to be relegated to a subordinate place in Australian policies, and objectives which were in theory eminently suited to United Nations action were now to be pursued independently of it. The two most important instruments of the new government's foreign policy were the Pacific Pact and the Colombo Plan. Both were regarded as supplementary to, and falling within the ambit of, the functions of the United Nations. The

---

[21] *Ibid.*, Vol. 208, 8 June 1950, pp. 4014-15.

important thing was that, despite the formal safeguarding of the primacy of United Nations, the new policies were now to be pursued outside it.

The Pacific Pact was envisaged as a defensive military arrangement having as its basis a firm agreement among countries that have a vital interest in the stability of Asia and the Pacific, and a capacity for undertaking military commitments. It was the historical successor to the abortive Pacific Pact proposed by Mr. J. A. Lyons in 1937. The British Commonwealth countries would form the nucleus of such a pact; it was hoped that other Pacific powers, particularly the United States, would be founding members. Although the pact was to conform to the type of regional arrangement envisaged in Article 52 of the Charter, no attempt was made to justify its provisions by reference to the Charter.

The Colombo Plan was designed to provide economic aid to Southeast Asian countries to facilitate basic developmental projects of each individual country's own choice. The two schemes formed part of a two-pronged plan to check Communist aggression in South Asia. Behind the military shield of the pact, stable and democratic governments could be established and maintained. Living standards could at worst be pegged, at best could be slightly raised, thus cutting at the roots of potential support for communism.

The chief Labour objection to the new Liberal policy lay in its changed emphasis, the reorientation away from the United Nations. Dr. Evatt reiterated his view that the United Nations was

> the sole working forum to-day for the resolving of international disputes. The bitterness of the differences between the Great Powers cannot affect their meetings, and the fact that those meetings do not take place at the top level as they did during the war, means that there is only one tribunal to resort to and that is the forum of the United Nations.[22]

There appeared to be an inconsistency between Mr. Spender's assumption of great power disagreement and his proposal that the

---

[22] *Ibid.*, Vol. 206, 16 March 1950, p. 912.

United Nations should attempt to solve the problems of atomic energy and disarmament. On the other issues, there was substantial agreement between the parties, particularly over the Pacific Pact. Dr. Evatt had earlier revived the Lyons proposal in an amended form; he regarded United States participation as essential to its success. If this were secured, "it could do nothing but good."

The outbreak of the Korean War in June 1950 led to swift Australian support for the decision of the Security Council and the despatch of Australian forces to resist aggression in Korea. The government felt that, while the Security Council's decision to resist was independent of any judgment of the causes of aggression, there was no doubt that there had been an infringement of territorial integrity.[23] Both Mr. Chifley and Dr. Evatt fully endorsed the government's action and pressed for even fuller support for the United Nations force. Few doubts were expressed by either party about the nature of the aggression: the pacific intentions of Syngman Rhee were never questioned. To both political parties, the war arose from resistance to unprovoked aggression. The war has been one of the occasions when the Australian government has, as a matter of principle, strongly supported the United Nations. It made a major contribution to the British Commonwealth contingent, and played an important role in the economic and administrative problems of the war through membership in UNCURK and financial backing for UNKRA.

The Korean War led to a parliamentary clash on Australian defence policy. Mr. Menzies made willingness to serve outside Australia a condition of enlistment in the regular and volunteer forces on the ground that this was necessary to enable Australia to meet its United Nations commitments. This raised a long-standing and bitter party issue in Australian politics: Labour's preference for

---

[23] *Ibid.*, Vol. 208, 6 July 1950, p. 4846 (Mr. Spender). For a discussion of government policy, see G. Sawer, in Gordon Greenwood and Norman Harper, eds., *Australia in World Affairs, 1950-55* (Melbourne: F. W. Cheshire, 1957), pp. 118-19.

retaining Australian armed forces in or near the Commonwealth. Mr. Chifley and Mr. Ward both pointed out that Australia's liability to the United Nations was not absolute. "In respect of any request that may come from the United Nations, we should continue to give assistance within our capacity; but that does not involve calling up men to serve in any part of the world on any pretext at all."[24]

During the next four years, the "new look" in Australian foreign policy and its attitude to the United Nations were confirmed. The Colombo Plan was implemented and its geographic scope extended. The Pacific Pact took a rather limited form with the signature of the ANZUS agreement in September 1951. It was later supplemented by the wider South East Asia Collective Defence Treaty, the SEATO Pact, signed at Manila on 8 September 1954. Liberal parliamentary support for the United Nations has been continuous, especially for the Organization's philanthropic and technical assistance activities. Except on occasions when the General Assembly has attempted action which, it was felt, infringed on domestic jurisdiction, the government has expressed cautious approval. With no high hopes that the United Nations could solve the fundamental problems of the world in the near future, the government has conceded to the United Nations a limited usefulness. As Mr. Casey stated in 1952:

> I do not . . . underestimate the . . . value of meetings of the Assembly. There, at least, countries on opposite sides of the Iron Curtain can meet and hear one another speak. Absence of contact might well be worse than vituperation.[25]

Dr. Evatt for his part has made no vigorous efforts to restore the United Nations to its original, and perhaps controversial, position of primacy in Australian policy. He criticized the Australian government for not pressing for the establishment of an organ to

[24] For Mr. Chifley's remarks, see *C.P.D.*, Vol. 210, 24 Oct. 1950, p. 1268. Mr. Ward at a later date seemed to suggest that Australia could (and perhaps should) have followed India's example and not sent forces to Korea (see *ibid.*, Vol. 214, 10 Oct. 1951, pp. 490-91).

[25] For Mr. Casey's views, see *ibid.*, Vol. 216, 22 Feb. 1952, pp. 270-71, and Vol. 217, 4 June 1952, pp. 1369-70.

give Australia and other participants greater powers of direction over United Nations forces in Korea.[26] He sought to enhance the importance of the Security Council by urging that it deal with the Indochina problem and Egyptian violations of the Anglo-Egyptian Treaty.[27] Such moves have been infrequent and not sustained. Foreign policy, particularly with regard to the United Nations, has increasingly tended to become bipartisan.

How far have there been important party differences over the role of the United Nations? Can permanent trends in national policies be detected? Within the Labour party, the earlier radical or left-wing trends, represented by stalwarts such as Mr. Beasley (the former Minister for Defence), have largely disappeared. A few back-benchers were frankly pessimistic about the possible success of the United Nations on the ground that the doctrine of class war precluded the possibility of peace through any association of governments. During the Korean War such views were confined to three elderly senators who continued to embarrass the party.[28]

A close study of the parliamentary debates until the cease-fire in Korea shows that Dr. Evatt alone in the Labour party retained some of his initial enthusiasm for the United Nations: commendation of its achievements and support for its principles rarely come from rank-and-file members. By March 1947 Mr. Beasley, from his important position of the speaker following the Minister in debate, openly disagreed with him, considering the United Nations to be ineffective and Australia's continued attacks on the veto as futile.[29] Dr. Evatt's stubbornly persistent attack on the veto also came under fire from Mr. Haylen, a consistent supporter of the government's foreign policy.[30] All the evidence suggests that

---

[26] *Ibid.*, Vol. 211, 28 Nov. 1950, p. 3182.

[27] *Ibid.*, Vol. 214, 16 Oct. 1951, p. 679, and *ibid.* (House of Representatives), Vol. 4, 5 Aug. 1954, p. 71.

[28] *Ibid.*, Vol. 215, 21 Nov. 1951, pp. 2384-85 (Senator Morrow); Vol. 216, 27 Feb. 1952, pp. 406-07 (Senator Cameron) and p. 422 (Senator O'Flaherty).

[29] *Ibid.*, Vol. 190, 9 March 1947, pp. 858-62.

[30] *Ibid.*, Vol. 193, 24 Sept. 1947, p. 155.

Dr. Evatt's leadership in the United Nations and his enthusiastic parliamentary support for it were personal: they did not represent a considered party attitude. Occasional party dissent, such as that of Mr. Beasley and Mr. Haylen, was tolerated because the subjects of criticism appeared to be marginal and remote.

Liberal and Country party opinion was much more guarded. Mr. Menzies and Mr. Casey, with their wide understanding of international problems, were more sympathetic to the United Nations than most of their colleagues. Many Liberals were lukewarm, although no one suggested withdrawal from the United Nations and there was no party support for three members who pressed for the exclusion of the USSR. There was consistent preference for collaboration with, and reliance upon, the British Commonwealth and the United States for security and the solution of economic problems. With the change in government in 1949, there was no evidence of waning enthusiasm for the United Nations. The difference in attitude was one largely of emphasis and of priority in policy. In October 1950 at the fifth session of the General Assembly, Mr. Spender was critical of the "Uniting for Peace" resolution. He pointed out the difficulties in the exchange of information by the military planners and the Collective Measures Committee, and urged strongly that the United Nations encourage the formation of regional security pacts.[31] This foreshadowed the development of Australian policy towards ANZUS and SEATO as limited but specific regional pacts, pacts however which might not fit easily into United Nations planning for collective security. Active support for the work of the United Nations continued under the Menzies government and United Nations contacts of all kinds have expanded rather than contracted. Australian participation has been active and very detailed, and many government departments have been drawn into these activities.

---

[31] General Assembly, Official Records (G.A.O.R.): 5th Sess., 1st Ctte., 356th Mtg., 10 Oct. 1950, pp. 74, 75.

Many of the detailed criticisms of the United Nations during the rough-and-tumble of parliamentary debate arose out of the British constitutional convention that it is the duty of the Opposition to oppose, and of the government to support, current policies. As parties changed sides in the House, so criticisms were modified in detail. By 1949 the facts of the "cold war" imposed agreement on political parties in Australia as elsewhere that the role of the United Nations was to be a relatively minor one. Even Dr. Evatt appears to have concluded, in the light of experience, that his earlier optimism was now untenable. At one level the change in attitude was reflected in government policy towards the Australian Association for the United Nations. Substantial financial assistance, granted by the Labour government, was considerably curtailed when the Liberal party took office; it has subsequently been maintained at that lower level but with constant unofficial co-operation.

With the development of the Indochina crisis in 1954 and the federal government's decision in 1955 to station troops in Malaya, the Australian Labour party became increasingly critical of government foreign policy. The criticisms coincided with the split in the Labour party and the emergence of the minority Democratic Labour party which first contested federal elections in 1955 and won one seat in the Senate. The split strengthened the influence of Dr. Evatt in the Australian Labour party, and this was reflected in the revision of the party's foreign policy platform. At the Hobart Conference in 1955 and the Brisbane Conference in 1956, the Australian Labour party strongly reaffirmed its support for the United Nations. Priority was given to membership of the Commonwealth of Nations, but at the same time, the party declared that:

> Australia must give greater practical support to the United Nations for the purpose of carrying out the principles of the United Nations Charter, and, in particular, for their wholehearted application in the Pacific and South-East Asia areas. These principles cover both collective action to repel military aggression, and . . . continuous action by way of conciliation

and peaceful intervention for the purpose of preventing war. . . .[32]

The Suez crisis in 1956 provided the opportunity for differing party assessments of the United Nations. When disputes had come before the Security Council or the General Assembly on previous occasions, Australia had been able to maintain some measure of detachment. Because Australian troops had been stationed in Egypt in two world wars, because of the important part that the Canal played in Australian communications with Europe, and because of the deep Australian sentimental attachment to the United Kingdom, it was difficult for Australians to approach the problem dispassionately. Mr. Menzies had himself been involved in the negotiations outside the United Nations and had led the five-member committee to discuss the views of the first London Conference with President Nasser. On his return to Australia, a brief debate took place in Parliament on 25 September when Mr. Menzies explained government policy and was then hotly criticized by Dr. Evatt. Further brief debates took place on 31 October and 8 November. The House rose on 8 November and did not reassemble until 19 March 1957 when a lengthy debate on foreign policy took place.

The crucial difference between the government and the Opposition lay in their relative assessment of the role of the United Nations in the settlement of the dispute over the nationalization of the Suez Canal and in dealing with the situation created by the Anglo-French invasion of Egypt and the Israeli attack upon Egyptian territory. Mr. Holt, a senior member of cabinet, summed up government policy:

> We support the United Nations organization. . . . We shall continue to do what we can to strengthen its effectiveness, but we do not allow ourselves to be blinded by its weaknesses and its imperfections. . . . We believe that Australia could exert a significant influence on world affairs, not by going it alone in

---

[32] Extracts are given in *C.P.D.* (House of Representatives), Vol. 14, 11 April 1957, pp. 814-15.

the councils of the United Nations organization, but through our intimate association with the United Kingdom and other countries of the British Commonwealth, through our strong friendship with the United States of America . . .[33]

Dr. Evatt, from the beginning, argued that the dispute over the Canal should be handled through the United Nations machinery for conciliation and mediation and that "our firm policy is to give unwavering support to the United Nations."[34]

Government preference for negotiation outside the United Nations was reflected in support for the discussions culminating in the Menzies mission to Cairo. On his return, Mr. Menzies, after outlining Australian policy, posed the alternatives facing the government should the Security Council be deadlocked over Suez:

> I state the choice in stark terms: we can organise a full-blooded programme of economic sanctions against Egypt, *or* we can use force to restore international control of the Canal, *or* we can have further negotiations, provided we do not abandon vital principles, *or* we can "call it a day," leave Egypt in command of the Canal, and resign ourselves to the total collapse of our position and interests in the Middle East. . . .[35]

It was the insistence that force might properly be used for purposes other than self-defence or to carry out a decision of the United Nations that led Dr. Evatt to attack government policy. Accepting Lord McNair's view that "armed force was no longer a discretionary instrument of policy but its use is regulated by law," he argued that "the Charter of the United Nations . . . provides that all other conflicting obligations are to give way to the rule of the United Nations Charter. . . ."[36] Use of force in the circumstances was inconsistent with the obligations that Australia had accepted as a member of the United Nations. The three power armed inter-

---

[33] *Ibid.*, 4 April 1957, p. 580; cf. Mr. Casey, *ibid.*, 11 April 1957, p. 831.

[34] *Ibid.*, Vol. 13, 8 Nov. 1956, p. 2124.

[35] *Ibid.*, Vol. 12, 25 Sept. 1956, pp. 825-26.

[36] *Ibid.*, pp. 827, 833.

vention in Egypt led Dr. Evatt to reiterate his point and to declare that the enforcement action they had taken was "contrary to the Charter of the United Nations."[37] It was an intolerable and illegal doctrine to assume that force could be used other than in self-defence. The Australian Labour party fully supported the action of the General Assembly in bringing about a cease-fire.

The creation of the United Nations Emergency Force was welcomed with varying degrees of enthusiasm by the Australian political parties. The Menzies government had over a period of years given increasing support to the Collective Measures Committee and by 1953 had urged that it be put on a permanent footing. Had this been done, the Egyptian crisis might not have come to a head in this particular way. When UNEF was established, the government supported it fully, but feared that it would produce no solution of the basic issues in dispute. Mr. Menzies bitterly criticized the exclusion of the United Kingdom and France from it.

> They are not allowed to participate in an international force—a force to consist of people from Portugal and Colombia and little groups and bits and pieces. But not Great Britain and France. I would have thought that around their forces could have been built a U.N. force which would have power, authority and could have got this canal going.[38]

No doubt he had in mind the analogy of Korea but that in fact was a completely different situation: the United Nations force entered South Korea at the request of the government to carry out decisions of the United Nations. UNEF moved into Egypt to prevent the United Kingdom, France, Egypt, and Israel from defying decisions of the United Nations.

The Suez crisis, coinciding in point of time with the Hungarian revolt, led the Menzies government to be acutely aware of the

---

[37] *Ibid.*, Vol. 13, 31 Oct. 1956, p. 2063.
[38] Mr. Menzies in a speech to the annual meeting of the Federal Council of the Liberal Party, *Sydney Morning Herald*, 16 Nov. 1956.

imperfections of the United Nations machinery. To Mr. Menzies, the Anglo-French intervention in Egypt had galvanized the United Nations into action; because of the inherent respect of Britain and France for the rule of law, they had complied with the recommendations of the General Assembly. Neither the Security Council, deadlocked on Hungary by a Russian veto, nor the General Assembly was able to secure the compliance of either Hungary or the USSR with United Nations decisions. Underlying government policy was the belief that Anglo-French intervention was justified in Egypt and that there was no case at all for Russian military intervention in Hungary. Mr. Casey, reflecting on the Suez crisis, concluded that

> the United Nations has had many of these questions before it for a number of years. Without wishing to be unduly critical, it can be said that it has reached no satisfactory solution to any of them. I believe this reflects the fact that we must recognize that the United Nations cannot always be counted upon to reach objective and fair and constructive conclusions on situations in which group pressures and the promotion of special interests have tended to weaken its effectiveness and its impartiality.[39]

Liberal criticisms of the United Nations centred around its inability to enforce decisions. The Security Council, paralyzed by the veto, was often powerless to act; when an agreement was reached (for example, on the six principles governing the future control of the Canal), it proved impossible to implement. Assembly decisions represented majority opinions in a body where equality of representation gives too great a voice to small powers, often not themselves democratic. Bloc voting and horse-trading tend to make it possible for officials to "predict, with a good deal of certainty and a very small margin of error, what the result of the vote will

---

[39] *C.P.D.* (House of Representatives), Vol. 14, 2 April 1947, p. 414; cf. 11 April 1957, pp. 828-30.

be."[40] The vital weakness of the United Nations lies in its inability to discipline members or to enforce decisions; this led some members of the Liberal party to suggest that "teeth" be given to the United Nations or that a peace force be set up.

The Australian Labour party strongly defended the United Nations in principle as "an earnest effort by the nations of the world to promote peace and prevent war." The debate showed a clear appreciation by Labour of the imperfections of the United Nations but an equally clear conviction that, despite these imperfections, it must be supported at all costs. The main criticisms of the Opposition were directed not so much against the United Nations itself as against a government which it felt had preferred to operate outside rather than inside the machinery of the United Nations, and preferred regional pacts to collective action in the United Nations as a means of preserving world security.[41] Above all, the Labour party stressed the importance of conciliation and mediation procedures while admitting the Organization's weakness in enforcement powers.

Has the existence of the United Nations made any considerable impact on the political parties or on overall Australian policy? There is abundant evidence of close and increasing Australian support for the activities of the United Nations. There is little evidence, on the other hand, that the United Nations has significantly altered Australian policy. Dr. Evatt's highly personal policy of enthusiastic support for the United Nations while he was Minister for External Affairs, and his attendant hesitation in attributing bad faith to Russia, left the major decisions unaffected. From the outset he appeared to have reservations. He endorsed Mr. Curtin's view that Australia must rely on Empire and national defence and not

---

[40] *Ibid.*, 11 April 1957, p. 789 (Mr. P. Hasluck); cf. *ibid.*, 4 April 1957, p. 532 (Mr. P. W. Stokes), pp. 547-48 (Mr. C. G. W. Anderson), and p. 589 (Mr. H. B. Turner); and 9 April 1957, p. 657 (Mr. Menzies).

[41] *Ibid.*, 4 April 1957, p. 556 (Mr. P. Haylen); and 11 April 1957, p. 785 (Mr. K. Beazley), p. 791 (Mr. F. Crean), pp. 814-15 (Mr. G. Duthie), and p. 822 (Mr. P. J. Clarey).

put its trust entirely in collective security.[42] His defence program, like that of his predecessors, was geared to imperial planning. He gave instant support to the Truman Doctrine and to the North Atlantic Treaty Organization. Regardless of any private reservations he may have had about great power negotiations, he sent the Australian air force to participate in the Berlin airlift. What is important is not his denial that his policy was conceived in terms of pre-war expediency and power politics, but rather that in execution it was one of support for British and United States policies on matters affecting world peace and Australia's vital interests.

Indonesia was probably the only important issue on which the Liberal party, had it been in power, would have followed a policy different from Labour's. Dr. Evatt openly stated at San Francisco that colonial misrule in Southeast Asia constituted a potential threat to Australia. An Indonesian government appeared more satisfactory for Australian interests than a Netherlands East Indies government. Labour's general views about imperialism rather than devotion to United Nations principles furnish the key to Labour policy in this case. The fear of the expanding influence of the Chinese Communists, however, has made impossible another Indonesian episode in Australian foreign policy. The San Francisco policies and their aftermath were a product of the depression and the fall of Singapore. The "cold war" in both Europe and Asia and continued prosperity at home ended the San Francisco interlude and changed the Labour party and its foreign policy.

The Labour party bitterly criticized government policy over Suez in 1956-57. The criticisms were directed against what Dr. Evatt termed the "niggardly and disloyal attitude"[43] which Mr. Menzies had adopted towards the United Nations. Dr. Evatt emphasized the need for conciliation and mediation and support for the general principles of the United Nations. But, as Mr. Menzies insisted,

---

[42] See Dr. Evatt's remarks, *ibid.*, Vol. 186, 26 March 1946, p. 630, in support of Mr. J. Curtin's statement, Vol. 179, 17 July 1944, p. 40.

[43] *Ibid.*, Vol. 13, 8 Nov. 1956, p. 2120.

taking a matter to the United Nations is not a foreign policy at all. Every nation must work out its own policy, the foreign policy that it wants to see adopted and operating, and when it has done that, it may then properly seek acceptance of that policy in the United Nations.[44]

While ceaselessly urging respect for the Charter and United Nations decisions, Dr. Evatt did not commit himself on specific issues. What part he would have played in the two London Conferences of canal users and at what stage he would have brought the dispute before the Security Council or the General Assembly is not clear.

THE ATTITUDE OF THE PRESS AND PUBLIC OPINION

In Australia it is impossible to make a distinction such as might be made in Britain between the mass circulation newspapers, only marginally interested in international affairs, and the smaller newspapers and weeklies that provide informed reporting and analysis of foreign news.[45] Both may assist in producing the climate of opinion in which those responsible for policy make their decisions and in which these policies may be analyzed by the public. The main Australian newspapers are primarily regional in their influence, an influence that radiates from the state capitals in which they are published; there are no national newspapers comparable to the London *Times* or the *Manchester Guardian*. In this, the Australian press resembles the American rather than the British pattern.

The Melbourne *Herald*, for example, with the largest evening circulation in Australia, has at the same time the greatest number of foreign correspondents, and devotes a considerable proportion of its leading articles to foreign affairs. The Melbourne *Sun*, although essentially a mass circulation pictorial, has a regular columnist

---

[44] *Ibid.*, Vol. 14, 9 April 1957, p. 655.
[45] For the circulation figures of Australian newspapers, see Appendix B, p. 378 below.

writing thoughtful articles on international problems. The Melbourne *Argus* (from 1950 until its demise in 1957 a tabloid) published numerous and provocative leaders as a matter of deliberate policy; its pungent daily comment on international affairs came from a skilled columnist. The *Sydney Morning Herald* and the Melbourne *Age* more closely resemble the traditional British newspapers than do other Australian dailies. While their influence on professional people is considerable, it would be unwise to ascribe to them any large part in shaping ministerial or official opinion. It is unusual for the Australian press to present information that is not more readily available to the government from other sources. Moreover, the press rarely attacks the government on foreign policy issues except in a crisis such as Suez. With the exception of the more popular dailies, which often ignore international issues, the leading articles in the Australian daily press are usually content to present the background to problems and the courses open to the participants. Criticism of government policies or the formulation of an independent line is uncommon except in the case of the *Sydney Morning Herald*, the *Age*, and, spasmodically, the *Argus*. There are no substantial weeklies of any weight at all, with the possible exception of the Sydney *Bulletin*, and it has never recaptured the influence it had at the beginning of the century.

The following table gives a rough picture of the quantity of editorial comment on foreign affairs in three Australian papers with high reputations. The London *Times* is included for purposes of comparison. The month of November 1951 (while the United Nations General Assembly was in session) was chosen at random. There is no suggestion that the geographic dissection of interest indicated in the table is a permanent or representative one. In classifying articles, those commenting on the merits of the United Nations or dealing primarily with its structure or functions are listed under "United Nations"; articles on disarmament come under "Great power relations"; those on Korea, unless included in the foregoing categories, are tabulated under "Pacific and Far East".

Leading Articles appearing November 1951

Subject	London Times	Sydney Morning Herald	West Australian	Melbourne Herald
Foreign Affairs (total)	43	26	15	15
Europe	9*	6**	4**	2**
Great power relations	5	3	2	5
Pacific and Far East	8	8	2	5
	(1 Japan 2 Korea 2 Malaya 2 India 1 Kashmir)	(5 Korea 1 Malaya 1 New Guinea 1 Far East)	(1 Korea 1 New Guinea)	(4 Korea 1 Malaya)
Middle East	10	7	4	3
Western hemisphere	1	1	1	0
British Empire and Commonwealth	5	0	1	0
United Nations	3	1	1	0

* excluding United Kingdom.   ** including United Kingdom.

Australian leader writers are rarely given to superlatives. Even the San Francisco Conference evoked at best a guarded optimism. The Sydney *Bulletin*, Australia's only political magazine with a substantial circulation, is non-party and expresses its views on most subjects intemperately;[46] it has been alone in direct and hostile criticism of the United Nations. Such optimism as existed in 1946 steadily evaporated as the international situation deteriorated during 1947 and 1948.[47] Yet on the whole editors were reluctant to conclude that the United Nations could serve no useful purpose.[48] Its value lay in providing a necessary forum where international prob-

---

[46] See, for example, article entitled "A bob as nob," 26 Nov. 1952.
[47] See, for example, *Sydney Morning Herald*, 11 Dec. 1947.
[48] See, for example, *Sydney Morning Herald*, 16 March 1948; Melbourne *Age*, 31 March 1948; and Adelaide *Advertiser*, 23 Sept. 1948.

lems and dangerous disputes could be discussed.[49] In 1949 pessimism abated somewhat, and the United Nations was credited with substantial achievements in Palestine, Indonesia, and Kashmir.[50] The invasion of Korea led a significant minority of Australian editors to predict that the United Nations would not rise to the occasion.[51] Support for the United Nations rallied when the Security Council reacted vigorously.[52] The "Uniting for Peace" resolution was regarded as strengthening the general structure of collective security.[53] With the success of United Nations forces in Korea and an improvement in the international situation, even some of the pessimists began to revise their views and print favourable assessments of the United Nations. By 1952 moderate praise became the order of the day: the United Nations appeared valuable as the one meeting place where East and West could discuss their differences.[54] As a general rule, these trends in the Australian press paralleled those in the British press, except that in Australia the descent to pessimism was less marked in 1948 and more quickly reversed in 1949. A graph of the Australian temperature chart would show less violent fluctuations than in the United Kingdom.

Public opinion polls indicate trends of opinion not markedly different from those expressed in Parliament and the press. In March 1946, 40 per cent of those polled in Australia thought prospects of world peace were worse than in 1919 and only 29 per cent thought

---

[49] See, for example, *West Australian*, 6 April 1949.

[50] See, for example, *Sydney Morning Herald*, 21 April 1949.

[51] Melbourne *Sun* and Adelaide *Advertiser*, 27 June 1950; *Brisbane Courier-Mail*, 28 June 1950; Sydney *Bulletin*, 5 July 1950. The Hobart *Mercury*, 27 June 1950, was alone in suggesting that the United States not send troops. It opposed the use of arms lest this should prolong a civil war without affecting the result.

[52] See, for example, Sydney *Daily Telegraph* and *Sydney Morning Herald*, 25 June 1951; *Brisbane Courier-Mail*, 22 Oct. 1951; Adelaide *Advertiser*, 24 Oct. 1951.

[53] *Sydney Morning Herald*, 20 Sept. 1950; *Sydney Morning Herald* and *West Australian*, 22 Sept. 1950; Hobart *Mercury*, 25 Sept. 1950; Sydney *Daily Telegraph*, 15 Nov. 1950.

[54] See, for example, *West Australian*, 4 Sept. 1952; Adelaide *Advertiser*, 18 Oct. 1952.

them better.[55] By August 1947, 35 per cent were expecting war within ten years; a year later this percentage had risen to 67.[56] (Australia
on this occassion had the dubious distinction of being more pessimistic than any other country participating in the poll.) The swift
change to extreme pessimism in 1948 at the time of the Berlin crisis
suggests caution in accepting the figures, particularly as polls in
other countries showed that over the same period, the percentage
of people satisfied with the work of the United Nations was rising.
In May 1946, according to the polls, the community was roughly
divided into thirds among those satisfied with the United Nations,
dissatisfied, and lacking opinions. Dissatisfaction mounted a year
later, but by December 1948 it had fallen below its original level.

Reactions to the United Nations[57]

	May 1946	*May 1947*	*December 1948*
Satisfied with UN	34%	26%	38%
Dissatisfied	34%	39%	29%
No opinion	32%	35%	33%

The subsequent increase in confidence evident in Parliament and the
press is paralleled in the polls: by October 1952, 62 per cent of the
respondents considered that the United Nations had been "reason-
ably successful," and by January 1956, the percentage had risen
to 67.[58]

Yet too much weight should not be attached to these expressions
of public opinion because it seems clear, but not surprising, that
the man in the street had little grasp of the details of specific issues
before the United Nations. His interest in and knowledge of inter-

---

[55] *Australian Gallup Polls* (Melbourne: Australian Public Opinion Polls),
Nos. 327-34, Feb.-March 1946. (The polls are hereinafter referred to as A.P.O.P.)

[56] *Ibid.*, Nos. 436-47, July-Aug. 1947; Nos. 548-58, Oct.-Nov. 1948.

[57] See *ibid.*, Nos. 559-68, Jan-Feb. 1949, for summary of the results of these
polls.

[58] *Ibid.*, Nos. 884-94, Oct. 1952, and Nos. 1143-49, Jan 1956.

national affairs were of a general character. He was inclined to place the responsibility for any deterioration in the international situation upon the United Nations and to regard any improved prospects for peace as a tribute to the efficiency of the United Nations. He often confused the outcome of power politics with the direct influence of the new international organization. There was a correlation but not the close causal relationship that he assumed. A poll in July 1945 indicated that of those questioned only one-third of the men and one-quarter of the women had followed the press reports of the San Francisco Conference.[59] A further poll in February 1947 dealt with the Bretton Woods proposals. The press had freely discussed these proposals and the federal cabinet had been sharply divided on the issue. Yet although 49 per cent of the people interviewed claimed some knowledge, the poll showed that 9 out of every 10 people were poorly informed about the specific proposals.[60] It would not be unfair to conclude that few of the 90 per cent of Australian adults who on the average spend 35 minutes each day reading a morning newspaper pay careful attention to the international news. Opinions held on complex United Nations issues are thus rarely well considered or soundly based.

In considering attitudes to the United Nations, editorial and public opinion regarding the USSR is particularly important. Confidence in the success of the United Nations in maintaining world peace in a polarized world is directly related to confidence in the peaceful intentions of the Soviet Union. Proposals to give teeth to the United Nations, possibly to the prejudice of its efficacy as an organ of conciliation, tend to presuppose answers to the question whether established Soviet policy permanently precludes a satisfactory settlement by conciliation. Attitudes towards disarmament are also directly related to estimates of Soviet policy.

The war-time optimism about continued collaboration among the members of the Grand Alliance carried over into the early post-war

---

[59] *Ibid.*, Nos. 284-93, Aug. 1945.
[60] *Ibid.*, Nos. 406-15, Feb.-March 1947.

period. Few Australians believed at this stage that Russia sought world domination.[61] Occasional leading articles favoured the immediate divulging of atomic secrets to the Soviet Union on the ground that it was wiser to share them in a friendly fashion than to wait for their discovery in the course of a new arms race.[62] Opinion steadily hardened over the next two years and the polls reflected the trends observable in Parliament. Among Labour voters the critics of Russia were in a majority; the supporters of non-Labour parties were even more suspicious.[63]

Date	Question	Labour Voters	Non-Labour Voters	General opinion
July 1946	Is Soviet policy aimed at			
	— world hegemony or	43%	58%	48%
	— security from attack?	33	19	27
May 1947	Who is to blame for the present US-USSR disagreement?			
	— USSR	32%	46%	37%
	— United States	15	6	11
	— Both	30	30	29
Dec. 1947	Are Soviet intentions			
	— aggressive or	51%	72%	61%
	— peaceful?	31	13	22

Editorial comment in a few papers up to the end of 1947 showed occasional sympathy for Russian attitudes with which the United States disagreed. The *West Australian* (19 September 1947) pointed

---

[61] *Ibid.*, Nos. 327-34, Feb. 1946. According to this survey, only 15% held this view.

[62] Melbourne *Sun*, 19 Oct. 1945; Sydney *Daily Telegraph*, 4 Oct. 1945; *Sydney Morning Herald*, 21 Feb. 1946; Hobart *Mercury*, 25 Sept. 1946.

[63] A.P.O.P., Nos. 365-74, Aug. 1946; Nos. 426-35, May-June 1947; and Nos. 470-77, Dec. 1947. Similar polls in the United Kingdom about the same time gave a very different result: 42% believed that the Soviet Union was aiming at security and only 26% felt that the main Soviet objective was imperialist expansion.

out that United States failure to recognize as permanent the pro-
visional Polish-German boundary would be regarded as hypo-
critical by Russia. The Hobart *Mercury* (3 October 1947) argued
that Russia was entitled to claim a seat for Eastern Europe on the
Security Council and criticized the vigorous United States opposition
to the election of the Ukrainian SSR to the Council. The *Sydney
Morning Herald* (20 March 1947) did not dispute the legality of the
Soviet claim to £2,500 million reparations out of Germany's current
production although it suggested that Russia reduce the amount.[64]

Leading articles at this stage sometimes weighed the possibility
that Western actions tended to defeat their objectives by intensi-
fying tension. The *Mercury* (17 January 1947), while supporting the
proposed alliance between Britain and France (signed 4 March 1947)
as justified and necessary, remarked that if it resulted in Russia's
turning back to suspicion and isolation, the price would be a heavy
one. In Australia, as in other parts of the world, Russia's rejection
of the Marshall Plan in July 1947 and the failure of the Foreign
Ministers' Conference held at London at the end of that year made
a deep impression: these were taken as positive evidence that the
division between East and West was rapidly passing the point of no
return.[65] Thereafter the Australian press was consistently critical of
the Soviet Union and pessimistic about the chances of conciliation.

There was an interesting contrast between the attitudes of the
Australian and British press to the establishment by the United
Nations of the Little Assembly in November 1947. In the United
Kingdom, fear of Soviet withdrawal from the United Nations was
more evident than in Australia. Several Australian papers were less
concerned with the possibility of Russian withdrawal than with the
lack of force behind the Assembly's decisions.[66] After 1947 there was

---

[64] See however *West Australian*, 1 April 1947.

[65] *West Australian* and *Sydney Morning Herald*, 4 July 1947; Melbourne *Herald*,
24 Nov. 1947; Sydney *Daily Telegraph* and Melbourne *Argus*, 17 Dec. 1947.

[66] Adelaide *Advertiser*, 18 Sept. 1947; *Sydney Morning Herald*, 19 Sept. 1947;
Melbourne *Argus*, 22 Sept. 1947.

a noticeable contrast between British and Australian press opinion concerning the relative emphasis to be placed upon the enforcement and the conciliation functions of the United Nations. This came out very clearly in the unreserved support of the Australian press in 1950 for the "Uniting for Peace" resolution.[67]

Certain specific issues before the United Nations have aroused special interest in Australia. Of these, one of the most important was the Korean War and the wider issues of security in the Pacific area. With these questions Australia was vitally concerned, both as a member of the Pacific community and as a participant in the Korean campaign. Complete agreement between the United Kingdom and the United States to defend South Korea did not preclude sharp disagreements on policies. These disagreements were followed with close attention in Australia.

The swift Council decision to resist the invasion of South Korea and the despatch of troops by the United States evoked enthusiastic press support and unanimous expressions of confidence in the future of collective security and satisfaction at the participation of Australian troops. A public opinion poll showed 70 per cent support for the despatch of a contingent to Korea.[68] The consensus of editorial opinion supported the advance into North Korea despite the risks involved.[69]

The entry of Communist Chinese forces into the Korean War produced no support for an attack upon China or for a formal declaration of war. Most editors urged a policy of caution and stressed the advisability of discussions with Peiping.[70] There was

[67] See, for example, *Sydney Morning Herald*, 20 and 22 Sept. 1950; *West Australian*, 22 Sept. 1950; Hobart *Mercury*, 25 Sept. 1950; Sydney *Daily Telegraph*, 15 Nov. 1950.

[68] A.P.O.P., Nos. 700-10, July-Aug. 1950.

[69] Melbourne *Age*, 18 Sept. 1950; *West Australian* and Hobart *Mercury*, 28 Sept. 1950; Melbourne *Argus* and Melbourne *Herald*, 30 Sept. 1950.

[70] Hobart *Mercury*, 9, 21, and 30 Nov. 1950; Melbourne *Argus*, 14 Nov. 1950; Melbourne *Age*, 22 Nov. 1950; Melbourne *Herald*, 27 Nov. 1950; Melbourne *Sun*, 27 and 30 Nov. 1950.

some support for the recognition of Communist China and general opposition to branding China as an aggressor.[71] Editors accepted the ban on the export to China of strategic materials provided that the ban were restricted to these materials.[72] Proposals to employ the atom bomb met with the disapproval of both the press and the public.[73] A public opinion poll in December 1950-January 1951 showed that only 17 per cent of those queried favoured the use of the bomb and 73 per cent opposed it; 36 per cent supported conventional bombing of Manchuria with 47 per cent opposed. A subsequent poll in February 1953 showed a smaller majority (57 per cent) opposed to the use of the A-bomb.[74] General MacArthur's threat to extend the war to China was universally criticized by the press and his dismissal from command accepted with relief.[75]

The Suez crisis touched the Australian people at several sensitive spots. The Australian press was almost unanimous in its condemnation of "an indefensible act of expropriation," by "an irresponsible leader dominating an irresponsible government, flouting international agreements at the mercy and caprices of a rabidly nationalist and fanatical public opinion."[76] There was a strong tendency to support collective Western action to secure an international settle-

---

[71] Melbourne *Age*, 8 Jan. 1951; Melbourne *Argus*, 9 Jan. 1951; Melbourne *Herald*, 11 Jan. 1951; *Brisbane Courier-Mail*, 1 Feb. 1951. The Melbourne *Sun*, Melbourne *Herald*, and Adelaide *Advertiser* (19 Jan. 1951), as well as the Hobart *Mercury* and *Brisbane Courier-Mail* (1 Feb. 1951), opposed the proposal to name China as an aggressor. The *Sydney Morning Herald* (11, 19, 24, 26, and 29 Jan. 1951) and the *West Australian* (1 and 2 Feb. 1951)—both moderate and influential independent papers—vigorously supported it.

[72] *West Australian*, 15 May 1951; Melbourne *Sun* and Hobart *Mercury*, 21 May 1951.

[73] *Mufti*, the organ of the Returned Soldiers' League (Aug. 1950), and the Brisbane *Telegraph* (7 Dec. 1950) were prepared to use the A-bomb.

[74] A.P.O.P., Nos. 732-43, Dec. 1950-Jan. 1951, and Nos. 906-15, Feb. 1953.

[75] Hobart *Mercury*, Melbourne *Argus*, and *Brisbane Courier-Mail*, 27 March 1951; *Sydney Morning Herald*, 31 March 1951; Adelaide *Advertiser*, 9, 13, and 23 April 1951; Melbourne *Sun*, 12 April 1951.

[76] Adelaide *Advertiser*, 31 July 1956. See also *West Australian*, 28 July 1956; Melbourne *Age*, 30 July 1956; *Sydney Morning Herald*, 31 July 1956; Melbourne *Herald*, 4 Aug. 1956.

ment rather than to press for mediation through the United Nations. The Adelaide *News* (3 September 1956) pointed out that the issue should be settled by negotiation rather than force because there was no clear-cut issue of naked aggression: "Here is a country of very different status [from the Soviet Union or China]—formerly a vassal state—repossessing something in its own territory. This is the heart of the matter." Australians, although strongly opposed to Nasser, were suspicious of "gun-boat diplomacy" and reluctant to use force to settle the Suez question: there was little dissent from America's abhorrence of force.[77]

While the Australian press preferred negotiation to force, there was a marked lack of enthusiasm in the first two months after the nationalization of the Canal for any action through the United Nations. The *Sydney Morning Herald* (5 October) put the matter bluntly by pointing out that Suez provided a crucial test for the United Nations: it "gives the United Nations the choice between redeeming itself in the eyes of those who have become cynical and acknowledging that the Charter represents no more than a pious hope." Dr. Evatt's broad proposals for reference of the dispute to the United Nations received scant support: the inability of the United Nations to resolve the running dispute between Egypt and Israel produced no confidence that the broader Suez question would be effectively dealt with in "the endless maze of the United Nations."[78] The breakdown of the London Conferences and the failure of the Menzies mission to Cairo led to some re-examination of the alternatives and a preference for negotiation through the United Nations rather than the use of force. This preference was not backed by any optimism about a Security Council solution: it arose out

---

[77] Hobart *Mercury*, 30 July 1956; *West Australian*, 31 July and 6 Aug. 1956; *Brisbane Courier-Mail*, 2 and 4 Aug. 1956; Melbourne *Age*, 2 Aug. 1956; *Sydney Morning Herald*, 3 Aug. 1956.

[78] Hobart *Mercury*, 16 Aug. 1956; cf. *Mercury*, 10 Sept. 1956 ("channelled from one futility to a worse one, the United Nations."). Adelaide *Advertiser*, 17 Aug. and 12 Sept. 1956; *West Australian*, 11 Sept. 1956.

of a conviction that world opinion should be respected and that a policy of economic sanctions outside the United Nations could be dangerous.[79] The Security Council, it was felt, would be unable to secure a solution which would meet basic Western principles or induce Egypt to accept an agreed compromise. Its unanimous acceptance of the six principles agreed upon privately by British, French, and Egyptian representatives was regarded as a moral victory for the West but nothing more.[80]

The Australian press was sharply divided by the Anglo-French invasion of Egypt. The *Sydney Morning Herald* (31 October 1956) condemned the Israeli attack upon Egypt as "the act of a nation which has temporarily lost all sense of reality .... The Western powers must call on Israel to withdraw at once, and if she refuses, they must intervene decisively, even if it means reoccupying part of the Middle East to preserve peace." The Melbourne *Age* (31 October and 1 November) urged swift United Nations action to prevent a general conflict, but when British paratroopers landed in the Suez zone, it wavered in its support for United Nations intervention. Torn between two conflicting loyalties it conceded that the United Nations had so far failed to resolve Middle Eastern conflicts and concluded that "the Anglo-French action . . . will be understood as politically inevitable." One section of the press was jubilant at the attack upon Egypt. "The Commonwealth of Nations should be delighted with the way Britain has asserted herself. This is more like

---

[79] Melbourne *Herald*, 10 and 24 Sept. 1956; *Sydney Morning Herald*, 14 Sept. 1956; *Brisbane Courier-Mail*, 17 and 26 Sept. 1956; Melbourne *Age*, 19 Sept. 1956. The Hobart *Mercury* was rather contemptuous of the United Nations: it felt (20 Sept.) that although it might be diplomatic to invoke United Nations action, it would be "as useful as referring it to the Eskimos." The *Sydney Morning Herald* (17 Oct.), after analyzing the operation of economic sanctions, suggested that an economic boycott might well affect the West more adversely than Egypt.

[80] Melbourne *Age*, 16, 25 Sept. and 2 Oct. 1956; *Sydney Morning Herald*, Hobart *Mercury*, Adelaide *Advertiser*, Melbourne *Herald* and Sydney *Bulletin*, 26 Sept. 1956; *Brisbane Courier-Mail*, 27 Sept. 1956. The Sydney *Bulletin*, 22 Sept. and 3 Oct. 1956, was Dr. Evatt's strongest critic. See also *Sydney Morning Herald*, 8 Sept. and 5 Oct. 1956; Melbourne *Herald*, 15 Sept. and 6 Oct. 1956; Adelaide *Advertiser*, 5 Oct. 1956.

the old Britannia." "For Britain the choice had become peace with economic extinction or a fight for survival."[81]

The *Brisbane Courier Mail* (1 and 2 November), disturbed at first, lost any doubts about British policy when bombing raids began on Egypt. "The Egyptian war confuses Australians with the barbarity of its beginning and the inadequacy of the reasons given for starting it. . . . The best service Australia can now give to Britain is to help her people get out of an unjust war into which the Eden government had thrust them." The Melbourne *Argus* (2 November) condemned the attack as having "no moral or legal authority. . . . The real object, and all the world has seen through it, is to seize the Suez Canal by force."[82] The condemnation or attempt at vindication of British action did not carry with it positive support for United Nations intervention. "It is not a repudiation of the United Nations to recognize that it cannot use a magic wand in the crisis." "The slogan 'jaw not war' is not good enough for the United Nations."[83]

The Canadian proposals for creating a police force, the beginnings of the United Nations Emergency Force, met with general approval ranging from a recognition of the positive value of such a force in helping keep the peace and the belief that it could act as a shield for the Canal Users' Association and a guarantee for the opening of the Canal to a patronizing support for a decision that, it was felt, should have been taken seven years earlier when the state of Israel was created.[84] The *Age* (9 November), while cautiously optimistic, declared that real peace in the Middle East "could never be achieved without the active intervention of the United Nations

---

[81] *Sydney Morning Herald* and Sydney *Sun*, 1 Nov. 1956; Hobart *Mercury*, 2 Nov. 1956.

[82] Cf. Adelaide *News*, 2 Nov. 1956.

[83] *West Australian* and *Sydney Morning Herald*, 3 Nov. 1956.

[84] Melbourne *Age* and Hobart *Mercury*, 5 Nov. 1956; *West Australian*, 7 Nov. 1956. For the steps leading to the setting up of UNEF, see William R. Frye, *A United Nations Peace Force* (New York: Oceana Publications for the Carnegie Endowment for International Peace, 1957), Chs. 1-3.

and, however unpopular the Anglo-French action was with most members, it is now clear that it has achieved precisely this result."

The Australian press, disturbed at the breakdown of Commonwealth consultation over Suez and at the contrast between the Anglo-French reaction to United Nations directives over Suez and the firm Russian refusal to sanction any kind of United Nations intervention in Hungary, felt that it was essential to establish an effective United Nations force: "The policeman must patrol his beat and he must carry a truncheon. . . . It may well be the final test of the United Nations' ability to enforce its authority in any danger spot in the world" (*Age*, 12 November). Australian editors failed to appreciate the complex legal problems involved in creating a United Nations force, particularly the questions of national sovereignty and the powers and functions of a force operating in Egypt. President Nasser undoubtedly raised these real issues in an attempt to make as much political capital as possible out of them. There was support for Mr. Casey's protests to the United Nations about "the absurd haggling that accompanies the piece-meal admission of Mr. Hammarskjold's troops to Egypt."[85] A United Nations force admitted to Egypt on Egyptian conditions would be merely a "sham United Nations force," a "large team of observers armed with more typewriters than rifles."[86] There was, too, an impatience at the delays in dealing with the situation and a fear that the end result could well be a stalemate of the kind that had existed between Egypt and Israel since 1949. It was important to deal not only with the "blunder of intervention" but also with the "provocation" by getting at "the root causes of conflict."[87]

The United Nations Emergency Force was finally accepted with little further criticism. But the whole Suez episode raised speculation about two further related problems: the difficulty of formulating

---

[85] Adelaide *Advertiser* and *West Australian*, 23 Nov. 1956.

[86] *Brisbane Courier-Mail*, 22 Nov. 1956; *West Australian*, 15 Nov. 1956; Melbourne *Herald*, 30 Nov. 1956.

[87] *Sydney Morning Herald*, 15 Nov. 1956; Melbourne *Herald*, 4 Dec. 1956.

a clear-cut United Nations policy, and the relative roles of the great and small powers. The contrast between the roles of the United Nations in Suez and Hungary was painfully obvious. The discussions in the General Assembly and the obvious manoeuvring of pressure groups in a United Nations whose membership had expanded considerably since 1945 aroused some concern. "If the United Nations is made the propaganda machine for any group of nations, if it ceases to fight for the peace and order of the world, it will have outlived its usefulness and sacrificed its authority."[88]

Although the Korean War and the Suez crisis provoked the widest comment on the United Nations in the Australian press, there has been some discussion of other issues that have come before the United Nations; the Indonesian dispute and the discussions in the General Assembly on racial discrimination and on the status of colonies were of particular interest to Australia. Prior to the Dutch "police action" in July 1947, the press had been sympathetic to the Dutch as European neighbours and war-time allies and uniformly hostile to the Indonesian leaders, whom they regarded as Japanese collaborators. The "police action" aroused wide criticism of Dutch policy.[89] Opinion shifted to the view that this was not essentially a matter of domestic jurisdiction but rather one that should be dealt with by the Security Council.[90] This is particularly interesting because the non-Labour parties, which the Australian press is usually inclined to support, took the opposite view.

During the next eighteen months, however, pro-Dutch sentiment gained ground, and in December 1948 criticism of the second Dutch "police action" was surprisingly mild. Although almost every paper spoke of Dutch tactics as unwise and unjustified, especially in view

[88] Melbourne *Age*, 27 Nov. 1956; cf. the bitter attack in the Sydney *Bulletin*, 21 Nov. 1956.

[89] *Brisbane Courier-Mail*, 24 July 1947; *Sydney Morning Herald* and Hobart *Mercury*, 25 July 1947; Melbourne *Age* and *Argus*, 1 Aug. 1947.

[90] *Sydney Morning Herald*, 28 July 1947, and Melbourne *Herald*, 31 July 1947, *West Australian*, 31 July 1947, alone supported the claim of domestic jurisdiction.

of the reaction they were bound to provoke in Southeast Asia, there was negligible support for the Indonesians, and several newspapers were inclined to favour Dutch policy.[91] The pro-Indonesian statements of the Australian Labour government were considered partisan and the bitter Australian attack upon the Netherlands in the Security Council was condemned.[92] However, only the *Sydney Morning Herald* (27 December 1948) thought it useless and undesirable to bring the issue before the Security Council. The Melbourne *Herald*'s view (22 December) that colonial wars, if they involved a threat to world peace, were outside domestic jurisdiction was balanced by that of the *Brisbane Courier-Mail* (21 December), which considered it dangerous for Australia as a colonial power governing Papua to attack Dutch sovereignty over its colonies.

Public opinion polls suggest that although Australian opinion was both hesitant and divided on the issue, more people favoured Dutch than Indonesian control. The following table is based on two polls taken in August 1947 and February-March 1949.[93]

How Indonesia Should Be Governed?

	Aug. 1947	Feb.-March 1949
Dutch control	23%	28%
Indonesian control	18	19
Joint control	15	11

With the achievement of Indonesian independence in 1949, Australian relations with Indonesia became formal but friendly. The only major point of difference was the status of West New Guinea (or West Irian). Australia has consistently supported the view that sovereignty resided in the Netherlands government and that the territory had not been transferred as a result of the round-table

[91] See, for example, *Sydney Morning Herald* and Adelaide *Advertiser*, 20 Dec. 1948; Melbourne *Argus*, 21 Dec. 1948.

[92] *Sydney Morning Herald*, *West Australian*, Melbourne *Herald* and *Age*, 27 Dec. 1948.

[93] See A.P.O.P., Nos. 569-78, Feb.-March 1949.

discussions in 1949. On 6 February 1952, Mr. Casey declared categorically that "Australia recognises Dutch sovereignty over Dutch New Guinea and agrees with the Dutch that their sovereignty should be continued . . . Indonesia has no real claims to the territory."[94] There has been no dissent from this view by Dr. Evatt or other members of the Opposition. "I agree with [Mr. Casey] that sovereignty over Dutch New Guinea without doubt resides in the Netherlands. Nothing has taken that sovereignty away. . . . The defence of New Guinea . . . is integral with the defence of Australia."[95] On each occasion since 1954 when Indonesia has attempted to raise the question of West New Guinea before the United Nations, Australia has opposed United Nations intervention on the ground that the matter does not fall within United Nations jurisdiction. Australia has argued that the indigenous people of Dutch New Guinea should be permitted to determine their own political future, even although it is obvious that this power of self-determination could not be exercised for some years to come.[96]

The Australian press has strongly opposed Indonesia's claim because it "had no basis in racial kinship, no substance in the facts of regional geography or ethnology and no compatibility with Australia's responsibilities, obligations and interests."[97] This is a succinct summary of a view very widely held in Australia, a view that has scarcely been modified in any way. Proposals have occasionally been made by bodies like the United Nations Association of Australia for the transfer of control over West New Guinea to the Trusteeship Council. This would be accompanied by a tripartite control (Indonesia, the Netherlands, and Australia) of the Nauruan type. The difficulty arises of selecting a mutually acceptable

---

[94] *Current Notes on International Affairs* (Dept. of External Affairs, Canberra), Vol. 23 (1952), p. 91.

[95] *C.P.D.* (House of Representatives), Vol. 5, 2 Nov. 1954, p. 2511.

[96] G.A.O.R., 9th Sess., 1st Ctte., 727th Mtg., 24 Nov. 1954, pp. 399-402.

[97] Melbourne *Age*, 13 June 1950 and 25 Nov. 1957; Melbourne *Herald*, 23 Sept. 1957; *West Australian*, 24 Sept. 1957; *Sydney Morning Herald*, 2 Nov. 1957; Melbourne *Advocate*, 28 Nov. 1957.

administering authority. There is no evidence of popular support for such a proposal. A public opinion poll on the question of the government of West New Guinea did not even pose this as an alternative. It showed overwhelming opposition to a transfer of sovereignty to Indonesia (only 4 per cent favoured such a move): 27 per cent preferred Australian rule and 28 per cent supported United Nations control.[98]

The controversies in the General Assembly in 1952 over the racial policies of South Africa and French policies in North Africa as well as the general discussion on the status of colonies evoked widespread editorial comment. It is doubtful whether any aspect of United Nations activities outside the security field has attracted such attention in recent years. The press was unanimous in both cases in opposing United Nations intervention. While there was some condemnation of French and South African policies, it was felt on balance that United Nations intervention would be illegal and that the acrimonious debates merely served to weaken and divide the United Nations.[99] The fear was also expressed that United Nations intervention would split the Commonwealth of Nations and perhaps provide awkward precedents which might be applied to Australian problems.[100]

A survey of the press, public opinion polls, and parliamentary opinion shows that interest in and enthusiasm for the United Nations even in the early years was considerably less than for the League of Nations in a comparable period. The guarded press optimism of 1945 reached its nadir with the 1948 General Assembly; it revived slightly with the outbreak of the Korean War, reached a new peak

---

[98] A.P.O.P., Nos. 1183-95, July-Aug. 1956.

[99] *Sydney Morning Herald*, 10 Nov. and 10 Dec. 1952; Hobart *Mercury*, 5 Nov., 9 and 18 Dec. 1952; *Brisbane Courier-Mail*, 7 Nov. 1952; *West Australian*, 10 Nov., 11 and 17 Dec. 1952; Melbourne *Age*, 11 Nov. 1952; Adelaide *Advertiser*, 17 Nov. 1952.

[100] Melbourne *Age*, 10 Oct. 1952; *Brisbane Courier-Mail*, 7 Nov. 1952; *Sydney Morning Herald*, 10 Nov. 1952; *West Australian*, 11 Dec. 1952. The Melbourne *Argus*, 14 Nov. 1952, alone put the case for intervention by the United Nations.

in 1951, and declined slightly in the following year. Few people believed that the United Nations had a crusading mission; the majority felt that it provided a means of conciliation in a troubled world. On this issue there was little substantial difference between attitudes in Australia and in the United Kingdom.

The Australian press, and opinion in general, has been concerned primarily with Pacific affairs: interest in Europe and the Middle East has fluctuated considerably. Initially, and for some time after tensions began to mount, the Australian press advocated a conciliatory policy towards Russia at least on some issues. As the "cold war" developed, attitudes hardened fairly rapidly. Some difference of opinion arose between the supporters of greater enforcement powers for the United Nations and those believing that this would limit the effectiveness of conciliation procedures. At no stage has any conflict arisen between an important national interest and a United Nations policy: should such a situation arise, support for the United Nations as indicated by public opinion polls would substantially decline.

chapter eleven

Charter Revision

The framers of written constitutions normally provide procedures for amendments on the assumption that such constitutions are never perfect documents. The San Francisco Conference set out procedures for simple amendment in Article 108, and then provided that a review conference might be called under Article 109(1). Article 109(3) made provision for placing on the agenda of the tenth session of the General Assembly a proposal to call such a conference if one had not been held by that time. This meant that a Charter review conference would probably be held in 1956 to consider a revision of the Charter based upon an examination of its operation during the first ten years of the life of the United Nations. At a review conference, the Charter could be amended by decision of two-thirds of the members of the conference, subject to ratification by two-thirds of the members of the United Nations including the five permanent members of the Security Council.

Australia felt in 1945 that there should be a considerable degree of flexibility in the Charter provisions concerning such a conference. Australia disliked the original proposal requiring a three-fourths majority of the General Assembly for calling a general conference and objected strongly to the provision that amendments recommended by such a conference would go into effect only if ratified by all the permanent members of the Security Council. The Australian delegate argued that "the voting procedure . . . for the ratification of amendments proposed by the Conference should be left to the good sense and wisdom of the members of that Conference." Because of this objection Australia abstained in the final vote in committee on the text of Article 109 of the Charter.[1]

The pressure for Charter revision today does not arise primarily from any constitutional necessity. It stems rather out of a rising sense of popular frustration, out of a growing conviction that the fundamental purposes of the Charter are in fact not being realized. The high hopes of 1945 have given place to a cautious cynicism and even indifference. Madison once observed that "the instability, injustice, and confusion introduced into the popular councils, have, in truth, been the mortal diseases under which popular governments have everywhere perished."[2] To many idealists, the United Nations was the first, halting step towards world government; it gave to the peoples of the world an opportunity to influence through an international forum the policies of governments. Although it fell short of popular government it pointed the way to it. After functioning for nearly ten years, the United Nations seemed to have been cursed with the "violence of faction," and "instability . . . and confusion" threatened its continued deliberations. This was the

---

[1] *Documents of the United Nations Conference on International Organization, San Francisco, 1945* (New York: United Nations Information Organizations, 1945), Vol. VII, pp. 229-30. Cf. pp. 145-46 and 468. Hereinafter cited as *UNCIO Documents.*

[2] Alexander Hamilton, James Madison, and John Jay, *The Federalist,* No. 10.

view of millions of people all over the world as atomic weapons and their control became a vital issue.

The San Francisco Conference completed its deliberations a bare six weeks before the first atomic bomb flashed over Hiroshima on 6 August 1945. In 1954, Mr. John Foster Dulles said that "had the delegates at San Francisco known that we were entering the age of atomic warfare, they would have seen to it that the charter dealt more positively with the problems thus raised."[3] The development of atomic power raised immediately the question of some form of international control of atomic weapons; the subsequent development of the H-bomb merely underlined the urgency in the popular mind of the need for control in the interests of world civilization. As the discussion on control shifted from full exchange of information to the right of inspection and then to detection of secret preparations, the question of the veto in the Security Council became, from both a constitutional and a practical point of view, of utmost importance. During the early discussion on the procedures for bringing about international control of atomic energy, Mr. James Byrnes assured the United States Senate that the interests of the United States could be protected at every step by a veto. Mr. Bernard Baruch, the first United States representative on the United Nations Atomic Energy Commission, held that there must be no veto to protect those who violate the agreements on atomic energy control. The proposals for punishments of violations went straight to the veto provisions in the United Nations Charter. It became clear that any veto over the process of inspection would immediately nullify all plans for control. This pointed the way to the reconsideration and perhaps elimination of the great power veto in the Charter.

Less drastic than the proposal for the complete abolition of the veto was the suggestion that the parties agree to waive the use of

---

[3] Statement by Mr. Dulles before the Charter Review Subcommittee of the Senate Foreign Relations Committee on 18 Jan. 1954. U.S. Dept. of State *Bulletin*, Vol. XXX, No. 762 (1 Feb. 1954), p. 172.

the veto in connection with the detection and punishment of violations of the atomic energy agreements. Mr. A. Gromyko stated that
the Soviet Union would insist that the great power veto be retained
"under any circumstances." The provisions of Article 51 of the
Charter were also discussed in this connection. Article 51 provides
that "Nothing in the present Charter shall impair the inherent
right of individual or collective self-defense if an armed attack
occurs against a Member of the United Nations, until the Security
Council has taken the measures necessary to maintain international
peace and security." If violations of an atomic treaty were brought
within the terms of a definition of an "armed attack," then members
would be legally free to take immediate preventive action, even if
the hands of the Security Council were tied by a great power veto.
This, however, did not suffice to protect states against the con-
tingency of a surprise attack with atomic weapons.

The situation then is that the USSR has consistently been unwilling
to forego its veto power. Although the United States took a similar
position at San Francisco, it has since stated that it would not be
stopped by a veto from organizing collective action against a great
power which threatened or broke the peace. The United States has
proposed that measures be taken for waiving the veto in the special
case of atomic energy control. The Vandenberg Resolution indicates
that the United States might also consider the abolition of the veto
on decisions involving pacific settlement of disputes and on the
admission of new members.[4] The USSR on the other hand insists
upon the broadest interpretation of the veto right which it will not
waive for any special purpose. This deadlock, coupled with a
growing public realization of the catastrophic dangers of atomic
or hydrogen warfare, has given an increasing urgency to the whole
question of Charter review in the minds of ordinary people.

---

[4] "Presumably, the United States would itself hesitate to go much further than
this in now surrendering its 'veto power'" (Mr. Dulles, *ibid.*).

THE ACHIEVEMENTS OF SAN FRANCISCO AND
THE PURPOSE OF CHARTER AMENDMENT

A realistic appraisal of events at San Francisco leads to the conclusion that at the Conference a war-time alliance, exceedingly comprehensive in membership, sought to realize the inchoate aspirations of member states by creating an international organization to facilitate co-operation among members, to reduce global tensions, and to minimize, if not eliminate, the dangers of a further major international conflict. These purposes were set out in the Preamble to the Charter: "We the peoples of the United Nations determined . . . to unite our strength to maintain international peace and security . . . have resolved to combine our efforts to accomplish these aims." Accordingly the United Nations was created; but, as one writer has pointed out, "the United Nations . . . never was intended to be the sole and exclusive means of conducting international relations. It did not replace the rest of the machinery of international relations; it only added a new piece of machinery."[5]

It is important to remember that the nations at San Francisco were exceedingly conscious of their sovereign rights and were acting in a highly charged emotional atmosphere at the end of the most devastating war in history. They were attempting to solve practical political problems. Although there was at the time considerable popular discussion of world federation, the statesmen at San Francisco were neither attempting an exercise in world planning nor seeking to restate theories of international peace. The San Francisco Conference made no attempt to create a "superstate." It could not do so because of the firm conviction of all members that national sovereignty should as far as possible be preserved. It was even more impossible for the states meeting at San Francisco to surrender national sovereignty than it had been for the thirteen

[5] Quoted from an address by the Hon. Paul Hasluck (Australian Minister for Territories) on 22 Oct. 1954, before the United Nations Charter Revision Convention held at the University of Sydney.

states meeting at the Philadelphia Convention in 1787, or for the six Australian colonies meeting through the decade 1890-1900, to jettison states' rights. The San Francisco Conference emphasized the independence and sovereignty of the member nations. The United Nations was an

> organization set up by agreement to accomplish certain specific objectives, the chief of which was to resist any aggression. The powers it had for this purpose it had as agent for the members, and they agreed to assist in the implementation. It had no legislative power, and it was not the form of organization on which legislative powers could be conferred. Its organs were not representative in the democratic sense. It did organize great changes in the structure of the world, but it did this through agreement on subjects on which its nations were in agreement. . . . The United Nations does not operate by fiat but by agreement, and it will always do this until the world structure is so strengthened that we can set up a world state which will exercise legislative power.[6]

This appraisal, nearly a decade later, by one of the participants in the San Francisco Conference, represented a common assessment of the limited achievements of 1945. From a brutal, realistic point of view the Charter was the result, in the words of Sir Carl Berendsen, of a "shot-gun wedding." Like the Australian and United States Constitutions, it represented a series of basic compromises. By no means an ideal or perfect document, it represented the widest possible area of agreement in what was an exceedingly favourable atmosphere.

Given the ardent attachment to the concept of national sovereignty, there is much truth in the view that "the United Nations created at San Francisco was more in the nature of an instrument of great power rule within the framework of certain collective

---

[6] A manuscript comment in 1954 by the late Sir Frederic Eggleston, formerly Australian Minister to China and the United States and adviser to the Australian delegation at San Francisco in 1945. See generally F. W. Eggleston, *Reflections on Australian Foreign Policy*, Norman Harper, ed. (Melbourne: F. W. Cheshire, 1947), especially Ch. 2.

security assumptions than a collective security arrangement designed to deal with great power rivalry."[7] What is astonishing, in view of the wide acceptance of power politics and the balance of power, was the large area of agreement: the middle and smaller powers, like Australia and the Latin American states, accomplished a significant modification of these views. Underlying this agreement, however, was a basic assumption: that the degree of great power unanimity, despite surface friction, would continue in the post-war world. One commentator, René de Lacharrière, has concluded:

> Sans cette hypothèse, les lacunes de la Charte deviendraient inexplicables. Tout s'éclaire, au contraire, si l'on admet comme donnée initiale un accord fondamental entre les grandes puissances, c'est-à-dire, sinon une identité de vues complète et immédiate sur tous sujets, du moins la possibilité constante de trouver un terrain d'entente en vertu d'une concordance générale des intérêts et des aspirations sur les fins des Nations Unies.[8]

He perhaps exaggerates this point, but it is a basic one. There was at San Francisco a general belief in the essential homogeneity of interests, political and social, among the states represented. What was overlooked in the aura of enthusiasm was the essentially temporary nature of any war-time alliance and the obvious semantic difficulties among such allies. Simple terms like "democracy," "aggression," and "fascism" had a totally different historical context to the San Francisco bedfellows. The ambiguities in the text of the Charter and the lack of precision in drafting mirrored these shortcomings in the area of agreement. The surprising thing was the relative infrequency of discussions at the Conference of semantic, and so of legal, differences. Since San Francisco such differences have become much more evident, the apparent homogeneity of

---

[7] Howard C. Johnson and Gerhart Niemeyer, "The Validity of an Ideal," *International Organization*, Vol. VIII (1954), p. 23.
[8] René de Lacharrière, "L'action des Nations Unies pour la sécurité et pour la paix," *Politique Etrangère*, Vol. XVIII (1953), p. 315.

w

interest has vanished, and the polarization of power has established a new heterogeneity of interests, intensified by suspicion. In other words, the preconditions for agreement, so much in evidence at San Francisco, scarcely exist today.

Any constitution is adapted to a particular kind of social and economic environment, domestic or international. Change is normally by the process of slow evolution. Conventions develop and precedents are established by experience; these tend to modify the original constitution. In this way the United Nations Charter has undergone a slow change. An alternative method of change is by the process of formal constitutional amendment. Provision for this is included in federal constitutions such as those of Australia and the United States, but it has proved to be an exceedingly difficult and laborious process. Neither country has seen fit to call a convention for drastic revision of the constitution, although proposals have recently been made in Australia for such a convention. Federal and unitary states alike have found that change is easier by the process of judicial interpretation. Because of the limited authority of the International Court of Justice this method had been hardly possible in the United Nations, which of course is neither a superstate nor even the most limited federation. Accordingly the procedure for the amendment of the Charter was laid down in Article 108 and special provisions for a general Charter review conference were set forth in Article 109. Jefferson recognized the fact that

> laws and institutions must go hand in hand with the progress of the human mind. . . . As new discoveries are made, new truths disclosed, and manners and opinions change with the change of circumstances, institutions must advance also, and keep pace with the times. . . . Each generation is as independent of the one preceding, as that was of all which had gone before. It has then, like them, a right to choose for itself the form of government . . . the most promotive of its own happiness.[9]

---

[9] Adrienne Koch & William Peden, eds., *The Life and Selected Writings of Thomas Jefferson* (New York: Random House, 1944), pp. 674-75.

Justice did not necessarily demand that the Social Darwinian philosophy of Mr. Herbert Spencer be written into the United States Constitution, or the world government concepts of Mr. Clarence Streit be read into the Charter of the United Nations; it does necessitate the recognition of the facts of progress, intellectual and scientific.

It cannot be emphasized too strongly that the purpose of convening a general conference under Article 109 is "the reviewing of the present Charter." The objective is not necessarily full or drastic revision which appears to be the primary purpose of so many of the plans which have been put forward, for example, the Clark-Sohn Proposals, the London Parliamentary Resolutions on World Government, the Federal Union-World Government Crusade Proposals, and the Pinder and Copenhagen Proposals. It is true that many of these plans distinguish, and rightly so, between interim and permanent reform. A real danger lies in a possible confusion between the limited function of a general conference to review the Charter and the very basic revisions advocated by the authors of the above proposals. It is exceedingly doubtful whether, as a matter of political reality, there is any greater chance of devising a better Charter today than there was at San Francisco. Given the growth of heterogeneous interests rather than the strengthening of homogeneous interests among the members of the United Nations, given the development of the "cold war" and the creation of power blocs, given the emergence of a numerically strong anti-colonial group and the creation of an Afro-Asian bloc, strong pressure for Charter revision could be fatal to the continued existence of the United Nations. A major surgical operation might well result in the death of the patient.

There seems little merit in the summoning of either a "propaganda" or a "showdown" conference: either could have dangerous or even fatal results. Given the general climate of international opinion, the prospects of anything more than minor tinkering with machinery would be very slim indeed, and until the political atmosphere improves a Charter review conference would have little chance of success. On this point there is no significant difference of opinion in Australia; only a tiny idealistic minority would go further than a sober reappraisal of the functioning of the Charter. Some would flatly reject even this. One of the Australian delegates to San Francisco has expressed the opinion that "the times are unpropitious to make the Charter any better, and we should not be led by disillusionment to lower the standards of international conduct which it sets."[10]

Charter review implies a re-examination of the functioning of the United Nations in the light of experience. It necessitates a reconsideration of the problem of implementing the purposes of the Charter, an examination of the possibilities and limitations of the present structure of the United Nations. Given the deterioration of international relationships, the real problem is how to develop the widest possible area of agreement. The major defect of the League of Nations was not a constitutional or legal one: it lay rather in the spiritual failure of the members, their reluctance or inability to recognize the real identity of national and international interests, their refusal to use the existing machinery to its fullest extent. A change of mental outlook is as important today as it was in 1939. The function of a *review* conference must be to explore the possibilities of using efficiently existing machinery and to make such minor amendments as will remove major blockages. On the other hand, a *revision* conference might well result in the dissolution of the United Nations with only a remote possibility of its reconstitution. The real art of politics is the realization of the possible: this would be the task of a review rather than a revision conference.

It is necessary to recognize that underlying the whole problem of the functioning of any kind of international organization is the issue of national sovereignty. The more thoroughly the functioning of the United Nations is examined, the more it becomes evident

---

[10] P. Hasluck, 22 Oct. 1954, *op. cit.*

that its ineffectiveness derives from a single underlying factor. Unless review is considered against this background, it becomes unrealistic. This single basic factor is called by different names: domestic jurisdiction, veto, self-determination. But whatever the name, it is still a manifestation of the age-old struggle of liberty and license, the sphere of enforceable and unenforceable law, the problem of national sovereignty. The Charter is a statement of principles with deliberately loosely-worded provisions for implementation agreed to by the original fifty-one member nations in their own interests. Having been ratified by the adherents, it is binding, but binding only to a point. There is no greater power to enforce obedience, although the penalty of expulsion provided for in the Charter may act as a deterrent. The Charter sums up the extent of the limitations upon national sovereignty which the signatories found it possible to accept. While all have ratified the text in good faith, each has retained the right to interpret the loosely-phrased clauses in the light of its own point of view, in relation to its own world position and responsibilities. The implementation of Charter principles is the fundamental problem to be solved; this is a matter of mutual confidence and good faith rather than of legal form or constitutional obligations. Attempts to devise a perfect system of implementation would split and destroy the Organization; as one legal loophole was closed, others would be found. No written document can ever eliminate the human factor.

Given the probability that the Charter represents the maximum acceptable limitation on national sovereignty, the problem of implementation appears to be partly a psychological one, and partly one of utilizing existing machinery. There has in fact been a considerable degree of Charter revision by formal or tacit agreement, and over twenty Articles have been modified in whole or in part. This has been the result largely of new conventions, of the process of procedural rather than substantive change, of the careful exercise or interpretation of existing powers. It has become accepted practice, for example, that if a permanent member of the Security Council abstains from voting, this does not constitute a veto in terms of Article 27(3). With the establishment of a semi-permanent committee to examine the reports on non-self-governing territories, a new organ of the United Nations has been created. This involved no amendment to the Charter, but rather the use by the Organization of its latent powers. The establishment of the Little Assembly, in the face of Soviet objections that it was an attempt to revise the Charter in the interests of a special group, was a move to transfer power to the General Assembly. The defence of the peace has become with experience more and more an Assembly matter: it was the General Assembly which eventually assumed primary responsibility for the Korean affair. There are real difficulties in this development as the General Assembly has only advisory power, and the great powers may well prove reluctant to accept the advice of a number of small powers which are not vitally concerned with an issue or which may have no direct responsibility in a specific problem. A fruitful field for study could well be procedures of the General Assembly and the Security Council and the manner of exercise of existing powers.

AUSTRALIAN ATTITUDES ON CHARTER REVISION

Before the meeting of the tenth session of the United Nations General Assembly, no official statement of Australian policy on Charter revision was issued and no political party had made any formal comment. Despite brief and sporadic discussion of proposals by a United Nations Charter Revision Convention in Sydney, N.S.W., on 22-23 October 1954, in which 72 delegates from 26 organizations directly or marginally interested in the United Nations took part, there has been little considered public discussion of the general problem of Charter review. Serious consideration of the problem has come primarily from groups established in connection with this study on Australia and the United Nations and also by small groups in some of the state divisions of the Australian Association for the United Nations. At the same time, the original Australian amendments at San Francisco and Australia's subsequent experience and policies in the United Nations do throw some light on official attitudes towards review or revision of specific Articles of the Charter. At the tenth session of the General Assembly the Australian government supported a draft resolution to consider the calling of a general conference of members to review the Charter, but its delegates had grave doubts about the possibility of such a conference achieving worthwhile results. "If . . . world conditions do not noticeably improve . . . we should consider whether a conference would run the risk of becoming an arena for quarrelsome and perhaps dangerous disputation."[11]

For Australia the fundamental guiding principle must be the preservation of the United Nations. No Australian government could support any policy which might lead to a permanent splitting of the world into two mutually antagonistic power blocs or the withdrawal of a major power from the United Nations. The increasing pressure for admission of small states to the United Nations and the failure of any power to leave it mean that all powers tend to place a premium on membership of the United Nations. Although Australian public opinion, in so far as it can be gauged, is occasionally critical of particular United Nations policies, it would not tolerate a policy of dissociating Australia from, or of drastically weakening, the United Nations.

MEMBERSHIP OF THE UNITED NATIONS

Of the theoretical desirability of universal membership there can be little question: only in this way can the processes of the United Nations be effective throughout the world. The danger of perpetuating in peace a war-time alliance is self-evident. The initial discussions at San Francisco showed a reluctance to admit former

---

[11] General Assembly, Official Records (G.A.O.R.): 10th Sess., 542nd Plenary Mtg., 17 Nov. 1955, pp. 305-06.

enemies and their supporters. Australia proposed that, while normally the General Assembly alone should decide on the admission of new members, in the case of former enemy states and their supporters, a recommendation of the Security Council should also be required. This proposal was, however, withdrawn. The Dumbarton Oaks draft provided that membership in the United Nations "should be open to all peace-loving states." Australia proposed that membership be open to "any state which accepts the obligations of this Charter and which is admitted to membership in accordance with the Charter."[12] The text finally agreed on reads as follows:

> Membership in the United Nations is open to all other peace-loving states which accept the obligations contained in the present Charter and, in the judgment of the Organization, are able and willing to carry out these obligations. [Article 4(1)]

Article 4(1) recognizes the desirability of universality of membership but regards this as a guiding rather than a determining principle. It is for the General Assembly, acting upon the recommendation of the Security Council (Article 4(2)), to decide on the fitness of applicants for membership. In practice decisions have been based almost solely on political considerations with injustice to unsuccessful applicants and to the detriment of the United Nations. Nine new members were admitted between 1946 and 1950, but by 1952, twenty-one other nations had unsuccessfully applied for admission. Many of these applicants were refused admission because of the exercise by the Soviet Union of the veto in the Security Council. It attempted to impose political conditions which had no real relevance to the provisions of the Charter. The political deadlock was broken at the tenth session of the Assembly in 1955. After considerable political manoeuvring and unofficial proposals for a "package deal," a reversal of policy by the USSR paved the way for the admission of sixteen new members on 14 December 1955. Australia supported the Assembly resolution. The applications of Japan and Outer Mongolia were deferred when no compromise

---

[12] See *UNCIO Documents, op. cit.*, Vol. VIII, p. 299, and Vol. III, p. 543.

between the United States and the Soviet Union proved possible. Japan was, however, admitted at the next session.

The first major problem is, how can the term "peace-loving state" be defined? The phrase is a political one with no precise meaning. In the vast majority of cases, there has been little effort to apply an exact or broad legal definition. Rather the question of admission has been one of political manoeuvring, of hard bargaining in the attempt to secure a "package agreement." This was particularly true with regard to newly independent and satellite states. The question has been raised significantly in connection with Communist China. China as such is a member of the United Nations and a permanent member of the Security Council. The controversy over Chinese representation could be viewed as a technical problem concerning the relative validity of credentials issued by Formosa and Peiping. Behind this question is the problem of the recognition of a *de facto* government. This, by international law, is the prerogative of each individual state. But the issue goes beyond the legal question of recognition to what constitutes a "peace-loving state." The role of Communist China in the Korean War and the condemnation by the United Nations of China's intervention therein raise a broad political problem as well as a vital moral question. The Australian government has not recognized the Peiping government and "will not at present consider the admission of Communist China" which has yet "to establish the bona fides of peaceful intent."[13] Representation in the Security Council is an independent but related problem. A growing body of unofficial opinion in Australia is moving towards supporting Communist China's claim for representation in the United Nations with a qualification as to timing of the seating of Peiping's representative in the Security Council.[14]

---

[13] Mr. R. G. Casey, *Sydney Morning Herald*, 9 July 1954.

[14] It is important to note that this view would not be accepted by members of the Roman Catholic Church nor by a powerful wing of the Australian Labour party, which includes many Catholics.

The Chinese case raises a further broad problem: should membership be automatic, once the conditions set out in Article 4(1) of the Charter have been met, or should membership be confined to "like-minded" nations elected by the General Assembly and the Security Council? The Clark-Sohn proposals and the London Resolutions propose textual amendments to Article 4(1) which would admit all independent states that accept Charter obligations. Some of the critics of such a proposal are prepared to go further and contract membership by exclusion of troublesome or uncooperative states. To do so would destroy the very character of the United Nations and convert it into a very different organization. Although Australia (among other nations) was opposed to the admission of Spain in the early stages because of the latter's conduct during the Second World War, Australia came to accept the view that the United Nations should include not merely "peace-loving states" but also those regarded by some as either law breakers or anti-social elements. Only in this way could a semblance of universality be attained.

The second major problem is the procedure for admission. The decision rests in the first instance with the Security Council (Article 4(2)). From the beginning Dr. Evatt would have preferred to entrust this power solely to the General Assembly, and he subsequently attempted to protect what he deemed to be the rights of the General Assembly. In the initial stages it was part of his campaign to locate the effective power of the United Nations in the General Assembly rather than the Security Council. Subsequent political developments merely confirmed his view of the importance of entrusting to the Assembly decisions on questions of admission. In 1947 he laid down the Australian view of the principles underlying Article 4. Each application must be considered separately on its own merits. The role of the Security Council was to determine, on basis of the facts, whether an applicant was a peace-loving state able to carry out its obligations under the Charter. If these conditions were in substance fulfilled, then it was the duty of the Security

Council to make the appropriate recommendation to the General Assembly. "While a favourable recommendation of the Security Council was a condition precedent to membership, the Security Council should act on the Assembly's view of the facts." Should the Security Council act upon irrelevant considerations, then the General Assembly should invite it to reconsider the applications.[15]

The Australian stand was buttressed at one essential point by the advisory opinion of the International Court of Justice. In its opinion of 28 May 1948, the Court declared that:

> A Member of the United Nations which is called upon, in virtue of Article 4 of the Charter, to pronounce itself . . . on the admission of a State to membership in the United Nations, is not juridically entitled to make its consent to the admission dependent on conditions not expressly provided by paragraph 1 of the said Article; . . . in particular, a Member of the Organization cannot, while it recognizes the conditions set forth in that provision to be fulfilled by the State concerned, subject its affirmative vote to the additional condition that other States be admitted to membership in the United Nations together with that State.[16]

Subsequently, although emphasizing less strongly the power of the General Assembly, Australia has consistently maintained the principle that extraneous considerations must be ignored by the Security Council in making recommendations on membership. Australia long refused to be a party to a "package deal"[17] and at the ninth session of the General Assembly sponsored with Pakistan and

---

[15] G.A.O.R., 2nd Sess., 1st Ctte., 99th Mtg., 7 Nov. 1947, pp. 347-51.

[16] International Court of Justice, Advisory Opinion on Conditions of Admission of a State to Membership in the United Nations, *Reports of Judgments, Advisory Opinions and Orders, 1948*, p. 12.

[17] For the Australian position, see G.A.O.R., 3rd Sess., *Ad Hoc* Pol. Ctte., 6th Mtg., 22 Nov. 1948, pp. 53-58; 4th Sess., *Ad Hoc* Pol. Ctte., 26th Mtg., 1 Nov. 1949, pp. 127-28; and 6th Sess., 1st Ctte., 497th Mtg., 22 Jan. 1952, p. 231.

Thailand the admission of Laos and Cambodia on the ground that these countries fulfilled the conditions set out in the Charter.[18]

The acceptance by the permanent members of the opinion of the International Court of Justice, which would have the effect of limiting the use of the veto on this issue, could prevent a deadlock over admission. It would not guarantee that all candidates would always secure sufficient affirmative votes. The issue remains a political one and also a psychological one: only the easing of power tensions can minimize the use of the veto. From its record one can assume that the Australian government would be prepared to accept an amendment to the Charter which would vest the power of admission either in the General Assembly itself or in the General Assembly acting on a recommendation from a sub-committee. It would prefer to abolish the veto on such decisions. The other interests of the permanent members of the Security Council would still be safeguarded by the provisions of Article 27(3) regarding voting powers. A somewhat hesitant unofficial Australian opinion would prefer an alteration in the procedure for admission to the political horse-trading involved in "package deals."

SECURITY COUNCIL

Veto: It is important to recall the situation in which the permanent members of the Security Council were given the right of veto. If one adopts the view that the United Nations was created as "an instrument of great power rule within the framework of certain collective security assumptions," then the right of veto becomes a necessary consequence. It must be remembered, however, that the right of veto was conceded only after a month's debate during which seventeen powers presented amendments. It was conceded partly out of recognition that the Security Council was given coercive powers to deal with outbreaks of aggression and that

---

[18] See G.A.O.R., 9th Sess., *Ad Hoc* Pol. Ctte., 17th Mtg., 29 Oct. 1954, p. 61, and 27th Mtg., 15 Nov. 1954, pp. 121-22.

members were obliged to take part in such collective measures as the Council deemed necessary. These provisions were designed to make swift action against an aggressor possible and thus increase the deterrents against aggression. There was an expectation of continued unanimity among the great powers, and a conviction that it would be impossible for the United Nations to condemn one of the permanent members as an aggressor. It was also crystal clear that without a veto, the great powers (notably the United Kingdom, the United States, and the USSR) would not have ratified the Charter. The veto was an essential precondition for the creation of a United Nations.

Criticism of the veto has arisen primarily out of its frequent, perhaps excessive, use by the Soviet Union. It has been used on organizational questions: the admission of new members and the appointment of the Secretary-General. It has also been used in questions involving the maintenance of peace and security: such as the cases of Syria and Lebanon, Spain, Greece, Indonesia, Czechoslovakia, Berlin, control of atomic energy, the reduction of armaments, and Korea.

The practical problem with regard to the veto is not its abolition but rather agreement as to the conditions under which it may be used. Given the present power structure in the world and the concept of the necessary relationship between power and responsibility, it would be completely unrealistic to attempt complete abolition of the unanimity principle. Nothing would sign the death warrant of the United Nations so speedily. No one of the great powers would consider it for a moment. It is interesting to note an Egyptian comment.

> It may be doubted whether the abolition or suppression of the veto is desirable from the point of view of the smaller nations. Such suppression would imply the possibility of applying sanctions against one or more of the Great Powers. . . . Moreover, as concerns the decisions of the Council relating to the maintenance or reestablishment of peace, that is to say in

relation to those matters which would be likely to have the greatest consequences for the smaller nations, how could we be sure that the vote of a simple majority would be the wisest and most just solution? Is it not better for the smaller powers, under the present structure of the international society, to be able to retrench themselves behind the veto, and to enjoy such security as may be found in the Balance of Power instead of submitting themselves to the law of the majority which might be controlled by one or more of the Great Powers themselves if the veto were eliminated.[19]

Since the United Nations is not a supranational body but one "based on the principle of the sovereign equality of all its Members," and since all members are at present irrevocably attached to the principle of national sovereignty and unwilling to abrogate it seriously, the problem of the veto perhaps becomes a more viable one. In the field of enforcement action, there can be at present no major change. There is an essential but necessary incompatibility between "the sovereign equality of all its Members" and the principle of unanimity as applied to the permanent members of the Security Council. With real power vested in a small minority of members, the General Assembly is far removed from being a World Parliament: political and military power rather than law and justice are the bases of the organization. Under the present provisions, the United Nations cannot involve a permanent member in a war against its will. Great power predominance is illogical in terms of equal sovereignty; it can also negate the work of the United Nations. But in the present climate of world opinion it is a necessary condition for the functioning of an imperfect international organization.

A further vital point of difficulty arises out of the application of the veto provisions to procedures of conciliation. At the San Francisco Conference the Australian delegation proposed a series

---

[19] This quotation is from a preliminary unpublished report by a group of members of the Egyptian Society of International Law, prepared in connection with the study, *Egypt and the United Nations*, another of the volumes in this series of National Studies on International Organization.

of amendments to the Dumbarton Oaks draft. These were designed in part to differentiate between voting on enforcement action and voting in relation to the settlement of disputes by peaceful means. Accordingly, Australia proposed that in the case of the former, the permanent members of the Security Council had to act in unison or not at all; in matters affecting pacific settlement, however, decisions should be taken on the vote of any seven members of the Council.[20] As the Australian delegate explained, "in a sentence, our view is . . . that conciliation, or peaceful means of settling a dispute, should be regarded not as a power of the Council but as the duty of the Council because by such means the dispute may be composed and the use of force may be prevented."[21] No compromise proved possible on this point in 1945.

The adoption of such a distinction would have eased the difficulties facing the United Nations and avoided some of the sense of frustration. Between January 1946 and December 1954, the Security Council had before it twenty-two "situations" and disputes. The discussion of some of these had been initiated in the General Assembly and then had been referred to the Security Council (e.g., the Palestine situation); in other cases, the discussion had begun in the Security Council and then, after a deadlock, the matter had been placed on the agenda of the General Assembly (e.g., Greece and Korea). As the "cold war" developed, the Security Council ceased to be an effective instrument for dealing with questions of security and the peaceful settlement of disputes. As its power declined, political disputes were handled more and more by the General Assembly, a development which had never been contemplated by Australia and other small powers at San Francisco. In addition, the great

---

[20] *UNCIO Documents*, Vol. III, p. 550. Australia also proposed that decisions about utilizing regional agencies in enforcement action be taken on the vote of any seven members, including at least three of the permanent members.
[21] *Ibid.*, Vol. XI, p. 123. See also Parliament of Commonwealth of Australia, *United Nations Conference on International Organization: Report by the Australian Delegates* (Canberra: Govt. Printer, 1945), p. 16.

powers increasingly tended to bypass the United Nations in settling important political issues, e.g., the Geneva Conference on Indochina in 1954 and the Geneva summit conference in 1955. The Indonesian and Egyptian questions were the only ones in which final settlements were effected as a result of direct mediation by the United Nations. Whether it is now possible to rehabilitate the Security Council by reviving the distinction between enforcement action and conciliation procedures and eliminating the veto from matters of conciliation is impossible to determine. Much depends on the willingness of the great powers to abandon the "chain of events" argument and on the degree of international tension. The distinction is one that merits examination at a review conference.

Apart from questions of peace and security, the veto can completely thwart action by the United Nations on such matters as the admission of new members (Article 4(2)) and the election of the Secretary-General (Article 97). The principle of great power unanimity also applies to any amendments to the Charter under Article 108 or any amendments recommended by a two-thirds vote of a review conference under Article 109(2). Of course, it was also true at San Francisco that each of the sponsoring powers had a "veto" over changes in the Dumbarton Oaks text. One can only hope that such a "veto" would not be exercised against changes recommended by a review conference which are clearly reasonable and have the support of overwhelming world opinion. Otherwise a review conference would be futile.

The desirability of universal membership in the United Nations has already been considered. The problem of the Security Council's power of veto could be handled in a number of ways. It could be curtailed by an amendment which would vest the specific power to admit new members in the General Assembly. Whether the permanent members of the Security Council would be prepared to relinquish control entirely to the Assembly is doubtful. On the basis of policies pursued so far, it is unlikely that the United States, for example, would be prepared to leave the question of the representation of Communist China entirely to an Assembly vote. An alternative would be a revision of the text of Article 4(1) to circumscribe further the area of legal argument and so the opportunities for the exercise of the veto. In practice, this would come back to the basic problem of the spirit in which members attempted to interpret their obligations under the Charter. Alternatively, if admission could be regarded as a purely procedural matter rather than a matter of substance, then under Article 4(2) the veto would not be applicable.

This in fact lends point to the view that a great deal could be accomplished by agreement within the present framework of the United Nations Charter. Precedent can be created by voting decisions. This would reduce the contentious area of legal amendments which could prove to be an intractable problem. A formal definition of "procedural matters" might be incorporated in the Charter itself or an informal agreement might be reached governing the way in which the Security Council should operate. There are difficulties in the way of obtaining such informal agreement or in establishing firm precedents. But these difficulties need to be faced in the attempt to narrow the field of controversy. This would appear to be one of the most profitable fields for exploration by a review conference.

The appointment of the Secretary-General is also a matter of vital importance, because all the administrative responsibilities of the United Nations devolve upon him. The permanent members have a peculiarly close interest in his functions, and presumably it is for this reason, as well as because of the doctrine of the relationship between power and responsibility, that it has been considered necessary that the permanent members agree on the appointment of the Secretary-General. The sharp divisions of opinion between the United States and the USSR in 1950 on the question of the appointment of a successor to Mr. Trygve Lie were resolved by a General Assembly decision to extend his term temporarily. This placed Mr. Lie in a false position and limited the effective exercise of his functions; in consequence he resigned during the seventh

x

session of the General Assembly. The dispute threatened to hamstring the whole executive work of the United Nations. The need for great power agreement could well prevent the appointment of the most competent person by producing a compromise choice. It is true, of course, that the United Nations could function, if necessary, with an acting Secretary-General. This would prevent a stalemate and enable the administrative work to be carried out adequately. Alternative solutions would lie either in the vesting of the power of appointment wholly in the General Assembly or in agreement to treat this as a procedural matter under Article 27(2), thus eliminating the possibility of a veto.

Composition of the Security Council: The San Francisco Conference recognized the prime importance of the great powers in maintaining peace and international security. It was equally evident that the responsibility for peace and security was no monopoly of the great powers and that the basis of the Security Council must be broadened as much as possible to obtain the active co-operation of the small and middle powers. It was necessary in determining the size of the Security Council to strike a balance between the two principles, to avoid a fragmentation of responsibility among a multitude of small powers which might paralyze action, and equally to avoid the danger of great power monopoly and the relegation of the small powers to a formal decorative function.

The assumption lying behind the acceptance of a special position for the Big Five was that their power would be both effective and durable. It was essentially a static assumption which allowed no play for the dynamism of history, for the inevitable fluctuations in power over a period of time. The Big Five represented in fact the temporary location of power as the result of a military victory in war, even although there were basic inequalities among the Five. Any other solution of the problem at that time would have been completely unrealistic.

A similar assumption lay behind the amendment to the Dumbarton Oaks draft, pressed by Canada and Australia, relating to the election

of non-permanent members. Australia proposed that they be selected on the basis of "their past military contribution to the cause of world security," and their ability and willingness "to assume substantial security responsibilities," and "make a substantial contribution to the maintenance of international security."[22] This proposal reflected both pride in war-time achievement and the ebullient nationalism consequent to it. The essence of the Australian suggestion was incorporated in Article 23(1) of the Charter; whether it represented a wholly sound general principle for the election of non-permanent members to the Security Council is another matter. The complex question of power shifts and the need to accommodate membership of the Security Council to them raise exceedingly delicate questions of face, particularly for the permanent members of the Security Council.

The problem of regional representation among the non-permanent members of the Security Council is an important one, but once again it is a matter that can be dealt with procedurally by Assembly vote. No Charter amendment is necessary. The criterion of the "contribution of Members of the United Nations to the maintenance of international peace and security and to the other purposes of the Organization" is one that has been ignored in practice. It is difficult to apply in any case, and is almost bound to become a matter of political convenience or arrangement. The second criterion, of "equitable geographical distribution," has also in practice been a matter of political negotiation with scant reference to geographic facts: the coincidence between membership and geographic regions has been largely fortuitous. Elections for non-permanent representation have led to fierce lobbying and canvassing.

The following table lists the countries that have been non-permanent members of the Security Council and indicates the geographical distribution of the occupants of the six non-permanent seats.

---

[22] See above, p. 53.

1946	1947	1948	1949
Australia	Belgium	Argentina	Cuba
Brazil	Colombia	Canada	Egypt
Poland	Syria	Ukrainian SSR	Norway
Egypt	Australia	Belgium	Argentina
Mexico	Brazil	Colombia	Canada
Netherlands	Poland	Syria	Ukrainian SSR

1950	1951	1952	1953
Ecuador	Brazil	Chile	Colombia
India	Netherlands	Greece	Denmark
Yugoslavia	Turkey	Pakistan	Lebanon
Cuba	Ecuador	Brazil	Chile
Egypt	India	Netherlands	Greece
Norway	Yugoslavia	Turkey	Pakistan

1954	1955	1956	1957
Brazil	Belgium	Australia	Colombia
New Zealand	Iran	Cuba	Iraq
Turkey	Peru	Yugoslavia	Sweden
Colombia	Brazil	Belgium	Australia
Denmark	New Zealand	Iran	Cuba
Lebanon	Turkey	Peru	Philippines

Western Europe

Netherlands (1946)
Belgium (1947-48)
Norway (1949-50)
Netherlands (1951-52)
Denmark (1953-54)
Belgium (1955-56)
Sweden (1957-58)

Eastern Europe

Poland (1946-47)
Ukrainian SSR (1948-49)
Yugoslavia (1950-51)
Greece (1952-53)
Turkey (1954-55)
Yugoslavia (1956)

Middle East

Egypt (1946)
Syria (1947-48)
Egypt (1949-50)
Turkey (1951-52)
Lebanon (1953-54)
Iran (1955-56)
Iraq (1957-58)

Latin America

Mexico (1946)
Brazil (1946-47)
Colombia (1947-48)
Argentina (1948-49)
Cuba (1949-50)
Ecuador (1950-51)
Brazil (1951-52)

Chile (1952-53)
Colombia (1953-54)
Brazil (1954-55)
Peru (1955-56)
Cuba (1956-57)
Colombia (1957-58)

Commonwealth of Nations

Australia (1946-47)
Canada (1948-49)
India (1950-51)
Pakistan (1952-53)
New Zealand (1954-55)
Australia (1956-57)

The most striking feature is the continuous representation of Latin-America by two members. Western Europe, the Middle East, and the Commonwealth of Nations, a non-geographic group, have always had representatives on the Council. The representation of other areas has been irregular. Africa has been represented intermittently by Egypt, although Egypt is essentially Middle Eastern rather than African. Eastern Europe was initially represented by members of the Soviet bloc, but since 1949 the Soviet-sponsored candidates have failed to win election. Eastern Europe continued to be represented geographically if not politically[23] through 1956. In 1957 the Philippines took over the seat occupied by Yugoslavia[24] and in the next election Japan defeated Czechoslovakia.

Until 1957 the most serious defect in representation had been the frequent omission of Asia from the Security Council. Technically, of course, the Middle Eastern countries form part of the Asian continent, but in fact there is a wide gulf of interest and a difference of problems between South and East Asia and the western Asian states. Until the Philippines was elected to the Council, India and Pakistan were the only Asian countries to have been elected as non-permanent members, and the time and circumstances of their election suggests that this arose out of their membership in the Commonwealth of Nations rather than for regional or geographic reasons. Non-Commonwealth countries in the Far East, members of the United Nations but so far unrepresented on the Security

---

[23] During the elections in 1949, Mr. Vyshinsky said that "Yugoslavia did not represent the countries of Eastern Europe, and no one could or would recognize it as having that capacity." Mr. Acheson then pointed out that the Charter referred to geographical and not to ideological considerations. For this exchange, see London Institute of World Affairs, *The Yearbook of World Affairs 1954*, (New York: Praeger, 1954), pp. 109-10. Turkey was elected to represent the Middle East for the 1951-52 term but in 1953 was elected to the Eastern Europe seat. Geographically, Turkey is in both regions, but this was an adroit switch from one bloc to the other.

[24] As a result of the deadlock in the elections for the 1956-58 term, a compromise was reached whereby Yugoslavia was elected on the understanding that it would resign at the end of 1956 and the Philippines would be elected to serve out the term.

Council, include Afghanistan (13 millions), Burma (20 millions), Indonesia (84 millions), and Thailand (21 millions).

It is clear that bloc voting has taken place regularly in the election of non-permanent members and that this has ensured permanent representation of the Arab-Middle East group, the Commonwealth of Nations, Latin America, and Western Europe. To be elected, a member must receive two-thirds of the votes cast. If in the first ballot less than three candidates obtain the necessary majority, additional ballots are conducted, "the voting being restricted to the candidates obtaining the greatest number of votes in the previous ballot, to a number not more than twice the places remaining to be filled."[25] Given the present voting procedures and the fact that twenty of the eighty members of the United Nations are Latin American states, the possibility of both Asia and Eastern Europe being represented on the Council at the same time appears to be remote.

The solution may lie in the adoption of a new formula or an agreed system of regional representation within the present structure of the Security Council. This could be brought about by a self-denying ordinance by one of the blocs (e.g., by the Latin American countries to limit their representation to one rather than two seats) and subsequent agreement to allot the seat to Asia. The problem might also be met by increasing the number of elected seats from six to eight or nine, a proposal that has been made officially by Mr. Casey.[26] This would provide for more adequate representation of geographic regions without so enlarging the Security Council as to convert it from a manageable executive body into a cumbersome second chamber. This would permit the reservation of a seat for the Afro-Asian bloc. As of the end of 1957, thirty-two countries from Asia and Africa were members of the United Nations. It might be expected that India and Pakistan

---

[25] Rules of Procedure of the General Assembly, Rules 95 and 96, in United Nations Doc. A/520/Rev.3, July 1954.

[26] G.A.O.R., 11th Sess., 588th Plenary Mtg., 21 Nov. 1956, p. 201.

would retain their conventional right to periodic election to the Commonwealth seat. Such an increase would also mean that one seat could be reserved for an Eastern European candidate: "cold war" tactics could then be eliminated from Security Council elections.

In November 1956 the Latin American countries proposed in the General Assembly that the Security Council be increased in size and that the voting procedure for elections be altered. The object was to provide more adequate and certain representation of the Afro-Asian and the Latin American blocs. The discussions in the Assembly took place in the context of the Soviet insistence that the status of Communist China be first determined and the desire of the sponsoring powers for fuller representation. Australia supported the Anglo-American proposal for an increase in the number of non-permanent members of the Security Council by two. Decision on the twenty-power draft resolution was deferred to the twelfth session of the General Assembly.[27]

A suggestion that has much to commend it is that the number of permanent seats be increased by the addition of India. This would rectify a serious anomaly in the Charter; it would be in accord with the realities of power in Asia and the world; it would recognize the historical fact of fluctuations in power and create a precedent for greater flexibility in the membership of the Security Council. Such a change, not yet publicly considered, would meet with considerable support in informed private circles in Australia. The whole issue of Asian representation in the Security Council is highlighted by the controversy over the seating of the Nationalist Chinese as distinct from the representatives of the Peiping regime. This however is not a matter of Charter review; it is rather one of politics and of moral principles.

The unofficial Australian view about the Security Council can be summed up as follows: the retention of the veto in matters of

---

[27] *Ibid.*, 629th Plenary Mtg., 20 Dec. 1956, p. 769, and 661st Mtg., 26 Feb. 1957, p. 1224.

enforcement; recognition of conciliation as a procedural matter; examination of the possibility of transferring to the General Assembly the power to admit new members (and perhaps also, but with considerable doubts, the power to appoint the Secretary-General); adequate representation of Asia on the Security Council, with a preference for the admission of India as a permanent member and additional Asian representation among the elected members. There is a widespread feeling that procedural action may provide a more practicable and fruitful approach than the difficult process of constitutional amendment.

GENERAL ASSEMBLY

One of the major issues for Australia at San Francisco was the enlargement of the powers of the General Assembly. Australia proposed that the Assembly should have the right to consider and make recommendations on "any matter affecting international relations," subject to the exception that the General Assembly should not make recommendations on matters actually being dealt with by the Security Council. In the end, Australia accepted the narrower phrase "any matters within the scope of the . . . Charter." Australia had been anxious to widen the powers of the General Assembly "over all matters of real international concern whether relating to security or welfare and whether particular or general in character."[28]

Since 1945 the overfrequent exercise of the veto and the gradual eclipse of the Security Council have led to a steady pressure to enlarge the real powers of the Assembly. This took the form at first of the creation of the Little Assembly. More significant was the "Uniting for Peace" resolution adopted on 3 November 1950.[29] This recognized the primary responsibility of the Security Council for the maintenance of peace, and the limitation under Article 12

---

[28] *Australian Report on UNCIO*, *op. cit.*, p. 20. See also pp. 58-59 above.
[29] General Assembly Resolution 377(V).

of the Charter upon the power of the Assembly to make recommendations on a matter before the Council. But this limitation exists only when the Council is effectively handling the matter, not when the veto paralyzes action. In such a situation responsibility still rests both on the individual members of the United Nations and on the General Assembly. The resolution at once ended the deadlock produced by the use of the veto, enabled the Assembly to play a decisive role in matters of peace and security, and kept Korea under United Nations consideration after the USSR returned to the Security Council. It circumvented the veto, and in so doing tended to invert the relationship between the Security Council and the General Assembly: it reflected clearly the increasing degree to which the Assembly had come to assume the role of the Security Council for the maintenance and restoration of peace. The resolution demonstrated the possibility of functional change within the present framework of the United Nations, perhaps obviating the need for Charter amendment. Its implications, procedural and substantive, have never been fully worked out. Its danger lies in the possibility of coalitions of a power and political kind developing within the United Nations, coalitions which might make the USSR more obdurate in the use of the veto and more reluctant to consider modifications either of procedure or of the Charter itself.

It is in part as a result both of the resolution and the dilemma which gave rise to it that proposals for drastic constitutional change have subsequently been devised. The Clark-Sohn proposals suggest that the General Assembly shall have the power "to enact legislation binding upon member Nations and all the people thereof," within specified fields and "in accordance with the strictly limited authority" to be delegated to it.[30] The London Resolutions, Plan B, provide

---

[30] See Grenville Clark and Louis B. Sohn, *Peace Through Disarmament and Charter Revision* (Preliminary Print, July 1953), p. 24. Citations in this chapter are to the *original* Clark-Sohn proposals which were substantially revised in the authors' book *World Peace through World Law* (Cambridge: Harvard University Press, 1958).

that "power shall be given by the Charter to the Assembly to legislate in order that States shall be governed by International Law more nearly as individuals are governed by the law of their States."[31]

Such proposals to convert the Assembly into a legislative body arise in part out of the conviction that tinkering with or eliminating the veto is futile: a minority can always prevent decisions from being carried out in many parts of the world. The devolution of greater, but defined, powers to the General Assembly represents a well-understood and workable federal principle. This has been the normal process of constitutional change in the Australian and United States federations. But it is a process at present entirely unsuited to the United Nations. To most thinking people some kind of world federation represents a long-term, and rather remote, objective. Not even the H-bomb has yet succeeded in telescoping the process of historical development or in creating a climate of opinion in which world federation is acceptable. The United Nations came into existence as a loose confederation of powers at best. It is no superstate: this was one matter on which there was complete and emphatic agreement at San Francisco. The Australian view is that nothing has altered the validity of this concept of the United Nations: at present and in the foreseeable future, it is not the form of organization on which legislative powers could be conferred. The remedy for the imperfections of the United Nations lies not in a devolution of legislative and other powers but rather in the fullest use of existing powers, machinery, and procedures; this in turn goes back to a changed climate of opinion. It is not impossible to get nations to agree to complicated international documents such as the Red Cross Convention. Legislative power can make this easier; it is not indispensable. Too drastic a swing toward world federation could, at present, involve the destruction of the whole organization.

---

[31] World Association of Parliamentarians for World Government, *The London Resolutions on World Government* (London, 1953), p. 10. Hereinafter referred to as *The London Resolutions*.

The question of devolution of powers is linked with that of improving the representative character of the Assembly. The London Resolutions suggest the adoption of "the principle of weighted voting possibly by establishing a bicameral Assembly and relating representation in one of the chambers to economic and/or population factors."[32] The Clark-Sohn plan presents a detailed proposal for representation on a basis of one delegate for each 5,000,000 of population or major fraction thereof, with a maximum of thirty representatives for any one nation. Countries with a population of less than 100,000 would be entitled to a single representative.[33] It is, on the surface, manifestly absurd that Iceland's 141,000 people have the same voting power as India's 387 millions. The United Nations is based on the principle of the "sovereign equality of all its Members"; that is embodied in the democratic principle of equal representation for members in the General Assembly. The principle of equality is applied to states, not to populations. It is an equality of states rather than of stature; it bears no relationship to inequality of resources or numbers. Many democratic states have recognized the need for some weighting of citizens for purposes of voting (e.g., by imposing educational qualifications); the same principle could be applied in the international sphere. There must continue to be some relationship between representation and resources, stage of development, and population. This is recognized in the London Proposals for weighted voting. Such proposals rest on the assumption that the conversion of the General Assembly into a world parliament would resolve most of the difficulties of the United Nations. This is largely a fallacious assumption: the problems are partly procedural and partly political; the constant tendency for bloc voting and the seeking of local domestic political advantage does much to stultify Assembly decisions. There would be no support in Australia for any immediate alteration in the system of Assembly representation. This is at present a totally unrealistic proposal.

---

[32] *Ibid.*, p. 9.

[33] Clark and Sohn, *op. cit.*, p. 21. (See note 30, p. 347 above.)

DOMESTIC JURISDICTION

Proposals to extend the competence of the General Assembly have also been conceived with an eye to concurrent amendment of the contentious domestic jurisdiction clause. The Clark-Sohn proposals deal with the question of domestic jurisdiction by the following redrafting of Article 2(7) of the Charter.

> Nothing contained in *this* Charter shall authorize the United Nations to *enact legislation concerning matters which by international custom are generally accepted* as essentially within the domestic jurisdiction of any *nation* or shall require the *member Nations* to submit such matters to settlement under this Charter, *save only to the limited extent that such legislation is authorized, or such settlement is required, by this Charter*. But this principle shall not *prevent the United Nations from making such recommendations concerning matters of an economic, social, cultural or humanitarian character as* are hereinafter authorized.[34]

The proposals are clearly linked to the enlargement of the powers of the Assembly, powers both to legislate and merely to recommend. Powers of legislation "would be narrowly confined to matters directly related to peace and security, and even in that field would be carefully restricted to the implementation of 'constitutional legislation.'"[35] The London Resolutions, Plan B, provide for less drastic modification of Article 2(7):

> Nothing contained in the Charter shall authorise the United Nations to intervene in matters which, in accordance with a decision of the International Court of Justice, are solely within the domestic jurisdiction of any State, or shall require the members to submit such matters to settlement under the Charter.[36]

The principle of domestic jurisdiction is, of course, merely one more, perhaps a basic, manifestation of national sovereignty. As

---

[34] *Ibid.*, p. 9. (See note 30, p. 347 above.)
[35] *Ibid.*, p. 12.
[36] *The London Resolutions, op. cit.*, p. 12.

such its recognition was a necessary condition for the creation of a United Nations in 1945 just as it had been for the League of Nations in 1919. The phrase, "essentially within the domestic jurisdiction of any state" was deliberately preferred to the phrase of Article 15(8) of the Covenant of the League of Nations, "solely within... domestic jurisdiction."[37] It was so preferred because the increasing interdependence of the world left few matters which could be shown to be "solely" within domestic jurisdiction. The London Resolutions revert to a phrase deliberately discarded in the Dumbarton Oaks draft as inadequate; the purpose is to contract the sphere of domestic jurisdiction and so enlarge the potential field for international action.

Construction of the phrase "essentially within the domestic jurisdiction" is no work for the layman. Too frequently arguments in the General Assembly, ostensibly over the interpretation of Article 2(7), have really been concerned with deeper issues. The protagonists have been those who wished to condemn the state involved and those who did not. Often abstention from voting has resulted from a desire to avoid establishing a precedent that could apply to other matters. In practice the General Assembly and the Security Council have ignored the intentions of the framers of the Charter and have defined domestic jurisdiction from case to case on purely political grounds. Disputes have arisen, not merely over political issues, but also over the activities of the specialized agencies and their instrumentalities. The operations of the Economic and Social Council and the activities of the International Labour Organisation likewise raised questions of domestic jurisdiction and intervention. Decisions taken under the express terms of reference of these bodies have raised the question of implementation by domestic or international means. With this have come assertions of a right of veto under cover of the domestic jurisdiction clause.

In the initial discussions in the Human Rights Commission Aus-

---

[37] For a fuller discussion of the domestic jurisdiction principle, see above, pp. 61-64 and 143 ff.

tralia advocated the establishing of an International Court of Human Rights; individuals as well as states would have access to, and full legal standing before, an international tribunal charged with the supervision and enforcement of the human rights covenants. Australia argued that compulsory judicial decisions of the Court of Human Rights must be accepted as limitations on national sovereignty. Subsequently this view was modified. The USSR insisted that measures of implementation must be left solely to the states themselves. Any international machinery for enforcement was an interference with domestic jurisdiction. Technically, this position is unassailable, but it does constitute an impasse which is not technical, for it is in the nature of unyielding dogmatism.

The concept of intervention itself raises difficulties. Does discussion constitute intervention? The view of the Australian government, enunciated in 1952, is that it does. "The whole purpose of bringing forward an item or a resolution is to modify or change the existing situation, which is, 'ipso facto', intervention."[38] The mere fact of raising an issue, of discussing it, constitutes a form of effective intervention. In practice, Article 2(7) has merely served to increase the possibilities of argument and to provide opportunities for the exercise of moral pressure or even political blackmail. Attempts to narrow the field of intervention have not prevented intervention of this kind where there appeared to be a gross disregard by a government of the commonly accepted principles of domestic jurisdiction. On the other hand, the decision of the International Court in the Anglo-Iranian oil case has made it clear that, in the words of a Belgian expert, "matters which normally belong to the domestic jurisdiction of a state do not lose that character because they have exceptionally become the object of a bilateral agreement unless that very agreement contains an express provision to that effect."[39]

---

[38] See above, p. 171.

[39] Henri Rolin, "The International Court of Justice and Domestic Jurisdiction," *International Organization*, Vol. VIII (1954), p. 44.

Revision of the phrasing of Article 2(7) to clarify its meaning would be difficult; diversity of legal interpretation over what constitutes intervention enhances the difficulty. Such disagreement as existed at San Francisco has been intensified rather than diminished and the possibility of agreement on a revised draft has become remote. Despite a certain ambivalence in the past, Australia favours today a rigid interpretation of Article 2(7) of the Charter, an interpretation which broadly defines the scope of domestic jurisdiction and so limits United Nations intervention. This attitude has been strengthened during the discussions of the West Irian problem. Moreover, no Australian government could survive an election or a vote in Parliament if it agreed that questions of immigration policy could be construed as coming within the ambit of United Nations intervention.[40]

No matter how amended, Article 2(7) will continue to occasion bitter debates, essentially similar to those in the past, on the competence of the United Nations to consider specific cases before it. Many of the discussions in the United Nations arise out of a misconception of the functions of the United Nations, and the initiation of such discussions is inimical to the Organization's best interests. Most Australians would agree with Sir John Latham's view that

> the United Nations should not be regarded as a means of conducting crusades against all the wrongs which exist in the world and in every country of the world. . . . If every country in the world tries to introduce into other countries the institutions in which its people believe there is no hope of peace for the world . . . The idea that the United Nations Organization should attempt to deal in public with wrongs everywhere represents a policy which it is impossible to carry into effect

---

[40] A considerable minority in Australia feels that there is some merit in discussion and disagrees with the government view that discussion constitutes intervention. The policy committee of the Victorian Division of the Australian Association for the United Nations went further (July 1954): "Australia should set an example in encouraging international co-operation on issues which might technically be stated as domestic."

and which may destroy the United Nations Organization itself.[41]

On occasion when a defence based on the domestic jurisdiction principle has been raised, Australia has initiated or supported proposals requesting advisory opinions from the International Court. Proposals to vest in the Court authority to interpret Article 2(7) and the Australian proposal requiring the acceptance by all members of the compulsory jurisdiction of the Court were defeated at San Francisco. The Court has therefore been a frail instrument for the interpretation of Article 2(7). Some doubts are felt in Australia about the wisdom of seeking advisory opinions from the Court. In all probability the majority of the Court would take a narrow view of the scope of domestic jurisdiction. A spate of such opinions might embolden those governments prepared to push the jurisdiction of the United Nations to such a point that, at best, the Organization could fall into disrepute through fruitless discussion, and, at worst, would be faced with the danger of secession by responsible and important governments.

COLONIAL PROBLEMS: NON-SELF-GOVERNING TERRITORIES AND TRUSTEESHIP

Both the principles of trusteeship and the operation of the trusteeship system have been subject to considerable criticism since 1945. The initiative at San Francisco for adding new chapters to the Charter dealing with non-self-governing territories came in large measure from Australia and the United Kingdom. Having strong views on colonialism in general and colonial administration in particular, Dr. Evatt proposed to extend principles of trusteeship to all dependent territories whether they were mandated territories or colonies exclusively controlled by a metropolitan power.[42] Although

---

[41] Sir John Latham, *Open Diplomacy* (Sydney: Australian Institute of International Affairs, 1953), pp. 19-20.

[42] See above, p. 72.

Australia was compelled to give ground, the specific undertakings in Article 73(a) and (d) were the result of persistent Australian pressure. This expression of the world's new-found sense of responsibility was one of the major gains at San Francisco.

Since all members of the United Nations have, by virtue of their membership, accepted Chapters XI-XIII of the Charter, there should be no fundamental differences on principles of colonial policy. The broad objectives are clearly set out—the primacy of native welfare, the obligation to promote self-government, the encouragement of respect for human rights and for fundamental freedoms. But fierce controversy has developed between the colonial powers and the administering authorities on the one hand and the anti-colonial powers on the other. Much of the pressure for change has come from the Afro-Asian and Latin American countries, emotionally interested in the fate of colonies and anxious to facilitate a rapid transition to autonomy, and from the Soviet bloc, actuated by an ideological interest and a desire to win Asian support. They have questioned the good faith of the administering powers, doubting whether they really accept the welfare of the native peoples as their primary objective and intend to introduce effective self-government. On the basis of the reports of visiting missions they have criticized in detail the administration of trust territories and have sought to extend the right of the United Nations to supervise such administrations. The issue has tended to become a political and economic one in which the welfare of the native peoples has been relegated to the background.

Pressure for review of Chapter XI of the Charter has centred around the proposal to extend the obligation of colonial powers under Article 73(e). These obligations are much vaguer than the corresponding trusteeship obligations clearly set out in Article 76. The proposals have been twofold: (1) to require the transmission of political information in addition to the "statistical and other information of a technical nature" which the administering authorities are already obligated to submit; and (2) to empower the

y

United Nations to make recommendations on the reports submitted.[43] At San Francisco the United Kingdom and other colonial
powers resisted proposals for the compulsory transmission of political information. Subsequent pressure for the revival of this proposal
has developed in the main from the increasing political tensions
of the "cold war."

Unlike some of the other colonial powers, Australia has regularly
forwarded political information. Such information is available in
administration reports regularly submitted to Parliament, printed
as parliamentary papers, and available through ordinary booksellers.
The major objection to the universal adoption of such a practice
would appear to be that the pressures for such reports arise primarily
out of a determination to cause political embarrassment to the
administering authority. The question of action by the United
Nations on reports received is another matter. The General Assembly
has decided to continue on a semi-permanent basis the special
committee to receive and consider information concerning non-self-
governing territories. The creation of the committee is an interesting
development of United Nations machinery within the framework
of the Charter, and its operation will be watched with interest to
see what educative functions it performs. It has no special competence to make recommendations and its activities will be carefully
scrutinized by administrators in colonial territories. The attitude
of the Australian government on the question of perpetuating the
committee will depend upon the way in which the committee performs its functions.

A further weakness of Chapter XI of the Charter lies in the
loose and inadequate definition of the phrase "non-self-governing
territories": there is no clear test for determining which territories
are non-self-governing. At present, the metropolitan powers have
the sole right to determine the status of "colonial territories."
Clarification of these difficulties might be a useful function for a
review conference.

---

[43] See, for example, Clark and Sohn, *op. cit.*, pp. 106-08.

Criticism of Chapter XII (Articles 75-85) and proposals for revision centre around the purely voluntary character of the trusteeship system, the lack of provision for revision or termination of trusteeship agreements, the designation of strategic areas, and the absence of adequate protection for trust peoples against the violation of agreements.[44] These issues are contentious and political in character, and there is little prospect of agreement on revision proposals, proposals which ideally may be desirable. Few responsible people in Australia feel that the obligations and restrictions on the admistering authorities are too rigid—that Australian power to control immigration and to defend Australia are dangerously restricted by the Charter. Article 84 permits the administering authority to use volunteer forces and facilities in the trust territory to carry out its obligations to maintain international peace and security as well as "for local defence and the maintenance of law and order within the trust territory." All sections of the Australian community feel New Guinea to be vital for defence: the only serious threat to Australian security has come through New Guinea. Any international action taken by the Australian government must reflect this fact. A revolutionary change in methods of warfare, such as the widespread introduction of atomic and nuclear weapons, which extended Australia's defence frontier to the mainland of Asia could make New Guinea strategically less valuable. But an equally revolutionary change in Australian public opinion would be required before there would be any shift in policy. This is at present a very remote possibility. There would be little support in Australia for proposals to make more rigid the obligations of administering authorities under Article 84. These are considered sufficiently precise and do in practice induce some impatience at uninformed criticism of the manner in which they are carried out.

The focal point of criticism in colonial questions is the position of the non-self-governing territories. The doctrine of international

---

[44] *Ibid.*, pp. 109-15.

accountability which underlies trusteeship in general has, on balance, much to commend it.[45] It is being pressed more vigorously now than in 1945. At a time when much of the earlier Australian enthusiasm for the doctrine has evaporated, the San Francisco suggestions for placing all colonies under trusteeship are being revived (e.g., the Federal Union Proposals).[46] The new Asian nations and the Arab countries are especially sensitive to colonial questions, particularly the rate of progress of colonial peoples towards self-government. There is an understandable impatience and at times suspicion of metropolitan policies. Principles of trusteeship tend to be sidetracked in political conflicts in which practical problems of administration are ignored in the attempt to score propaganda points. The Trusteeship Council has often been little more than a political forum.

The specific form of accountability under the trusteeship system recognizes that the administering authority has complete and exclusive powers of administration in the trust territory. The only limitation upon this control is the obligation to carry out the duties imposed by the Charter. The Charter empowers Australia to provide for the defence of New Guinea (Article 84) and so for the safety of Australia; it gives to Australia the right to control immigration to and commercial relations with the territory (Articles 76(d) and 80). The administering authority is therefore not merely an agent of the United Nations. Australia would firmly oppose any attempt to vest sovereign authority in the United Nations or to take the determination of policy out of the hands of the administering authority.

---

[45] See above, pp. 211 ff.

[46] See *United Nations Reform: Proposals for a Federal United Nations*, Joint Commission on U.N. Charter Reform established by the Federal Union and the Crusade for World Government (London, July 1953), p. 18. Compare the Belgian view as presented in *La Mission sacrée de civilisation. A quelles populations faut-il en étendre le bénéfice? La thèse belge* (New York: Belgian Information Center, 1953).

The Charter provides that the function of review should be exercised by the United Nations through the Trusteeship Council and the General Assembly. A bitter deadlock has repeatedly developed in the Trusteeship Council, where administering and non-administering powers are equally represented. The provision for equal representation was adopted as a precaution against dominance of the Council by either group and so the forcing of an extreme view, of either type, on the United Nations. The result has been that the administering powers, under constant pressure from the anti-colonial powers, have tended to belittle the Trusteeship Council as an ignorant political busybody. In consequence, there has sometimes been a tendency to ignore Council recommendations and to do as little as possible to fulfil the letter of obligations. A drastic change in the composition of the Trusteeship Council has been suggested as a remedy. The Clark-Sohn plan proposes an increase in the representation of non-colonial powers.[47] Rightly or wrongly the administering authorities have long smarted under what they consider ill-informed criticism, especially from the Soviet Union. The peculiarly complex problems of New Guinea have only recently been appreciated by members of the Council's visiting missions and, as a result, pin-pricking criticism may well disappear. The fundamental weakness of the Trusteeship Council lies precisely in the ignorance and lack of realism of some of its members who have no first-hand experience with colonial administration. A new voting formula which placed administering members in a minority would not cure this weakness. It would receive little support from Australia.

Another proposal is for the creation of a committee of experts, a nonpolitical body resembling the Permanent Mandates Commission of the League of Nations. Such a committee, by its intimate knowledge, could assist and advise both the General Assembly and the administering authority. It could act under the Trusteeship Council and be represented on all visiting missions. Because of their

---

[47] Clark and Sohn, *op. cit.*, pp. 116-18.

integrity and lack of bias, the opinions of these experts would carry more weight than the views of governmental representatives. Most administering authorities would prefer such a solution; it would certainly be to the advantage of the colonial peoples themselves. It would be far less acceptable to the Arab-Asian bloc which would prefer an altered balance of power within the present Trusteeship Council. Australia, formerly critical of visiting missions because of the embarrassment caused to the administration, has come in-increasingly to appreciate the useful educative value of having non-expert members visit trust territories.[48] Despite the deadlock in the Trusteeship Council, official and a large segment of private opinion in Australia would prefer to leave Chapter XII of the Charter unamended, although there is some minority support for the creation of a non-political committee of experts.

THE ECONOMIC AND SOCIAL COUNCIL (ECOSOC)

The proposal of a committee of the International Bar Association, that the Economic and Social Council and the Trusteeship Council should become subsidiary rather than principal organs of the United Nations,[49] raises a basic question concerning the purposes of the United Nations. The Preamble to the Charter suggests that the underlying purposes of the United Nations are four-fold. The primary one is to "save succeeding generations from the scourge of war"; the fourth is "to promote social progress and better standards of life in larger freedom." The purposes are set forth more specifically in Article 1 where again the emphasis is on the maintenance of "international peace and security." Paragraph 3 of Article 1 recognizes the need to "achieve international co-operation in solving international problems of an economic, social, cultural, or humanitarian character."

---

[48] See above, pp 213-14.
[49] International Bar Association, *Report of the Committee on the Constitutional Structure of the United Nations* (1 Jan. 1954), p. 32.

There is an obvious connection between these two objectives. As Field Marshal Smuts has pointed out, one of the most prolific causes of war is economic and social unrest. Much of the idealism behind the setting up of the United Nations arose out of the acceptance of Franklin D. Roosevelt's Four Freedoms Speech of 1941, the main points of which were written into the Atlantic Charter of 14 April 1941. No organization, national or international, can survive without strong support at the grassroots level. In a world of sovereign national states, it is difficult to find any real sense of community. The twin concepts of freedom from fear and freedom from want go far to provide just such an emotional integration of peoples. Without it there is a danger of atomization and disintegration. Abstract ideas in themselves provide no real cement. To millions of ordinary people in the plains of the Punjab, or the pampas of South America, the paddy fields of Java, and the factories of Western Europe, the "scourge of war" is an endemic reality, but the Security Council and General Assembly tend to become rather remote and meaningless abstractions. Their contacts with the United Nations, as a matter of experience, have been with the economic, social, cultural, and humanitarian work of the specialized agencies. For the purpose of giving these peoples an enduring interest in the United Nations so that ultimately they can collaborate more fully at the political level, it is necessary that this should continue to be so. Because "the work of these welfare agencies reaches right down into the lives of millions of people, it may engender a sense of international community strong enough to support eventually an effective organisation with powers of government."[50] It is imperative that both the Trusteeship Council and ECOSOC continue to function as principal rather than subsidiary organs of the United Nations.

One of the major Australian criticisms of the Dumbarton Oaks draft lay precisely in the weakness of its social and economic chapters and the omission of provisions dealing with non-self-governing

---

[50] *The London Proposals, op. cit.*, p. 11.

territories. The struggle over full employment and the Australian attempt to convert the Dumbarton Oaks draft from a "frigid" into a "full-blooded document" arose from the conviction that there is a necessary causal relationship between war and economic and social distress. As Dr. Evatt pointed out during the debate in the Australian Parliament on acceptance of the Charter, one of its great merits was that it "set in motion practical steps for achieving freedom from want as well as fear."[51] The arguments valid in 1945 are even more cogent today. It is essential that a principal organ of the United Nations be empowered to function continuously, be capable of making prompt recommendations on vital matters of world interest (e.g., the checking of economic crisis), and be able to deal on a global scale with problems of economic distress. The appropriate organ is ECOSOC and Australia sought at San Francisco to enhance its status. The success of its work depends largely upon its ability to find the necessary funds and to attract first rate personnel for its work.

The proper function of a review conference, then, should be to examine the operations of ECOSOC in order to eliminate weaknesses and slough off unnecessary duties rather than to attempt a reduction of its status. As to the composition of ECOSOC, which is largely an incidental question, the Clark-Sohn proposals contain an interesting suggestion for a change. Instead of the present system of electing eighteen member states to the Council, it is proposed that the General Assembly elect twenty-four representatives (no two of the same nationality) to serve on the Council.[52] The weakness of so many United Nations committees and organs is that their members can never forget their national allegiances, that at least one eye is turned or one ear cocked towards their own countries. The danger is the greater where the members represent governments. One of the strengths of the International Labour Organisation is

---

[51] See above, p. 83. Note the Australian proposals for amendments to the Dumbarton Oaks draft, *UNCIO Documents*, Vol. III, pp. 546-48.

[52] Clark and Sohn, *op. cit.*, pp. 97-98.

the broadness of its base: employers and employees as well as governments are represented. The Clark-Sohn proposal for reform could in some degree remove the purely national character of representation in ECOSOC.

The major weakness of ECOSOC lies in its amorphous character as both an independent agent and the coordinator of the work of specialized agencies. ECOSOC has become so cluttered with functions of a social and economic nature that it is impossible for it to concentrate on essential and vital tasks: major questions of economic policy or planning are thrust to one side by the burden of its administrative duties. There is a great deal to be said for the proposal that it should concentrate on its intended functions of coordination, and that by a redefinition of its responsibilities nonessential duties should be sloughed off. Those economic and social questions which do not come within the ambit of existing specialized agencies could be handed over to a new and independent body. The special merit of this proposal is that it involves a procedural rather than a constitutional change. As one writer has commented:

> . . . the changes can be effected in practice without any modification of the Charter. ECOSOC could suspend its commissions, as it has already, without suppressing its obligations to appoint them; the Assembly could by a provisional working arrangement with ECOSOC appoint the Commission on Human Rights and request it to report directly instead of via the Council; ECOSOC could abstain from submitting recommendations about human rights, while retaining the constitutional right to do so . . . Article 59, empowering ECOSOC "when appropriate to initiate negotiations among States concerned for the creation of any new specialized agencies required for the accomplishment of the purposes set forth," at the beginning of Chapter IX, was not inserted by accident.[53]

This accords with the Australian view that the necessary changes

---

[53] A. Loveday, "Suggestions for the Reform of the United Nations Economic and Social Machinery," *International Organization*, Vol. VII (1953), p. 336.

in the United Nations system are largely procedural and mechanical in character rather than constitutional, and that they can best be carried out within the framework of the present Charter rather than through Charter revision.

INTERNATIONAL LAW AND THE
INTERNATIONAL COURT OF JUSTICE

Some of the controversy over the functioning of the United Nations has developed from the imprecise phrasing of the Charter. This was in part a necessary consequence of the circumstances in which the Charter was framed. Just as compromises had to be made at the Philadelphia Convention in 1787, and the Australian constitutional conventions of the 1890's, so the San Francisco Conference had to content itself with political and legal compromises in order to increase the area of agreement and to obtain the accept- ance of the Charter. Loose drafting was no historical accident but rather a. matter of necessity.

A number of the key words and phrases in the Charter are ambiguous. What is meant by "war," "nations"? What constitutes "intervention"? What does the phrase "essentially within the do- mestic jurisdiction of any state" mean? What are "non-self-governing territories"? Proposals have been made to give proper legal inter- pretation to amorphous phrases such as these.[54] They arise partly out of a feeling of continued frustration, partly out of a tendency to press the analogy between national and international law too far. A prime difficulty is that many so called "legal" issues are themselves political.

The problems of precise legal definitions are extraordinarily difficult. A detailed definition of "war," for example, might easily be evaded by describing operations as "police action" or as "measures

---

[54] See, for example, the *Report of the Committee of the International Bar Association, op. cit., passim.*

of self-defence." International jurists are themselves sharply divided over the meaning of "intervention."[55] The lengthy discussions in the General Assembly merely add point to the controversy. The authors of the Chatham House study on nationalism point to the diverse, shifting meanings of that term which tend to vary from state to state.[56] Political phrases hardly belong in the realm of precise legal definition at present. This is not to argue that no long-term attempts at definition should be made; it does mean that the growth of international law and of juridical definition of difficult semantic terms must be a slow gradual process. The task is one not for the General Assembly or the Security Council, but rather for the patient work of lawyers and statesmen. An Australian jurist, Sir John Latham, has said: "To give to U.N.O. a power 'to declare and modify international law' would . . . destroy any prospect of putting international law upon a firm basis. I doubt whether any Government would genuinely accept such a proposal."[57]

What is the proper role for the International Court of Justice? Australia proposed at San Francisco that the Charter require all members to accept the obligations contained in the "optional clause" of the statute of the old Permanent Court of International Justice.[58] This would have given the International Court limited but compulsory jurisdiction over contentious matters likely to provoke conflict or breaches of the peace. This proved unacceptable to the Conference and was abandoned. In 1930 Australia itself accepted, with certain reservations, the compulsory jurisdiction of the old Court. A fresh declaration in 1940 added to the list of exceptions disputes arising out of events occurring while Australia was at war. The jurisdiction of the new International Court of Justice, the

---

[55] See above, Ch. 6 *passim*, especially pp. 176-79.

[56] See *Nationalism: A Report by a Study Group of Members of the Royal Institute of International Affairs* (London: Oxford University Press, 1939), pp. xvi-xx.

[57] See his comments on the *Report of the Committee of the International Bar Association*, *op. cit.*, p. 64.

[58] See above, p. 64.

principal judicial organ of the United Nations, is defined in Article 36 of the Statute. It includes an "optional clause" according to which parties to the Statute of the Court may at any time accept the jurisdiction of the Court in legal disputes. Australia accepted the "optional clause" upon certain conditions. These were redefined by a new declaration on 6 February 1954 which extended the list of exceptions to disputes relating to the continental shelf and cognate matters unless the parties ". . . have first agreed upon a *modus vivendi* pending the final decision of the Court."[59] In 1953 Australia accepted Japan's submission to the Court of a dispute arising out of an Australian proclamation defining territorial waters in the region of the continental shelf.

There has been a tendency on the whole towards a contraction of the area of effective jurisdiction of the Court. It could be used with greater advantage to facilitate the smoother functioning of the United Nations. This could be done through more frequent reference to the Court for advisory opinions: Australia has frequently associated itself with other powers in supporting this practice. In many instances proceedings at the United Nations are delayed or complicated by formal objections to jurisdiction. On closer examination these objections often turn out to be more political than legal in nature. The sorting out of legal and political issues and the clarification of the jurisdiction of the different organs of the United Nations would be of immense practical value to their successful functioning. An eminent Australian jurist, Professor Sawer, suggests that:

> It should be a general rule of United Nations procedure that any Power objecting to an organ of the United Nations taking a proposed subject under consideration should state whether the objection is legal or political, or both. If the claim is made that the objection is wholly or partly legal, then without further discussion the question should be referred to a judicial body to decide in the first place the question of jurisdiction.

---

[59] International Court of Justice, *Yearbook 1953-54*, pp. 210-11.

The International Court is an obviously appropriate body to decide such questions.[60]

The practical objection that the Court is too far from United Nations headquarters could be met by the organization of a panel system by which a number of judges of the Court could always be present in New York. The adoption by the tribunal of an expeditious and less formal process would expedite the work of the United Nations and also enhance the prestige and utility of the Court itself.

Proposals to extend the jurisdiction of the International Court to all commercial transactions involving points of private international law have far-reaching implications. This could drastically limit the jurisdiction of national courts in such cases and could give to the International Court an appellate jurisdiction. Discussions over human rights have been accompanied by proposals to create an international judicial tribunal to deal with all cases of alleged violation of human rights. Judicial determination of economic rights is virtually impossible. A court may be confronted with a certain unqualified obligation in the covenants on human rights, and simultaneously with a government claim of incapacity to provide the required economic conditions. As to political rights, Sir John Latham's comment is to the point: "The constant and complex litigation in the U.S.A. upon the provisions of the 'Bill of Rights' illustrates the difficulty of the subject, in a community where the judgments of courts are enforced as of course."[61] In the international sphere judgments in this field would at present be completely empty, perhaps even productive of harm. The multiplication

---

[60] Professor G. Sawer suggests the adoption of a subsidiary series of rules for the International Court: (i) in a tribunal of five, there must be four votes in favour of jurisdiction before jurisdiction is established; (ii) if the question is whether there is jurisdiction merely to discuss a matter, the general presumption is in favour of jurisdiction; (iii) if the question is whether there is jurisdiction to discuss and to take any further step (e. g., the making of a recommendation) then the presumption should be against jurisdiction. (Manuscript comment.)

[61] *Report of the Committee of the International Bar Association, op. cit.,* p. 62.

of international courts would appear to be a matter for careful consideration at a later stage when a sense of international community has developed and where effective enforcement is possible.

CONCLUSION

Any proposals for Charter revision must be considered in the context of the present power conflict, a conflict aggravated by the intrusion of ideological factors. The conditions under which the Charter was drafted and the situation to which it was expected to apply no longer exist. Great power unanimity has vanished, and with it some of the possibilities of international collaboration envisaged in 1945. In the high noon of San Francisco, it was widely believed that the United Nations could maintain international peace and security; such optimism has now largely evaporated. The system of collective security envisaged under Articles 43-50 has been still-born and the sketchy improvisation of the "Uniting for Peace" resolution has never been adequately tested. ". . . the United Nations today [1954] is in fact powerless to deal with any major threat to security. There would be little prospect that, in the event of such a threat, the procedures for peaceful settlement laid down in the Charter would in fact be invoked to the full, or that the enforcement measures against any breach of peace would in fact be taken."[62]

It was a guarded optimism about the ability of the United Nations to maintain peace that led most members to trust in the United Nations but at the same time build up their own defence forces. From the outset Australia has relied for security upon its own preparedness and collaboration with the other members of the Commonwealth and the United States. Australia, in company with the vast majority of members, has never regarded the United Nations as an adequate shield in itself. At best the United Nations provided a framework for co-operation with other like-minded

---

[62] Hasluck, 22 Oct. 1954, *op. cit.*

powers. Australia has consistently sought to organize regional pacts within the ambit of the Charter: ANZAC (1944), ANZUS (1951), and SEATO (1954). These afforded more certain prospects of security in a darkening world than Security Council resolutions. Even in the early stages of development only a handful of idealists supported proposals to "put teeth" into the Charter.

Given the present polarization of power, many of the apparently logical proposals for Charter revision are purely academic. Charter review must be considered in the light of present realities. That is not to say that in a dynamic world proposals for change must be completely discarded. Australian estimates of them could be very different given a different situation. A full-scale revision conference would have little chance of success at present despite, and perhaps because of, the moral pressures that might be brought to bear. Australia would oppose the holding of such a conference unless the climate of world opinion changed drastically. However, a *review* conference, aimed at accomplishing something much more limited and positive, could do much to explore technical weaknesses and indicate the possibilities of procedural as distinct from constitutional change.

Finally, many of the difficulties of the United Nations stem not so much from structural defects as from the atmosphere in which it functions. It has been suggested that the location of the United Nations in a small neutral state, remote from the power conflict, would assuage feeling and be conducive to a more rational discussion of issues. Some Australians would agree. Of more importance in its effect on the atmosphere in which the United Nations functions is the widely held view that democracy demands open diplomacy. The cult of open diplomacy owed much to the moral convictions of Woodrow Wilson and the general revulsion in 1919 against the secret treaties characteristic of the pre-World War I power balance. The pendulum, in the opinion of many Australians, has swung too far in the opposite direction. Diplomacy today tends to operate through headlines. Debates in the General Assembly and the Security Council are pitched beyond the chambers to domestic or international audiences. Members of committees can rarely serve in a private capacity as experts. Irreparable damage is done to international goodwill as well as to international peace and security by debate over the microphone or through the tele-printer. Round-table discussions of disputes *in camera*, without benefit of press, would reduce the acerbity of feeling.[63] Only when agreement has been arrived at or a decision effected should publicity be given to the terms. International accountability and responsibility could still be preserved, and with them goodwill and a capacity to manoeuvre.

---

[63] See, for example, Sir John Latham's suggestion in the *Report of the Committee of the International Bar Association, op. cit.,* p. 65: "Except in cases in which two-thirds majority of members voting decides to the contrary, debates and discussions in the General Assembly and the Security Council shall be held in private." It is doubtful whether such a view would be supported by Dr. Evatt, who is a firm believer in the value of the pressure of world opinion.

APPENDICES

TABLE 1

GOVERNMENTS AND CHIEF MINISTERS 1943-58*

Date	Party	Prime Minister	Treasurer	External Affairs	Defence	Air	Army	Navy	Territories
Sept. 1943	Labour	Curtin	Chifley	Evatt	Curtin	Drakeford	Forde	Makin	Ward
6 July 1945	Labour	Forde	Chifley	Evatt	Beasley	Drakeford	Forde	Makin	Ward
13 July 1945	Labour	Chifley	Chifley	Evatt	Beasley	Drakeford	Forde	Makin	Ward
Nov. 1946	Labour	Chifley	Chifley	Evatt	Dedman	Drakeford	Chambers	Riordan	Ward
Dec. 1949	Liberal-Country	Menzies	Fadden	Spender	(1) Harrison (2) McBride (Oct. 1950)	White	Francis	Francis	Spender
May 1951	Liberal-Country	Menzies	Fadden	Casey	McBride	(1) McBride (2) Townley (July 1954)	Francis	(1) McMahon (2) Francis (July 1954)	Hasluck
Jan. 1956	Liberal-Country	Menzies	Fadden	Casey	McBride	(1) Townley (2) Osborne (Oct. 1956)	Cramer	(1) O'Sullivan (2) Davidson (Oct. 1956)	Hasluck

* Some minor changes in the composition of the Menzies government have not been included.

POLITICAL PARTIES AND GOVERNMENTS IN AUSTRALIA

Table 1 lists the governments and chief ministers for the period 1943-1958. Table 2 sets out the comparative strength of the main political parties as reflected in the elections for the House of Representatives. (The House is elected by compulsory voting on a preferential system; ballots cast for the candidate with the fewest votes are progressively transferred to the second choice indicated on the ballot until one candidate has an absolute majority.)

TABLE 2

DISTRIBUTION OF SEATS
HOUSE OF REPRESENTATIVES(a)

Party	Aug. 1943	Sept. 1946	Dec. (c) 1949	April 1951	May 1954	Dec. 1955
Labour	49	43	47	53	57(d)	47
Liberal	15(b)	17	55	51	47	57
Country	10	12	18	17	17	18
Others	—	2	1	—	—	—
Total	74	74	121	121	121	122 (c)

(a) Excludes representatives of the Northern Territory and the Australian Capital Territory. These two representatives vote only on territorial questions; they usually side with the Labour party.

(b) Figures for 1943 are for the United-Australia party, predecessor to the Liberal party.

(c) Prior to the 1949 elections, the electoral boundaries were redrawn and the number of seats increased from 74 to 121. In 1955 an

additional seat was created as a result of a population increase.

(d) Includes 7 members who left the Labour party in 1955 to join
the Democratic (Anti-Communist) Labour party. All of them
were defeated in the 1955 elections.

The Australian Labour Party: Labour parties were formed in
several states before federation and a nationally organized Labour
party developed gradually, contesting the first federal election in 1900.
In 1921 the party adopted as a general objective "the socialization of
industry, production, distribution and exchange," an objective to
be achieved constitutionally. At the same time, the extension of
the socialist sector of the economy would still allow a place for
private enterprises which were regarded as being consistent with
national welfare.

The Australian Labour party has been primarily a party of
workers backed by the trade unions organized into two rival bodies,
the Australian Council of Trade Unions and the Australian Workers
Union. The party has been troubled by factional differences almost
since its inception and the conflict between the right and left wings
has tended periodically to produce splits and the secession of right-
wing elements to other parties. Irish immigrant influence has been
considerable and one of the traditional lines of fission has been a
religious one. Although the Labour party has had the support of
many civil servants and middle class voters, it has a tradition of anti-
intellectualism.

During the Second World War, Mr. John Curtin and Mr. J. B.
Chifley succeeded in maintaining party unity and averting a clash
between the hostile factions. With Mr. Chifley's death in June 1951,
Dr. H. V. Evatt became party leader. A former president of the
United Nations General Assembly (1948-49), Dr. Evatt has been
largely responsible for formulating the party's foreign policy.

Dr. Evatt's leadership of the party has been challenged, unsuccessfully, on several occasions by the right wing elements of the party.
A split in 1955, beginning in Victoria, led to the formation of the

Democratic (Anti-Communist) Labour party. At the federal elections in December 1955, this group lost all the seats it held in the House of Representatives but won one seat in the Senate.

The Liberal party was formed by the merger of non-socialist radicals with conservative free traders in 1909. It has developed as a combination of right-wing groups with business support, and from time to time has absorbed dissident right-wing labour groups (e.g., the groups led by Mr. W. M. Hughes and Mr. J. A. Lyons). The party name has been periodically changed: "Liberal," "Nationalist," "United-Australia." In December 1944 the non-labour groups combined to form the Liberal party under the leadership of Mr. R. G. Menzies.

It is a party primarily of private enterprise and urban business interests with a good deal of middle class support. It has advocated policies of private ownership of property, tariffs to protect Australian industry, anti-communism, court-controlled secret ballots for trade unions, national health and social services, a measure of government business enterprise free of political control, and the maintenance of a federal system which would recognize states' rights. It has, on questions of foreign policy, strongly supported close cooperation with the United Kingdom and with the Commonwealth of Nations.

The Country party is essentially a sectional economic party which emerged in Western Australia in 1914 as a farmers' party, and then began to organize in other states. It entered federal politics in 1919, winning ten seats, and today has considerable strength in Queensland, New South Wales, and Western Australia. As a minority party it has never been able to govern in its own right, and its role has been largely that of negotiating concessions from the other major parties in return for political support. It merged with the Nationalist party in 1922, but in 1931 preferred to act as an independent party. In 1940, it supported the United-Australia party and gradually moved in the direction of another merger with the Liberal party at the federal level in 1944. Under the leadership of Mr. A. Fadden (now Sir Arthur Fadden), it formed a coalition government under Mr. Menzies in 1949. Although it has been a party favouring private enterprise and private ownership and control of land, it has advocated a modified rural socialism. It has supported government provision of rural credit and government stabilization of prices for primary products, with government price supports if necessary.

The Communist party, organized in 1922, has never exerted any political influence at the federal political level. In 1943 it reached its greatest strength, polling 1.98% of the House votes. It has never won a federal seat in either the Senate or the House, and has won only one seat in the state legislatures (Queensland).

The main influence of the Communist party has been exerted at the trade union level where, because of its militant union policy, it has won the support of left-wing labour elements. This has given it control, from time to time, of key unions, especially waterside workers (dock men), seamen, miners, and railway workers. In matters of foreign policy it has strongly supported the policies of the USSR.

AUSTRALIAN METROPOLITAN NEWSPAPERS

Australian newspapers are, with minor exceptions, not owned or controlled by political parties. The Australian Labour party has from time to time controlled small metropolitan papers in all the major capital cities with the exception of Melbourne and Perth. These have, however, been largely ephemeral, and their circulation has been limited. During the period 1945-56 none of them has ranked among the important daily newspapers. A number of the metropolitan dailies have developed under family influence, but these have been limited to single cities. The late Sir Keith Murdoch owned a number of inter-state newspapers. Until his death in 1952 these included the Melbourne *Herald* and *Sun*, the *Brisbane Courier-Mail*, and the Adelaide *News*. Since his death the Brisbane *Telegraph* has become part of the *Herald* group but the Adelaide *News* has left it.

Some of the Australian dailies (e.g., *Sydney Morning Herald*, *Brisbane Courier-Mail*) have tended to be conservative in their views and have consistently supported the Liberal-Country parties. Three newspapers (Melbourne *Age*, Sydney *Daily Telegraph*, and *West Australian*) in particular have followed an independent policy and have exerted considerable influence on public opinion at different times. The Melbourne *Argus* has followed a variety of policies as it has changed hands. In 1949 it was purchased by the London *Daily Mirror;* its editorial policy on foreign affairs, particularly Asian affairs, was largely independent. It ceased publication in January 1957.

There are few weeklies. The Sydney *Bulletin* is intensely conservative and nationalistic in its views. The Melbourne *Advocate* is a Roman Catholic paper. Monthly journals have been ephemeral, with *Voice* (Sydney) expressing a moderate Labour viewpoint. Of the quarterlies, *Australian Outlook* and *Australian Quarterly* are both independent, non-party journals.

CIRCULATION OF AUSTRALIAN NEWSPAPERS*
(Daily average net sales)

	1945	1 Oct. 55—31 March 56
ADELAIDE		
Advertiser (M)	128,021	171,804
News (E)	78,191	121,601
BRISBANE		
Brisbane Courier-Mail (M)	158,338	228,569
Telegraph (E)	122,502	155,000
HOBART		
Mercury (M)	31,520	43,293
MELBOURNE		
Age (M)	113,163	125,723
Argus (M)	121,901	168,861
Herald (E)	330,110	437,805
Sun (M)	327,777	455,156
PERTH		
Daily News (E)	64,525	92,592
West Australian (M)	96,824	142,231
SYDNEY		
Daily Mirror (E)	288,240	309,957
Sun (E)	275,376	315,190
Sydney Morning Herald (M)	273,700	310,185
Telegraph (M)	276,566	319,000

(E) Evening   (M) Morning

* Circulation figures from the *Australian Encyclopaedia* (Sydney: Angus and Robertson, 1958), Vol. 6, p. 321.

TRUSTEESHIP AGREEMENTS

I. TRUSTEESHIP AGREEMENT FOR THE TERRITORY OF NEW GUINEA[1]
(As approved by the General Assembly on 13 December 1946)

Whereas the Territory of New Guinea has been administered in accordance with Article 22 of the Covenant of the League of Nations and in pursuance of a mandate conferred upon His Britannic Majesty and exercised on his behalf by the Government of the Commonwealth of Australia; and

Whereas the Charter of the United Nations, signed at San Francisco on 26 June 1945, provides by Article 75 for the establishment of an International Trusteeship System for the administration and supervision of such territories as may be placed thereunder by subsequent individual agreements; and

Whereas the Government of Australia now undertakes to place the Territory of New Guinea under the Trusteeship System, on the terms set forth in the present Trusteeship Agreement,

Therefore the General Assembly of the United Nations, acting in pursuance of Article 85 of the Charter, approves the following terms of trusteeship for the Territory of New Guinea, in substitution for the terms of the mandate under which the Territory has been administered:

Article 1

The Territory to which this Trusteeship Agreement applies (hereinafter called the Territory) consists of that portion of the island of New Guinea and the groups of islands administered therewith under the mandate dated 17 December 1920, conferred upon His Britannic Majesty and exercised by the Government of Australia.

---

[1] United Nations *Treaty Series*, Vol. 8, No. 122, pp. 182-86.

Article 2

The Government of Australia (hereinafter called the Administering Authority) is hereby designated as the sole authority which will exercise the administration of the Territory.

Article 3

The Administering Authority undertakes to administer the Territory in accordance with the provisions of the Charter and in such a manner as to achieve, in the Territory, the basic objectives of the International Trusteeship System, which are set forth in Article 76 of the Charter.

Article 4

The Administering Authority will be responsible for the peace, order, good government and defence of the Territory and for this purpose will have the same powers of legislation, administration and jurisdiction in and over the Territory as if it were an integral part of Australia, and will be entitled to apply to the Territory, subject to such modifications as it deems desirable, such laws of the Commonwealth of Australia as it deems appropriate to the needs and conditions of the Territory.

Article 5

It is agreed that the Administering Authority, in the exercise of its powers under article 4, will be at liberty to bring the Territory into a customs, fiscal or administrative union or federation with other dependent territories under its jurisdiction or control, and to establish common services between the Territory and any or all of these territories, if, in its opinion, it would be in the interests of the Territory and not inconsistent with the basic objectives of the Trusteeship System to do so.

Article 6

The Administering Authority further undertakes to apply, in the Territory, the provisions of such international agreements and such recommendations of the specialized agencies referred to in Article 57 of the Charter as are, in the opinion of the Administering Authority, suited to the needs and conditions of the Territory and conducive to the achievement of the basic objectives of the Trusteeship System.

Article 7

The Administering Authority may take all measures in the Territory which it considers desirable to provide for the defence of the Territory and for maintenance of international peace and security.

Article 8

The Administering Authority undertakes, in the discharge of its obligations under article 3 of this agreement:

1. To co-operate with the Trusteeship Council in the discharge of all the Council's functions under Articles 87 and 88 of the Charter;

2. In accordance with its established policy:

   (a) To take into consideration the customs and usages of the inhabitants of New Guinea and respect the rights and safeguard the interests, both present and future, of the indigenous inhabitants of the Territory; and in particular, to ensure that no rights over native land in favour of any person not an indigenous inhabitant of New Guinea may be created or transferred except with the consent of the competent public authority;

   (b) To promote, as may be appropriate to the circumstances of the Territory, the educational and cultural advancement of the inhabitants;

   (c) To assure to the inhabitants of the Territory, as may be appropriate to the particular circumstances of the Territory and its peoples, a progressively increasing share in the administrative and other services of the Territory;

   (d) To guarantee to the inhabitants of the Territory, subject only to the requirements of public order, freedom of speech, of the press, of assembly and of petition, freedom of conscience and worship and freedom of religious teaching.

II. NAURU TRUSTEESHIP[2]

Article 5

The Administering Authority undertakes that in the discharge of its obligations under article 3 of this Agreement:

---

[2] *Ibid.*, Vol. 10, No. 138, pp. 4-8.

1. It will co-operate with the Trusteeship Council in the discharge of all the Council's functions under Articles 87 and 88 of the Charter;

2. It will, in accordance with its established policy:

(a) Take into consideration the customs and usages of the inhabitants of Nauru and respect the rights and safeguard the interest, both present and future, of the indigenous inhabitants of the Territory; and in particular ensure that no rights over native land in favour of any person not an indigenous inhabitant of Nauru may be created or transferred except with the consent of the competent public authority;

(b) Promote, as may be appropriate to the circumstances of the Territory, the economic, social, educational and cultural advancement of the inhabitants;

(c) Assure to the inhabitants of the Territory, as may be appropriate to the particular circumstances of the Territory and its peoples, a progressively increasing share in the administrative and other services of the Territory and take all appropriate measures with a view to the political advancement of the inhabitants in accordance with Article 76b of the Charter;

(d) Guarantee to the inhabitants of the Territory, subject only to the requirements of public order, freedom of speech, of the press, of assembly and of petition, freedom of conscience and worship and freedom of religious teaching.

III. Parallel provisions in the Western Samoan and Ruanda-Urundi Agreements

Western Samoa[3]

Article 5

The Administering Authority shall promote the development of free political institutions suited to West Samoa. To this end and as may be appropriate to the particular circumstances of the Territory and its peoples, the Administering Authority shall assure to the inhabitants of West Samoa a progressively increasing share in the administrative and other services of the Territory, shall develop the participation of the inhabitants in advisory and legislative bodies and in the Government of the Territory, and shall take all other

---

[3] *Ibid.*, Vol. 8, No. 115, pp. 74-76.

appropriate measures with a view to the political advancement of the inhabitants of West Samoa in accordance with Article 76(b) of the Charter of the United Nations.

RUANDA-URUNDI[4]

Article 6

The Administering Authority shall promote the development of free political institutions suited to Ruanda-Urundi. To this end the Administering Authority shall ensure to the inhabitants of Ruanda-Urundi an increasing share in the administration and services, both central and local, of the Territory; it shall further such participation of the inhabitants in the representative organs of the population as may be appropriate to the particular conditions of the Territory.

In short, the Administering Authority shall take all measures conducive to the political advancement of the population of Ruanda-Urundi in accordance with Article 76(b) of the Charter of the United Nations.

---

[4] *Ibid.*, Vol. 8, No. 117, p. 110.

ATTITUDES OF THE NATIVE PEOPLES OF PAPUA AND NEW GUINEA TO THE UNITED NATIONS 1945-54

by Camilla Wedgwood, *Australian School of Pacific Administration*

Any attempt to assess the attitude of the native peoples of Papua and the trust territory of New Guinea[1] towards the United Nations is extremely difficult: their attitude necessarily depends upon what the natives know about the United Nations, and how far they understand what they know.

The natives of these territories may be roughly divided into four groups. The first comprises those who have had no contact with white people or whose contact is confined to occasional meetings with administrative officers, missionaries, and men engaged in searching for minerals or recruiting native labour. It is safe to assume that such natives have never heard of the United Nations.

The second group comprises those who have been in contact with Europeans for perhaps two generations or more. The male members of this group have for many years been accustomed to

[1] The territory of Papua was annexed by Great Britain in 1884 and in 1906 was transferred to the Commonwealth of Australia. The trust territory of New Guinea was administered by Australia as a class C mandate on behalf of the League of Nations from 1921 until it became a United Nations trust territory in 1946 with Australia as the administering authority. The two territories were united for administrative purposes in 1949, but the Trusteeship Council and its visiting missions have been concerned only with New Guinea, the north-eastern half of the island. Ethnically, the differences between the native peoples of the two territories are negligible and there is little difference in their levels of sophistication (N.D.H.).

working as contract or occasional labourers for European employers, but they still live in the villages and cultivate their gardens very much as their forefathers did. It may be safely assumed that these natives also know nothing of the United Nations, although it is possible that some who have been away from their villages have heard the name if they happened to have listened to the broadcasts given in a special Native Peoples' Session on United Nations Day. It is also possible that some of the villagers in this second group may have seen the members of one of the United Nations visiting missions and listened to addresses by them. It is doubtful, however, whether they understood much of what was said on these occasions, whatever the skill and conscientiousness of the interpreter.

These two groups form probably no less than 70 per cent of the adult native population of the two territories. The children of the second group may be less ignorant of the United Nations than their parents, for in many villages they attend primary schools and an appreciable number have proceeded to village higher schools. An annual lesson on the United Nations is given on 24 October (United Nations Day). It is improbable, however, that the content of the lesson means much to them or that they are sufficiently interested in it to remember it.

The third group consists of those natives who live in close contact with European communities; their present manner of life is very different from that of their forefathers since it is deeply influenced by contact with European culture. The degree to which this influence has penetrated varies, but generally it is particularly noticeable in the fields of economic, social, and political organization. In this group are the natives living in the neighbourhood of the European townships, particularly Port Moresby, Rabaul, and Lae, and those who have attached themselves, more or less permanently, to the life of the European, visiting their villages only for occasional holidays. The latter group includes men and women who are permanent residents on a mission station, and those who have for many years been employed in some department of the administration or in a commercial firm. A very large proportion of the natives within this group have received at least eight years' schooling; most of them are literate in a local vernacular language or in a *lingua franca* (though some, particularly among the women, may have reverted to illiteracy), and all speak a *lingua franca* which enables them to communicate with Europeans, Asians, and natives of different mother tongues. In Papua a considerable number have some knowledge of English, but this is not sufficient to enable them to read an English newspaper or book, or to listen to a radio talk in English with real understanding. In the territory of New Guinea prior to 1946 there were few schools that taught English, and the number of natives with a working knowledge of English is therefore much smaller than in Papua.

The fourth group is, relatively, a very small one. It comprises those educated natives who have a good mastery of English, as well as some who, though they can neither read nor speak English, have first-hand experience of the world beyond the boundaries of Papua and New Guinea, have the intellectual ability and sufficient general education to learn by this experience, and so have come to understand something of European ideas and the European way of life. Most of the individuals within this group have lived in close contact with Europeans, and nearly all of them are male.

For convenience we may refer to members of the third group as "sophisticated" natives, and to members of the fourth group as "educated" natives. It is within those two groups that one may look to find some knowledge of the United Nations and some understanding of its aims and of the principles upon which those aims are based. But even among these people who do know something about the United Nations, it is extremely difficult to assess their attitude towards it. We can only hazard some guesses.

What are the channels through which the "sophisticated" and the "educated" natives may learn about the United Nations? There are, in the main, four: the European press, the news-sheets and papers issued for native readers, the radio, and the meetings with members of the United Nations visiting missions during the triennial visits. The number of "educated" natives who can read the English newspapers and magazines available in the territory, and read them with real understanding, is extremely small. Probably only the small number of natives working as compilers on the *Papuan Times* and the *Rabaul News* are accustomed to reading the more serious articles and items of news in the English papers.

Of the news-sheets and papers produced specially for native readers, some are official publications issued by the Department of Education; some are issued under the aegis of religious missions; one, a monthly in the Motu language, is an independent native production originally aided if not sponsored by the Department of Education. The weekly news-sheets issued in the trust territory are written in pidgin English (the only common language in which a large number of the natives of this territory are literate) and consist usually of two foolscap pages of mimeographed material. It is mainly concerned with local news, government notices (which often include some instructions aimed at improving native agriculture or living conditions), information about local native sporting events, and occasionally some overseas news of special local interest. The activities of the United Nations are sometimes touched upon and there is an attempt to interpret the United Nations in terms comprehensible to the political experience of the native readers. In the second or third week of October every year all these news-sheets contain something about United Nations Day and about the work of the United Nations in promoting peace and in the field of international aid. The 1950 and 1953 visits of the United Nations visiting missions also occasioned articles on the United Nations in these news-sheets. Earlier, in 1948, several issues of these news-sheets contained articles and notices about the appeal of the United Nations Children's Fund and listed the sums contributed by the various villages.

There is a monthly newspaper issued in English by the Depart-

aa

ment of Education. It resembles a school magazine rather than a newspaper. About once every year an illustrated article on the United Nations is published in it, usually in connection with United Nations Day. It has not been possible to examine the news-sheets issued in pidgin or in the vernacular by the religious missions. It seems that they resemble parish magazines and are concerned with the immediate interests and needs (spiritual and material) of those for whom they are written. In the Motu monthly, issued by the Hanuabada Native Club, there has been only one mention of the United Nations, a brief article inspired by a broadcast given by a former administration officer who had recently been working at United Nations Headquarters. Only in the *Papuan Times* is the United Nations frequently referred to. This is a weekly newspaper of about six double-sided foolscap sheets, written in English and produced in mimeographed form by native Papuan members of one of the missionary societies. It makes a serious attempt to give its readers some knowledge of international happenings, and articles have appeared in it on the United Nations technical assistance work, on the Korean War and the peace talks, as well as more general articles on the composition and aims of the United Nations; excerpts from the debates in the General Assembly and the Trusteeship Council have also been published in it.

The Commonwealth broadcasting station gives time daily to the Department of Education, which broadcasts in English, in the two *lingua franca*, Police Motu and pidgin, and in seven of the more important vernaculars. Some of the broadcasts are designed for school children, but most are directed towards adults. On United Nations Day each year talks are given on the United Nations and its work, and on the occasions of the visits of the United Nations visiting mission listeners are told something about the members and the purposes of the mission. The United Nations Children's Fund was also mentioned over the air. Mostly, however, the amount of time allocated to informative talks is devoted to topics of immediate interest to the natives or important to native welfare: improved methods of agriculture, the control of pests, health and sanitation, etc.

United Nations visiting missions visited the trust territory on two occasions, in 1950 and in 1953.[2] During both visits the members held public meetings in a number of places (mostly at government stations, though some were held in villages), and natives from many villages could come to see and hear them. They also visited schools, hospitals, agricultural stations, and other institutions where they came into contact with the natives. But in terms of the whole territory the number of places they actually visited was very limited; the visits themselves were necessarily brief, so that the contacts they did have with the natives were superficial.

It will be seen, then, that there are relatively few occasions on which the adult native population has an opportunity to learn about the United Nations. We must now ask how far the natives profit by the occasions that do arise. To what extent do the natives—the "sophisticated" and the "educated"—read the articles in the news-sheets and listen to the broadcasts on the United Nations and its subordinate organizations? To what extent do they understand or get an accurate idea of what the writers and speakers are trying to convey? Are they interested in seeing and hearing members of a United Nations visiting mission and what do they understand of the purpose of the mission or of the Trusteeship Council which has sent it?

The weekly news-sheets issued by the Department of Education in the trust territory are distributed free and probably reach the hands of a large proportion of the "sophisticated" and "educated" male natives living in the neighbourhood of the European centres. They probably also reach some who live in villages further away. There is so little reading material for natives who are literate, but not literate in English, that a considerable number of those who receive a news-sheet probably read it. (The quality of paper used

---

[2] A third visiting mission was sent in 1956.

for these news-sheets is unsuitable for rolling cigarettes—for this Australian newsprint is much in demand—and we may therefore assume that the news-sheets are not taken for this purpose). Doubtless the local news and sports sections interest them most, but any reading material has an attraction for them. It is impossible to tell, however, how many natives do in fact read the articles about the United Nations when they appear in the news-sheets. The *Papuan Times*, which gives much more space to the United Nations and its activities than any other native newspaper, is sold. The number of its regular subscribers is uncertain, but it is probably read by a considerable proportion of those natives in and around Port Moresby and Samarai who speak and read English. It is also known to some of the English-reading natives in the trust territory.

As to the radio, it is impossible to tell how many natives listen to broadcasts about the United Nations. It is very difficult to estimate how many natives hear the Native Peoples' Sessions. Attempts to install and maintain receiving sets in a number of villages have not been very successful. On government stations, mission stations, and some plantations, natives are enabled and encouraged to listen in; it seems that in some places large numbers do so. But there is nothing to show to which talks they listen with their minds, and which they merely hear with their ears.

The important question, however, is not how many people read about the United Nations, or listen to talks about it, but what do they understand of what they read or hear. How far, if at all, do those natives who know of the existence of the United Nations understand its composition, its aims, the ideals underlying those aims, the work which it does?

In nearly all the articles about the United Nations published in the news-sheets and elsewhere, sincere attempts are made to explain these things in terms of native experience. The difficulties of communication are very great, and there is reason to believe that, except among the "educated" natives, the attempts are only very partially successful. People who are only slowly and painfully beginning to realize the possibility of a political unit larger than the village (the native villages seldom consist of more than 350 persons and are often much smaller) and for whom loyalty to kin is still the supreme loyalty, can have but a very inadequate concept of what a nation is, let alone an organization of nations. Three quotations from articles illustrate the ways in which these unfamiliar ideas are presented to the natives. They are translated from three of the pidgin news-sheets.

The first is from the *Rabaul News* of 20 October 1951:

> When the war was still on, leading men in Australia and England and America and all the countries which were together with them considered much and discussed together: "It would be a good thing if we joined together in peace time also." Why did they want to join together?
>
> The first reason was so that they could guard against another big war happening. The second reason was so that they could see to it that no country in the world should suffer disaster for lack of money or for lack of food or for lack of anything else. . . . The third reason is so that they could prevent a country from suffering disaster on account of sickness; could ensure that there shall be enough schools for everybody; could ensure that everyone shall have good government as there is in all those places which are ruled over by our king, King George VI.
>
> They wanted everyone, in every place to be able to talk without fear about anything which he thinks wrong. They wanted everyone to be able to get enough of all that he needs so that he is not hungry and so that everyone shall live in safety and security. They want things to be so that no honest man and no honest country shall have cause to be afraid of any other man or of any other country nor of the Government; so that every person has a right to attend his church and no other man, and no other country or Government can make trouble for him on account of his church.
>
> When the war ended, all these countries that I have just been talking about, in all 51 countries, met together and formed

UNO (United Nations Organisation). The work of UNO in assembly is to bring about all these things that I have just mentioned. All those places (countries) which are within UNO have the right to send some men to this Assembly. Everything was finally settled on 24th October, 1945, and they continually meet in assembly. They make a good job of a lot of work.

If two countries have a quarrel and are about to fight, it is the practice for UNO to meet and to settle the quarrel. If one of the countries refuses to obey the decision of UNO, all the countries belonging to UNO have the right to say: "Very well, if you intend to fight, look out! I have the right to help this other country."

In Korea, a place far away, there was a country which attacked another. Soldiers of many countries belonging to UNO all joined together with the other country and they are still fighting. What UNO wants to do is to teach all countries that they cannot attack another country with impunity.

If a country wants to undertake a big piece of work for the purpose of improving the living conditions of the people, and has not got enough money for it, UNO has the authority to send someone and if this person thinks that the work is good, UNO has the authority to help by sending a man who knows a great deal about money. This is what was done in Pakistan and in India and in many other places.

If UNO knows that the food has been ruined in a country, and the people are starving, UNO has the authority to send food and money for the people. This is what UNO has done in Greece, China, India, Italy and many other places.

If there is serious sickness in a country, UNO has the authority to send doctors and medicine to this country to overcome the sickness. This is what happened in Egypt, and in the same way there are some men belonging to UNO who are going to many places to overcome malaria, TB and all kinds of sickness which are found in places like New Guinea.

If there are not enough schools in a place, UNO can send someone to investigate and to help the people about schools. UNO also helps places where there are not good schools by taking some people (from these places) and sending them to school in another place.

UNO has the authority to do all this work, and lots of other work. UNO wants everyone, in every place to work together like brothers. It is trying hard all the time to make this happen.

It is true that there are irresponsible men in every place, and there are also some irresponsible countries which will not co-operate with UNO, and frustrate UNO's work. Nevertheless, UNO has achieved good work, and has the power to do more good work.

I don't know whether it will overcome the irresponsible men and the irresponsible countries so that everyone can work together like brothers. Certainly it is a big task, but it would be well to achieve it.

The second excerpt is from an article published in *Lae Garamut* on 6 November 1948:

Now I am going to tell you about a large association called United Nations. Do you know what a nation is? Well, Australia, and England and America, each of these is a nation; all the districts within each has the same law. "United" means gathered together; the ones which are in this large association are called United Nations. All the people who belong to all the nations in the world can meet together and discuss all those things which are good for all the people in the world.

In some of your villages you have got associations and sometimes all the village councillors meet together and talk with the Government officer about things which will be for the good of all the villages. If all villages do this, and all the village councillors (of all the villages) work together, they are "united", and you could speak of the 'United Village Councils'. That is like the "United Nations". . . .

The third extract is taken from the closing paragraph of an article in *Lagasai* (published at Utu in New Ireland), written on 5 August 1950 to explain the action of the United Nations in Korea:

The United Nations Organisation is just like the police in Papua and New Guinea. If two villages begin a fight about something, the police go out and stop it. Then, when the fighting has stopped, the Government and the two warring villages discuss the matter and the dispute is settled. The United Nations is like the police. It sends men to any place where there is trouble, and they stop it; and when the dispute has been finally settled, its men go again. The United Nations Organisation has no navy or army or air force of its own, but if it decides to stop this war in Korea, it has the right to ask all the countries to help. It asked America, England, Australia, New Zealand and several other countries to send some troops—army, air force and navy . . .

In an article on United Nations Day published in the October 1953 edition of the English language monthly, the *Papua and New Guinea Villager*, the United Nations is likened to "a very large co-operative society" "which is planning to give help to all needy people"; the work of the Food and Agriculture Organization, World Health Organization, and the United Nations Educational, Scientific and Cultural Organization is outlined and specific mention is made to the relief work carried out in Greece after the earthquake of 1953.

Thus the United Nations is likened to the collaboration of soldiers of different nations during the Pacific War, to an association of village councils, to the police force, and to a co-operative society. In each case the analogy is to some extent appropriate, but also to some extent misleading.

From their experiences during the Pacific War, a large number of the natives recognize the difference between Australian and United States troops and the alliance between them for purposes of fighting was doubtless intelligible to the natives, for in olden days temporary alliances were often made between two villages to carry out an attack on a third village. But such alliances were always temporary and for war purposes only. The idea of a more permanent association for mutual aid in peaceful matters would be unfamiliar (such reciprocal services in the indigenous societies are performed on the basis of kinship ties) but it would not be totally incomprehensible. The village council is not an indigenous institution; it has been introduced within the last few years by the administration as a first step towards developing a system of responsible native local government along Western democratic lines. As yet they have been established only in areas where the natives are "sophisticated," and where relations between neighbouring villages have been sufficiently friendly, and old antagonisms sufficiently forgotten, to make it possible for such villages to form a single, effective economic and political local group. It is rather unfortunate that in the passage quoted above the reference to the village councillors meeting with the government officer unintentionally emphasizes the fact that the village councils are alien institutions. However much a government officer is liked and respected, he is still an alien and represents to the natives an alien authority to which they perforce submit.

The likening of the United Nations to the police force has the same disadvantage, but in a more marked degree, for the native constabulary exists for the purpose of enforcing the law which the alien government has imposed. Though a very large proportion, even of the unsophisticated natives, freely admit that the suppression of inter-village fighting by the government has been a blessing, nevertheless the native constabulary is to them the instrument of alien authority, and it can hardly be said that the ordinary villager regards it with a wholly trustful or wholly friendly eye. Moreover, as far as the vast majority of the natives knows, the native constabulary is concerned only with the conduct of natives and does not take action against the European; thus it seems to uphold a system of differential treatment which conflicts with the principles which determine the composition or guide the deliberations of the United Nations.

The likening of the United Nations to a co-operative society is a happier analogy. The co-operatives are, it is true, alien in origin, but they have not been imposed upon the people; they are truly voluntary organizations, and during the last decade a considerable number have sprung up in many parts of Papua and New Guinea. Moreover, where they have been formed the natives do in fact manage them—under the guidance of a European certainly, but not at his behest and not merely by carrying out his instructions. So far, however, the membership range of each of these native co-operatives is geographically very restricted; traditional village antagonisms are not to be overcome quickly or easily. The weakness of the analogy is therefore that it wholly fails to suggest the world-wide character of the United Nations and the important principle that within it there shall be no distinctions on the basis of locality, colour, or faith. The co-operatives, too, are purely economic organizations: they have no functions similar to those carried out by FAO, WHO, or UNESCO. When disaster hits an area in New Guinea, through earthquake, volcano, drought, or floods, it is the government, not the local co-operative society, which provides relief.

The association, in the minds of the natives, of the United Nations with their own alien government is probably strengthened rather than weakened by their experience with the United Nations visiting missions. The members of the missions have been either Europeans or Asians dressed in European garb, and the latter have in general features resembling the Chinese whom the natives know and dislike, or the Japanese of whom they have bitter memories. While on their tours the members of the visiting missions are accompanied by an officer of the administration. Contact with any large groups of natives has been through occasional "public meetings," at which whatever is said on either side has to be transmitted to the other by an interpreter who is, if not supplied by the administration, at least very certainly conscious that the administrative officer is listening to him. The link between the visiting mission and the administration must seem all the closer when natives are invited (to them it may even appear to be a command) to come to the government station to meet the mission. There is no published record of what has actually been said at these "public meetings."

Statements by the members of the mission about the aims of the United Nations and the Trusteeship Council, and the purpose of their visit, probably conveyed nothing to the minds of the natives of the "bush" villages whom they addressed, and little enough to the more sophisticated natives. However, the sight of the members of the missions may have helped the more sophisticated to realize the existence of the United Nations by incarnating it, as it were, in the persons of the visitors.

Contacts between natives and members of the missions during visits to schools, hospitals, and other institutions have also necessarily been superficial. The native inmates must have viewed these visits as an official inspection by a high-ranking administrative official in company with very distinguished strangers, and they were no doubt engulfed by that atmosphere of artificiality and restraint which inevitably characterizes the visits of royalty to similar institutions in Australia. In the minds of most of them, there would probably be little relation between what they may have been told or may have read about the aims and ideals of the United Nations and these alien, awe-inspiring visitors who were being shepherded by an equally awe-inspiring administration officer.

On the occasion of the tour of the first United Nations visiting mission two petitions were presented by natives. One, presented on behalf of a group of sophisticated villages near Rabaul, asked for more and better educational facilities, and complained of differential treatment vis-à-vis Europeans and of a deliberate policy on the part of Europeans in commerce and in the religious missions to prevent native advancement. The other petition came from a group of villages in New Ireland (a region which has been in close contact with Europeans since the early years of this century). It expressed a wish for the continuance of the Australian administration and a strong distaste for Indonesians, Chinese, Japanese, and Germans; it asked for a school teacher, more medical services, and a guarantee of fair prices to natives in the Chinese trade-stores. The fact that these petitions were presented indicates that at least a few natives sufficiently understood the purpose of the mission to know that they could make this approach, and to believe that it was worthwhile to do so. The response to these petitions may have suggested to them, however, that the United Nations was not deeply concerned with their grievances and was unwilling to act on their behalf. With their limited knowledge it was not to be expected that the native petitioners should understand the true situation. Thus, the mission's recommendation in respect of the complaint in the first petition (that the Europeans were deliberately preventing the natives from advancing) was that the United Nations Trusteeship Council "should reassure the petitioner" that this "was a misapprehension." Such a reply would hardly convince or impress the petitioners. During the tour of the second visiting mission in 1953 no petitions were presented by natives.

Thus everything the natives read or hear about the United Nations (if indeed they read it or listen to it at all) tends to make the United Nations something alien to them. At most it is something wielding power and authority over them—like the police, an instrument for imposing upon them an alien will, which, however beneficial, is nevertheless alien—something in which they have no say and, except if it actively interferes with their personal lives, no interest. It is true that when the United Nations Children's Appeal was launched in 1948, there were a number of broadcasts on the subject, as well as articles in the news-sheets, and the natives in villages around Rabaul, Lae, and other European townships responded very generously. In doing so, however, they were responding directly to a practical situation; they were told of the crops destroyed by the war, and of children who were starving. The natives know what it is for their gardens to fail or be destroyed by war; they know what it is to have their children crying with hunger; and generosity with food is a virtue in which natives are trained from babyhood. The appeal therefore concerned something they understood out of their own experience. Their conception of the role of the United Nations in this context—if they formulated one—was probably of a number of persons (possibly government officers) who bought food with the money and handed this food to crowds of hungry children.

In its report, the United Nations visiting mission of 1953 wrote that:

> ... it did not find in the Territory any appreciable knowledge concerning the aims and activities of the United Nations or of the basic objectives of the Trusteeship System among the indigenous inhabitants. In a few schools there were United Nations posters, none of which appeared to the Mission to be particularly appropriate or of much significance to the students in view of their general lack of knowledge regarding the United Nations.
>
> The people had been informed of the Mission's visit but with a few exceptions they did not indicate that they understood the purpose of its visit or even had a clear idea of the Mission's identity. For example in the Rabaul area, one of the most sophisticated in the Territory, the Tavuilui Committee [sic] addressed its welcome to the United Nations Missionaries. Mission, to the indigenous people, in the past has always been associated with one or another of the religious groups in the Territory. In fact the Mission noted that, to avoid confusion in the minds of the people, interpreters often substituted in pidgin the more significant title United Nations "line"[3] in place of United Nations Mission.
>
> After observing the degree of advancement of the indigenous people, the Mission believes that although the information now sent to the Territory may be satisfactory for the non-indigenous population, in general it is of little value for the rest of the population. Aside from the occasional exceptions when information is given via radio or in the news-sheets published in pidgin English by the Department of Education, there exists a complete lack of information material in any form comprehensible to them, and consequently an absence of knowledge regarding the United Nations.

---

[3] The pidgin word *lain* (English "line") is used primarily for a set of age-mates, and metaphorically or by derivation for a group of men associated together to perform a task.

> The Mission feels that the preparation of special material
> on the United Nations in a medium which the people could
> readily understand would go a long way toward remedying
> the situation.[4]

This can be accepted as a true estimate of the situation regarding knowledge or understanding of the United Nations. It is doubtful whether this ignorance of the natives about the United Nations is primarily due to any lack of effort on the part of the administering authority to disseminate information or even to the unsuitability of the type of information material (such as posters) to the experience and understanding of the natives. The people of Papua and New Guinea, like people all over the world, are interested in those things which they can see affecting their lives: they will listen to and take the trouble to understand those things which they feel to be of immediate and obvious importance to them. The United Nations does not fall within this category. Except for a small number of educated natives, the people of Papua and the trust territory of New Guinea are fully occupied with their wives and children, their gardens and their pigs, and the daily interests of a peasant population. If their attention can be directed to the United Nations, they can only think of it as something which the European has devised, something which is perhaps like many things which the Europeans do, irrational or incomprehensible. That some of the educated natives, both in the trust territory and in Papua, have some real understanding of what the United Nations is and what it stands for is certain. At present, however, they form a microscopic minority of the total native population. It is they, rather than any European, who will probably be the best people to interpret the United Nations to their fellow countrymen.

---

[4] Trusteeship Council, Official Record: 12th Sess., Supple. No. 4, U.N. Visiting Mission to Trust Territories in the Pacific, 1953: Report on New Guinea, pp. 69-70.

Index